KT-214-298

CHILDREN'S BRITANNICA

CHILDREN'S BRITANNICA

Volume 18
Tree to Wayfaring Tree

Encyclopædia Britannica, Inc.

AUCKLAND/CHICAGO/GENEVA/LONDON/MANILA/PARIS

ROME/SEOUL/SYDNEY/TOKYO/TORONTO

First edition 1960
Second edition 1969
Third edition 1973
Fourth edition 1988

International Standard Book Number: 0-85229-218-X
Library of Congress Catalog Card Number: 89-84047

Typeset, printed and bound in Great Britain by
BPCC Hazell Books Ltd
Member of BPCC Ltd
Aylesbury, Bucks, England

TREE. A tree is a woody plant usually with a single stem. A large elm or oak is easily recognized as being a tree. It has roots in the soil, one main stem, or trunk, and a crown of branches. The woody plants called shrubs and bushes are usually smaller than trees and have usually more than one main stem. The difference between trees and shrubs, however, is not always clear. Some plants that normally are considered to be trees may, under certain conditions, be shrub-like. Others, normally shrubs, may at times be tree-like. (See SHRUB.) Trees are the largest living things on the Earth, and they live longer than any animals.

The biggest trees are the giant sequoias of California. The largest of these, nicknamed "General Sherman", stands 83 metres (272 feet) high. The tallest trees are mountain-ashes and Douglas firs, which have grown to well over 100 metres (330 feet). The oldest trees are the Californian bristlecone pines, some of which are more than 4,500 years old. Trees are found in all regions (except where the soil is very thin, in deserts and in the Arctic and Antarctic). In the tropics they form dense, hot forests with climbing plants binding the trees together. In northern regions such as Canada, Siberia, and Alaska mighty forests of fir trees grow.

Trees draw in water through their roots, which may spread long distances under the earth, or—as in the case of the mangrove—arch down from the trunk into the soil. Like all other green plants they build up food by means of their leaves. *Deciduous* trees lose their leaves for a season, usually winter, and then grow new ones, the buds containing the new shoots and leaves often being protected with scales against cold weather. Most deciduous trees have wide, flat leaves and so are called *broad-leaved* trees. *Evergreen* trees are always covered with leaves, although actually they are constantly losing small numbers of leaves and new ones replace them. Most evergreen trees have narrow, sharp leaves and bear cones, so they are called *needle-leafed* trees or *conifers*. In areas where many deciduous trees grow, the woods and forests are bare during the winter, but in the tropics, where most trees are evergreen, the landscape looks much the same all the year round.

The age of a tree can be told by counting the rings in the trunk. In most kinds of temperate trees, new wood is formed each year in a layer outside the wood of the previous year. The layers of wood, as seen on the cut end of a felled tree, are circular and are called annual rings. Each ring in the wood of the trunk represents one year of the tree's life. In a year of good rainfall, the ring formed is wider than one formed in a drier year. A record of rainfall can thus be read in tree rings.

Trees reproduce by means of fruits, which appear after the flowers have fallen. Some trees have more obvious flowers than others. It can be seen at first glance that the white blossom of a cherry tree consists of flowers, but it is not so clear that the dangling catkins of a hazel tree are flowers. (See POLLINATION.) The same can be said about fruits. Ripe plums are at once seen to be fruit, but the conifers, such as firs, pines, and larches, reproduce by means of tiny winged seeds hidden in their cones.

Trees are vital to our world for a number of reasons. Like all green plants, they build up their food by the process known as *photosynthesis*. The by-product of this process is oxygen which is given off into the air and replaces the oxygen which human beings and other animals take from the atmosphere as they breathe.

The Value of Trees

The great forests have been called the "lungs of the world", since they make much of the oxygen we need to live. Trees also prevent erosion and flooding by "binding" the soil together with their roots. Innumerable animals make their homes in trees, using them for food and shelter. Virtually every part of a tree—wood, bark, sap, roots, leaves, fruits, and seeds—has been used by people. Trees supply wood, which is used for fuel and is made into lumber, paper, plywood, plastics, fence posts, railway sleepers, and countless other products (see FORESTRY). Certain trees

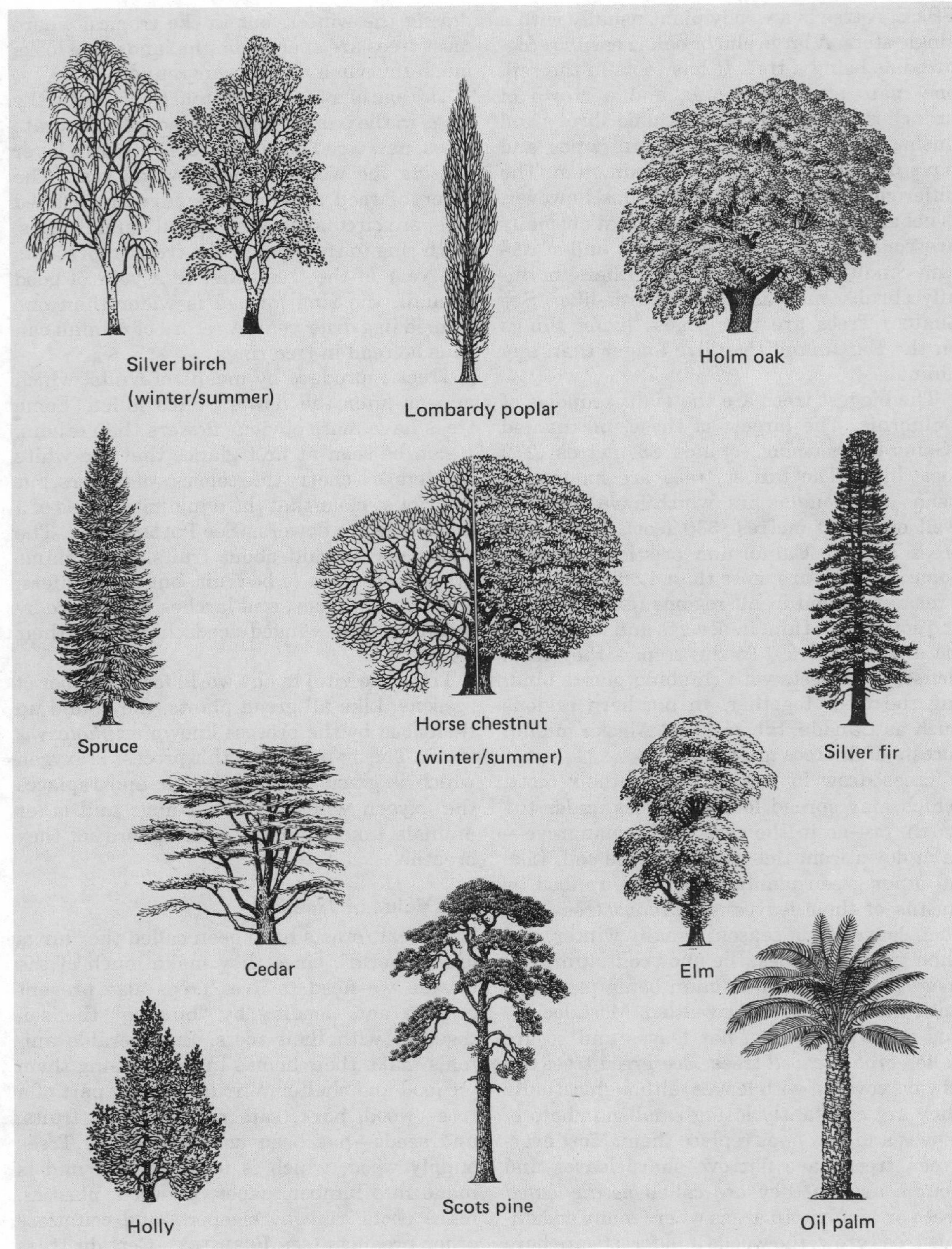
Silver birch
(winter/summer)
Lombardy poplar
Holm oak
Spruce
Horse chestnut
(winter/summer)
Silver fir
Cedar
Elm
Scots pine
Holly
Oil palm

are of value as sources of foods, including fruits—such as apples, oranges, peaches, and dates—and nuts—such as pecans, walnuts, almonds, and cashews. Well-known spices that come from trees are cinnamon, cloves, and nutmeg.

Coffee and cocoa are beverages made from tree seeds. Among other tree products are cork; tannins (from wattle bark and quebracho wood), used to make leather; rubber; turpentine; useful gums and resins (gum Arabic, amber, and myrrh); essential oils (camphor and eucalyptus); fatty oils (olive and tung); waxes (carnauba); sugars (maple and palm); medicines (quinine and cascara); and fibres (kapok). In addition, trees are planted for ornament, shade, and soil erosion control, and as windbreaks. Millions of trees are cut annually for use as decorations at Christmas. Trees, providing shelter and food, are necessary for wildlife.

Sally & Richard Greenhill

Trees have a special place in childhood. Children love climbing and making "dens" in them.

As well as these functions, woodland and forest give people areas of recreation where they can relax. The beauty of trees and great forests has been celebrated throughout the ages in art and literature.

In many parts of the world, trees are being cut down at a terrifying rate. Often the animals and other plants that depend on them are destroyed. No new trees are planted to take their place. Instead, after a few years of being farmed for crops, the land becomes eroded and useless. The destruction of our woods and forests is one of the great problems affecting the world.

Trees of the World

The traditional tree in many European and North American areas is the oak. The elm is nowadays less common in many areas because of the fungus called Dutch elm disease, carried by a wood-boring beetle, which rots away the wood.

The evergreen yew lives to a great age and belongs to a very ancient plant family, the gymnosperms, which have grown on the Earth for many millions of years. The dark leaves and fruits of yew trees are poisonous to many animals. Cedars can easily be distinguished by their size and by the way their branches grow in flat tiers, or layers. The best-known kind is the cedar of Lebanon, which used to grow in great forests on Mount Lebanon in the Middle East.

The emblem of Canada is the five-pointed leaf of the maple. From the sugar maple, which grows in Canada and the United States, comes maple sugar, obtained by boring a small hole in the trunk and collecting the sap as it oozes out.

In Australia eucalyptus trees grow, which include the blue gum. Eucalyptus trees may grow to a height of more than 90 metres (295 feet), and a strong scented oil comes from the leaves.

Stinkwood from South Africa (called stinkwood because of the unpleasant smell when the trees have just been cut) provides strong and handsome wood which is much used for furniture making. Mahogany, from Central America, and teak, a heavy wood, are used for furniture making and shipbuilding.

A very useful tree from the tropics is the palm. Different kinds of palm produce coconuts, sago, and dates, and an oil used in making candles and soap is obtained from the oil palm. The trunks, branches, leaves, and bark are all used in various ways. Another beautiful and useful tropical tree is the rubber tree. It is grown in great plantations in Sri Lanka, Malaya, and other places and the liquid rubber is collected from the stems by making cuts and catching the resin in tins placed underneath them.

In the islands of the South Pacific the breadfruit tree grows. It has glossy green leaves and large, starchy fruits.

There are separate articles on most of the trees mentioned here, and also on BARK; CONIFER; FLOWER; FOREST; GYMNOSPERM; LEAF; PHOTOSYNTHESIS.

TREE or **BROWN CREEPER.** A bird that looks like a brown and white mouse running up a tree trunk is almost certain to be the bird named tree creeper in Europe and brown creeper in North America. It is about 12 centimetres (5 inches) long, with mottled upper parts of brown, black, and yellow and pure white underparts. The feathers of its brown tail are stiff and act as props when it is clinging to a tree. The bill is very fine and curved.

A tree creeper investigates bark for insects, gripping with its clawed toes and propped up by its tail.

Tree creepers are always found in woods or wooded country. They fly from tree to tree with shrill calls, exploring crevices in the bark for insects and their eggs, grubs, and pupae. Unlike nuthatches (see NUTHATCH), tree creepers cannot run down a trunk but have to fly down and start again.

In spring these birds build tiny nests, made of wood chips, twigs, moss, wool, and feathers, and fit them behind the bark of dead trees. The hen bird lays from four to seven white eggs with red spots.

There are about six species of tree creeper (*Certhia*) which are distributed over the northern hemisphere.

The six species of Australian tree creepers (*Climàcteris*) are blackish-brown or reddish-brown mottled birds with a reddish band across the wing. They have brush-tipped tongues and behave rather like honeyeaters (see HONEYEATER). Their tails are not stiffened, and they have loud, piercing calls.

TREVITHICK, Richard (1771–1833). The Cornish mining-engineer Richard Trevithick was a pioneer of steam engines (see STEAM ENGINE). He succeeded in harnessing high-pressure steam to drive fixed pumping engines in the Cornish tin mines. The use of steam at high pressure (which James Watt thought too dangerous) enabled smaller and lighter engines to be built. In 1801 Trevithick built

Courtesy, Science Museum, London

Trevithick's third steam locomotive, built in 1808.

his first "steam carriage", which one Christmas Eve he drove up a hill in Camborne, Cornwall.

In 1803 he built a second steam carriage, which he drove through the streets of London. He then designed the world's first steam locomotive, which in 1804 hauled 10 tonnes (11 US tons) of iron and 70 men along 15 kilometres (10 miles) of cast-iron track in South Wales. Trevithick built two more locomotives, but then turned his attention to other schemes as the cast iron tracks available at the time could not bear the weight of his engines. He used his engines to drive an iron-rolling mill, a barge, a steam dredger, and a threshing machine on a farm. He made improvements in boiler design, creating what became known as the Cornish boiler.

Although a brilliant engineer, Trevithick was no businessman. He went bankrupt and sailed off to South America, hoping to make a fortune designing engines for the Peruvian silver mines. When he came back, penniless, he found that other engineers had profited from his pioneer work, and he died in poverty.

TRIAL is the legal procedure carried out by a court of law to decide whether a person is guilty of a crime or to decide an issue between two opposing parties to a civil dispute.

The different kinds of court are described in the articles COURT, JUDGE, and JURY. For an explanation of legal systems in various countries and the difference between criminal and civil law, see CRIME; LAW; POLICE.

Trials almost always take place in public, although filming and broadcasting are not normally allowed. Trials *in camera* (Latin, meaning "in a vaulted room" or private chamber) take place where state security or public morality is involved.

Except for minor criminal offences and disputes involving small sums of money, people appearing in court are usually represented by a lawyer, although they may always represent themselves if they wish. Some countries provide financial help for poorer people. For information about the different kinds of lawyer and their work, see LAWYER.

Where legal systems are based on the common law (such as in most of the United States and Canada, as well as England, Australia, and New Zealand), the procedure at trial is said to be "adversarial". This means that the opposing sides in the trial (the "adversaries") present the evidence and question the witnesses. In countries where the legal system is not based on common law (such as France and most other countries in Europe), the method used is "inquisitorial". In this case the judge plays a larger rôle in questioning witnesses and discovering the facts for himself. This article describes what happens in trials under the common law legal system.

Where a jury is used, it is the jury's function to listen to the evidence and decide the facts. The judge advises the jury on the law and makes decisions about procedure. If there is no jury the judge must decide the issue of facts himself.

In a criminal trial the person accused of the crime is usually known as "the defendant" and his lawyer is "defence counsel". The lawyer representing the police or the prosecuting authority is known as "the prosecution". Serious cases are prosecuted by a public prosecutor who has a different title in each country.

In a civil trial the person taking action, or bringing the case, is usually called the "plaintiff", and the other side is known as "the defendant".

Rules of procedure and evidence are laid down to provide a fair hearing for both sides.

Beginning the Trial

In a criminal trial the defendant is first asked if he pleads guilty or not guilty to the charges. If he pleads guilty, no evidence is called and the judge proceeds to sentence him. If he pleads not guilty and a jury is being used, the jury must then be selected and sworn in. Both the prosecution and defence have the right to challenge the suitability of potential jurors, and in a case with several defendants it may take some time before a jury is constituted (see JURY). "Swearing in" means that each juror makes a promise according to his religious belief (or he "affirms" if he has no religion) to listen carefully to the evidence and make a fair decision.

The trial is opened by the person bringing the case. In a criminal trial this is the prosecution; in a civil trial, the plaintiff. This person bears the *burden of proof*, that is, he must convince the judge or jury to convict the defendant or find in favour of the plaintiff.

There is a difference in the burden of proof in a criminal trial and a civil case. In a criminal trial the prosecution must prove the defendant guilty *beyond reasonable doubt*; in other words, the jury must be *absolutely sure* that the person is guilty of the crime before he can be convicted. In civil cases the burden of proof is not so high. The plaintiff must prove his allegations *on a balance of probabilities*; in other words, it must be *more likely than not* that what the plaintiff alleges did really happen.

Admissibility of Evidence

Evidence that is agreed between the parties need not be proved. Such evidence may include such facts as the financial damage suffered by a plaintiff in a personal injury case and evidence from a doctor about injuries. Then the only issue to be proved is whether the defendant was responsible for causing the injuries.

Everything in dispute must be proved. Most evidence will be given by witnesses on oath. Like the jurors, witnesses must swear that they will tell the truth. If they are later found to have been lying, they can be prosecuted for the offence of *perjury*.

A witness can only *testify* to what he has seen or otherwise perceived for himself. Anything else would be "hearsay"; he would merely be repeating what someone else has told him.

When giving evidence for the person who has called him, the witness must not be "led". That means he must not be persuaded to say something by the lawyer suggesting it to him. A "leading question" is one which suggests a particular answer.

Once a witness has given his evidence he can be "cross-examined" by the lawyer for the other side. At this stage the defence counsel will put the case for the defence to the prosecution witnesses and will probably try to persuade them that they are wrong. Again, there are complicated rules about the kinds of question that may be asked, and the opposing lawyer may object if the questions are irrelevant or otherwise improper.

It is always the judge who must decide on questions of evidence and procedure in court, and if people disobey him they may be guilty of *contempt of court*. The judge has power to send people to prison for contempt of court if they seriously disobey him.

In a criminal trial, once the case for the prosecution has been heard, the defence may claim that there is "no case to answer", that is, that the evidence does not support the charge. If this claim is successful, the defendant will be set free without having to put his case. Similarly, in a civil trial, the judge may decide the plaintiff's claim does not stand and it may be dismissed.

In most cases the trial continues with the case for the defence. The rules of evidence are the same. The defendant's previous convictions (if any) may not normally be revealed in court in case they influence the jury's decision.

After the evidence has been heard, the lawyers for both sides may summarize their cases to the judge. In a jury trial they will address the jury. The prosecution usually speaks first and the defendant therefore has the last word. The judge then sums up all the evidence. He must instruct the jury on their rôle and remind them to convict only if they are sure beyond reasonable doubt.

Decision

The jury retires from court to reach its verdict. In some countries a majority decision is allowed; in others it must be unanimous (see JURY). When the decision is made, the jury returns to court to give it. If the jury cannot agree on a verdict there must be a retrial. If the defendant is found guilty the judge must pass sentence, although in some places the jury plays a part in the sentencing. (For the kinds of sentence that may be given, see CAPITAL PUNISHMENT; PRISON; PROBATION: and articles on various crimes.)

In a civil trial the judge gives his decision and the reasons for it in open court. He may award damages: compensation in the form of money to a person who has suffered an injury. Other remedies include an order to prevent someone from carrying out an unlawful act; this is called an injunction. (See DAMAGES; INJUNCTION.)

After sentencing in a criminal trial or the judgement in a civil trial the judge makes an order for costs. The costs of a prosecution usually come out of public funds. In a civil case the person who loses usually has to pay the costs of both sides.

Appeal

An appeal to a higher court may be allowed by a defendant found guilty in a criminal trial or by the losing side in a civil trial. In a criminal trial it may be an appeal against conviction or sentence or both. In a civil trial it may be an appeal against the decision or the remedy or both. The issue of who is to pay the costs may also be disputed. For more about appeal courts, see COURT; JUDGE.

TRIESTE is a city and small province covering 212 square kilometres (82 square miles) on the Adriatic coast of northeast Italy. During its history, it has changed hands several times. In Roman times, Trieste was a fortified harbour. During the Middle Ages, it was for a time an independent city-state but later came under Austrian rule.

Trieste was the chief port of the Austro-Hungarian Empire during the 19th century. Most of its people, however, were Italians and for this reason it was decided in a secret treaty after World War I (in which Austria-Hungary was defeated) that Trieste should be handed over to Italy. Italian troops marched into the city in 1918 and, although Trieste became less busy as a port, new industries such as ship-building, steel mills, and oil refining were started.

During World War II (1939–45) Trieste fell into German hands, but was captured by Yugoslav troops in 1945. For a while it was under the joint control of Britain, the United States, and Yugoslavia until in 1954 Yugoslavia agreed to divide Trieste with Italy. Yugoslavia took over most of the land around

Authenticated News

The Castle of Miramare, on the Adriatic coast just north of Trieste. It was designed by a Viennese architect for Archduke Maximilian of Austria.

Trieste, while the city and port itself was returned to Italy. The port's activity increased once again and became the basis of its economy. The population of Trieste today is 246,305 (1984).

TRIGONOMETRY. Trigonometry is concerned with measurement based on triangles. It is important in geometry and in physics. It was used by surveyors and astronomers as a method of calculating distances long before modern sophisticated equipment was invented.

To introduce the idea, let us consider a fishing rod, 1 metre long, with the fishing line dropping vertically into the water.

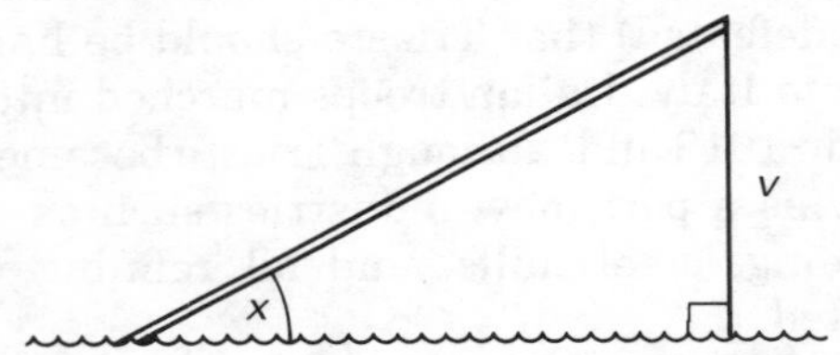

The height of the rod above the water, which we have called v, will change according to the angle between the rod and the water, which we have called x. So we have a function

$$x \rightarrow v.$$

The function involved here is known as a *sine* function (see FUNCTION), or "sin" for short. A sine is a special number associated with an angle and in our example it is equal to v divided by the length of the fishing rod which we shall call 1 unit.

This means that

$$\sin x = \frac{v}{1}$$

and therefore

$$v = \sin x.$$

We can draw the rod at different angles (that is, different values of x) and measure the corresponding values of v. These results can then be put on a graph. The figure at the bottom of the page shows a way of doing this.

In theory we can continue increasing the angle past 90°,

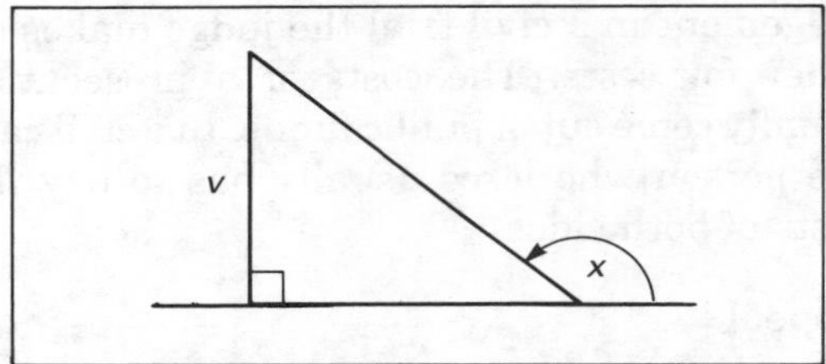

and even past 180°, when v will be negative, because the "height" is now downwards.

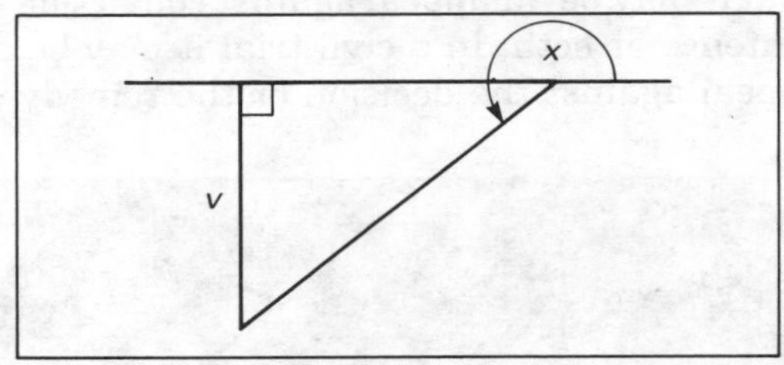

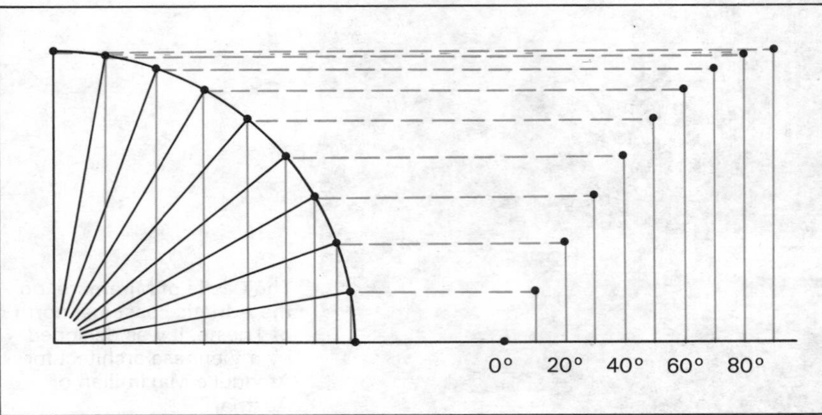

The coloured lines in this drawing show the different values of *V* corresponding to different angles. If we plot them on a graph (in the right of the diagram) we get a curve called a *sine curve.*

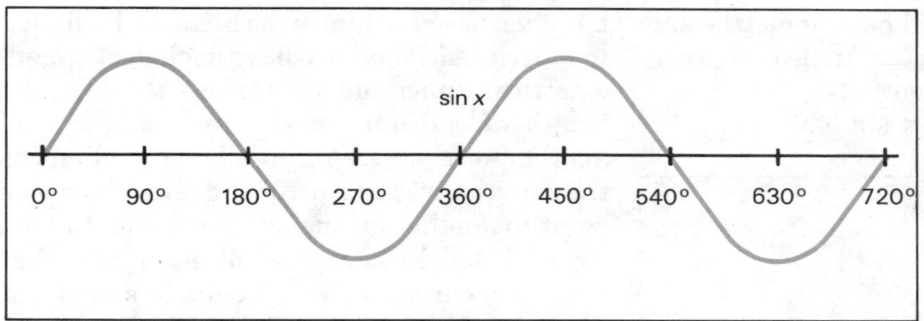

A sine wave is a cyclic function that repeals itself every 360°. Its maximum positive value is 1, and its maximum negative value is −1. It passes through zero every 180°. Sin 0° equals 0.

And when we reach 360° we can begin again, with the function repeating itself every 360°. Such a function is said to be *cyclic*.

The graph looks like the one above and is sometimes known as a *sine wave*. Sine waves are important in the wave theory of sound, light, electricity, and radio. If you plot a graph of sunrise or sunset times throughout the year, you will see that these also correspond to sine waves.

If we look instead at the horizontal distance between the fishing line and the bottom of the rod, marked h in this diagram,

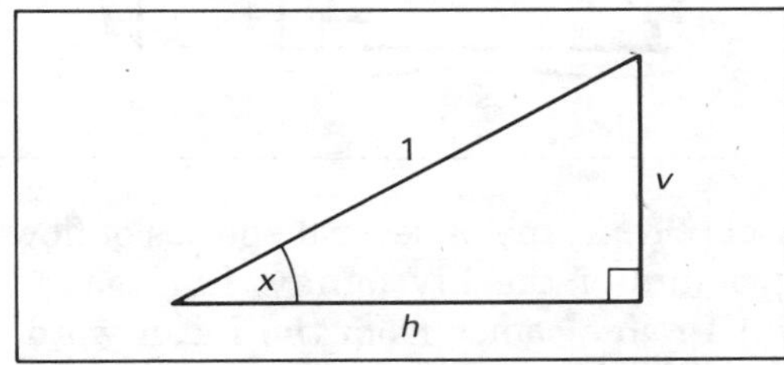

we can see that this will change too as the angle x changes. This function is the *cosine* function, or "cos" for short. The cosine of x equals h divided by 1, so we can say

$$h = \cos x.$$

The graph (at the bottom of the page) turns out to have the same shape as the sine wave, but moved along.

If x is between 0° and 90° then we can summarize what we have learned so far in the following diagram.

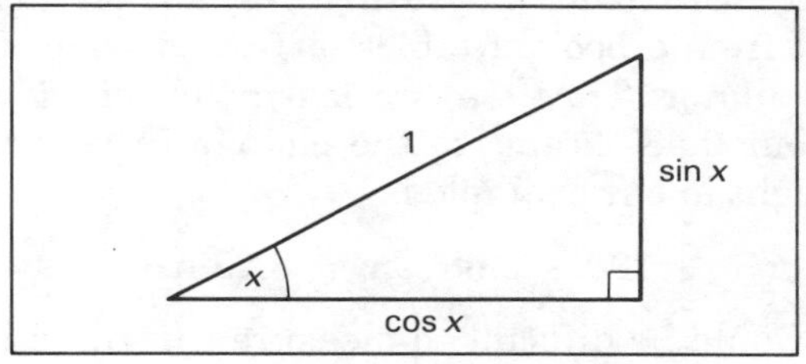

If the fishing rod is, say, 3 metres long instead of 1 metre, then the whole triangle will be enlarged by a factor of 3, so the sides will be as shown here:

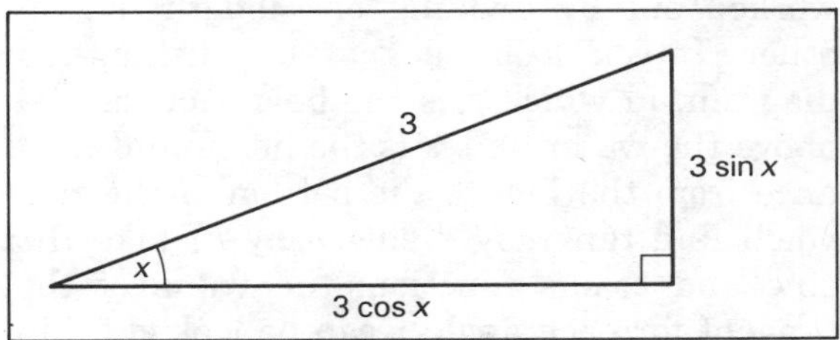

but the sine and cosine of the angle equivalent to x will remain the same.

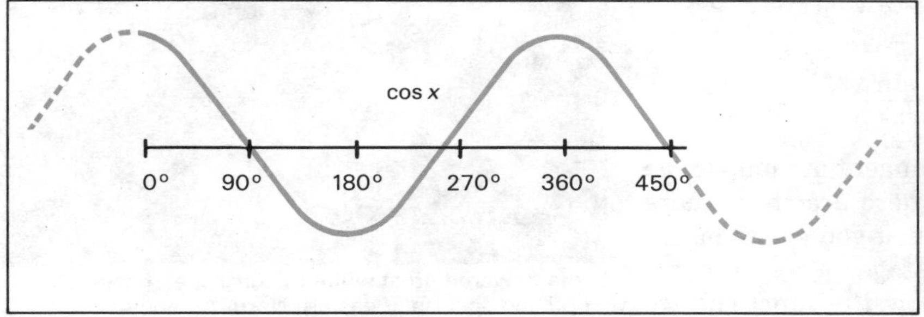

This cosine curve has the same shape as a sine wave and also repeats itself every 360°. But it starts at its maximum positive value. So cos 0° equals 1, while cos 90° equals 0.

If we travel along a road for 100 metres and the road is going uphill at an angle of 5°, then the following diagram shows that the change in vertical height is 100 × sin 5°.

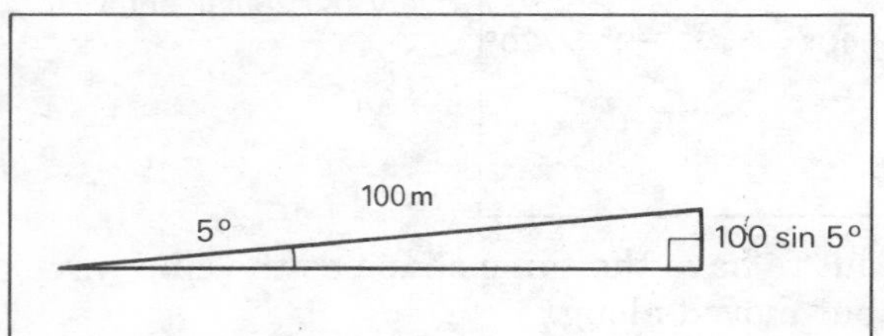

Because sines and cosines are constant values when related to the angles they come from, we can use them for measuring. We can find them out from a book of tables or from a scientific calculator. Thus we can learn that sin 5° is about 0.0872, and so the change in vertical height in our example is

$$100 \times 0.0872\text{m} = 8.72\text{m}.$$

It would be difficult to measure this directly. Trigonometry gives us a way of calculating it.

Another commonly used trigonometrical function is the *tangent*, or "tan" for short. Like the sine and cosine functions, the tangent of an angle is a special number that can be worked out by dividing one length by another. If you look back at our fishing-rod diagram, in which v is the height of the rod above the water and h is the horizontal distance from the line to the bottom of the rod, you'll find tan x by diving v by h. Like the sine and cosine function, the value of the tangent for each angle x can be looked up in special mathematical tables or worked out by means of a scientific calculator. You will also find that tan, sine, and cosine functions are all linked together by this very useful formula:

$$\tan x = \frac{\sin x}{\cos x}.$$

The sine, cosine, and tangent are only three functions of an angle. There are three more that you will come across if you study mathematics to an advanced stage.

Finally, we will see how the functions we have discussed so far can be historically linked to a circle. Although we have spoken of trigonometrical functions as ratios—that is, the length of one line divided by the length of another—they were originally worked out as the lengths of certain lines drawn from one point to another on the arc of a circle. In fact, we still speak of a tangent as a line that touches a curve, such as the arc of a circle, at one point. This diagram shows which lines are involved.

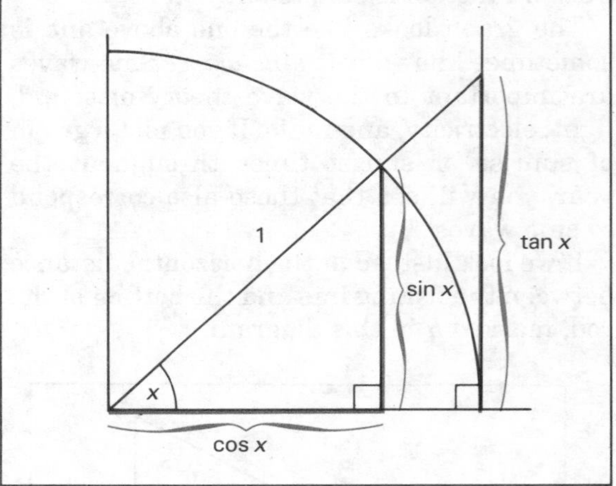

TRILLIUM is any of several species of flowering plants of the lily family, Liliaceae. The plant's name comes from the Latin word for three. The blossoms of trilliums have three petals, three sepals, six stamens, a three-celled ovary, and a cluster of three leaves.

NHPA/John Shaw

Large flowered great white trillium, one of several woodland species of eastern North America.

Trilliums are woodland plants of North America and Asia. They grow in damp, shaded areas. About 25 different species are known.

One of the species of trillium with large flowers is the great white trillium, or trinity lily (*Trillium grandiflorum*). Its blossoms have broad petals, each 7.5 centimetres (3 inches) long, and a pleasant scent. Days after blooming, the flowers change from white to pink. The so-called purple trillium (*T. erectum*) really has dark-red petals. The blossom has a most unpleasant odour.

Perhaps the prettiest of the trilliums is the painted trillium (*T. undulatum*). Its narrow, pointed petals are white, marked with deep pink or maroon. The nodding trillium's (*T. cernuum*) white flowers droop and are almost hidden by the leaves.

When trilliums are picked, they wilt quickly, and the plant forms no seed for the next year. It is best, therefore, to let the flowers stay in their natural woodland home.

In 1927 the trillium was made the official flower of Ontario, Canada.

TRILOBITES were once the most abundant sea animals on Earth. Their fossil remains are plentiful in rocks in many parts of the world. Trilobites looked rather like woodlice. They had hard, jointed bodies, divided lengthways into three lobes or sections—hence the name *Tri* ("three")-*lobite* ("lobed").

Trilobites first appeared in the seas at the beginning of the Cambrian Period, roughly 570 million years ago but they were all extinct by the end of the Permian, 225 million years ago. Some were quite large, more than 45 centimetres (18 inches) long; others were much smaller. Most lived on the sea floor. Some could swim; others could burrow in the mud.

Courtesy, Institute of Geological Sciences

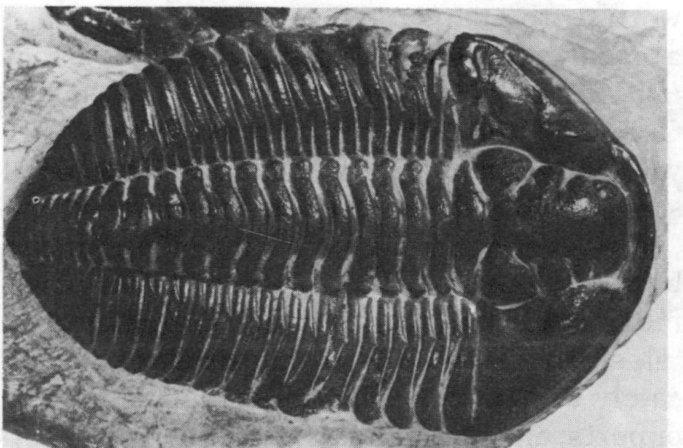

The three-lobed, armour-plated body plan of a trilobite is clearly shown by this fossil.

The trilobite's armoured body consisted of a head, usually with eyes and antennae, a segmented middle portion, and a tail shield. Each segment had a pair of limbs that were used for walking, and also for finding food on the seabed. The swimming forms were lightly built and carried spines, while the burrowing types were spade-shaped. Trilobites grew by shedding their outer skeletons and growing new ones.

TRINIDAD AND TOBAGO are two islands which form a single independent country in the West Indies. Trinidad is the most southerly of the West Indian islands (see WEST INDIES). It is about 80 kilometres (50 miles) from north to south and about 60 kilometres (40 miles) broad. Tobago is much smaller, 43 kilometres (27 miles) long and 12 kilometres (7 miles) broad.

FACTS ABOUT TRINIDAD AND TOBAGO

AREA: 5,128 square kilometres (1,980 square miles).
POPULATION: 1,223,000 (1987).
GOVERNMENT: Independent republic; member of the Commonwealth.
CAPITAL: Port-of-Spain.
GEOGRAPHICAL FEATURES: Trinidad is crossed from east to west by three ranges of thickly wooded hills. Tobago is a volcanic mountain mass, thickly wooded in many parts.
CHIEF PRODUCTS: Petroleum, natural gas, sugar, cocoa, citrus fruits, copra, asphalt, cement.
IMPORTANT TOWNS: Trinidad: Port-of-Spain, San Fernando, Arima. Tobago: Scarborough.
EDUCATION: Education between tha ages of 5 and 15 is free.

Trinidad has two long peninsulas stretching from its western corners. At their tips these peninsulas come within 14 kilometres (9 miles) of Venezuela on the mainland of South America, and between them they enclose a wide area of shallow water called the Gulf of Paria. The waters of the gulf are sometimes

ZEFA

The tourist's view of Tobago is one of swaying palms, gleaming white beaches and a beautiful warm, clear sea.

greyish-green because of mud brought into the gulf by the Orinoco River. The narrow northern entrance to the gulf, broken up by islands, is known as the Dragon's Mouth. The southern entrance is called the Serpent's Mouth.

A ridge of wooded mountains across the north of Trinidad and called the Northern Range rises to its highest point at Mount Aripo which is 940 metres (3,084 feet) high. Among the most striking natural features are the Maracas Falls, 95 metres (312 feet) high, at the head of a valley in the northwest. Wildlife includes colourful birds such as flamingoes, egrets, ibis, and hummingbirds. On the small bird sanctuary of Little Tobago birds of paradise live in the wild—the only place they do so, outside Australia and New Guinea.

The tropical climate of Trinidad is warm and damp, although the nights are fairly cool. The average temperature is 24°C (75°F). It seldom rises above 34°C (93°F) or drops below 21°C (70°F). The dry season runs from January to May; the rainy season for the rest of the year.

When Trinidad was discovered by Christopher Columbus in 1498, the island was inhabited by Arawak Indians, and Tobago by the warlike Carib tribe. Columbus vowed to dedicate the first land he saw on this voyage to the Holy Trinity, and by a strange coincidence he sighted land just where three peaks rose above the horizon. He therefore called it in Spanish *La Trinidad*, meaning "the Trinity". Columbus took possession of the island for Spain but few Spanish settlers came.

Then in the 18th century Trinidad was visited by a French planter from the island of Grenada. He was impressed by the fertility of the soil and, in 1783, persuaded the Spaniards to allow settlement by foreigners. The only condition they made was that the new settlers should be Roman Catholic. A few years later the French Revolution caused many French planters in the West Indies to move with their African slaves to Trinidad. In 1797 a British force from Martinique captured Trinidad from the Spaniards. British possession of the island was confirmed by the Treaty of Amiens in 1802.

When in 1834 the slaves in the British colonies were freed, many of the Africans left the hard and miserable conditions of the sugar plantations. To replace them, workers were brought from India, China, and the Portuguese island of Madeira during the years 1845–1917. Indians now form more than one-third of the population. English is the language generally spoken. Hindi is also widely spoken and is taught in some schools. Over half the people are Christian, but there are also many Hindus and Muslims.

The influence of the mixture of many races can be seen when Trinidad holds its carnivals. Many exotic and colourful costumes are worn in the bands and processions. There is a good opportunity to hear the steel bands and calypsos for which Trinidad is noted. Calypsos are humorous ballad songs with words often made up on the spot, often about some event or person in the news.

The steel bands specialize in calypso music, but they also play jazz, Spanish, and classical music with unusual rhythms. The adjective "steel" refers to petrol drums, heated and delicately tuned by beating into small segments, or parts; and also to scrap metal such as motor-car brake drums. Exciting effects are obtained when the instruments are played by beating with rubber-headed sticks (see also POPULAR MUSIC).

Agriculture and Industry

The soil of Trinidad is very fertile and most kinds of tropical produce flourish. The chief crops are grown on plantations and include sugar, cocoa, coconuts, grapefruit, limes, oranges, bananas, and coffee. Rum is made from sugar, and the scented flavouring called Angostura Bitters is made according to a secret recipe kept by one family from generation to generation. Another product is the tonca bean (sometimes called coumara nut), which is the seed of a special kind of forest tree and has a sweet smell like new-mown hay. It is used for making perfumes. Although it employs fewer people than farming, the oil industry brings most of Trinidad's wealth, for the island is a large producer of petroleum. Petroleum from Trinidad and some from Venezuela and Saudi Arabia is refined at Pointe-à-Pierre and Palo Seco in the southern part of Trinidad. Asphalt is also exported. It comes from the Pitch Lake in the southwest of Trinidad.

The capital of Trinidad is Port-of-Spain, which lies towards the northern end of the west coast. It is the chief harbour for traffic between the islands and its modern port handles worldwide passenger and cargo ships. Pointe-à-Pierre and Point Fortin are important offshore petroleum loading berths. Other important towns are San Fernando and Arima. Trinidad is a popular beach holiday resort and many hotels have been built.

From 1958 to 1962 Trinidad was the seat of government of the West Indies Federation. After the Federation broke up, Trinidad and Tobago became independent. Its first prime minister was Eric Williams. Living standards improved in the 1970s, as oil exports increased. In 1976 the country became a republic.

Tobago

Tobago is about 30 kilometres (18 miles) northeast of Trinidad. It is a bean-shaped island which rises to a thickly wooded mountain ridge some 550 metres (1,800 feet) high along the centre. Its capital is Scarborough (formerly called Port Louis), which is on the coast in the southwest. Most of the people are engaged in producing copra (see COCONUT), limes, bananas, and cacao beans (for chocolate and cocoa).

TRIPOLI is the name of two important cities on the shores of the Mediterranean Sea, one in Libya, the other in Lebanon (see LEBANON; LIBYA). Both cities are known by their Arabic name Tarabulus as well as Tripoli.

ZEFA

Tripoli, the capital of Libya, is a handsome North African city, a mixture of old and new.

"Western" Tripoli is the capital and chief seaport of Libya. It was founded by the Phoenicians. Its eastern and southern parts consist of modern white buildings and the streets are lined with palms and flowered, scented oleander trees. To the west is the old Arab town with its twisted, arched streets, busy markets and workshops and beautiful mosques.

The Gurgi Mosque, with its high minaret (tower), is almost alongside a magnificent Roman archway of white marble (built in AD163 in honour of Marcus Aurelius), which was once the chief entrance to the city. Tripoli owes its importance to its harbour which, together with the modern part of the city, began to be developed during the years of Italian rule from 1911 to 1943. Much of Libya's foreign trade, including its oil, now passes through Tripoli. The city is the trading centre of a fertile oasis growing olives, vegetables, citrus fruit, tobacco, and grains. Fishing is important and in the city are carpet and tanning industries. The airport is 34 kilometres (21 miles) south of the city. The population is about 858,000 (1981).

"Eastern" Tripoli is a seaport in Lebanon about 65 kilometres (40 miles) north of the capital, Beirut. It is an industrial centre handling oil, as well as making soap and cotton goods. Sponge fishing is also important. There are several historic sites including mosques.

Tripoli was also founded by the Phoenicians. It later saw Roman, Muslim, and Crusader occupation. Muslims retook the city after a period of economic and educational progress under the Crusaders. Later came Ottoman rule followed by Egyptian, then British occupation. In 1946 it became part of the Republic of Lebanon. Its population is about 180,000 (1982).

TROJAN WAR. Long ago, about the year 1200 BC, a fleet of seafaring people from mainland Greece is said to have crossed the Aegean to the ancient city of Troy in Asia Minor (modern western Turkey). There they fought the Trojan people, besieging and eventually capturing and burning Troy itself (see TROY).

Nobody knows for certain whether or not this expedition actually took place, but the stories about it became part of Greek mythology. The original expedition, or raid, was transformed into a war that lasted ten years. The two epic poems of Homer, the *Iliad* and the *Odyssey*, were set against the background of this war (see HOMER; ILIAD; ODYSSEY). The Roman poet Virgil also used the story as part of his great epic the *Aeneid* (see AENEID; VIRGIL).

The Trojan War, according to legend, was caused by an event at the wedding feast of Thetis, a sea goddess, and Peleus, a mortal. The goddess of strife and discord suddenly appeared among the guests with a golden apple inscribed "For the fairest". This was claimed by three goddesses: Hera, the queen of the gods, Athena the goddess of wisdom, and Aphrodite, the goddess of love and beauty. Paris, a Trojan prince, was called on to choose between them. Hera promised him power, Athena offered wisdom, and Aphrodite promised him the most beautiful woman in the world for his wife. Paris gave the apple to Aphrodite.

Now the woman whom Aphrodite had chosen for Paris was Helen, a daughter of Zeus. She was already the wife of Menelaus, King of Sparta. Paris came to Menelaus' court and succeeded in persuading Helen to leave her husband and sail away to Troy with him. Menelaus, determined to get Helen back, appealed for help to his brother Agamemnon, king of the splendid city of Mycenae. The two brothers summoned together all the heroes of Greece to join them in an attack on Troy. Achilles, the son of Thetis and Peleus, was the mightiest fighter of all. The brain of the company was Odysseus, who was always ready with cunning plots. Nestor was respected for his wisdom.

The Greeks set sail for Troy with a splendid fleet. But Troy, under its wise King Priam and Hector, the noblest of his sons, was a mighty city protected by great walls. The Trojans refused to give up Helen, and the Greeks could do nothing but camp on the surrounding plains.

For nine years the siege of Troy went on, neither side gaining much advantage. Then at the end of that time a quarrel broke out between Achilles and Agamemnon. This is the point at which the *Iliad* begins (see ILIAD). In the battles that followed, gods and goddesses took part. Hera and Athena, still angry at the judgement of Paris, were on the side of the Greeks, while Aphrodite and Apollo, god of the sun, supported the Trojans. In a terrible fight between the two heroes Hector and Achilles, Achilles slew Hector and dragged his enemy's body three times round the walls of Troy tied behind his chariot. Priam personally retrieved it for burial.

Scenes from the Trojan War are portrayed on this sarcophagus from the time of Alexander the Great. It was found in the Lebanon.

Courtesy, The Ancient Art & Architecture Collection

Still, however, Troy would not give in. As the siege continued, Achilles was shot with an arrow by Paris, and Paris himself suffered the same fate at the hands of another Greek hero Philoctetes. As the war dragged on, Odysseus decided that it was time to use cunning. He ordered Epeius, a skilful Greek carpenter, to make a hollow wooden horse large enough to contain armed men. A group of Greek heroes, including Odysseus, Menelaus, and Epeius himself, climbed in and shut the concealed door. The Trojans were made to believe that the Greeks had abandoned the siege and were returning home. Accordingly all except one man, called Sinon, embarked and sailed away, hiding on the isle of Tenedos near by.

The Trojans came cautiously out of Troy and examined the deserted camp. The huge wooden horse standing on the plain astonished them greatly and they agreed among themselves to drag it into the city. Only Laocoon, a priest of Apollo, opposed this. Troy, however, was doomed to fall, and so the gods, in order to make the Trojans believe that Laocoon was lying, sent two great snakes over the sea. These terrifying creatures crushed Laocoon to death, together with his two sons. This convinced the Trojans that the horse was a sacred object which he had insulted. Then, as final proof, Sinon was found and brought before Priam. He said that he had deserted the Greeks and that the horse would protect the city if it were taken inside. The Trojans needed no more persuasion. Singing with joy they dragged the horse within the walls by ropes. As they entered, Cassandra, Priam's daughter warned them of terrible calamity. But although she could see into the future it was her fate never to be believed.

The Trojans feasted and made merry that night. When the city was still, Sinon crept to the horse, opened its secret door, and released the armed Greeks who proceeded to attack the sleeping city. Signal fires were raised for the fleet, gliding back from Tenedos, and the rest of the Greeks burst in to help in the destruction of Troy. Soon every street was filled with fighting men and the buildings of Troy were on fire. Priam took refuge at the altar of Zeus, but was slain by Achilles' son Neoptolemus.

One of the Trojan heroes succeeded in escaping from the city. This was Aphrodite's son Aeneas, who, with his father, his son, and some companions, set sail from the doom-stricken city. For years he wandered until he reached Italy, becoming the founder (according to legend) of the Roman people. His story is told in the *Aeneid*.

After the sack of Troy, Odysseus wandered for ten more years before he reached his island home of Ithaca and his wife Penelope. Homer made the story of his many adventures into another great poem, the *Odyssey*. (See ODYSSEY.) Agamemnon reached home to find that his wife Clytemnestra had taken a lover. The two murdered him. Menelaus, on the other hand, lived happily with Helen for many years afterwards. He had found her during the fighting in Troy and brought her back with him to Sparta.

TROLLOPE, Anthony (1815–82). In his numerous novels about English social life during the Victorian period, the writer Anthony Trollope created many memorable characters. He placed them in settings described in such careful detail that reading his books today gives a wonderful understanding of what it was like to live in Victorian England.

BBC Hulton Picture Library

The novelist Anthony Trollope was an accurate and witty observer of Victorian society in England.

Trollope was ignored and bullied at school because his father was poor. This unhappy experience gave him a bad start in his career working for the post office in London. In 1841, however, he took a new job working for the post office in Ireland, which suited him better. He grew happier, married in 1844, and began to write.

Trollope is given credit for inventing the "novel sequence", a succession of books describing the lives and fortunes of a group of characters over a number of years. His two great novel sequences are the Barchester and the Palliser novels. The Barchester novels are set in an imaginary county in England which he called Barsetshire. The town of Barset is a cathedral town, and the novels describe the interwoven lives of families with church connections. The Palliser novels deal with the fortunes of a family with political ambitions and great wealth. Trollope based the political novels on his own unsuccessful attempt to be elected to parliament.

Trollope wrote 47 novels in all, as well as travel books, biographies, short stories, and a fascinating autobiography. He combined his writing with a highly successful career in the post office. He introduced the letter box, and helped to make the delivery system more efficient.

Among his other well-known novels are *The Three Clerks* (1857), *He Knew He Was Right* (1869), *The Way We Live Now* (1875), and *The American Senator* (1877).

TROMBONE FAMILY. Trombones are heavy-sounding brass instruments that are generally used when the orchestra is playing the loud, powerful parts of a piece of music. They are also used for filling in the harmony (see HARMONY) "below" the trumpet and horn parts. Trombones are related to trumpets in having a tube of cylindrical shape and a cup-shaped mouthpiece. But instead of having valves, a trombone is fitted with a movable slide, which, when pulled out, allows the range of notes that can be played to be extended downwards for six semitones. (See HARMONY; TRUMPET FAMILY.) The old name of the trombone was "sackbut" and it is thought that the first part of this word came from an old French word meaning to pull, or draw, an obvious reference to the action of the slide. The slide can be in any of seven positions, the ordinary one and six lower ones. When it is in any of them the player can, by tightening or slackening his lips, sound the series of natural notes (called harmonics) like those of the hunting horn (see HORN FAMILY).

There are different sizes of trombone. In the orchestra nowadays there are usually two medium-sized, or tenor, trombones and one large, or bass, trombone. Mozart's *Requiem*, Schubert's *Great C Major Symphony*, and Stravinsky's ballet *Petrushka* are works in

Erich Auerbach

The trombones of an orchestra add both power and brilliance to the tone of the brass section.

which trombones are used very effectively. They are also used for brilliant effects in military bands. In jazz and dance bands they are generally heard playing a smooth song-like melody.

TROPICAL DISEASES. Tropical diseases are those that are common in tropical areas, causing much misery, ill-health, and death. The climate is warmest in the band around the middle of the Earth, the tropics, where the majority of the world's plants and animals dwell. They include many bacteria, protozoa, and other microscopic living things that can cause disease.

Tropical diseases are mostly infections and are mostly contagious (spread from person to person under suitable conditions). The World Health Organization lists six major tropical diseases on which research, information, and treatment are most urgently needed. These are malaria, leprosy, schistosomiasis (bilharzia), trypanosomiasis, filariasis, and leishmaniasis. Other diseases common in tropical areas include yaws, hookworm, sleeping sickness, dysentery, cholera, yellow fever, plague, and, until recently, smallpox. (There are separate entries on CHOLERA; HOOKWORM; LEPROSY; MALARIA; SCHISTOSOMIASIS; SLEEPING SICKNESS; YELLOW FEVER.)

Hundreds of millions of people are ill with tropical diseases. Up to 50 million people catch malaria each year. There are probably 20 million sufferers from leprosy.

Some diseases can occur only in the tropics. For example, the water snails that harbour the parasites causing schistosomiasis can live only in fairly warm water. Similarly, the tsetse flies that spread sleeping sickness need temperatures of at least 25°C (77°F) to live and breed.

For other diseases, warmth is only part of the story. Cholera, malaria, leprosy, and other "tropical" diseases can also occur in cooler temperate regions north and south of the equator. Isolated cases and small epidemics of tropical diseases crop up regularly in North America, Europe, and southern Australia, well outside the tropics.

Many tropical countries are poor and have little money to spend on doctors, drugs, and health services. Few people are immunized or are told about the importance of hygiene, food preparation, and safe disposal of sewage and wastes. Many do not have enough food to eat and so are more at risk of illness. Drinking-water is polluted and people have to live in overcrowded and dirty conditions. All of these factors increase the risk of disease.

By contrast, countries in temperate regions tend to be richer. People are generally more healthy and better fed. Babies are immunized against certain diseases. The medical services are well organized and many different drugs are available. As soon as a disease outbreak occurs, people know what to do and the doctors give the appropriate treatment. Drinking water is cleaner and most people understand the need for hygiene and safe cooking. (See HEALTH AND HEALTH CARE.)

Tackling Tropical Diseases

Nearly all of the tropical diseases can be cured, usually by drugs. But there are many obstacles to distributing these drugs where they are needed most. They may be too expensive to be bought by poor countries. They may not find their way into the country areas, where people suffering from diseases tend to be, and these people may not even know that drugs can help them.

Many health campaigns have been launched in tropical countries to fight tropical diseases.

Yet sometimes it is difficult to teach basic lessons, such as the importance of boiling water before it is drunk or used in cooking. People need to be shown why such measures are needed, because their old traditions and way of life have not recognized them as being important.

Organizations involved in the battle against tropical diseases include the World Health Organisation (WHO) and the United Nations Educational, Scientific and Cultural Organisation (UNESCO). The battle is being fought on many fronts. Money, doctors and nurses, drugs and equipment have to reach the regions that need them most. The most basic health measures, such as clean drinking-water and proper waste and sewage disposal, have to be made commonplace. People must have enough healthy food to eat. There have to be campaigns against individual diseases, to make medicines and expert help available.

TROPICS. On either side of the equator (0 degrees latitude) are two other imaginary lines: the Tropic of Cancer (23 degrees 27 minutes North latitude) and the Tropic of Capricorn (23 degrees 27 minutes South latitude). These lines are the northernmost and southernmost places on Earth where the Sun ever appears directly overhead. The zone between them is described as tropical, or within the tropics.

A glance at the map of the world shows that the following land areas are within the tropics: north Africa from the Sahara and the Sudan to Zimbabwe in the south; in Asia, southern Arabia, the southern half of the Indian peninsula, Burma, Thailand, Vietnam, Laos, Kampuchea, Malaysia, and Indonesia. The northern part of Australia and most of the Pacific Islands are also in the tropics. In America, the southern half of Mexico, the West Indies, Central America, and the northern half of South America are all tropical.

The word tropic means "turning point". It is so named because of the apparent movement of the Sun in the sky throughout the year. The Sun does not really move but its position in the

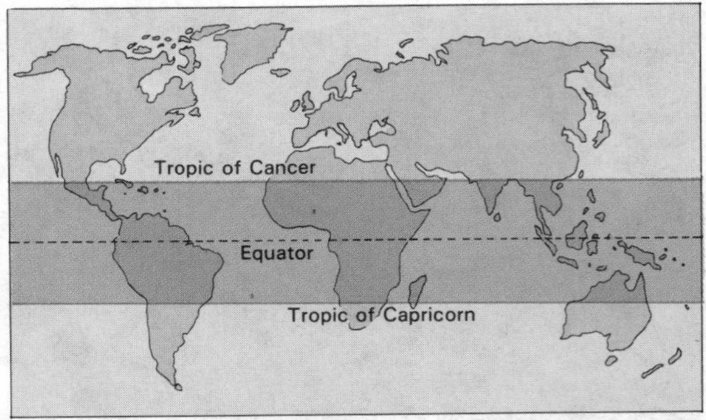

sky is seen to change from day to day because of the angle the Earth's axis makes with the plane of the Earth's path around the Sun. On 22 March, the Sun is directly overhead at the equator. The overhead Sun then appears to move north, reaching the Tropic of Cancer on 21 June. It then apparently returns south. On 22 September, it is again overhead at the equator and, on 21 December, it is overhead at the Tropic of Capricorn. This is more fully explained in the article SEASON.

One feature of the tropics is that the Sun rises and sets at about six o'clock. There is no long twilight before dawn or after sunset. The Sun's heat is highly concentrated in the tropics, making the region the world's warmest. Temperatures are high except in high uplands.

Areas near the equator are mostly rainy, and dense forests thrive in the hot, wet conditions. North and south of these forests are regions with wet and dry seasons. Here the forests merge into tropical grasslands. Further north and south, the rainfall decreases and the grasslands merge into hot deserts. There are separate articles on DESERT; RAIN FOREST; SAVANNA.

TROTSKY, Leon (1879–1940), was one of the chief organizers, along with Lenin, of the Russian Revolution of November 1917. Born of Jewish parents near Odessa in the Ukraine, Trotsky's real name was Lev Davidovich Bronstein. After he left the University of Odessa, he joined with those planning a revolution in Russia. At this time many Russians were unhappy under the harsh, undemocratic government of the tsars, the rulers of Russia. Because of this activity he was arrested in 1898 and exiled to Siberia. In 1902 he escaped by using the name Trotsky on a forged passport. He then took this name as his own.

BBC Hulton Picture Library

Leon Trotsky came second to Lenin in the Soviet leadership following the Communist revolution in Russia.

After escaping from Siberia, Trotsky went to London where he met Lenin. In 1905 he returned to Russia to resume his work for the revolution, but he had to flee in 1910. For a number of years he lived in various European cities where he lectured against the capitalist systems of government and World War I. In January 1917 he went to the United States to edit a Russian-language newspaper in New York City. However, when the revolution broke out in Russia in March, he returned to join in the struggle.

Trotsky soon became a Bolshevik, as members of the leading Communist faction were called at that time. He quickly rose to leadership within the party, achieving a position second only to Lenin. The Bolsheviks overthrew Alexander Kerensky's provisional government (which was trying to set up a democracy) in November 1917, and set up their own Soviet government. Trotsky became the people's commissioner for foreign affairs. He later took charge of organizing the Communist armies.

After Lenin's death in 1924, Trotsky was opposed by Joseph Stalin in a bitter struggle for power. Trotsky lost and was exiled in 1928. He finally settled in Mexico City. Twelve years later a political enemy murdered him in his home there. Many believed the murderer was acting on orders from Stalin.

Trotsky wrote numerous books: some are in English, including: *Defence of Terrorism* (1920), *Lenin* (1924), *Problems of Life* (1924), and *The Revolution Betrayed* (1937).

See also COMMUNISM; LENIN, VLADIMIR ILICH; STALIN, JOSEPH.

TROTTING see HORSE RACING.

TROUT are popular and well-known fish closely related to salmon. They differ from salmon in that their upper jawbone extends past the eye, and the tail-fin is straight rather than deeply scooped.

Familiar members of the trout family include the brown trout (*Salmo trutta*), rainbow trout (*Salmo gairdneri*), and cut-throat trout (*Salmo clarki*). Females of all these and other trout species use their tails to dig redds (shallow depressions) in the bottom of a stream just above a pool. The female lays her eggs here, and at the same time the male sheds his sperm (milt) which fertilizes them. Trout fishing is a favourite sport and many fishing clubs have their own hatcheries for breeding trout.

There are two main types of brown trout, non-migratory and migratory, or sea trout.

Top: A migratory sea trout; **Bottom**: Brown trout.

The non-migratory brown trout live in streams, rivers, and lakes and do not migrate, or journey, to the sea. Sea trout migrate like salmon and so are often wrongly referred to as salmon-trout.

Brown trout usually have heavy dark spots on a green or brown background. Sea trout are more silvery with fewer spots. The brown trout is a European fish that has been introduced into many other countries. It was introduced into the United States in 1883.

The rainbow trout is a beautifully coloured fish which, like the brown trout, has a migratory form, called the steel-head. The rainbow trout is native to the rivers of the west coast of North America, and Mexico. It feeds on insect larvae, molluscs, and crustaceans, It is a popular game fish because of its fighting qualities and grows fast when reared in fish farms. The cut-throat trout, also from Pacific coast rivers (from California north to Alaska), gets its name from orange or red blotches on its throat.

Other fish called trout include fish of the genus *Salvelinus*, also of the salmon family. These fish tend to live in northern lakes and migrate up rivers to breed. They include the brook trout or charr (*Salvelinus fontinalis*) of northeastern North America, and the lake trout (*Salvelinus namaycush*), a beautiful fish with a dark green back, light belly, and orange anal fins. It takes part of its scientific name from the North American Indian name "namaycush".

The young sea trout hatch in rivers, where they remain for two or more years. During this time they are called parr, and are very similar in colour and form to salmon parr. (See SALMON.) Later they change into silvery fishes called smolts and migrate to the sea. They do not go as far as salmon. After about six months some return to the rivers for a few weeks, and during this time a little less than half of them breed. Afterwards they return to the sea. Those that do not spawn will return to breed at a later date. Others may stay a year or more in the sea before returning to the river to spawn for the first time. Sea trout, unlike salmon, may spawn two or three times in their lifetime.

Unlike salmon, sea trout feed during their stay in the river. They grow quite large—fish weighing 10 kilograms (22 pounds) have been caught on rod and line. The males are reddish in colour and the females are silvery.

Brown trout parr look exactly like sea trout parr. The adult trout are handsome spotted fish which vary greatly in colour and size according to where they are found. Even the trout in one part of a river may differ from those in another part of the same river. In some mountain streams where many brown trout live and there is not much food for them they are rarely more than 25 centimetres (9.8 inches) long. In other waters, however, they may weigh over 8 kilograms (17.6 pounds).

Trout are found throughout the northern hemisphere, including North America, Europe, Asia, and Africa. They have been introduced into many other countries, such as New Zealand. Trout are also reared commercially in fish farms for use as food.

TROY. Greek legends told of a ten-year war between the Greeks and the people of Troy in Asia Minor (Turkey). Homer, the greatest of Greek poets, wrote a wonderful poem, the *Iliad*, about this war and the people who took part in it. The articles ILIAD and TROJAN WAR tell the story of this famous struggle.

There were, however, other stories about Troy besides that of the Trojan War. It was said to have been founded by a man called Teucer, who became its first king. Under his great-grandson Tros the city became known as Troy, and under Ilos, the son of Tros, it received another name, Ilium.

According to the legend, the son of Ilos was Laomedon, who became known as a cheat and a liar. Apollo, god of the sun, and Poseidon (Neptune), god of the sea, built a wall round Troy for him, but Laomedon refused to give them the payment he had promised. In revenge, the gods sent a sea monster to ravage Troy, but the hero Hercules promised to kill it on condition that Laomedon would give him

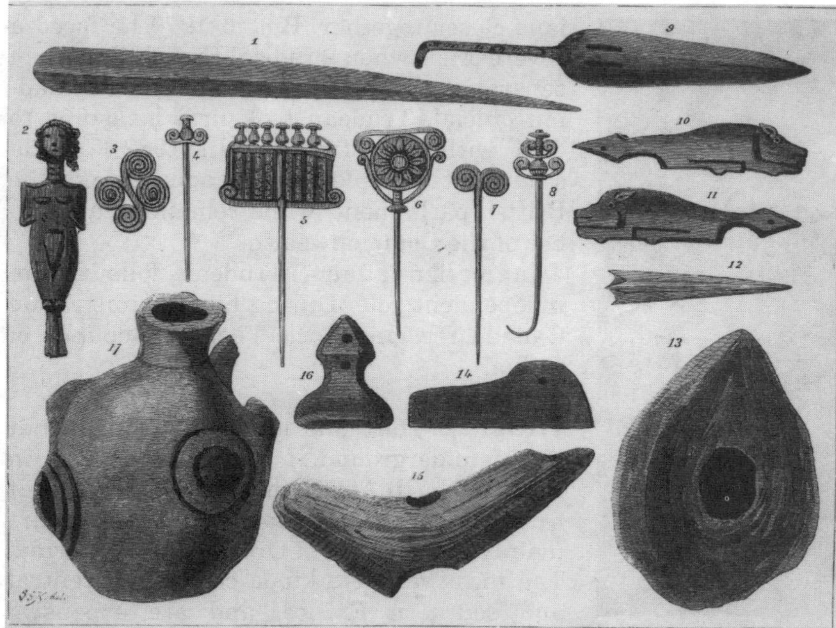

Objects found by Heinrich Schliemann at Troy: **1** tool made of bone; **2** idol; **3** gold ornament; **4–8** gold hairpins; **9** steel knife; **10 and 11** ivory tools for weaving; **12** ivory arrow-head; **13** stone hammer; **14** article made of terracotta; **15** stick handle of bone; **16** stone tool; **17** terracotta vase.

Mary Evans Picture Library

his horses. Hercules kept his word, but Laomedon again broke his, so Hercules in a rage killed Laomedon and sacked Troy. However, he spared Laomedon's son Priam, who was king of Troy at the time of the Trojan War.

Troy was not just a legendary city. Archaeologists digging at Hissarlik in Asiatic Turkey, close to the narrow strait known as the Dardanelles, have discovered the remains of no fewer than nine towns, the seventh oldest being Priam's Troy. The Trojan War was probably fought more than 3,000 years ago, but Troy in those days stood on a site which was already old and had been occupied for a long time.

The first Troy was little more than a village, although it had a wall. Gradually the succeeding towns grew larger until in the 13th or 14th century BC, there was a fine city with great gates in the walls and large houses. This was wrecked by an earthquake but was rebuilt, larger and finer still. Traces of the great civilization that flourished on the island of Crete and at the Greek city of Mycenae were found in this city, which was the Troy of Priam.

Troy rose again after its destruction, this time as a Greek city. In Christian times it was rebuilt and remained in existence until about the 5th century AD.

The man who unearthed Troy was a German called Heinrich Schliemann (see SCHLIEMANN, HEINRICH). He went to Hissarlik, which was not then believed to be the site of the city, in 1870, and began to dig there, convinced that the lowest—and therefore the oldest—remains would be those of Priam's Troy. He dug down to the second city, which had been burnt, and discovered there a hoard of rich gold ornaments. This, he was certain, was Priam's Troy, but shortly before his death it became clear that what he had found was a far older town. A United States expedition in the 1930s concluded that the so-called Troy VIIa, a walled town which bore signs of overcrowding, siege, violence, and finally fire, was in fact the Troy of the *Iliad*.

TRUDEAU, Pierre Elliott (born 1919), Canadian statesman, was his country's prime minister from 1968 to 1984 with one brief interval.

Trudeau was born in Montreal, Quebec. His mother was Scottish and his father French Canadian, so Trudeau grew up learning to

Popperfoto
During Pierre Trudeau's terms of office he established Canada's independence from the British parliament.

speak both French and English fluently. He was educated in Montreal and earned both his bachelor's degree and his law degree with honours.

In 1951 Trudeau began practising law in Quebec and also began to write and speak on important political issues. After a period as a law professor, in 1965 he won a seat in the House of Commons. He joined Prime Minister Lester B. Pearson's Liberal government as parliamentary secretary and later as minister of justice. Trudeau succeeded Pearson as head of the Liberal party. When Pearson retired in April 1968, Trudeau became prime minister. In the election that followed in June, Trudeau, with his ideas for change, led his party to victory. He was replaced in 1979 when the Progressive Conservative Joe Clark became prime minister. Trudeau, however, regained the office some nine months later.

As prime minister, Trudeau worked to create what he called a "Just Society" and to cope with Canada's major problems: unemployment, poverty, and urban growth. He tried to bring French- and English-speaking Canadians closer together. But in 1970 he faced a severe crisis when a radical French Canadian separatist group murdered a French Canadian official. Trudeau took firm measures to deal with the situation. In 1982 Canada secured its complete independence from the British parliament, while remaining a member of the Commonwealth.

In foreign affairs, Trudeau followed an independent role. During his administration Canada recognized the People's Republic of China.

TRUFFLE. The truffle is an edible fungus that grows underground. It is quite common in Europe, North Africa, and the Near East but rare in the United States where it occurs mainly in the states of Oregon and California. The most valuable kinds come from central and southern France, and are expensive delicacies.

Yan Toulouse

The Périgord black truffle from southwest France is highly prized and used to flavour goose pâté.

Truffles are round and weigh very little. Most are about the size of a hen's egg when ripe. The skin is covered with warts and darkens with age. When cut the flesh is brown or black and has a strong yeasty smell. Most European truffles grow near the roots of trees. For example, the valuable Périgord truffle (*Tuber melanosporum*) of French cookery is often found by the roots of oak trees or holm-oaks, in southwestern France.

Truffles were highly prized by the ancient

Greeks and Romans and were a favourite dish among European noblemen after the Renaissance. Truffle-hunting, using either pigs or dogs specially trained to scent the truffles, became a regular occupation among country people.

Truffles are eaten in many ways, especially with poultry, when they are traditionally prepared by first being peeled, cut into quarters, and then cooked in pork fat.

TRUMAN, Harry S. (1884–1972), was the 33rd president of the United States. He had the difficult task of succeeding Franklin D. Roosevelt, who was famous abroad as well as in his own country for his extrovert nature, and as a defender of people's rights. Truman believed in "middle-of-the-road" policies and was hardly known abroad, but he was shrewd, honest, loyal, and likeable. He took difficult and courageous decisions during and after World War II.

Harry Truman was born on 8 May 1884 in Lamar, Missouri, the son of a mule trader and farmer. Harry went to school at Independence, Missouri, but was unable to go on to the Military Academy of West Point because of an eye defect. Nor could his family afford to send him to college. He worked in Kansas City for a time but then returned to the family farm.

Truman showed bravery in action in France during World War I (1914-18). He returned home as a captain and married his childhood friend Bess Wallace. A haberdashery business which he started in Kansas City failed in the economic depression of 1921. Truman then entered local politics with the support of "Big Tom" Pendergast, the political "boss" of the Missouri Democratic party. He became a county judge and later a presiding judge. In 1934, with a reputation for honesty and the aid of the Democratic party organization he was elected to the United States Senate. In spite of Pendergast's disgrace and imprisonment for taking bribes, Truman was re-elected in 1940.

After a quiet start to his political career Truman attracted attention in 1941 when he was appointed head of a special Senate committee to investigate corruption and waste in the defence programme. President Roosevelt, who was about to run for a fourth term, admired Truman's skilful work and chose him as his "running mate" (candidate for the vice-presidency). Truman was nominated on the second ballot at the Democratic National Convention and became vice-president in 1945.

Harry S. Truman, 33rd US president, 1945–53.

Popperfoto

Roosevelt died less than three months later on 12 April 1945, and Truman then became president. In his first speech before Congress he promised to continue Roosevelt's policies. Things began well. Germany surrendered on 7 May 1945. In the summer Truman met with the British and Soviet leaders at Potsdam in Germany. What was probably Truman's most difficult decision resulted in the dropping of the first atomic bombs on Hiroshima and Nagasaki in Japan. Truman was anxious to shorten the war and save the lives of perhaps 500,000 American servicemen. The bombs caused appalling casualties and damage but hastened Japan's surrender, which took place on 14 August 1945.

Congress voted to approve American membership of the United Nations, but in general things became more difficult as Americans demanded an end to wartime controls and a return to normal peacetime conditions. Prices rose quickly. Strikes affected the coal mines, steel mills, and railways. In 1947 Congress, now controlled by the Republican party, passed the Taft-Hartley Act in spite of Truman's veto (rejection). This law reduced the power of the labour unions.

Nevertheless, Truman believed the federal government should be concerned with the welfare of all the people. He proposed a far-reaching programme of reform called the "Fair Deal". He asked for laws that would protect civil rights, provide good housing, broaden both unemployment insurance and social security benefits, and give health services and medical care to all. Truman wanted to give control of the atomic energy programme to civilians; to enlarge the conservation programme by starting projects similar to the Tennessee Valley Authority; and to provide more aid to farmers. Few of these measures were passed by Congress.

United Press International

The "Summer White House" at Independence, Missouri, Truman's retirement home.

Truman only just won the Democratic nomination in 1948 against opposition from the left and the right. To most people's surprise, however, he comfortably won re-election against Republican Thomas E. Dewey.

The cold war with the USSR increased in bitterness as Communist governments were set up in most East European countries. Truman followed a policy designed to prevent the further spread of Communism. A dramatic airlift of food and other supplies was the answer to the USSR blockade of routes into West Berlin in 1948. The military alliance called the North Atlantic Treaty Organization (NATO) was set up in 1949 by the North American and West European nations. Under the Point Four Programme the United Nations gave economic aid to developing countries. Truman obtained Congressional approval for all these measures.

On 25 June 1950 North Korea invaded South Korea. Backed by the United Nations, Truman sent American armed forces to help South Korea. He showed his authority when he dismissed General Douglas MacArthur, who had criticized Truman's refusal to allow bombing or invasion of Chinese territory.

Truman retired in 1953 to his home in Independence, Missouri. An extremely popular figure, he continued to speak out on public issues.

TRUMBULL, John (1756–1843), was an American painter, architect, author, and revolutionary patriot. In the rotunda of the Capitol building in Washington, DC, are four of his paintings commissioned by Congress in 1817 and completed in 1824. They show important events during the American Revolution. They are *The Declaration of Independence*; *The Surrender of Cornwallis*; *The Surrender of Burgoyne*; and *Washington Resigning his Commission*.

Trumbull was born in Lebanon, Connecticut, the son of Connecticut Governor, Jonathan Trumbull. He graduated from Harvard College and then studied painting in Boston. When he was 19, he became a map maker for General George Washington during the revolutionary war. Having retired from the army, Trumbull went to London, England, in 1784 to study painting under Benjamin West, the distinguished American-born painter. Among his best portraits are those of Washington and Alexander Hamilton. Trumbull's paintings are known for their fine colouring.

Although Trumbull served his country as soldier and diplomat (in London from 1794–1804) and continued his interests in architecture and map making, he never gave up painting. In 1831, the Trumbull Gallery was established at Yale University. It was the first university art gallery in America, and Trumbull gave his finest works to the gallery in exchange for an annuity. His *Autobiography* was published in 1841.

TRUMPET FAMILY. The trumpet is among the oldest of the brass instruments. The earliest trumpet known is that found in the tomb of the Egyptian king Tutankhamun. Like this very old instrument, the tube of the modern trumpet is still cylindrical in shape. It has a cup-shaped mouthpiece and ends in a moderate-sized bell. The trumpet has a more brilliant and penetrating tone than that of the bugle or horn. It has been used as a military and ceremonial instrument for centuries.

As in other brass instruments, sound is produced by the player pressing the mouthpiece to his mouth and making his lips vibrate within it. The buzzing sound he makes in this way sets the column of air inside the tube of the instrument vibrating in sympathy. When the player's lips are fairly slack all the air in the tube vibrates, and this produces the lowest note of the instrument. As the player tightens his lips he makes a higher buzzing sound, and so only fractions of the air column vibrate. These fractions produce the higher notes, which are called the *natural harmonics*. Each tube produces a different set of natural harmonics depending on its length. Thus the player can regulate the sounds he produces simply by altering the tension of his lips. The natural harmonics provide only a very limited range of notes tied to one or two keys only. But the player of the modern trumpet can add other sounds, lower in pitch, by pressing down valves that open extra lengths of tubing.

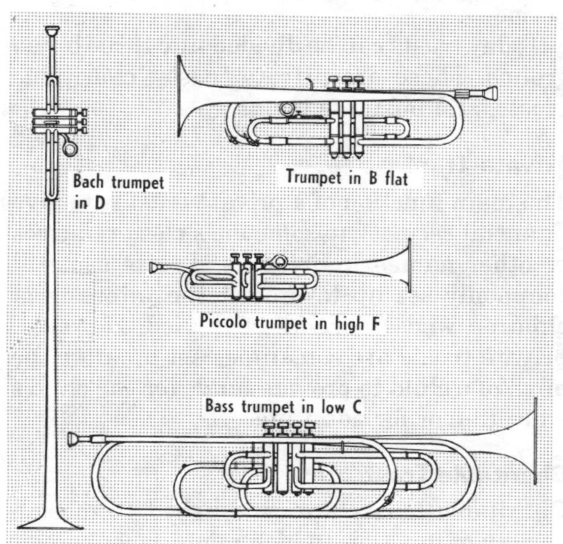

Musical wind instruments of the trumpet family.

Rex Features
Louis Armstrong was one of the greatest jazz trumpet players of all time. He was known as "Satchmo".

In the modern orchestra two or three trumpets are generally used. Their range is higher than that of the other brass instruments and trumpeters can play more quickly than other brass instrument players.

Before the 15th century the only trumpet in use was a simple natural trumpet without valves. It could only play the notes of its harmonic series. A slide trumpet was introduced at the Burgundian court in eastern France. It worked on the same principle as the trombone (see TROMBONE FAMILY). A slide trumpet of different design was used in 17th-century England. Known as a flat trumpet, it could play in minor keys. From the 17th to the 19th centuries, the natural trumpet was often used with a set of extra tubes called *crooks* (see HORN FAMILY). The familiar three-valve trumpet of today was first made in the 1820s and soon came into general use.

Most composers of orchestral music write for the B flat trumpet. However, there are other trumpets made in low F (a contralto trumpet used in some Russian music); in low C (a bass trumpet with a deep sound like a horn and built for the orchestral music in Wagner's series of operas, *The Ring of the Nibelungs*); in D (the "Bach" trumpet, often made with a straight tube); in high F (another instrument used for the rapid trumpet music of Bach); and in high D (used in some of the works of Stravinsky and Ravel).

The tone of the trumpet can be changed in several ways when a mute—a cone made of cardboard, fibre, felt, or metal—is placed in the bell of the instrument.

The cornet is an instrument similar in appearance to the ordinary B flat trumpet and in the same key. It has a cup-shaped mouthpiece, but its tube, which is shorter than that of the trumpet, is partly cylindrical and partly conical. The tone of the cornet, which is much used in military bands and has been popular in jazz, is mellower and less strident than that of the trumpet. The cornet was invented in Paris in the late 1820s.

TRUST. In the business and financial world there are many different forms of trust, but they all have a common feature. People or corporations put their money or property into a trust which is looked after by a trustee. The trustee may be an individual, a group of people, or an organization such as a bank.

For example, when someone dies, their possessions may be left in trust to their young children. An appointed trustee looks after the possessions until the children become adults. The trustee is responsible for making sure that the inheritance is managed in the children's best interests.

Trusts have a very long history, going back to medieval times in England. In those days if a landowner died without making a trust arrangement for his children, a feudal overlord (see FEUDALISM) looked after the land until the children grew up. The overlord could use the land for his own benefit, for example by growing crops or cutting timber. He could also take payment from the estate. To avoid this, a landowner could place his land with a trustee who would use it for the children's benefit. In this way, he could prevent the overlord from using up his estate's resources before his children were old enough to take control of their inheritance.

Trusts were also used at this time to get around laws aimed at preventing people from giving land to religious establishments. The land would be placed with trustees and the income that came from it would then be used for the benefit of a religious order.

These early trusts were all concerned with land, but were found to be so useful that they were later extended to cover other things such as money, property, and stocks and shares.

The form of trusts has also changed. In the 16th and 17th centuries there was an expansion in the number of charitable foundations in England. These were set up by rich merchants to help the sick, the homeless, and the elderly, as well as to provide education and religious instruction for poor children. Unlike private trusts, where the property is administered for named individuals, these foundations or charitable trusts administer the property to aid a particular cause. Charitable trusts are permitted by law to run for ever, while private trusts have to end within a given period.

Today trusts can be divided into three broad groups. These are private trusts, charitable trusts, and business trusts.

Private Trust

The main function of a private trust is to give financial security to someone's close relatives or other named individuals. Trusts are still commonly set up to protect the interests of children whose parents have died. However, private trusts are sometimes set up after the birth of a child to provide funds for the child's education or for adult life.

Charitable Trust

Charitable trusts are established to meet a variety of functions which might be of benefit to the whole community. Some are set up with money donated by wealthy individuals. The first great charitable trust in modern times was founded in the late 19th century by Andrew Carnegie, a Scot who made a fortune in the American steel industry. Carnegie dedicated his fortune to the benefit of mankind, and the Carnegie Trusts now give money to help education, community services, health, and the arts (see CARNEGIE, ANDREW).

Since then many other rich people have established similar trusts. The Ford Foundation and the Rockefeller Foundation (see FORD, HENRY; ROCKEFELLER FAMILY) are two examples from the United States, while in Britain there is the Rowntree Memorial Trust and the Nuffield Foundation. They are all named after their benefactors.

Trust funds have been established to provide and maintain museums, art galleries, and theatres. In addition, many universities, schools, and hospitals benefit from money donated to them.

People interested in historical buildings and the preservation of the countryside have also given money to be used for conservation. The National Trust in the United Kingdom, for example, acquires and maintains land and buildings of interest and beauty so that they can be enjoyed by the whole community. Anyone can contribute to the National Trust by making a donation. Many such charitable trusts rely on public contributions to continue their work.

In the United States, many towns, cities, and villages use a form of trust for the benefit of the community. Such trusts are called Community Chests, Community Funds, or Community Crusades. A committee uses funds collected from members of the community in many different ways, for example, to help the local needy and handicapped. Any surplus funds may also be used to help local hospitals, clinics, and schools.

Business Trust

The word trust is also applied in business and commercial world to a situation where one company, the "Holding Company", gains financial control of several other businesses. The stocks or shares of these businesses are acquired by a single group of trustees. In the United States in the 1880s, oil (cottonseed, linseed, and petroleum), salt, and sugar trusts were created.

One advantage of such trusts is that the "Holding Company" can buy raw materials in very large quantities for all its subsidiaries. Buying in large quantities, called "bulk buying", helps to keep costs down. The companies can also share research costs and knowledge about new technology. Finally, they may also enjoy the financial benefits of mass production, since they can produce more goods while employing fewer people.

However, if a trust acts as a *monopoly*, or single seller, of the products produced by its companies, then the government may oppose it. A monopoly could reduce the amount of goods on sale, leading to higher demand, and so raise the selling price. People who want the product must either pay the high price or go without, because there is no other producer from whom they can buy. This is considered an unfair method of selling.

These business trusts have been a major concern in the United States and a law called the Sherman Anti-Trust Act was passed in 1890 to restrict their powers. Other laws have since been added. Large companies and "conglomerates" still flourish but they are controlled by the government to see that they do not act as monopolies.

In some countries, such as Canada, the trust corporations provide normal banking services. In Australia trusts have existed for well over 100 years.

TSETSE FLY. This very harmful fly gets its name "tsetse" (meaning a fly which destroys cattle) from Botswana, Africa. It is small and much like an ordinary house-fly to look at. There are about 21 species of tsetse fly (*Glossina*), most of which occur south of the Sahara Desert in Africa. The tsetse fly lives on the blood of wild animals, of cattle, and of people, and some species spread a disease that causes the victims to fall sick and very

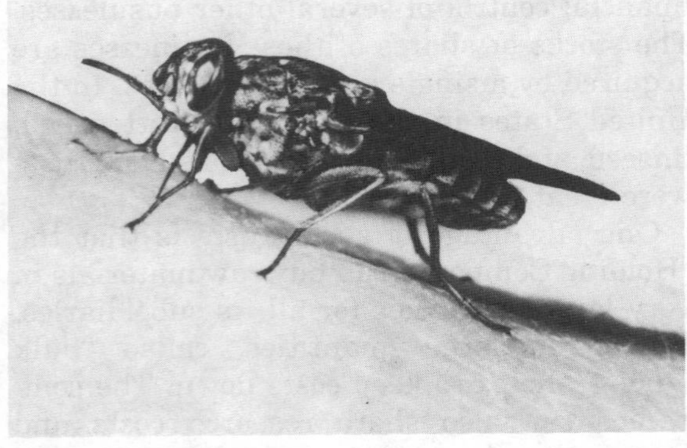

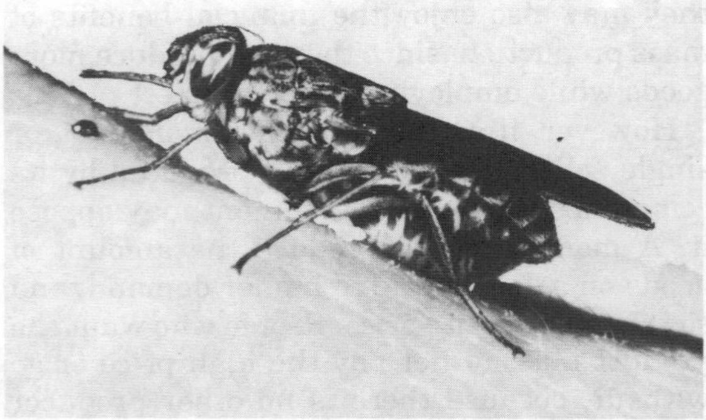

NHPA/Stephen Dalton

Tsetse fly before (top) and after (above) its human blood meal. Blood is needed for the eggs to develop.

often to die. This disease is caused by a very tiny animal called a trypanosome carried by the tsetse fly. This trypanosome lives in the blood of wild animals, so that when the tsetse fly sucks the blood of one it is very likely to swallow some trypanosomes as well. Once inside the fly's body these go through very complicated changes and eventually escape into the blood of another animal when the fly bites it. If this second animal is a person he or she develops sleeping sickness; if it is a cow or bullock, it gets *nagana*. Of the tsetse flies that attack people, over 80 per cent are males; females usually attack larger animals.

There are drugs that will cure these diseases, but scientists are trying to destroy the fly completely. The methods include clearing away the jungle undergrowth in which they breed.

The tsetse, instead of laying eggs as other flies do, gives birth from eggs inside the female's body to fully grown grubs which at once turn into pupae. Each species of tsetse fly has its own habitats and preferred places where it gives birth to its grubs. So, by destroying these places and killing the grubs and pupae wherever they can, scientists have managed to drive the tsetse out of some areas and to make them safe for raising cattle.

See also SLEEPING SICKNESS.

TUATARA. In New Zealand lives a reptile called the tuatara (*Sphenodon punctatus*) which has no close relatives, for all the other reptiles like it have died out. The tuatara itself is now very rare. It looks much like a lizard, but its skeleton is quite different, and it is actually closer to the tortoises. It has two large eyes with pupils like narrow, upright slits, and on the top of its head the remains of a third eye can be seen under the skin.

The tuatara grows about 70 centimetres (28 inches) long and is greyish-black in colour with a few yellow spots. Spine-like yellow scales form a crest which reaches from the neck to the end of the tail. Because of this the reptile was given the name *tuatara*, which is a Maori word meaning "having spines".

The tuatara is a night-living animal, spending the day in deep burrows which it digs for itself with its strong limbs. It feeds on earthworms, slugs, and insects and when kept in captivity it will eat frogs, mice, and small pieces of raw meat.

M. F. Soper/Bruce Coleman

The tuatara is a lizard-like reptile of New Zealand. It has no living close-relatives.

Female tuataras generally lay from eight to ten eggs at a time, and these usually take more than 12 months to hatch. The tuatara is a good swimmer and can remain under water for hours. Tuataras have been known to live for 100 years.

TUBA FAMILY. The musical instrument called the tuba produces the deepest sound of all the brass instruments. Usually only one is used in the orchestra, and it supplies the bass notes for the brass family in the same way as the double bass (see VIOLIN FAMILY) supplies them for the stringed instruments.

ZEFA

The tuba player (far right) plays a fundamental role in a town band as well as in an orchestra.

There are many different designs of tuba in use in different countries. In addition, those used in brass and military bands are different in shape from those used in orchestras. The brass tube of the orchestral tuba is coiled like that of the trumpet and horn, but because the instrument is so heavy and awkward to hold, it is placed on the player's lap. The large circular opening, called the bell, faces upwards and to the player's right or left. If the player wishes to make the pitch of the instrument deeper he can use up to four valves which open more tubing. Some tubas have five or even six valves.

The German composer Richard Wagner had special tubas made for the orchestral music in his series of operas called *The Ring of the Nibelungs*. They included the tenor tuba, which had a narrowish tube and a funnel-shaped mouthpiece like a horn; a bass tuba, also horn-like in design; and a double-bass tuba, which had a wide conical tube and a cup-shaped mouthpiece like a trumpet.

The tubas used in military bands are sometimes very large indeed. Specially designed to be carried on a bandsman's shoulder, they include the euphonium, which reaches down to a low B flat; the E flat bass, which is lower still; and the double B flat bass, which is the lowest of all. When made in a circular shape the double B flat bass is known as a helicon. The sousaphone, named after the American bandmaster John Philip Sousa, is a circular form of the E flat bass.

TUBERCULOSIS is a disease caused by a tiny rod-shaped germ, of which there are several varieties. One type, known as the human bacillus, is spread in tiny drops coughed into the air by an infected person and breathed in by someone else. Another kind, the bovine, can be caught from the milk of infected cows.

Tuberculosis (generally known as TB) can be very dangerous because it causes its victims to waste away and sometimes to die. In the 19th century many people died of tuberculosis of the lungs, which was also called consumption. The disease causes lumps, or "tubercles", to form in the lung tissue. Nowadays, however, in countries with good medical services, tuberculosis is becoming rarer. This is partly due to better living conditions and also because chest X-ray examinations detect the disease in the earliest stage. If a person is found to have tuberculosis, specific antibiotic drugs will make him better and non-infectious. The people he has been in contact with will also be traced and checked to make sure that they are not harbouring the disease.

The bovine type of the disease, which tends to affect the glands and the bones of the body, can also be prevented by testing cows to make sure that they are free of tuberculosis. A special form of heat treatment, known as pasteurization after the great French scientist Louis Pasteur, is applied to milk to make certain it is safe.

Another method of control is by a skin test which gives evidence of infection. People at risk can be inoculated against tuberculosis with a vaccine called BCG. In many countries, BCG vaccinations are given routinely to school children at risk. The vaccine is made from a special strain of the tuberculosis bacillus, which is called after the French scientists Léon Calmette and Camille Guérin who discovered it in 1906.

TUBMAN, Harriet (*c.*1820–1913), was a United States abolitionist and a key figure in the Underground Railroad that helped runaway slaves to freedom (see ABOLITIONISTS).

Harriet Tubman was herself born a slave on a plantation in Maryland. She escaped to the North in 1849, assisted by abolitionists in the Underground Railroad. The next year she returned to Maryland to help guide members of her family in their escape. After that trip she became one of the most active "conductors", or guides, on the Underground Railroad. Her efforts helped to free more than 300 slaves.

Before the American Civil War, John Brown consulted her about the famous raid on Harpers Ferry (see BROWN, JOHN). During the war Harriet Tubman was a nurse and laundress with the Union army. She also became a spy for the Union forces, seeking information behind Confederate lines.

Following the end of the war she worked to improve education for black people in the state of North Carolina. Widely respected for her strength and courage, she was sometimes called "the Moses of her people".

See also BLACK AMERICANS.

TULIP. The brilliant colours of tulips and their graceful shapes have appealed to gardeners and flower lovers in many parts of the world for hundreds of years. In parts of Europe, Asia, and North Africa tulips grow wild, and they are the ancestors of all the different garden kinds.

Ever since the 17th century, when tulips became extremely fashionable, Holland has been the chief tulip-growing country. There, during the 1630s, the people had such a passion for tulips that one bulb of a new variety might be sold for two or three thousand florins. This "tulipomania", or tulip madness, lasted for about five years and in that time some people made enormous sums of money while others lost all they had by buying and selling tulips. Then, when tulipomania had nearly ruined the country, it died down, but tulip growing remained one of the chief occupations of the Dutch. In England and also in Turkey tulipomania took hold of the people, but not to the same extent as in Holland. Turkey's craze was roughly between 1702 and 1720 and England's was at its height about 1710.

NHPA/M. W. F. Tweedie

A wild southern tulip growing in the Algarve, Portugal.

Tulips belong to the lily family, Liliaceae, and are generally grown from bulbs rather than from seed. In the cultivated kinds each bulb usually bears one flower only at the top of a long stem. From the lower part of the stem

A–Z Collection

A variety of *Tulip kaufmanniana*, from Turkistan.

two large leaves grow out, either strap-shaped or wide and thick.

The flower is cup-shaped and has three sepals and three petals, all looking alike. They may be rounded or pointed, or have wavy edges like a fringe. The colours range from pure white through pinks and reds of all shades to a very dark purple which is called black, and from the palest cream to a deep golden yellow. Some flowers are striped with two colours, and others have a patch of a different colour—sometimes black—inside the base of the petals.

Names have been given to certain types of tulips according to the different shapes of the flowers, heights of the plants, and times of flowering. There are the Early Single and Early Double varieties that flower in early spring and are about 30 centimetres (12 inches) high; the Early Doubles, as their name shows, have more than one set of petals. Triumph tulips are stiff-stemmed plants about 50 centimetres (20 inches) tall. The tall Darwin tulips bloom later in spring and have large flowers whose petals stand away from each other. Cottage tulips also flower late and are tall, hardy plants with more rounded heads than the Darwins.

Three types with rather special shapes are the Lily-flowered, the Peony-flowered, and the Parrot tulips. The first has long flowers with pointed petals that turn back, the second is a double kind shaped like a small peony, and the Parrots have fringed edges and open widely.

Besides these garden varieties, there are several dwarf tulips for rock gardens. These are about 15 to 25 centimetres (6 to 10 inches) high and some have four or five blooms on one stem. The flowers themselves may be very tiny or quite large. Most tulips have a faint scent but some have a stronger smell and some have none.

TULIP TREE. The tall and lovely tulip tree (*Liriodendron tulipifera*) is related to the magnolia. It grows in central and eastern North America. The tree may take 200 years to reach a height of up to 60 metres (190 feet).

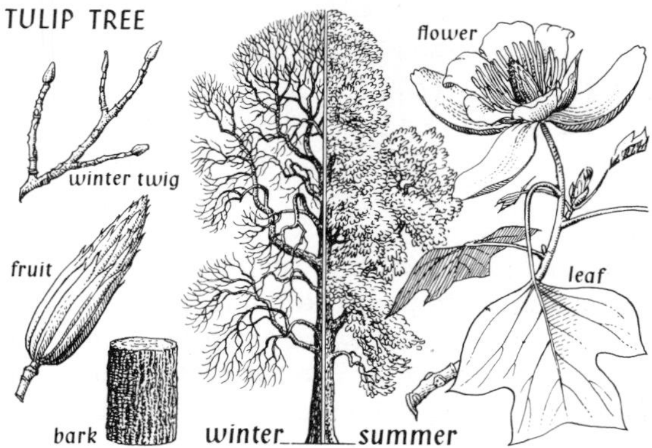

The trunk is straight, with evenly ridged grey bark. The blossoms, shaped like big bowls, appear in June or earlier. They are greenish on the outside and creamy yellow within, with deep orange centres and a sweet scent. The glossy leaves are bright green and have a large notch or indentation instead of a tip at the end. They turn a rich golden-yellow in autumn. The fruits, which are dry, brown, and cone-shaped, split into many flat scale-like parts when ripe. The tulip tree has been planted as an ornamental tree in parks throughout the world, and is a useful shade tree where there is space available.

Tulip wood looks rather like poplar wood and in the United States it is called poplar. It is imported into England under the name of canary whitewood. The wood is light, easily worked, and polishes well.

TULL, Jethro (*c.*1674–1741), was an English agricultural writer and inventor whose ideas improved British agriculture in the 18th century. He was born at Basildon, Berkshire, although the exact date of his birth is unknown. He studied at Oxford University and trained as a barrister, but chose instead to work on his father's farm in Berkshire.

Mary Evans Picture Library

Jethro Tull's seed drill, invented in 1701.

In the 17th century, seeds were sown by scattering them over the fields by hand. Tull realized that if they were sown in neat rows, fewer seed would be needed and it would be easier to pull out the weeds. The workers on his farm would not co-operate with him, so by 1701 he had built a machine, called a seed drill, to do the work.

While travelling in France and Italy, Jethro Tull noticed the methods of cultivation used in vineyards and decided to try them out when he returned to England. He realized that it was better for the plants to grow in loose earth as water could then get to the roots more easily. He built a horse-drawn hoe to cultivate the soil in this way. He also wrote a book explaining his methods called *Horse-hoeing Husbandry* (1731). Tull was accused of using other people's ideas and criticized by people who believed in the old methods. However, his ideas were used by Thomas Coke and Lord Townshend, other revolutionary farmers, and they gradually gained acceptance.

See also AGRICULTURE, HISTORY OF; TOWNSHEND, CHARLES.

TUMOUR is a mass of abnormal tissue. The word tumour in the broad sense means simply a swelling. In modern medical usage, however, it refers to enlargements caused by new growths or abnormally growing tissue. Swellings resulting from inflammations such as boils, abscesses, or an injury, are not true tumours.

The precise cause of true tumours is not known. Normal growth is controlled by the body. Plants and animals grow to maturity and then stop growing. In the same way, when tissue is injured, it heals naturally. When healing has been completed, the new growth stops. Tumours develop when normal growth and repair run wild. Then tumours, or new growths (neoplasms), are formed.

Tumours are of two main types—*benign* and *malignant*. A benign tumour is one that continues to grow in the place where it starts. It sends out no branches into neighbouring tissues, and no wandering cells to become new tumours in distant parts of the body. Malignant tumours (called cancers) invade the body and start new growths elsewhere, called secondaries or metastases.

Benign or malignant tumours may arise from any kind of tissue in the body—skin, muscle, or gland. Malignant tumours of the glands, membrane, or skin are *carcinomas*. Malignant tumours of muscle, bone, or cartilage are *sarcomas* (see CANCER). The most common benign tumours are fatty tumours under the skin and muscle tumours of the uterus (fibroids). The fatty tumours cause no trouble. The muscle tumours may be a serious threat to life or health because of bleeding, size, or pressure on nearby organs. Hollow tumours filled with fluid are cysts. They may be benign or malignant.

Tumours may or may not require treatment, depending on their size, location, growth, and malignancy. A small benign tumour in certain locations may be ignored. Benign tumours that cause problems are usually removed by surgery. A malignant tumour, however, must be dealt with, no matter where it is or how small it is, before it can spread into neighbouring organs. Removal may be by surgery, radiation treatment (radiotherapy), or drugs (chemotherapy), or by a combination of these, again depending on the size, location, and character of the tumour.

TUNA. One of the most important food fishes is the tuna (also called tunny), the largest member of the mackerel family. It occasionally reaches a weight of 450 kilograms (992 lbs).

Tuna are among the most swift and powerful of ocean fish. They are wonderfully streamlined, with no projecting bumps on their bodies to slow down their movements. When swimming rapidly their dorsal (back) fins and the pectoral and pelvic fins on the underside can be fitted into little grooves in the body to allow them to increase their speed still further.

The first part of the dorsal fin is made up of 13 or 14 spines. Behind these the rays of the fin are soft. At the hind end of the body, on both the back and the underside, is a row of eight to ten finlets. These and the soft part of the dorsal fin act as balancers. The back of the tuna is a dark, metallic blue colour, the sides are greyish and the underside is silvery white.

Tuna are always on the move chasing their prey, which consists of such fishes as herring, sardine, and flying fish. Their journeys have interested people for centuries. It has long been known that shoals of tuna arrive at some places regularly at certain times of the year and disappear after a stay varying from a few weeks to several months. It is now thought that the tuna follow the fish on which they feed and these fishes in turn follow the planktonic life on which *they* feed. (See PLANKTON.)

The blue-fin tuna (*Thunnus thynnus*) is probably the world's largest bony fish, up to 4.3 metres (14 feet) long and weighing as much as 900 kilograms (2,000 pounds).

Tuna flesh is full of oil and suitable for canning. The fish, eaten fresh, has been an important source of food to Mediterranean peoples since the time of the ancient Greeks. Tuna is also eaten fresh by the Japanese. There are tuna fisheries in many countries and the methods of catching the fish vary from complicated nets to harpoons and baited hooks.

The most important commercial tuna is the skipjack (*Katsuwonus pelamis*), which has long belly stripes. It is mainly caught in giant nets, or seines. Tuna have a worldwide distribution but prefer warm waters of not less than 10°C (50°F).

TUNDRA is the word which geographers use for the vast plains in northern North America, Europe, and the Soviet Union, where it is too cold and windy for trees to grow. To the north of the tundra are the ice- and snow-capped polar regions. To the south, the tundra ends at the northern tree-line, where the taiga begins (see TAIGA). Tundra plants include mosses, lichens, sedges, bilberries, some dwarf shrubs, and a few stunted aspens, birches, and Arctic willows.

During the long winters, when the Sun may not rise above the horizon for several weeks or months, snow blankets the land and the soil is frozen hard. Average temperatures rise above

Courtesy, Bureau of Commercial Fisheries, Honolulu Biological Laboratory, US Fish

A shoal of skipjack tuna, distinguished by their long belly stripes. This is a commercially important species.

B. & C. Alexander

Despite the long cold winter, the tundra supports a variety of flowering plants, lichens, and mosses.

freezing point for only two to four months of the year and, even at the height of summer, the average monthly temperature does not exceed 10°C (50°F) and frosts are common. But the snow melts and the top layers of the soil thaw. Beneath the surface layers, the soil remains permanently frozen. This frozen subsoil is called *permafrost*. Houses in the region have to be constructed so that the warmth they produce does not melt the permafrost, causing them to sink into the subsoil.

Because of the permafrost, water cannot drain away and so the land surface becomes muddy and marshy. Enormous numbers of insects, including blackflies, midges, and mosquitoes, breed in swampy hollows. People regard these insects as pests, but they are a rich source of food for birds, including swans, geese, ducks, and many species of wading birds. These birds migrate to the tundra in summer, nest and breed, and then fly south when winter starts. Migrating animals, such as caribou, musk oxen, and reindeer, graze on the tundra in summer. Other animals include Arctic foxes, bears, hares, lemmings, and wolves.

The tundra is thinly populated, though a few people, including Eskimos and Lapps, live there. The tundra contains mineral resources, including oil and natural gas, and these reserves are now being mined and drilled.

The southern hemisphere has little tundra, because there are no large land masses far enough south for it to occur. Tundra is found only on the northernmost parts of Antarctica and on a few islands. However, similar treeless regions, known as Alpine zones, occur on high mountains between the snow-line and the tree-line.

TUNGSTEN is a heavy grey or white metallic chemical element. The name comes from the Swedish *tung* (meaning heavy) and *sten* (stone). It is also known as wolfram and from this name comes its chemical symbol, W. Tungsten is almost twice as heavy as lead. Its melting point is 3,410°C (6,170°F), the highest of any metal.

The metal was first isolated in 1783 by two Spanish brothers, Juan José and Fausto Elhuyar. Tungsten minerals are mostly found in the rocks of mountainous regions; the minerals from which commercial amounts of tungsten are extracted are wolframite and scheelite. The main areas that are sources of tungsten are in China, Burma, South Korea, Brazil, Portugal, the Soviet Union, and the United States.

In the production of tungsten, the ores are first crushed and washed with water. Heavy tungsten minerals separate out, and the lighter rock particles are washed away. The concentrated ore is chemically treated to produce a soluble tungsten compound which dissolves, leaving behind insoluble impurities. Chemical refinement continues until tungsten oxide is obtained. Treatment of this oxide with hydrogen or carbon yields pure tungsten. Because tungsten's high melting point makes it difficult to melt, the powdered metal is compressed into bars, heated, and hammered into smaller-diameter rods. These rods can be rolled or hammered into sheets or drawn through dies to produce fine tungsten wires.

Pure tungsten is used primarily in the electronic and electrical industries. The element expands with heat at about the same rate as glass and it is used to make glass-to-metal seals. Electrical contact points in the distributor and spark plugs of many internal combustion engines are made partially of tungsten. Tungsten wire is used for electric-lamp filaments. Another major use of tungsten is in the manufacture of tough steel alloys (see ALLOY). These alloys retain their hardness and strength at high temperatures and are used in jet engines, missiles, and high-speed cutting tools.

The most important compound of tungsten is tungsten carbide, which is made by the combination of tungsten and carbon at high temperatures. It is one of the hardest materials made by man and is used in place of diamonds for cutting and drilling.

TUNIS is the capital and largest city of Tunisia in North Africa. It is near the country's northern coast on a shallow inlet (Lake of Tunis) of the Gulf of Tunis. A channel across this lake connects Tunis with the port of La Goulette. This places the city near the east-west trade routes through the Mediterranean Sea. The ancient Phoenicians saw the advantages of this location and in the 9th century BC captured the site of Carthage near present-day Tunis from the Libyans who had founded it (see also CARTHAGE). The climate of Tunis is Mediterranean, with cool, wet winters and hot, dry summers.

A pleasant mixture of Muslim and European atmosphere exists in the city. The narrow, winding streets of the Muslim section are an interesting contrast to the wide streets and modern buildings of the European section. A part of the Muslim section is the ancient area, called the Medina. It has changed little in modern times. One of the entrances to the Medina is through a large structure known as the Bab el Khadra Gate. There is also a famous mosque, and ancient Roman thermal baths. In the Medina are many individual markets, or *suqs*, where the products of the city's handicraft industries are sold. They include carpets, textiles, pottery, and leather and metal goods. The factories process the products of the rich agricultural area that surrounds Tunis. Olive oil production, canned fruit, chemicals, and tourism are the chief industries.

Tunis has grown rapidly, and it is by far the largest and most important Tunisian city. The population of Tunis, is 596,654 (1984).

TUNISIA is a republic in North Africa. Its neighbours on the shores of the Mediterranean Sea are Algeria to the west and Libya to the east.

In the north, spurs of the Atlas Mountains cross Tunisia in a northwesterly direction, rising in places to 1,500 metres (5,000 feet). Between the mountain ranges there are wide fertile valleys. Further south there are low tablelands and plains, and south of Gafsa begins the Sahara Desert. The chief river is the Medjerda, which over the years has formed large coastal plains in northeast Tunisia.

Near the coast, Tunisia has a pleasant climate with hot summers. In the inland regions it is very hot for most of the year. Most of the rain falls in winter. In northern Tunisia there are forests of oaks and cork-oak trees, with some pines. Further south the trees give place to thorny bushes and grasses. A few deer and leopards live in the mountains. Other wild animals include antelopes, jackals, hyenas, and pigs.

Most Tunisians are Berbers or Arabs (the Berbers were the original inhabitants of the region), and are Muslim. The main language is Arabic, but French is widely understood. The capital and chief port of Tunisia is Tunis (see TUNIS). On the north coast is the port of

ZEFA

View of the harbour of Mahdia, a fishing port on the Mediterranean coast of eastern Tunisia.

Bizerta, which is the northernmost city of Africa and is situated at the narrowest part of the Mediterranean.

The chief occupation is farming. Wheat and other grain crops are grown in the north. Other important crops are olives, grapes (for making wine), oranges, lemons and, in the southern oases, dates. Cattle, sheep, and goats graze on the central tablelands.

FACTS ABOUT TUNISIA

AREA: 154,530 square kilometres (59,664 square miles).
POPULATION: 7,636,000 (1987).
GOVERNMENT: Independent republic.
CAPITAL: Tunis.
GEOGRAPHICAL FEATURES: The country is mountainous in the north, covered by plains in the central and eastern areas, and in the south extends into the Sahara.
CHIEF PRODUCTS: Wheat, barley, oats, olives, dates, grapes, citrus fruits, vegetables; phosphate rock, iron ore, lead, zinc, natural gas, oil.
IMPORTANT TOWNS: Tunis, Sfax (Safaqis), Aryanah, Bizerta.
EDUCATION: Education is free.

Tunisia is fairly rich in minerals. Phosphate rock is used as a fertilizer and for making phosphorus. It is mined near Gafsa and sent abroad through the port of Sfax. Iron is mined in the northwest and other metals obtained are lead and zinc. Some natural gas and petroleum oil have been discovered in the southern part of the country. Their production is becoming more and more important to the economy. There are few factories, although carpets, leather goods, and pottery are made locally. Tourism is the country's leading industry.

Northern Tunisia is linked by rail with Algeria. The railways in central Tunisia serve chiefly to carry phosphate. Al 'Uwaynah near Tunis is a large airport.

History

After Carthage had been destroyed by the Romans in 146 BC, most of what is now Tunisia became part of the Roman province of Africa. The country was invaded in the 7th century by the Arabs, and Christianity and Roman civilization disappeared. In 1574 the Turks who had already conquered Algeria, took Tunisia and made it a Turkish province. Their rule was very slack, and the leaders of the coastal Arab tribes gave up most of their time to piracy, preying on ships sailing through the Mediterranean.

In the 19th century piracy was stopped but Tunisia continued to be badly governed, most of its fertile land being uncultivated and its people crushed by heavy taxation. When in 1869 the country could pay its way no longer, its money affairs were taken over by the French, Italians, and British. In 1881 French forces occupied the country from Algeria.

Tunisia became more prosperous under the French, but there was a good deal of discontent, both among the Arabs who wanted to be independent and also among the numerous Italian settlers. When in 1940 Italy declared war on France, the conquest of Tunisia was one of the Italian aims.

Tunisia became a battleground for six months of 1942–43 during World War II. After the war, the people demanded an end of the French protectorate and from 1951 onwards rioting and disorders were frequent. France granted self-rule to Tunisia in 1955, followed by independence in 1956. In 1957 the bey, or monarch, was deposed and Tunisia became a republic with Habib Bourguiba as president. Bourguiba remained as president into the

ZEFA

Tunisia has an ancient history, and the capital, Tunis, has seen many conquerors come and go. Its old city walls today attract tourists rather than repel armies, as they once did.

1980s; his rule was one of the longest in recent African history.

TUNNEL. A level or gently sloping artificial underground passage is called a tunnel. Tunnels may be made for roads, railways, and canals, and are often used for water, sewage, gas mains, electric cables, and in mining. A vertical underground passage is called a shaft.

One of the earliest known tunnels was made in the 22nd century BC in Babylon (now Iraq). It passed under the Euphrates River from the palace to the temple on the other bank, and was built of arched brickwork, being 3.6 metres (11.8 feet) high and 4.5 metres (14.8 feet) wide. Other ancient tunnels were built for water supplies and for drainage.

In the old days tunnels had to be dug by hand. A 5.6-kilometre (3.5-mile) tunnel dug by the ancient Romans to drain a lake in Italy occupied thousands of labourers over a period of 11 years. When tunnelling in rock they sometimes used fires to heat the working face. Then they raked the embers back and used cold water to chill the hot rock and make it splinter. More rapid progress came with the use of gunpowder for blasting away the rock. Gunpowder was first used in mining in the 17th century. Later, drills driven by compressed air or hydraulic power were developed. With these drills, holes are bored in the rocks, the holes being arranged in a pattern and charges of explosive rammed into them. The charges are fired in a particular order, usually so that those in the centre explode first and the outer ones a fraction of a second later.

Except in the very hardest rock, tunnels usually require a built lining. This is strongest and lightest if the tunnel is circular in shape. Formerly, tunnels were lined with masonry or bricks; nowadays, cast-iron or concrete sections—sometimes reinforced—are more often used.

When driving a tunnel through soft or crumbling soil the tunnellers must prevent the collapse of the walls and roof before the lining is put in place. For this, a special shield was invented by the engineer Marc Isambard Brunel (see BRUNEL, ISAMBARD KINGDOM). The shield was first used for driving a tunnel through the London clay beneath the River Thames between Wapping and Rotherhithe. Brunel's tunnel, which was opened for foot passengers in 1843, is now used for the underground railway.

The modern tunnelling shield was developed from Brunel's by the British engineer J. H. Greathead (1844–96) and was used by him for making the tunnels for London's tubes, or deep underground railways (see UNDERGROUND RAILWAY). The Greathead shield is a steel cylinder with a width approximately equal to its length. The front end of the cylinder has a cutting edge. Powerful hydraulic jacks push the shield forward while people working in the front part of it dig out the earth.

Sometimes shafts are sunk from the surface along the route of the tunnel, thus allowing work to proceed in several places at once. The shafts also help in ventilation. Artificial ventilation by means of huge fans is necessary for tube railways, and also for long road tunnels under rivers.

If a tunnel is being driven through waterlogged soil, it may be necessary to keep out the water by pumping air under pressure into the tunnel. The working space can then be entered

Above: Marc Isambard Brunel's tunnelling shield at work on the first Thames tunnel, in the 1830s. There were three separate compartments in which the tunnellers worked. The shield was moved forward by screw jacks and the tunnel was then lined with bricks. **Left**: By contrast, a huge mechanical "mole" was used in 1974 to dig the second tunnel under the Mersey in Liverpool. It had a cutting face armed with 55 steel discs.

Mary Evans Picture Library (above) Courtesy, Edmund Nuttall Ltd. (left)

through an air-lock (a chamber with two doors, only one of which can be opened at a time). It is dangerous to work in such pressurized tunnels, however. So nowadays, only the face of the tunnel is pressurized. This area is sealed off with a slurry (thin mud) mixture, and the soil is excavated by a rotating cutting wheel.

Some Famous Tunnels

One of the longest railway tunnels is the Simplon tunnel under the Alps between Switzerland and Italy. It is 20 kilometres (12.5 miles) long and has twin tunnels, the first of which was completed in 1905 and the second in 1921. The greatest depth of this tunnel beneath the surface is 2,102 metres (6,896 feet). London's underground railway system has some long tunnels, the longest measuring 27.8 kilometres (17.3 miles), between East Finchley and Morden. The longest underground railway tunnel in the world is in Moscow, between Belyaevo and Medvedkovo (30.7 kilometres or 19 miles long).

The longest road tunnel in the world is the St. Gotthard tunnel in Switzerland which passes under the Alps between Göschenen and Airolo. It is 16 kilometres (10 miles) long and was opened in 1980.

The world's widest tunnel runs beneath the Scheldt River in Belgium. The tunnel carries road as well as rail traffic and forms part of the E3 European motorway which will eventually link Stockholm to Lisbon. The tunnel, 57 metres (187 feet) wide and 10 metres (33 feet) high, passes under the Scheldt at Antwerp where the river is 480 metres (1,575 feet) wide.

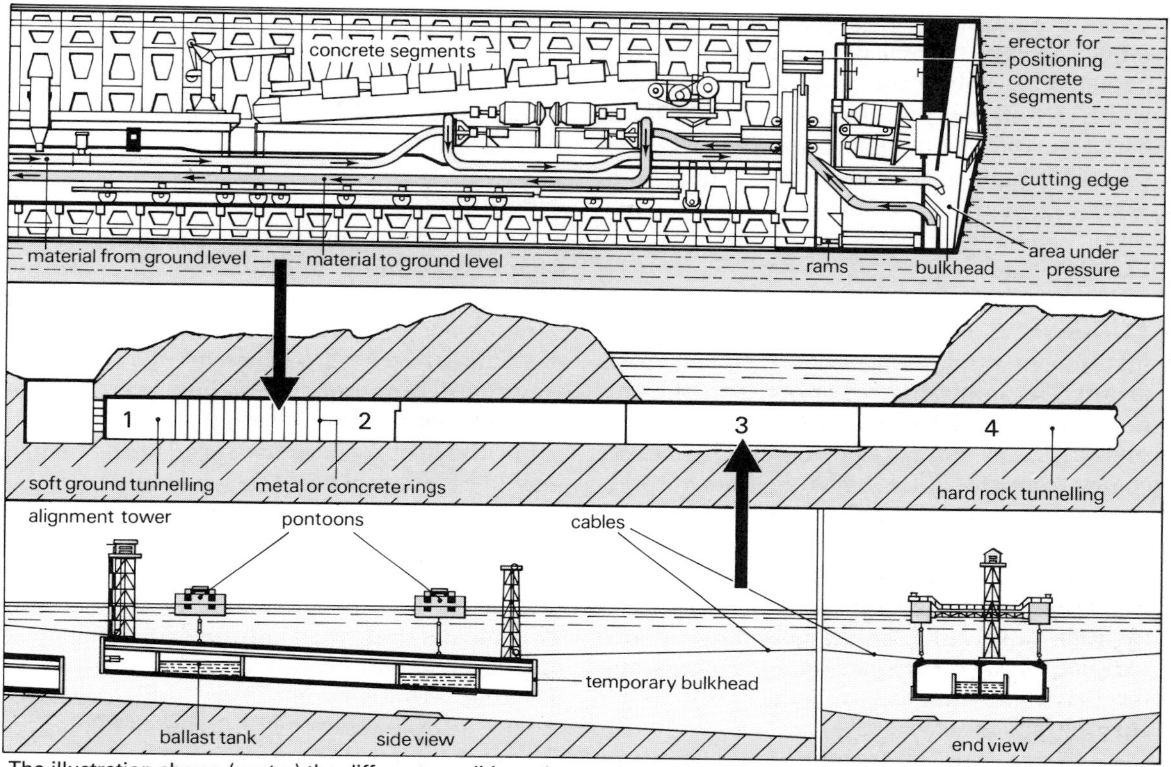

concrete segments
erector for positioning concrete segments
cutting edge
material from ground level
material to ground level
rams
bulkhead
area under pressure
1
2
3
4
soft ground tunnelling
metal or concrete rings
hard rock tunnelling
alignment tower
pontoons
cables
temporary bulkhead
ballast tank
side view
end view

The illustration shows (centre) the different conditions that engineers have to deal with when digging tunnels. In section 1 the ground is soft. A round tunnelling shield with a tough steel cutting edge is used (top). Hydraulic jacks push the cutting edge forward by pressing it against a concrete bulkhead. In section 2 the soil is waterlogged. A rotating cutting wheel excavates the soil from a pressurized area at the front of the shield. In section 3 the tunnel is being constructed under shallow water. Prefabricated sections of tubing are capped and floated into position (bottom, left and right). They are sunk by filling ballast tanks with water. They are then attached to the previous sections and uncapped. Section 4 is being tunnelled through hard rock. Holes are drilled at specific depths and filled with explosives. After the blast, machines take out the rock fragments and the process is repeated.

The submerged sections are composed of five caissons which were constructed in an enormous dry dock and then floated into position and sunk. Each weighs 47,000 tonnes (51,819 US tons). The tunnel has six lanes for road traffic, two railway tracks, and a smaller lane for cyclists and motor cyclists.

The idea of building a tunnel which would link Great Britain and France has been discussed many times. Work actually started in the 1970s, but was stopped because of rising costs. However, there were new plans in the late 1980s for a rail tunnel running beneath the English Channel.

Many tunnels carry water, either as canals or to supply cities, irrigate land, or for providing electric power. Some of New York City's water is supplied through the Delaware Aqueduct, a circular tunnel bringing water from the

ZEFA

The construction of a concrete tunnel at Zurich International Airport in Switzerland.

Catskill Mountains. It is 168 kilometres (105 miles) long and in some places runs 750 metres (2,500 feet) below the ground. Its greatest width is 5.8 metres (19 feet). It was built between 1937 and 1953 and was extended several times until 1965. (See IRRIGATION; WATER POWER; WATER SUPPLY.)

TUNNY see TUNA.

TURBINE is a type of engine powered by a fast-moving fluid, such as water, steam, or gas or air. The main difference between the turbine and other types of engine is that its only movement is rotary, or turning. Its name comes from the Latin *turbo*, meaning "something that spins or twirls". The pistons of engines such as those of a locomotive or motor car have a to-and-fro movement which has to be changed to a rotary movement by connecting rods and cranks. This is not necessary in a turbine, whose rotary movement is convenient for driving dynamos, propellers, and other turning machinery.

An early type of turbine was the water wheel, which has been used for over 2,000 years (see WATER POWER).

Modern turbines are of two basic types. Impulse turbines have fast-moving jets of fluid (a liquid or gas) hitting the blades, and the force and velocity of impact turns the rotor. In reaction turbines, a large volume of high-pressure fluid is forced through the blades which turn mainly as a result of the weight or pressure of the fluid.

Steam Turbines

A steam turbine consists of a cylinder-shaped casing containing a drum-shaped *rotor*, or turning part. Steam from the boiler is led through nozzles fixed to the casing so that jets of steam strike *blades* which are mounted in a ring round the rotor. The casing prevents any energy from the steam being lost.

For the best results, the speed of the blades should be roughly half the speed at which the steam comes out of the nozzles. Steam at a pressure of 14 bars (203 pounds per square inch, or about 14 atmospheres) comes out at more than 600 metres (2,000 feet) a second. This means that, with only one ring of blades, an enormous rotor speed is needed for efficient working. To overcome this difficulty, the steam, after leaving the first ring of blades on the rotor, is led through another row of fixed blades, or *stators*, on the casing. These redirect the steam on to a second row of moving blades, from which it is led through a second row of fixed blades and so on. In this way the speed of the steam is decreased little

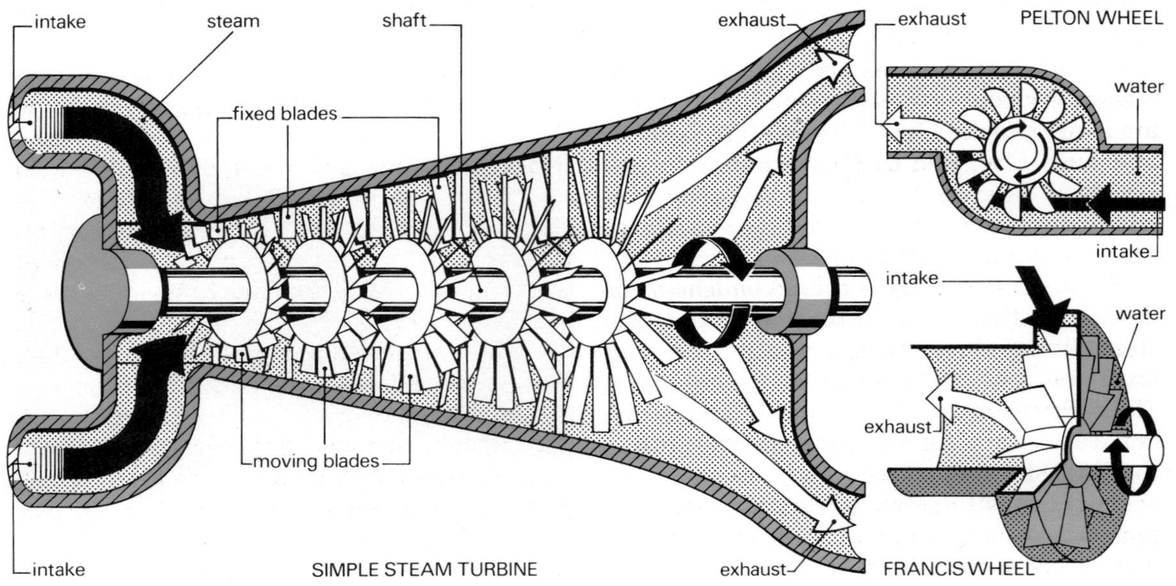

SIMPLE STEAM TURBINE

FRANCIS WHEEL

by little as it passes through each row of blades, and when the steam leaves the row of blades at the far end of the rotor most of the energy has been taken from it. As the speed of the steam decreases, the pressure becomes lower, and the steam takes up more space, so the successive turbine stages must increase in diameter (as shown in the diagram).

This type of turbine was developed by the British engineer and inventor Charles Parsons and is the kind used all over the world for driving generators in power stations and for propelling steamships. The original Parsons turbine was built in 1884. Its power was about 7.5 kilowatts (10 horsepower) and it drove a dynamo for making electricity. (See PARSONS, SIR CHARLES.)

Turbines of this type are economical, smooth, and quiet, and are made in very large sizes. Powers of 500 and 660 megawatts (670,000 and 885,000 horsepower) are common, and steam turbines of more than 1,000 megawatts (1,340,400 horsepower) have been built. Others of 2,000 megawatts (2,680,700 horsepower) are being designed.

Small high-speed steam turbines with a single row of blades were developed in 1887 by the Swedish engineer Carl Gustaf de Laval (1845–1913). It was de Laval who invented the special reduction gearing which allows a turbine rotating at high speed to drive a propeller or machine at a comparatively low speed. (See GEAR.) Steam turbines used in ships are always geared because high-speed propellers are inefficient. The first turbine ship, the *Turbinia*, was designed by Parsons and built at Wallsend-on-Tyne, England. It had three turbines producing a total power of 1,492 kilowatts (2,000 horsepower).

Steam turbines may be either *condensing* or *non-condensing*. In a condensing turbine the steam goes from the turbine into a condenser and is cooled by cold water circulating in pipes. The steam becomes water and a vacuum is created because the water takes up less space than the steam does (see HEAT; VACUUM). The vacuum helps force steam through the turbine. The water is then pumped back into the boiler to be made into steam again.

In a non-condensing turbine the steam which has passed through the turbine is used to provide heat for buildings or in other industrial processes.

Water Turbines

The chief use of water turbines is for driving generators in hydroelectric power stations. (See WATER POWER.) Both impulse turbines and reaction turbines make use of the energy of water under the influence of gravity. The distance of fall, or *head*, corresponds to steam pressure. A high head or a high steam pressure results in high water velocity or high steam velocity.

Impulse turbines known as Pelton wheels are used for heads above 300 metres (1,000 feet) (the highest used being about 1,650 metres or 5,400 feet) just as impulse steam turbines are used for high steam pressures. For heads of between 30 and 300 metres (100 and 1,000 feet), reaction turbines, of the Francis type with a fixed blade propeller is used. The Kaplan type, with a movable blade, is used for heads below 30 metres (100 feet).

In the Pelton wheel the water passes through nozzles which direct high-speed water jets at cup-shaped buckets fixed around the rim of the wheel. The whole is enclosed in a steel casing. Usually Pelton wheels are mounted with the shaft horizontal but some are mounted vertically.

The Francis turbine has a runner with curved blades fixed along its length parallel to the shaft, enclosed in a spiral casing on the inside of which are mounted guide vanes which direct the water on to the runner. The guide vane angle can be adjusted to control the turbine speed by changing the direction of water flow. Most Francis turbines are mounted vertically.

Kaplan turbines have a runner shaped like a ship's propeller but working on the opposite principle, being forced round by the water instead of being turned by an engine and forcing the water backwards to drive the ship forwards. The pitch or angle of the turbine runner blades can be altered to give the best results. The largest water turbines are in the

Soviet Union, where turbines of more than 500 megawatts (670,000 horsepower) output capacity have been installed. Speeds of water turbines vary from 1,200 revolutions per minute (r.p.m.) down to 75 r.p.m.

Gas Turbines

Gas turbines work on the same principle as steam or water turbines but are driven by hot gas which is produced by burning a liquid fuel such as paraffin (kerosine) or a gas such as natural gas. The hot gas is compressed by a rotary compressor and blown into the gas turbine. Gas turbines are explained in the article INTERNAL COMBUSTION ENGINE and some of their features are discussed in JET PROPULSION. Developed originally for aircraft, their outputs and sizes have been increased greatly. They are now also used for ship propulsion and in power stations.

Air and Wind Turbines

Windmills, used to grind grain and pump water, were an early form of air or wind turbine. However, in modern times air turbines have been developed for a number of other uses.

Tiny air turbines, driven by compressed air and turning at 250,000 r.p.m., are used for dentists' drills. At this speed the drilling of a tooth is quickly completed and there is less vibration than with an electric drill. Because of the high speed of rotation, cooling water is sprayed on to the tooth to prevent it from heating up due to friction.

At the other end of the scale are wind turbines for generating electrical power. These may be horizontally or vertically rotating, and have two or more blades. Provision is made to keep them facing into the wind to use its full energy. (See WIND POWER.)

TURBOT see FLATFISH

TURGENEV, Ivan (1818–83). The Russian novelist, poet, and playwright Ivan Sergeyevich Turgenev was born in Oryol, some 300 kilometres (200 miles) south of Moscow. His father was a retired cavalry officer and his mother came from a rich landowning family. He was educated at the universities of Moscow and St. Petersburg (Leningrad), and in 1838 went to Berlin to study philosophy. There he met educated Russians who admired Western European culture and government. Turgenev joined them and retained his admiration for Western Europe all his life.

After returning to Russia in 1841, Turgenev began writing short pieces about country life on Russian estates. These pieces, condemning the serfdom in which Russian peasants were forced to live, were collected in 1852 under the title *A Sportsman's Sketches*. That same year Turgenev was banished to his estate by Tsarist authorities for praising the Russian author Nikolai Gogol (see GOGOL, NIKOLAI).

Turgenev now began work on his novels, and *Rudin* was published in 1856; *A Nest of Gentlefolk*, in 1859; *On the Eve*, in 1860; and his masterpiece, *Fathers and Sons*, in 1862. In this great novel he portrayed the new generation of radical Russian youth. The book was unfavourably received in Russia, however, and Turgenev, hurt by its reception, began spending more and more time in France and Germany. His last major novels, *Smoke* (1867) and *Virgin Soil* (1877), did not regain his lost reputation in his homeland. Turgenev was worldly, sophisticated, and brilliant; and he was the first Russian novelist whose works were admired throughout Europe. Yet he remained an exile. He died at Bougival, near Paris, France.

TURIN is an important industrial and transport centre in the northern part of Italy on the banks of the Po River (see PO RIVER). It lies in a rich agricultural area. The main railway line leading to France and western Europe from Italy passes through the city.

Swift-flowing streams from the Alps to the north provide hydroelectric power for the city's factories. They produce textiles, clothing, metal goods, rubber, paper, and glass. Turin is most important, however, as the centre of the Italian motor vehicle industry.

Turin is a city of elegant squares lined with arcades, and rich in religious architecture

ZEFA

Turin, though an industrial city, is rich in architecture. This is a view of the Piazza Vittorio Veneto and the River Po.

and palaces. Outstanding buildings include Palazzo Madama; Palazzo Reale (royal palace); the red-brick Palazzo Carignano; and the Academy of Sciences. The Chapel of the Holy Shroud in the Cathedral of St. John the Baptist houses the famous linen cloth which is said by some to be the burial shroud of Jesus Christ. The University of Turin, founded in 1405, is famous for its medical and scientific departments.

Although founded as a Roman town, Turin's growth did not begin until the 13th century, when it was made the capital of the dukedom of Savoy. During the following centuries it became one of the great cities of Europe. In 1720 it was made the capital of the kingdom of Sardinia. In the middle of the 19th century the kings of the Italian states met in Turin to plan the union of Italy. From 1861 until 1865 Turin was the capital of Italy.

Because of its importance as an industrial and transport centre, Turin was heavily bombed by the Allies during World War II (1939–45). The resulting damage was largely repaired by the 1960s and the population was boosted by emigrants from southern Italy. The population is 1,030,011 (1986), making Turin the fourth largest Italian city.

TURKEY is a republic partly in southeast Europe but mostly in Asia. Iran and the Soviet Union are on the east, the Black Sea on the north; Iraq, Syria, and the Mediterranean Sea lie along the southern border, while Greece and Bulgaria lie to the west. The Asian part of Turkey is much the bigger of the two. The European part, which includes the Gallipoli Peninsula, is separated by the Sea of Marmara and by the narrow straits of the Bosporus and Dardanelles from Anatolia, which is the Asian part. The islands of Gökçeada (Imroz) and Bozcaada (Tenedos) off the Dardanelles are Turkish, but most of the main islands near the coast are Greek.

European Turkey is a fertile, rolling country with some lowlands and swamps and a pleasant climate. Anatolia has a fertile coastal belt which is fairly narrow except on the west

coast and in the southeast, and rises inland to a high tableland. The Taurus Mountains in the south and others in the north and west surround the Anatolian tableland, which towards the east becomes wild and rugged. In the extreme east of Anatolia, near the point where Turkey, Iran, and the Soviet Union meet, rises the great snowclad dome of Agri Dagi (Mount Ararat) 5,185 metres (17,011 feet) high, and the tallest in Turkey.

The Anatolian plateau contains wide areas of steppe and salt marshes and has a very harsh climate with little rain. Many of its rivers are almost dry in summer. Although the great rivers Tigris and Euphrates rise in Turkey, the largest river wholly within the republic is the Kizil Irmak, or Red River, which is also the most important. The largest lake in Turkey is Lake Van in eastern Anatolia. The lake lies 1,720 metres (5,640 feet) above sea-level and its waters have a high soda content.

Most of the people live on the fringe of the Anatolian tableland and in the coastal districts, where the climate is less severe and the soil more fertile. Much of the Black Sea coast is well wooded, mostly with pines and oaks. The Black Sea coast of Turkey is famous for its fruit trees, and the word "cherry" comes from Cerasus, which is the old name for the town of Giresun. Wheat and other cereal crops are grown on large areas of the Anatolian tableland. Those parts which are not cultivated are mostly scrub and heath. Even the deserts along the Syrian border are green and fresh in spring, but generally speaking the greatest need of Anatolia is water.

FACTS ABOUT TURKEY

AREA: 779,452 square kilometres (300,948 square miles).
POPULATION: 55,059,000 (1989).
GOVERNMENT: Independent republic.
CAPITAL: Ankara, 2,235,000.
GEOGRAPHY: The central part of the country is a treeless plateau, or tableland, surrounded by mountain ranges. European Turkey and Asiatic Turkey are separated by the Dardanelles, the Sea of Marmara, and the Bosporus.
CITIES: Istanbul, 5,475,982; Izmir, 1,489,772; Adana, 777,554; Bursa, 612,500.
ECONOMY. Products and exports.
  Agriculture: Wheat, sugar beets, barley, potatoes, grapes, apples, dry onions, olives, sunflower seed, lentils.
  Mining: Iron, chrome ore.
  Manufacturing: Cement, fertilizers, steel ingot, crude iron, pig iron, beer, wine.
  Exports: Textiles, agricultural products, livestock, chemical products.
EDUCATION: Children must attend school between the ages of 7 and 12.

Among the larger animals, a few bears and wolves still live in the wooded regions. Wild sheep, ibexes, deer, lynxes, martens, and hares are found. Kites are common and in the spring storks nest.

Picturepoint

ZEFA

Top: Mount Ararat, Turkey's highest mountain.
Left: The Islamic mosque at Dogubayazit in eastern Turkey dates from the 18th century.
Above: The port of Marmaris, southwestern Turkey, lies in a sheltered bay opposite the Greek island of Rhodes.

Spectrum

Bursa in northwestern Turkey is famous for its fountains and ancient silk industry.

People and Cities

The Turks are descended from a number of different peoples who ruled the country at various times during its history. The earliest of these were the Hittites, an Indo-European people who had set up a powerful empire in Anatolia by 1800 BC.

Almost all the people of Turkey are Muslim, although Islam is no longer the official state religion. Religion remains important in private life in spite of the many changes that have been seen since the republic was founded in 1923.

Until 1923, when Turkey became a republic, its capital was Istanbul – formerly known as Constantinople – on the European shore of the Bosporus (see ISTANBUL). Turkey's first president, Mustafa Kemal Atatürk moved the capital to Ankara in central Anatolia (see ANKARA). The third city of Turkey is Izmir (formerly Smyrna), which is beautifully situated at the head of a long gulf leading to the Aegean Sea. Its main street stretches along the busy waterfront and most of its buildings are modern, as much of the city was destroyed by fire in 1922. Not far to the southeast are the ruins of Ephesus, where once stood the famous Temple of Diana (see SEVEN WONDERS OF THE WORLD). Other important cities are the cotton centre of Adana near the northeast corner of the Mediterranean, the beautiful city of Bursa, which is set in a fertile plain near the Sea of Marmara and is famous for its fruit and vegetables, and the railway and agricultural centre of Eskişehir in Anatolia.

Agriculture and Industry

Just over half of the Turkish people earn their living from agriculture, mostly on small family farms, although cotton is grown on larger estates. The chief crops are wheat, barley and other grains, sugar beet, cotton, tobacco, olives, figs, raisins, nuts such as hazelnuts and pistachios, fruit, vegetables, and tea. Oxen are still seen pulling carts and ploughs, but tractors are commonly used. Sheep and goats are the commonest farm animals as they can live on poor pasture. The Angora (Ankara) goat, whose thick hair is used for making mohair, is widely bred. Cattle-breeding is important in the uplands of eastern Anatolia.

Coal is mined near Zonguldak on the Black Sea coast and iron in eastern Anatolia. Turkey is now one of the world's chief producers of chromite, from which chromium metal is obtained. Petroleum is obtained in southeast Anatolia.

There are iron and steel works at Karabuk and Eregli north of Ankara, and at Iskenderun in the southeast. Paper, sugar, cement, and fabrics such as cottons, woollens, man-made fibres and silk are also produced, together with carpets and most household goods. Several West European firms make motor vehicles in Turkey. Dams across the Sakarya and Kizil Irmak rivers provide water power and irrigation for the parched tableland of western Anatolia. The dam at Hirfanli on the Kizil Irmak formed a lake 70 kilometres (43 miles) long. The largest new dam is at Keban on the Euphrates.

The Turkish railways are state-owned and in the west are linked with the European rail system. Passengers and goods have to cross the Bosporus to Haydarpasa, where the

ZEFA

Stocking up with provisions at a general store in Refahiye, a small town in east-central Turkey.

Anatolian railway starts. There are also road bridges to carry traffic. In eastern Anatolia a line joins with the railway to Tiflis in the Soviet Union, but this stretch is little used. Other branches link Anatolia with Syria, Iran, and Iraq. There are bus services with neighbouring countries and most of the country towns. Ferry services run along the Black Sea and Mediterranean coasts.

Turkey has a state-owned airline and several international airports. The chief seaports are Istanbul and Izmir. Others are Trabzon, Giresun, Samsun, and Zonguldak on the Black Sea, Haydarpaşa on the Bosporus, and Mersin and Iskenderun on the Mediterranean.

Tourism is an important source of revenue for Turkey. Several million people each year visit the country on holiday. Bodrum, the site of the ancient Mausoleum of Halicarnassus (see SEVEN WONDERS OF THE WORLD) and a large crusader castle, is a popular resort. Kusadasai, near the ruins of ancient Ephesus; Marmaris on the Aegean coast; and Antalya and Alanya on the southern Mediterranean, also attract many visitors. Others go to Cappadocia in central Anatolia, a region of strangely shaped hills known as fairy chimneys, and of medieval churches hollowed out of the soft rock.

History

The people known as the Seljuk Turks came from central Asia in the 9th century AD and formed an empire in Persia (now Iran), Iraq, and Syria. They spread to Anatolia after defeating the emperor of the Byzantine Empire, which was the eastern part of the Roman Empire, in 1071. Before that, some of the Armenians and Greeks in Anatolia had been among the earliest people to practise Christianity, but under the Seljuks most of the country became Muslim.

The western fringe of the Seljuk lands was somewhere near Eskişehir. This region was held by a ruler named Osman, who conquered the surrounding district and became the real power in the land when the Seljuk kingdom ended in about 1308. He founded the Ottoman Empire. The word "Ottoman" is a European form of "Osmanli". (See OTTOMAN EMPIRE.)

The Ottoman sultans (kings) captured the remaining Byzantine possessions in Anatolia and crossed into Europe in 1345. Once in Europe they could not be dislodged and were seldom defeated. By 1389 they had conquered most of the Balkans. The spread of the Ottoman Empire was checked in 1402, when the ruthless Tatar conqueror Tamerlane led his tribesmen in a victorious battle against the Turks at Ankara. (See TAMERLANE.)

However, a few years later the Turks continued their attacks against the remains of the Byzantine Empire. In 1453 they took Constantinople, which they called Istanbul. The Turkish forces were victorious at sea as well as on land. A whole family of Turkish admirals and sea-rovers called Barbarossa (meaning "red beard") terrorized the Mediterranean in the early part of the 16th century. The Turks captured Rhodes, Cyprus, Algiers, Tunis, Tripoli in Libya, and Aden.

The Turks conquered Syria and Egypt in 1517 and Iraq in 1534. In 1526 they defeated the Hungarians at the Battle of Mohacs and occupied a large part of Hungary. By this time the Ottoman Empire was at the height of its power, and its ruler was Süleyman I, the Magnificent, (1494–1566). However, the Ottoman advance was stopped before the walls of

Vienna in Austria and in Malta in the Mediterranean. In 1683 Turkish forces besieging Vienna were defeated by King Jan (John) Sobieski of Poland. From that time on, the power of the Ottoman Empire gradually became less.

In the 18th century, Turkey fought several unsuccessful wars against Russia. In the 19th century there were rebellions in the Turkish territories of Greece, Serbia (modern Yugoslavia), Bulgaria, and Egypt, and Algiers and Tunis were lost to France. The Turkish government, with help from French advisers, introduced reforms in its army, laws, and education.

Great Britain and France supported Turkey in a successful war against Russia in 1854–55 (see CRIMEAN WAR), but as a result of the Russian-Turkish War of 1877–78 the Ottoman Empire lost most of its lands in the Balkans. When the 19th century ended, Turkey's only friend seemed to be Germany, which saw how useful it would be to have an ally whose territory stretched from Europe to Arabia.

During a war with Italy in 1911 Turkey lost its province in Libya, and the Balkan wars (1912–13) resulted in the loss of Crete, most of the Aegean Islands and the country on the European mainland west of the Maritza River. As a result of defeat in World War I (1914–18), when Turkey sided with Germany, the Turkish possessions in Arabia, Iraq, Syria, and Palestine were lost.

Modern Turkey

World War I also saw the rise to power of a soldier named Mustafa Kemal (1881–1938), who brilliantly defended the Gallipoli Peninsula against an Allied invasion in 1915. After the war he was stationed in northeast Anatolia and there he planned to restore Turkish power and lands. He resigned from the army and persuaded the Anatolian people to support his struggle. In 1920 he created a separate government at Ankara and in the following year was put in command of the Turkish armed forces in the war against Greece. In 1921 he held the Greeks at the Sakarya River and defeated them finally in 1922 at Dumlupinar, east of Izmir. Britain and France were not willing to go to war about Turkey and in 1923 they signed a peace treaty in Lausanne that restored some territory and set Turkey's present boundaries.

Turkey became a republic, with Kemal, who had been given the surname Atatürk ("father of Turks"), as its first President. He continued as president until his death. There were to be no more sultans.

Atatürk carried out a huge programme of reforms that changed Turkey from a backward country into a modernized republic. He removed the influence of the Muslim religion from politics, education, and law-making. He introduced universal education, the equality of all citizens, and a new code of laws based on a Western model. He abolished the use of the Arabic alphabet for writing in favour of the Roman alphabet and ordered the metric system of weights and measures to be adopted. Also he forbade the men to wear fezzes and turbans.

Women were allowed to vote in elections, to become members of parliament and to take part in the affairs of the country, instead of being mere veiled servants in the background. Sunday was introduced as the weekly day of rest instead of Friday. The old Turkish titles, such as "pasha" and "bey", were abolished and family names were introduced, as in the West. A number of reforms were carried out to establish or improve Turkish industries.

Kemal Atatürk also made no attempt to seek glory by conquering foreign lands, but developed better relations with Turkey's old enemies, the Soviet Union and Greece, as well as with the European states. Although Atatürk ruled with total power he did nothing to hinder the establishment of a democratic form of government. The result was that his successor, Ismet Inönu, gradually introduced a democratic state, with a government elected by the people. Nevertheless, Atatürk's party remained in power until 1950.

In World War II, Turkey joined neither side until February 1945 when it declared war on Germany. After the war, the Soviet Union attempted to obtain a share in the control of the Dardanelles and Bosporus and claimed territory in northeast Anatolia. Turkey's refusal of these demands was later supported by the United States and Britain. Turkey became a member of the North Atlantic Treaty Organization (NATO) and has received help from the United States in the form of money, war material, and machinery. It was one of the first countries of the United Nations to send troops to help South Korea in its struggle against the Communist attack in 1950. In 1959 Turkey and Greece agreed that the British colony of Cyprus (see CYPRUS), where Turks and Greeks lived together, should become an independent republic.

However, fighting later broke out among Greek and Turkish Cypriots and war between Greece and Turkey was only narrowly avoided. In 1974 Cypriot troops, led by Greek officers, overthrew the Cypriot government. It seemed that Cyprus might come under Greek control and so, to protect the rights of Turkish Cypriots, troops from Turkey landed and captured the northern part of the island. (See also CYPRUS; GREECE.) Although this offended all Greeks, war was again averted.

At home Turkey has not always been peaceful, due mainly to weakness in its economy. Political unrest has led to military take-overs, most recently in 1980.

TURKEY. Domestic turkeys are descended from a breed of turkey which is still found wild in Mexico and the southern parts of the United States. They have white tips to their tails. Wild turkeys (*Meleagris gallopavo*), which are also found in North America as far north as the Canadian border, have brown tail tips.

Some domestic turkeys have white plumage, but that of the most usual kind is black and bronze with a glossy green sheen. The head and neck are bare and red and the cock bird has a wattle, or fold of flesh, hanging over the bill and a long tuft of hairs on the breast. When it is excited or angry it raises its tail and spreads it out like a fan, droops its wings and struts up and down, blowing out its throat. Turkeys often make a dull gobbling sound, from which they get the name "gobbler".

Wild turkeys are birds of the forest and usually haunt the densest parts, although they are also found on swampy land. They generally live in flocks, each cock having several wives. As the cocks eat the eggs and even the young if they can, the hens hide their nests carefully. Each lays between 10 and 14 eggs.

Hans Reinhard/Bruce Coleman

A cock turkey displaying its tail feathers.

The brush turkey (*Agriocharis ocellata*) lives in Belize, Guatemala, and the Yucatan Peninsula. The bird is smaller than the common turkey, and is named from the eye-like spots on its tail feathers. The head and neck skin is blue rather than pink or red.

Other unrelated birds called brush turkeys, megapodes, or mound builders, live in Australia (see MOUND BUILDER.)

Turkeys were first kept for their meat by the Aztecs, in Mexico, where they were observed by the Spanish explorer Cortes. Shortly after, in 1524, they were first introduced to Europe. Now they have become highly prized as table poultry, and they are associated with festivals such as Thanksgiving Day and Christmas.

TURKMENISTAN. The Turkmen Soviet Socialist Republic is a constituent republic of the Soviet Union. It is located on the eastern shore of the Caspian Sea. The republic is traditionally called Turkmenistan. It is bordered by the Kazakh Soviet Socialist Republic to the north, the Uzbek SSR to the north and east, and Iran and Afghanistan to the south. It covers an area of 488,100 square kilometres (188,500 square miles).

Turkmen SSR is an extremely dry land with great extremes of temperature. January temperatures in some places average about −4°C (25°F), and July temperatures may rise to an average of about 32°C (90°F). Most of the republic has only 100–200 millimetres (4 to 8 inches) of rainfall yearly.

More than four-fifths of this land is covered by the dry Kara Kum (Black Sand) Desert, a lifeless wasteland with little vegetation or water. The people live mostly on the fringes of the desert, near the Kopet Dag Range along the southern border, or along the Amu-Darya, Murgab, and Tedzhen rivers.

Most of the people are Turkmen and are Sunni Muslims by religion. They speak a language that resembles the Turkish of Turkey. Before Turkmenistan became a part of the Soviet Union, these people were largely nomads. They raised livestock and moved seasonally to favourable pasture lands. After they came under Soviet control, many of the people settled in villages. They began growing crops with the aid of irrigation in addition to livestock. Many Turkmens now work in manufacturing. Russians now make up the next largest group, followed by the Uzbeks. The Russians generally hold the positions of leadership, and the Russian language is taught in schools. Children must attend school, which is free, from the ages of 6 to 16.

Industry and Agriculture

The major resource of the republic is petroleum, which is mined in the west. Turkmen SSR is the third largest petroleum producer in the Soviet Union. A pipeline transports petroleum to a refinery on the Caspian Sea. Chemicals, mining, and natural gas are also important industries. Fisheries are located on the Caspian Sea.

Light manufacturing industries have developed in the republic's major cities. Ashkhabad, the capital, has important cotton and silk textile industries. Other major cities in the republic include Chardzhou, Krasnovodsk, and Mary (Merv). Turkmen industry depends mostly on railways for transport. Industry has surpassed agriculture in value, but many Turkmens still farm. Principal crops include cotton, silk, grapes, corn, and wheat. Karakul sheep, horses, and camels are the chief forms of livestock.

The Turkmens occupied the region east of the Caspian Sea in the 11th century. After its defeat by the Russians in 1881, Turkmenistan

John Massey Stewart

The ruins of Nissa, near Ashkhabad in southern Turkmenistan. Nissa is thought to have been the capital of ancient Parthia at one time.

John Massey Stewart

Turkmenistan is famous for growing cotton and melons. This collective farm is near the Iranian border.

became a part of the Russian Empire. After the revolution it became a Soviet Socialist Republic in 1924. The population is 3,361,000 (1987).

TURKS AND CAICOS ISLANDS. These islands lie in the Caribbean Sea, at the south-eastern end of the Bahamas and roughly 145 kilometres (90 miles) to the north of the Dominican Republic. There are eight Turks islands and six main islands in the Caicos group. Altogether, the islands have a land area of 430 square kilometres (166 square miles).

Eight of the Turks and Caicos islands are regularly inhabited, and the people are mainly descendants of African slaves. The islands are flat, and surrounded by coral reefs. The soil is poor and the area suffers frequent hurricanes. Chief exports are crayfish, dried conchs, and conch shells. At one time there was a flourishing salt industry. However, the industry lacked the funds to invest in modern machinery for salt mining, and has declined in recent years.

The islands were first discovered by Europeans in 1512, when the Spanish explorer Juan Ponce de Leon visited them. At that time they were uninhabited, and they remained so until 1678 when they were occupied by British settlers from Bermuda who established a salt industry there. From 1874 until 1959, the islands were a Jamaican dependency. They became a British colony in 1962.

The capital of the colony is Grand Turk, on the island of the same name. On this island, too, the United States has two military bases.

The Turks and Caicos islands have a population of around 10,000.

TURNER, J. M. W. (1775–1851). Joseph Mallord William Turner was an English painter, famous for the gorgeous colours in his pictures. Most of them were landscapes – paintings of the countryside or outdoor scenes – and sea-pictures. At first he copied carefully from nature, but as he grew older he was less interested in the shapes of natural things and instead made them seem in his pictures as if they were dissolved in a pool of brilliant colour, shimmering with light.

Turner was the son of a barber in London and had very little schooling. In his early teens he was already at work, colouring pictures for an engraver (see ENGRAVING) and making drawings himself which he sold in his father's shop. In 1789 he went to the Royal Academy schools and was soon producing illustrations of views and scenery for books and magazines. Before he was 20 he had tramped through England and Wales collecting material for drawings and paintings. He had an amazing memory and was able to paint a scene, months later, with only a rough sketch to guide him. Take as an example his picture of a snowstorm at a harbour mouth, reproduced on the next page, which was painted from memory. The superb way in which he painted the waves was due to the fact that he had himself tied to the mast of a ship in order to experience a storm, so that he should be able to paint it afterwards.

In 1802 Turner visited France and one of the pictures he painted as a result was *Calais Pier* (National Gallery, London), in which he first showed his genius for putting the energy and movement of waves into paint. His other visits to France and Italy later increased his determination to make a special study of light and of the way in which it could be shown in painting by using brilliant colour and by leaving out the small details of a scene. One of his best pictures done like this is *The*

Snow Storm—Steam-boat off a Harbour's Mouth is one of Turner's later oil paintings, dating from 1842. In his later works, he became less interested in the natural shapes of objects, and more concerned with light and colour.

Courtesy, Trustees of the Tate Gallery

Fighting Téméraire, in the National Gallery, London. In the 1820s he also started to paint in oils, and these works are greatly admired.

Always a secretive and lonely man, Turner died under an assumed name in Chelsea. He had made a comfortable fortune, partly from his engravings and drawings published in a book called *Liber Studiorum* (A Book of Studies). He left to the nation more than 20,000 drawings and water colours as well as some oil paintings. A special wing of the Tate Gallery, London, to house the Turner collection was opened in 1987.

TURNIP is a root vegetable belonging to the family Brassicaceae. There are two kinds, the true turnip (*Brassica rapa*) and the Swedish turnip, or Swede (*Brassica napobrassica*), also known as the rutabaga. They store their food in the upper part of their roots during their first growing season. They are only left in the ground to grow if their seed is wanted. Usually they are dug up and eaten or fed to farm animals.

Turnips were introduced to England from Flanders during the 18th century. It was found that if they were given to sheep and cattle to eat the animals thrived on them and meat, milk, and wool production increased (see TOWNSHEND, CHARLES). Later in the 18th century swedes were introduced from Sweden. They can be told apart from true turnips by the stem or "neck" on the top of their roots. From this "neck" grow the leaves. Swedes are grown extensively in Great Britain, Canada, and northern Europe, but not in the United States. Turnip leaves are hairy while swede leaves are waxy and less green than turnip leaves. Swedes keep better than yellow-fleshed turnips and much better than white-fleshed ones.

The varieties of turnips grown as vegetables for people to eat have smaller and firmer roots than the varieties grown for farm animals.

The swede (left) is distinguished from the turnip (right) by the "neck" from which the leaves grow.

TURNSTONE. There are two species of turnstone, wading birds with a short, flattened bill, slightly upturned at the tip. The turnstone uses its bill to flick over pebbles and shells in search of food.

The ruddy turnstone (*Arenaria interpres*) is about 22 centimetres (9 inches) long with a plump body rather short legs and a short, strong bill. In summer the upper parts are a mixture of reddish-brown and black, like a tortoiseshell cat, the head and breast are black and white and the underparts are white. In autumn the upper parts become dull brown, but in flight turnstones look black and white because they have white bars on their wings. Their legs are yellow and their bills are black. They breed chiefly in the Arctic near stony or rocky coasts. On the breeding ground the male may make many false nests, while the female makes a single, true nest.

Gordon Langsbury/Bruce Coleman

A flock of turnstones on a shingle beach. The colour of the birds blends with the pebbles on the shore.

The ruddy turnstone spends its winters far to the south, on the coasts of South America, South Africa, Australia, and New Zealand.

The black turnstone (*Arenaria melanocephala*) breeds in Arctic Alaska and winters as far south as Mexico. It is dark coloured with a black and white wing pattern.

Turnstones utter a rapid call like "tuk-a-tuk". They are often seen in the company of other wading birds (see WADING BIRDS).

TURTLE AND TORTOISE. Turtles and tortoises are reptiles with shells (see REPTILE). In North America the name turtle refers to all shelled reptiles. But within the general term turtle, a few slow-moving land forms are called tortoise, and a few edible aquatic (water-living) forms are called terrapins. In Britain the name turtle generally refers only to the types that live in fresh or seawater. There are few freshwater European shelled reptiles and there are many African land forms. In contrast, the New World is rich in mainly aquatic forms, hence the general use of the word "turtle".

All turtles and tortoises have a scaly skin, and a protective shell that covers most of the body. They breathe air through lungs, and have a sharp, horny beak instead of teeth. The feet have claws and sometimes webs between the toes for swimming. Turtles usually breed once a year; the female lays her whitish, rounded eggs on land, usually in a hole she has dug with her hind claws. Turtles hibernate during cold weather in mud, earth, or under vegetation. The largest number of turtles are found in the southeastern United States and Southeast Asia.

The largest freshwater turtles are the snapping turtles. The alligator snapping turtle (*Macrochelys temmincki*) lives in the lower Mississippi Valley in the southeastern United States. It has a worm-like flap of skin on the inside of its bottom jaw with which it attracts fish within snapping range. This turtle reaches a length of over 60 centimetres (2 feet) and a weight of 90 kilograms (200 pounds). The common snapping turtle (*Chelydra serpentina*) often lies buried in the mud in shallow water. It eats both plant and animal food.

The common North American painted turtle (*Chrysemys picta*) has a neck and limbs streaked with red. It is often seen in groups basking in the sun on logs in the middle of a pond. The box turtle (*Terrapene carolina*) has a raised sculptured shell and is one of the few North American turtles that can withdraw its body completely into its shell. It lives in damp woods and by streams.

The North American diamondback terrapin (*Malaclemys terrapin*) lives in salt marshes and coastal waters from New England to the Gulf of Mexico. It is named for the raised patterns on its shell. The flesh of this terrapin was considered very tasty to eat during the 19th and early 20th centuries. There are also

A western painted tortoise from Utah, USA.

NHPA/R. J. Erwin

many races of turtle (*Pseudemys*) in North America, called terrapins, cooters, or sliders.

Soft-shelled turtles are a distinct group with a flat leathery shell, and nostrils at the end of a long, snorkel-like extension to the snout. They lie in quiet waters to ambush their prey.

There are about 35 species of snake-necked turtle mainly from South America and Australia. They all have long necks which they bend sideways instead of pulling them back into the shell. The Eastern snake-necked turtle (*Chelodina longicollis*) is a common Australian species that lives in swamps, billabongs, and lakes.

David Hughes/Bruce Coleman

The green turtle is highly valued for turtle soup. It is named after the greenish colour of its fat.

Sea Turtles

The largest marine turtle is the leatherback (*Dermochelys coriacea*), which usually grows to a length of about 2 metres (7 feet) and a weight of about 540 kilograms (1,200 pounds), although much larger specimens have been reported. Its long, ridged shell is made up of a number of small bones, instead of bony plates like those of other turtles. The leatherback is the best swimmer of all the turtles, and perhaps the oldest.

The green turtle (*Chelonia mydas*) (so called because of the colour of its fat) is relatively common. Like the leatherback, it is found in tropical seas and feeds on fish, molluscs, and other sea creatures. This is the turtle that is made into turtle soup. It may be 1 metre (3 feet) long and weigh 180 kilograms (400 pounds).

Loggerhead and hawksbill turtles also feed on fish and molluscs. The loggerhead (*Caretta caretta*) was given its name because of its enormous head. It may weigh over 200 kilograms (440 pounds). It eats smaller animals, and can give a bad bite. Loggerheads are often found as far north as the Mediterranean Sea and parts of the Atlantic. The hawksbill (*Dermochelys imbricata*) is smaller than the other turtles, with a shell rarely more than 55 centimetres (22 inches) long. From its shell, which consists of horny shields of dark brown and yellow, tortoiseshell is obtained.

The ridleys are small sea turtles with wide, rounded shells.

Turtles make long migrations to the beaches where the females lay their eggs. Little is known about these journeys and scientists are still mystified at the way in which turtles find their way across the sea to the same beaches year after year. It is when they come ashore to breed that the turtles are most in danger. Their eggs are easily dug up, many young turtles are eaten by predators, such as birds and crabs, which gather as they scramble towards the sea, and the slow moving adults are killed for food by hunters. Turtles are also caught in the open sea, and are becoming rare because so many have been killed.

Tortoises

The most interesting tortoises are the giant tortoises (*Geochelone elephantopus*), sometimes growing to a length of over 1.3 metres

Jane Burton/Bruce Coleman

A leatherback turtle digs a nest for her eggs. Sea turtles lay their eggs at night, for safety.

Udo Hirsch/Bruce Coleman

There are more than ten varieties of Galapagos giant tortoise. The largest weigh well over 150 kilograms.

(4.2 feet) with a weight of about 140 kilograms (300 pounds). They are now found only on Aldabra Island in the Indian Ocean and the Galapagos islands on the equator.

The name of these islands (which belong to Ecuador) comes from *galapago*, the Spanish for "tortoise", and when the islands were discovered in the 16th century they were swarming with giant tortoises. However, the coming of man to these remote islands meant the destruction of some of the interesting forms of life there. The early travellers to the Galapagos found that the giant tortoises were good to eat and could be kept alive for many months without food. In those early days, when ships had no refrigerators to keep meat fresh, giant tortoises were kept alive on board ship and killed when food was needed. Domestic animals such as pigs, goats, and rats were also responsible for their decline as they ate both the eggs and the young turtles.

The European common tortoise (*Testudo graeca*) is a close relative of the giant tortoise. It has a brownish shell marked with black and is the tortoise that is commonly kept as a pet in Britain and Europe. However, the number of tortoises has declined through over-collecting. Also, tortoises are known to carry disease and this, too, has made them less popular as pets.

There are four species of North American gopher tortoise (*Gopherus*). They have flattened limbs that act as spades to shovel earth when burrowing. The desert tortoise (*Gopherus agassizii*) lives in deserts and scrubland of the southwestern United States and Mexico. It feeds on annual wildflowers and grasses in the spring and autumn, and builds up enough fat to see it through its winter hibernation.

TUSSAUD, Marie (1761–1850). Marie Tussaud was the founder of the famous waxworks show in London known as Madame Tussaud's. But before she went to London she had spent the most exciting years of her life in Paris.

She was born at Strasbourg in France. Her soldier father, Joseph Grosholtz, died about the time of her birth, and Marie was brought up by her uncle, Philippe Curtius. He was a doctor in Berne, Switzerland, but he was so skilled at making wax models that he was persuaded to move to Paris, where he started a successful museum of waxworks. It quickly became famous for its life-size models of royal persons and other notable characters.

Marie learned her uncle's skill and soon was able to assist him with his work. In 1780, when she was 19, she was invited to teach her art to the king's sister, Madame Elizabeth of France. For the next nine years Marie lived at Versailles in the royal household.

In 1789 came the French Revolution, bringing terror to anyone who was associated with the royal family of France. Marie's uncle made her leave Versailles and return to him in Paris in case her life should be endangered. For three months she was a prisoner, but much worse was the fact that time and again she was compelled by the revolutionaries to make casts, or models, from the actual heads of people who had been guillotined (beheaded). Among the casts she made during this time were those of King Louis XVI, Queen Marie Antoinette, and the revolutionary leaders Robespierre, Danton, and Marat.

Courtesy, Madame Tussaud's

Wax model of Marie Tussaud (1761–1850), French-born founder of Madame Tussaud's museum of wax figures.

In 1795 Marie married François Tussaud, and in 1802 she brought her waxwork collection to England. She spent the rest of her life in London, where the exhibition became permanently established. It is still run by Madame Tussaud's descendants.

TUTANKHAMUN (*c.* 1370–1352 BC). The most exciting discovery of ancient Egyptian remains was that of the tomb of the pharaoh (king) Tutankhamun who had ruled Egypt in the first half of the 14th century BC. It was found in 1922 by an Englishman called Howard Carter who was a member of an expedition led by Lord Carnarvon. The tomb was in the Valley of the Kings, near Luxor, southern Egypt, where many Egyptian kings were buried. This tomb was probably not one of the most important but it was alone among the other royal burials in being the only one that had not been broken open and robbed of its treasures.

When Howard Carter gained entry into the innermost chambers of this fascinating tomb he discovered what he described as "wonderful things". The mummy (preserved body) of Tutankhamun himself was enclosed in a decorated coffin of gold, which in its turn was inside two wooden coffins covered in gold and a stone one called a sarcophagus. The face of the mummy was covered with a gold death mask, decorated with precious stones, and there were gold ornaments on the head.

The tomb included three other rooms besides the one in which the body lay. In these were found statues, beds, chairs, chests, boxes, chariots (in pieces), weapons, clothes, jewellery, wines, and preserved food. The furniture was overlaid with gold and gems and included a throne of wood covered with gold plating and decorated with lions' heads. The greatness of this treasure showed how rich Egypt must have been in the 14th century BC. But there is good reason to believe that Tutankhamun's burial was in fact a modest one by the usual standards of Egyptian royal tombs. As many of the objects in his tomb had been used by the king in his lifetime, it became possible, by examining them, to find out much about the daily lives of the ancient Egyptians that had not been known before. The archaeological finds even included a trumpet that was still playable.

Picturepoint

A decorated panel from Tutankhamun's throne.

Michael Holford

Tutankhamun with his wife and the god Osiris, who in Egyptian mythology is identified with dead rulers.

Most of the contents of the tomb were put in the national museum at Cairo, although the mummy and outer sarcophagus remained at Luxor.

Tutankhamun became king of Egypt through his marriage to one of the daughters of Akhenaton, the pharaoh who had changed the state religion from worship of several gods to worship of only one, Aton, the Sun god. (See AKHENATON.) At his birth Tutankhamun had been named Tutakhaton. He was only about nine when he became pharaoh, and for most of his reign Egyptian affairs were in the hands of a group of court officials led by his chief priest Ay. Akhenaton's religious changes were overturned, and the young king altered his own name to Tutankhamun to show that he agreed with the return to the traditional gods. Tutankhamun's death at the age of 18 was an unexpected shock for Egypt. Preparations for his burial had to be made in haste, and it has been suggested by some authorities that he was placed in the tomb that Ay had built for himself. Tutankhamun was a minor figure on the stage of history, and even the location of his tomb was forgotten. If it had not been found, his name might well have remained unknown to all but a few experts. As it is, Tutankhamun is the best-known pharaoh who ever lived.

A curious superstition sprang up about the tomb of Tutankhamun. It was said that the people who had broken it open were committing sacrilege (an offence against something sacred) and that they would meet sudden death as a result. Lord Carnarvon died from a mosquito bite and pneumonia five months after the finding of the tomb.

TUVALU is a country consisting of a group of nine islands in the Pacific Ocean lying 4,000 kilometres (2,500 miles) to the northeast of Australia. The various islands have a total area of 26 square kilometres (10 square miles).

The islands are coral atolls, long and narrow in shape. The climate is hot and humid ranging from 26°C to 32°C (79°F–90°F). Lizards, turtles, tuna, crabs, and flying fish are among the islands' wildlife. Little grows on the poor soil, and the chief occupation of the islanders is fishing and tourism. Coconut plantations provide some income, as does the sale of postage stamps, and traditional crafts. The people of Tuvalu are Polynesians (see POLYNESIANS; PACIFIC ISLANDS).

Europeans first discovered the islands in the 18th and early 19th centuries. From 1888 they, along with the Gilbert Islands, were administered as a British colony called the Gilbert and Ellice Islands.

In 1975, after a long-standing rivalry between the two islands, the colony was divided in two, and the Ellice Islands took the new name Tuvalu. The country became independent in 1978. Its capital is Funafuti. The country has a parliament and is a member of the Commonwealth.

Tuvalu has a population of around 8,000.

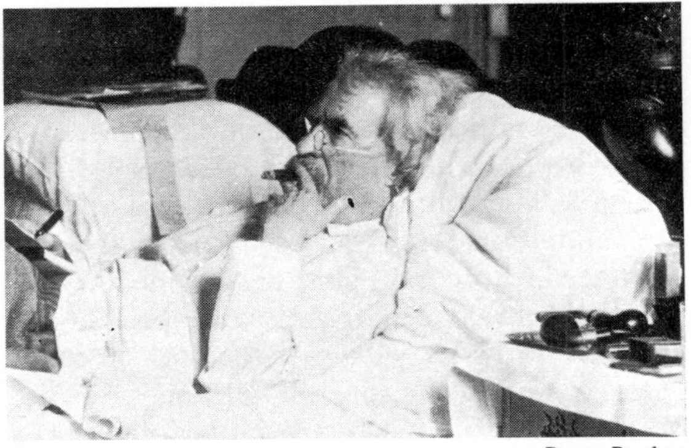

Brown Brothers

Mark Twain did much of his writing in bed. In his later years he wrote constantly to pay off debts.

TWAIN, Mark (1835–1910). Tom Sawyer and Huckleberry Finn were the boy heroes of two of the best-known books by the American author Mark Twain. The adventures of Tom and Huck took place in the rough pioneering days of the United States. Mark Twain himself lived during these times, on one occasion becoming a gold miner in the West.

Mark Twain was a pen name used for his books and other writings, and the author's real name was Samuel Langhorne Clemens. He was born in the state of Missouri and grew up in the Mississippi River town of Hannibal. When he was 11 years old his father died leaving the family almost penniless. Sam had hardly any proper education, but he was surrounded by the romance and excitement of life on the Mississippi River. His first job was helping his brother on the local newspaper, but his boyhood ambition had been to become a river pilot on the Mississippi, and eventually after a travelling job he came home and set to work "learning the river". In 1861 came the American Civil War; trade on the river ended and Samuel Clemens set out for the West. After unsuccessful attempts at goldmining, he became a journalist and took the name of "Mark Twain"—one of the calls used by the Mississippi pilots when testing the depth of the river and meaning "two fathoms deep".

Once Mark Twain had started as an author, success came quickly. His down-to-earth, humorous writings were read all over the United States, especially a set of letters that he wrote about a voyage round the Mediterranean in 1867, published as *The Innocents Abroad* (1869). In 1870 he married and settled down to a full-time career of authorship. As well as *The Adventures of Tom Sawyer* (1876) and *The Adventures of Huckleberry Finn* (1884), his books included *Roughing It* (1872), in which he described his experiences travelling by stage coach, *Life on the Mississippi* (1883), and *A Connecticut Yankee in King Arthur's Court* (1889).

TWEED is the name given to a wide variety of cloths woven in different colours, usually from wool, or wool and other fibres, such as cotton rayon, or acrylic. Although it was originally coarse and heavy, many tweeds are now light, smooth cloths that are made into elegant coats and suits. The pattern depends on the weave; that is, on the order in which the threads are interlaced. (See WEAVING.)

B. & C. Alexander

Loading bobbins to weave tweed fabric in a factory on the Scottish island of Islay.

The name tweed is not derived from the River Tweed which flows along the border between Scotland and England, although cloth was manufactured there. It comes from "twill", a fabric with the threads interwoven in such a way that they appear as slanting lines.

Many tweeds are named after places where they were originally manufactured, such as Harris (an island in the Outer Hebrides, Scotland), Yorkshire in England, and Donegal in Ireland, and Welsh tweed from Wales. The patterns may be checked or striped, or a "heather mixture" of many tones and hues. Tweed should not be confused with tartan, another woollen cloth made in Scotland (see TARTAN).

See also SPINNING; TEXTILES; WOOL.

TWINS are two children conceived by and born to the same mother at the same time. The article REPRODUCTION describes how a baby starts when a sperm from the father fertilizes an ovum (egg) from the mother, and how this fertilized ovum becomes implanted in the wall of the mother's uterus (womb). It grows there, nourished through the placenta until it is big enough to be born and breathe air and feed on milk.

The father deposits many millions of sperms in the mother's vagina, but normally a woman only releases a single ovum from one or other of her ovaries each month. This ovum, if fertilized, multiplies into two cells, then four cells, then eight and so on until an embryo made of many millions of cells is formed.

However, occasionally this ball of cells divides into two separate halves very early in its development. Each half continues to develop on its own and they grow into two separate babies. These two babies have been formed from a single fertilized ovum, so their genes will be identical (see the article on HEREDITY AND GENETICS). This is how identical (or *monozygotic* or *monovular*) twins are formed. They will always be of the same sex and they will be identical in those characteristics which are controlled by heredity. If they are brought up in very different environments, they may develop differently so that, for example, if one twin has a very inadequate diet it may not grow as tall as the other.

Very rarely the two halves of the early embryo do not separate completely. Each half develops into a separate baby but they are joined together by some part of their anatomy. This is how "Siamese twins" are formed. Siamese twins get their name from a very famous pair of joined twins called Chang and Eng, who lived in the 19th century. They grew up and married (still joined together) and lived till they were aged about 60. Nowadays if

ZEFA

Identical twin girls. They developed from a single fertilized egg which divided into separate embryos.

Siamese twins are born, surgeons can sometimes separate them after birth.

More common than identical twins are dissimilar (or *dizygotic* or fraternal or *binovular*) twins. These are formed if a woman releases two ova at the same time and both are fertilized. Due to the principles of inheritance, each ovum will carry a different selection of the mother's genes. The two ova will be fertilized by two different sperms, each carrying a different selection of the father's genes. Each fertilized ovum embeds itself in the wall of the mother's uterus and develops into a baby. These babies will be born at the same time but can be of different sexes and will be no more alike than are all brothers and sisters.

Twins are not born at the same moment. Always one is born first and then minutes, or even hours, later the other is born. So there is always an older and a younger twin, because a person's age is calculated from when he or she is born, not from the time of conception. Triplets are three babies born at a single birth. Quadruplets (quads) are four babies born at a single birth, and quintuplets (quins) are five babies born at a single birth. They may be identical, non-identical, or a mixture of the two. The tendency to have twins often runs in families, and is usually transmitted through the mother. About 1 pregnancy in 80 produces twins. Certain kinds of drugs, given to women to help them have babies, can increase the chances of giving birth to quads or quins.

TYNDALE, William (*c.*1492–1536), was an early Church reformer who devoted much of his life to translating the Bible into English.

Tyndale was probably born in Gloucester, England. He was educated at Oxford University, and by 1521 he had entered the Church. He became convinced that to understand the Bible fully, people must be able to read it in their own language, and he determined to translate it from the Greek.

The Church authorities persecuted Tyndale for his views, and he fled from England to continue his work in Germany. By 1525 he had finished translating the New Testament and 3,000 copies were printed. Many were smuggled into England, where most of them were seized by bishops.

Tyndale had begun the task of translating the Old Testament when, in 1536, he was arrested, accused of heresy (acting against the teachings of the Church), and executed.

At the time of his death 50,000 copies of his New Testament had been printed. Tyndale's work became the basis for most subsequent English translations of the Bible.

TYNE AND WEAR is a region in northeast England. From 1974 to 1986 it was the name of a metropolitan county, formed as the result of local government reorganization. The region takes its name from two rivers, the Tyne and the Wear, around which developed one of Britain's foremost industrial regions. The Tyne and Wear region covers part of the former counties of Durham and Northumberland, and is centred on the city of Newcastle upon Tyne (see DURHAM; NORTHUMBERLAND). It has an area of 540 square kilometres (208 square miles) and a population of 1,139,900 (1985).

The Tyne River is about 100 kilometres (62 miles) long. It is formed by the joining near Hexham in Northumberland of two small rivers, the North Tyne and the South Tyne. The North Tyne rises in the Cheviot Hills, on the border between England and Scotland, while the South Tyne rises in Cumbria. Both branches flow through pleasant green valleys and moors covered with heather. The Tyne flows into the North Sea at Tynemouth. Its historic crossing point is between Gateshead, on the south bank, and Newcastle upon Tyne on the north bank.

The Wear rises near Wearhead in County Durham, England, and flows into the North Sea at Sunderland. The ancient city of Durham (see DURHAM) stands on the Wear. From Bishop Auckland, the river flows across coalfields, so that the Wear, like the Tyne, has become an industrial river the nearer it approaches the sea. The rivers enter the North Sea within 11 kilometres (7 miles) of each other.

Along both rivers are located a number of industrial towns. Newcastle upon Tyne is the most important on Tyneside and stands on the Northumberland and Durham coalfield (see NEWCASTLE UPON TYNE). Other Tyneside towns are Blaydon, Gateshead, Wallsend, Hebburn, Jarrow, Tynemouth, and Whitley Bay. Sunderland is the chief city of Wearside. Inland lies the new town of Washington.

History and Industry

The Romans built a fort at Pons Aelii (Gateshead) to guard the main east-coast route between Scotland and England. Later, the Normans built a fort at Newcastle to control the river crossing.

Coal was the region's most valuable raw material; and it was mined from the 13th century and shipped to London by sea from Newcastle. By the 17th century, Sunderland was rivalling Newcastle as a coal port, and during the Industrial Revolution of the 18th and 19th centuries the Tyne and Wear region saw a huge expansion of industry. Deep mines were dug, and coal transported by steam railway and iron ships. Shipyards and engineering works sprang up along the rivers. Farming villages became mining villages.

Being so dependent on coal and heavy industry, the area was unable to adapt easily to changing industrial needs. By the 1950s many shipyards and factories were out-of-date. Although new industries have been started, the area today has high unemployment.

Greg Evans Picture Library

The Tyne Bridge links Newcastle and Gateshead at the highest navigable point of the River Tyne.

The Tyne ports and Sunderland are not large enough to handle the biggest modern cargo ships, but still take fishing vessels, coasters, and ferries crossing to Scandinavia. Road communications were improved by the construction of the Tyne Tunnel in 1967.

Local government is in the hands of district councils, following the abolition of the metropolitan county councils in 1986. These districts are called Newcastle upon Tyne, Sunderland, Gateshead, North Tyneside, and South Tyneside.

TYPEWRITER. Modern business depends greatly on typewriters, machines with which it is possible to write faster and more clearly than with a pen. The people who use them are called typists and they usually learn *touch typing:* that is, typing without looking at the keyboard. Speed comes with practice and a good typist can type as many as 100 words a minute.

The typewriter *keyboard* has about 40 to 50 keys (depending on the make and model) which are struck by the fingers. The keys are marked with different characters; that is, letters, figures, punctuation marks, and signs such as %, &, and ?. They are arranged in a similar order on every make of machine, and each key controls two characters. To type capital letters, or the character on the top of the key where there are two, a *shift-key* must be pressed before pressing the character key. Keyboards are made for all written languages, including those written from right to left, such as Hebrew or Arabic.

Electric typewriters need very little pressure on the keys and produce an even, finished result. There are two basic designs of machine. One is the *single-element* or "golf ball" typewriter (introduced in 1961) which prints by means of a single, sphere-shaped typing element, roughly the size of a golf ball, bearing all the characters the machine can use. The typing element is mounted on a carrier and travels along the paper by running along a metal bar during typing. It rises and turns very quickly to strike the paper through the ribbon with the character of the key being pressed. The element can be unclipped and replaced with a different type style (such as *italic*) when required.

The second design is the *type-bar* typewriter, where levers connect the keys with bars carrying *type-blocks* with raised steel characters. The type-bars lie side by side, and when a key is tapped its character swings up to strike the paper through the ribbon. With this method, the paper is moved along in front of the type-bars on a *carriage* which is returned to the left margin each time a line is finished.

When the paper is put in, it is fed between the ribbon and a hard roller called the *platen*. Special paper inserted at the same time can be used to make copies. Inked fabric ribbons, which can be reused many times, often have two colours—black and red—which the typist selects by using the *colour-change lever*. Carbon ribbons, available in a number of individual colours, can be used once only, but they have the advantage of producing a clearer print than fabric ribbons.

After each letter or sign has been made, the typing position moves one space to the right (or left for Arabic and Hebrew).

Typewriters normally type to a certain measure. The most common gives ten characters to the inch (four characters per centimetre). There are larger or smaller styles to suit special work. For home and travel use, lightweight portable typewriters are available. These are manually, or electrically (mains or battery) operated.

Many typewriters have an error-correction key which operates a device for erasing mistakes. Other machines contain electronics similar to those used in computers (see COMPUTER), enabling them to type semi-automatically. For example, certain machines

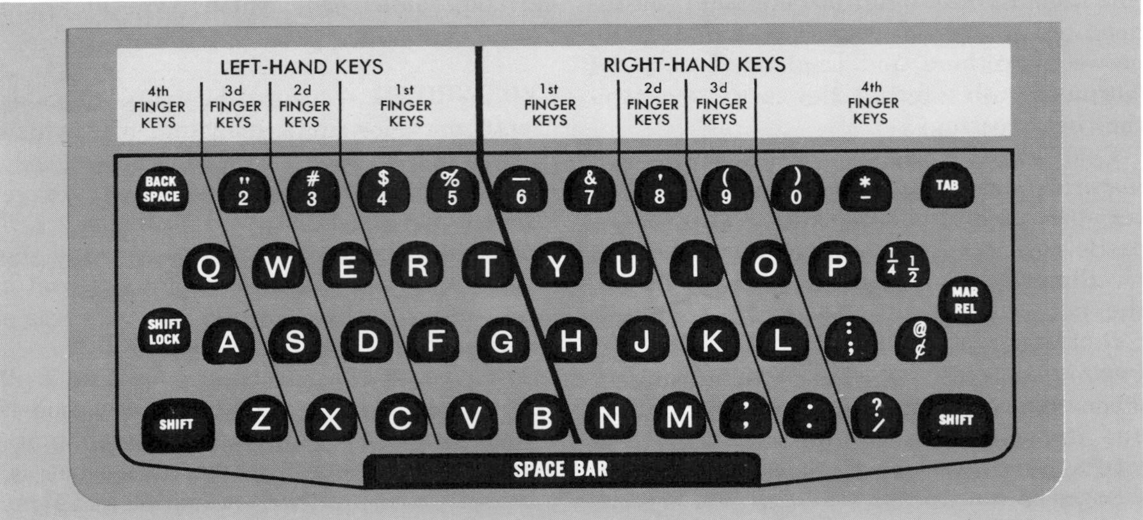

Certain fingers should be used for certain keys in touch-typing, so that the typist learns to look at the work, not the keys.

Courtesy, Olivetti

On a modern electric typewriter corrections can be made at the touch of a key.

can "store" magnetically the work which has been typed and allow corrections to be made. It is then typed out at very high speed using a *daisy-wheel* type element which works in the same way as the "golf ball", or a *dot matrix* printer which forms each character from a series of closely-spaced dots. Typewriters can also be linked to computers or have small computers built into them to do *word processing*, which needs the speed and calculating ability of computer technology (see WORD PROCESSOR).

TYPHOID FEVER. This disease and its milder forms, paratyphoid A and B, are sometimes known as enteric fever, from *enteron*, the Greek word for the intestine, as they affect the small intestine. Nowadays typhoid is very rare in countries where sewage (waste matter) is properly disposed of and where drinking water and foods are clean.

The rod-shaped bacteria (germs) of typhoid and paratyphoid live inside people, who may sometimes have these diseases so slightly that they do not feel ill at all. A few people may become what are known as "carriers", which means that they go on passing germs out of their bodies, in the faeces, for years without knowing it. This is why so much trouble is taken at sewage works to make certain that live germs are dealt with properly.

In some countries hygiene is poor and there is overcrowding and poverty. Under these conditions typhoid germs may get into water or soil in which food is grown. It is therefore unwise to drink water which has not been boiled or to eat raw fruit and vegetables in these places. Flies and other creatures help to spread the germs from the faeces of infected people to water and food.

Typhoid starts with feverishness, and ten days later small red spots appear on the skin. There is usually constipation or diarrhoea and large ulcers, or open sores, appear on the inside of the intestine. The person loses fluid and becomes very exhausted. Antibiotic drugs can cure the disease, but in many places where it occurs, these drugs are not available or are too expensive. Travellers to areas where typhoid or paratyphoids A and B are common can be protected by injections given before they leave.

TYPHUS FEVER is the main one of a group of serious infectious diseases. The germs causing the diseases are smaller than bacteria and are called *rickettsiae*. They are carried from an infected to a healthy person by insects such as body lice. Because they are spread in this way, typhus fever and its relatives are most common during wars and famines. If people eat poorly and live crowded together without sanitary facilities, the body louse can quickly spread.

In a case of typhus fever, between one or two weeks after the bite by an infected body louse, there are sudden chills, fever, and severe headache. Nose bleeds, eye soreness, and mild cough may then appear. Fever continues into the second week followed by delirium, unconsciousness, and, in severe cases, heart failure.

A doctor will suspect typhus if a person develops these symptoms and if there is any chance that he might have been bitten by body lice. The disease can be shown to be present by the antibodies that form in the patient's blood to fight the rickettsiae. Antibiotic drugs and good nursing can cure the patient. The use of antibiotics has greatly improved the chances for a cure.

Typhus-like epidemics have been described since the 16th century. However, typhus fever was not clearly shown to be different from typhoid fever until 1837. Some of the symptoms and treatments are the same for both diseases. (See TYPHOID FEVER.)

The spread of typhus fever can now be controlled by isolating the sick, by vaccinations, and by delousing. Delousing means cleaning and spraying infected people to kill body lice.

Diseases closely similar to typhus include Rocky Mountain spotted fever, scrub fever or tsutsugamushi fever (spread from rats and mice to human beings by mites), tick fever (also spread by mites), and murine typhus (spread from rats to human beings by fleas). Like typhus itself, all these infections can be cured by antibiotic drugs and good nursing care.

TYRE see TIRE.

TYRE AND SIDON were two mighty cities of the ancient world, often mentioned in the Bible. They were built by the Phoenicians, the great seafaring and trading nation of the Mediterranean during pre-Roman times (see PHOENICIA).

ZEFA

Castle ruins at Sidon, an ancient Mediterranean port in Southern Lebanon.

Sidon (modern Saida) on the coast of what is now Lebanon, was the older of the two cities, founded before 2000 BC. Tyre, 30 kilometres (19 miles) south, was originally a colony of Sidon and was founded before the 14th century BC. It was built on an island off the coast, but has long been joined to the mainland by the building of causeways (raised roads). Now Tyre is a peninsula, not an island, and is called Sur.

Both Tyre and Sidon were rich and flourishing cities with their own kings for a time. Sidon, however, was conquered by the Philistines and the Assyrians, Babylonians, Macedonian Greeks, and Romans. In Roman times it was famous for its glass industry. Now it is important as the Mediterranean terminus of the pipeline from the Saudi Arabian oilfields.

Tyre's most famous industry was the manufacture of the precious dye, known as Tyrian purple, from a mollusc (shellfish) called murex. The Phoenicians of Tyre founded many other colonies in the Mediterranean region, including Carthage in North Africa, which later became the rival of Rome. (See CARTHAGE.) Hiram, one of the kings of Tyre, traded with Solomon. Another king was the father of the pitiless queen Jezebel, wife of the Israelite king Ahab.

Tyre was besieged for 13 years by the Babylonian Emperor Nebuchadnezzar in the 6th century BC and was captured after a seven-month siege by Alexander the Great more than 200 years later. It too became a Roman town, and was not deserted until it was destroyed by the Muslims in 1291.

Both Tyre and Sidon suffered much during the 1980s as a result of the conflict in Lebanon. Sidon was a centre for Palestinian refugees and Maronite Christians.

UGANDA is a landlocked country lying on the Equator in the eastern part of central Africa. Its neighbours are Sudan in the north, Kenya to the west, Zaire to the east, and Rwanda and Tanzania to the south.

The country has a tropical climate and very

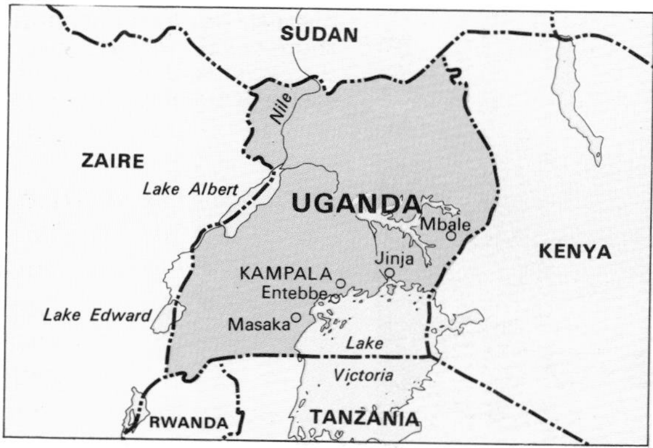

varied scenery. For the most part it consists of a high tableland which in the south is covered with small, rounded hills. Near the lakes and mountains, elephant grass grows more than 3 metres (10 feet) high. Elsewhere there are wide stretches of forest, some of which contain valuable timber trees such as mahogany, ironwood, and African teak. On the slopes of the Ruwenzori Range there are giant groundsels and lobelias over 6 metres (20 feet) tall. The lower slopes are the home of chimpanzees, colobus monkeys, and wild pigs. In the more open country of western Uganda, elephants, buffaloes, lions, leopards, and many kinds of antelope are common. Rhinoceroses live in the Kabalega (formerly Murchison) Falls National Park in the northwest. Hippopotamuses and crocodiles abound in the lakes and in the River Nile, whose biggest fish are the great Nile perch.

People and Economy

Bantu-speaking Africans make up a large section of the population, but there are also many other African groups. English and Swahili are commonly spoken. Most of the people are Christian, but there are also followers of African religions and of Islam.

Most Ugandans are crop farmers growing millet, plantains (cooking bananas), sweet potatoes, maize, and vegetables for their own food. Traditionally, women do most of the work of planting, hoeing, and harvesting. The farmers also grow some crops to sell. Chief among Uganda's export crops are cotton and coffee. Sugar, tobacco, and tea are also grown. Production of hardwoods is increasing and more use is being made of the huge freshwater fisheries. Copper mining is also important to the economy.

The Owen Falls dam controls the flow of the River Nile from Lake Victoria. It is 760 metres (2,500 feet) long and 30 metres (100 feet) high and has raised the water level so that it now covers the Ripon Falls, by which the river leaves the lake. The dam supplies electric power for Uganda's small-scale industries, which include the manufacture of textiles. Cement is made near Tororo on the eastern border.

The capital, Kampala, has a population of about 500,000. Other important cities are Jinja, Masaka, and Mbale.

FACTS ABOUT UGANDA

AREA: 241,140 square kilometres (93,110 square miles).
POPULATION: 16,164,000 (1987).
GOVERNMENT: Independent republic; member of the Commonwealth.
CAPITAL: Kampala.
GEOGRAPHICAL FEATURES: Uganda consists of plateaus broken up by wide, steep-sided valleys. About half of Lake Victoria is within its boundaries. The highest peak is Margherita at 5,118 metres (16,791 feet). There are large areas of grassland, with patches of tropical forest.
CHIEF PRODUCTS: Coffee, cotton, maize, sugar, tea, tobacco, livestock; wolfram (tungsten ore), copper.
IMPORTANT TOWNS: Kampala, Jinja, Mbale, and Masaka.
EDUCATION: School attendance is not compulsory.

History

The name Uganda comes from the ancient kingdom of Buganda, which was ruled through a feudal system rather like that of Europe in the Middle Ages; a royal court with elaborate customs and ceremonies; on the shore an army and on the lake a fleet of war canoes able to carry more than 16,000 warriors. The countryside was cultivated with endless rows of bananas and had good roads. Arab slave- and ivory-traders reached the country in the 1840s, and in 1862 the first European explorers John Speke and James Grant crossed the land in their search for the

Kampala lies near the north shore of Lake Victoria. It is the capital and commercial centre of Uganda.

Picturepoint

source of the Nile. Christian missionaries followed soon after.

Uganda was taken under British protection in 1894. In the following year the building of the Uganda Railway began, to Kisumu on the northeast corner of Lake Victoria, which at that time lay in Uganda. Later a line was brought in by stages through Tororo and across the Nile at Jinja westwards almost to the Zaire border. Most goods-traffic into and out of the country travels by rail and steamer services across Lake Victoria.

Uganda became independent in 1962 with Dr. Milton Obote as its first Prime Minister. In 1967, Uganda was declared a republic. Dr. Obote's government was overthrown in 1971 by a military revolt led by Major-General Idi Amin who later became President. Amin ruled as a dictator.

A Ugandan attack upon Tanzania in 1978 led to a counter-attack, and as the Tanzanian troops advanced through the country they were joined by many Ugandans. As a result President Amin was overthrown in 1979 and was succeeded by two provisional presidents. Milton Obote was elected to the office of president in 1980 but he was again deposed by a military coup in 1985.

UKRAINE is the third largest and one of the richest of the 15 Soviet Socialist Republics forming the Soviet Union.

The Ukrainian Republic stretches from the Carpathian Mountains on the borders of Poland and Czechoslovakia to the Donets River. On the southwest it is bordered by the Moldavian SSR and Romania; on the west by Hungary, Czechoslovakia, and Poland; on the north by the Belorussian SSR; and on the northeast and east by the Russian SFSR. The Ukraine is in the agricultural area of the western Soviet Union that borders the northern shores of the Black Sea and the Sea of Azov. It covers an area of 603,700 square kilometres (233,100 square miles), much of which consists of vast flat plains called steppes (see STEPPE). In many parts the steppes are covered with a thick layer of fertile black earth which is ideal for growing grain.

The climate, too, is good for agriculture. Winters in the Ukraine are cold. Summers are warm and sometimes very hot in the south. Rainfall is generally light. It ranges from 300 millimetres (12 inches) a year in the south and east to about double that in the northwest. About ten per cent of the Ukraine – chiefly in the northwest and in the hilly areas – is covered with birch, beech, maple, larch, and ash forests. Most of the Republic, however, is grassy, treeless plains.

The chief crops of the Ukraine are winter-sown wheat, maize, barley, sugar beet, and sunflowers. Sunflower seeds are crushed to provide an oil used for cooking and for making margarine and soap, while the remains provide cattle cake. There are also very large numbers of cattle, pigs, sheep, and goats.

The industrial wealth of the Ukraine is based on the iron of the Krivoi Rog district, which lies in the middle of the great eastward bend made by the Dnieper River as it flows through the centre of the republic, and also on the coal and other minerals of the Donets basin further east. These two regions contain many industrial cities and huge factories. Kharkov specializes in making farm tractors, agricultural machinery, and electrical equipment. Two of the most important industrial towns, which produce aluminium, steel, and chemicals, are Zaporozhe and Dnepropetrovsk. Both use electricity from the giant hydroelectric power stations on the Dnieper, at Zaporozhe and Kakhovka. Nuclear power stations have also been built in the Ukraine including the one at Chernobyl that exploded with devastating results in 1986. Natural gas and oil are found in the republic, as well as one of the world's richest deposits of manganese. Under the "five-year plans" by which the industry and agriculture of the Soviet Union were developed, many new towns and factories were set up in the Ukraine. By 1940 the republic was producing about half the coal, iron, and steel of the Soviet Union.

Many of its factories were destroyed during World War II when the Ukraine was occupied by the Germans from 1941 to 1944. They were rebuilt after the war but the Ukraine lost some of its importance in comparison with the other republics of the Soviet Union. This was because agriculture was developed further east in the middle Volga region, in Kazakhstan, and in western Siberia. In the same way, the development of industries in towns on the Volga and east of the Ural Mountains has meant that iron and steel and machinery are produced in other centres besides those of the Ukraine. Tourism is also an important industry on the Crimean coast with the beaches of Yalta, Gurzuf, and elsewhere attracting visitors from all over the Soviet Union. The capital of the Ukraine is Kiev (see KIEV) and the population of the republic is 50,994,000 (1986), making it the second most populous in the Soviet Union.

Picturepoint

A main street in Lvov, in the western Ukraine. This city was part of Poland until World War II.

ULSTER see IRELAND, NORTHERN.

ULTRASONICS. Sounds are produced by an object vibrating so as to move the particles in the air in its immediate vicinity. Solids and liquids also transmit sounds but a vacuum does not. (See SOUND.) The number of vibrations made in one second is called the frequency of the vibrations. The hertz (symbol Hz) is a unit of frequency; one Hz is equal to one full vibration per second. Frequencies below 16 Hz are too slow to be heard by human beings and are known as infrasonic; those above 20,000 Hz (the usual limit for the human ear) are known as ultrasonic.

Ultrasonic waves occur in nature; bats utter squeaks at frequencies between 40,000 and 100,000 Hz. These sounds are reflected back from an object to a bat's large ears and from the interval between squeak and echo, it knows the distance of the object. This method of distance measurement is called echo-location, or sonar, and the bat uses it to detect flying insects on which it feeds. It is also used by porpoises and dolphins to detect fish. Ultrasonic impulses can be sent in a narrow beam and this enables both direction and distance to be found. (See ECHO; SOUND.)

Man has applied ultrasonics to industry. Ultrasounds can be produced in two ways: by sending a high-frequency alternating current through a crystal of quartz causing the crystal to vibrate (the *piezoelectric* method) or by reversing the direction of an alternating current through a coil of wire wound round a metal rod to produce ultrasonic pulses (the *magnetostrictive* method). Both these devices are known as transducers and can change electric current into sound, and sound into current.

Ultrasonics can be used in a variety of ways. The echo-ranging device known as *sonar* can detect submarines under water by sending out ultrasonic pulses which are reflected by the submarine's hull. The same method is used for locating shoals of fish and for finding the depth of seas and lakes.

ZEFA

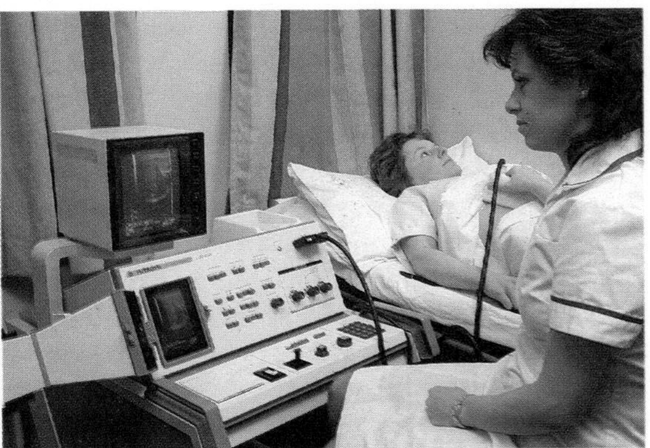

An ultrasonic scanner has a cathode-ray tube that can display the progress of a baby's development in a mother's womb. Ultrasound is safer than X-rays.

Transducers can be made to detect gaps and holes in solids. Ultrasonic pulses can detect cracks or flaws in materials and also measure the thickness of steel plate and tubes to keep watch on corrosion. Farmers can also use the pulses to measure the fat on pigs.

Ultrasonic waves travel through flesh and soft tissues and can be used by doctors in place of X-rays to produce images of the internal organs and tissues of the human body. The transducers used are of the piezoelectric type and work at frequencies of 1 million Hz, displaying their results on a cathode-ray tube (see ELECTRONICS). At low power, these ultrasonic waves have no harmful effects on the body and are used for investigation and diagnosis. The so-called whole body scanner uses ultrasonics to help in the detection of tumours and blood clots. Ultrasonic scans are frequently given to pregnant women to make sure that the baby is growing at the right rate. The scan also checks for physical abnormalities, such as spina bifida, and whether there is more than one foetus in the mother's womb. With modern equipment doctors can obtain moving pictures of processes inside the body.

By increasing the power output of the transducer the beam of ultrasonic waves can be concentrated, like a laser beam (see LASER). In this form ultrasonics can be used in surgery. The ultrasound waves can destroy nerve fibres and blood vessels, and can be used in brain surgery and also in the treatment of arthritis and rheumatism.

If a metal object is put into a tank of liquid which is subjected to high-power ultrasonic vibrations, the agitation will clean the metal surfaces. Mixtures of liquids in which one liquid is contained in the other in tiny droplets (so-called emulsions—see SOLUTION AND SUSPENSION) can be made in a similar way. Ultrasound can clear fog and smoke by causing the particles of dust and moisture in the air to cling together. It can also be used for clearing wine by making the solid particles it contains settle to the bottom of the vessel.

An ultrasonic drill can drill a square hole. The tool is held against the surface with some grinding paste between the two, and then vibrated ultrasonically, biting through the surface without turning. Ultrasonic welding is done by clamping two pieces of metal between a flat support and a rounded pressure head. When vibrated by a transducer, the pressure head causes the metal to rub together at high speed. The resulting friction heats the two pieces until the metal melts to form a welded joint. Magnetostrictive transducers are used for ultrasonic drilling and welding.

UMBRELLA. The earliest umbrellas, which were probably used in China in the 12th century BC, were really parasols—the difference between a parasol and an umbrella being that a parasol is used to keep off the sun and an umbrella the rain. The word umbrella comes from the Latin word *umbra*, meaning shade. The ladies of ancient Rome also used parasols. The Japanese still have very elegant parasols which are part of their national costume.

Cephas Picture Library/Mick Rock

An umbrella repairer in Sri Lanka. In a hot, wet climate umbrellas are used against both sun and rain.

In the East the umbrella was long regarded as a sign of rank. The emperor of China was protected by a special one with four canopies on the same stick. Today in parts of Africa tribal chiefs still have umbrellas to distinguish them from ordinary people.

Umbrellas in medieval Europe were also used for ceremonial purposes. They were part of the equipment of people such as the doge (chief magistrate) of Venice, of bishops, and of popes. Indeed, the pope may still be accompanied by two umbrellas when he goes in procession. One is open to represent his temporal (earthly) power and one is closed to represent his spiritual power.

The ordinary everyday umbrella was slow to find favour in Western Europe. In the 17th century it was a heavy, clumsy thing covered with leather or with sticky oiled silk. It was too heavy to be carried by a person using it and so had to be held up by a servant. The use of whalebone for the ribs caused umbrellas to become a good deal lighter and easier to use. Gradually they also became more elegant in design, and in the 18th century French parasols were made with ornamental handles and fringed covers.

Also in the 18th century, umbrellas were kept at London coffee houses, to be hired to customers during heavy showers. Parishes had special umbrellas too, which were lent to clergymen for funerals. Nevertheless, it was some time before people began to use umbrellas of their own, for they were regarded as a sign that their owners did not keep a carriage. The first person who began to use one regularly was a man named Jonas Hanway. He appeared in the streets of London with an umbrella in 1750 and was greeted with jeers and catcalls and even attacked. Soon, however, other people followed his example.

Metal began to be used for the ribs instead of whalebone and alpaca replaced heavy silk for the covers. Then, in about 1850, Samuel Fox was inspired by the sight of the tubular bridge over the Menai Straits between Anglesey and the mainland of Wales to invent a grooved steel frame which combines strength with lightness. The handles of 19th-century umbrellas, however, were still generally of carved ivory or onyx.

UNDERGROUND RAILWAY. One form of rapid transit system developed all over the world is the underground railway or subway. These exist in many capital cities and regional centres to relieve road traffic congestion by providing a fast, efficient, and cheap method of moving passengers, especially at peak travelling times.

Underground lines run in tunnels beneath streets and houses and sometimes rivers, but include sections at ground surface level and elevated above it. The earliest underground trains were steam-hauled. Electric traction is usually used today, in conjunction with computer-assisted train control.

Internationally, the best-known underground railways are those in London, Moscow, New York, and Paris, partly because they were for many years the only major systems and also because of their well-known decorative features. "Métro" is the name used for both the Paris and Moscow networks. It is a shortened form of the word *métropolitain*, the French word for metropolitan, meaning "of a chief city" and derived from the Greek words *meter* (mother) and *polis* (city).

In the 1980s there were 175 rapid transit and underground railways throughout the world, with dozens more due for completion during the 1990s. Thirty-two systems operate in the United States, 21 in the Soviet Union, 10 in Japan, 6 in Britain, and 4 in the People's Republic of China. Many systems have been built in very recent times.

Transit systems which run primarily underground or incorporate tunnel sections include those in Boston, Chicago, Cleveland, San Francisco, and Washington, DC, in the United States; Edmonton, Montreal, Toronto, and Vancouver in Canada; Recife, Rio de Janeiro, São Paulo, and Santiago de Chile in South America; London, Glasgow, and Newcastle-upon-Tyne, in Britain; Beijing in China; and Nagoya, Osaka, Sapporo, and Tokyo in Japan.

Among such systems in other parts of Europe are those in Athens, Barcelona, Berlin, Brussels, Budapest, Copenhagen, Hamburg, Helsinki, Kiev, Leningrad, Lisbon, Madrid, Milan, Munich, Naples, Oslo, Paris, Prague, Rome, Sofia, Stockholm, Vienna, and Warsaw. In addition, there are systems in Australia—Adelaide and Melbourne; in the Middle East—Alexandria, Baghdad, and Cairo; in India—Calcutta; and in Southeast Asia—Bangkok and Singapore.

Purpose of Underground Railways

Metro or light railway systems can offer a solution to the problems of overcrowded roads, and are a useful means of transporting people where other forms of transport are limited or non-existent. Filled to "crush" capacity, a single train may carry 400 to 600 people. If as many people went by road, at least six buses or 100 cars would be needed to carry them.

When a rapid transit system is planned, the first problem is deciding who will pay the capital costs of investment in construction and equipment, and the running costs, which are unlikely to be recovered through receipts (fares paid by passengers). To encourage people to use the system, the fares must be kept reasonably low. The controlling transport authority (usually a body with powers delegated by central government or a city authority) must usually raise the necessary money.

The railway planners must also consider other factors, such as population growth, car-ownership levels, leisure habits, and travel preferences. They must plan the links with other means of transport, including cars, buses, mainline and suburban railways, and travel by air and sea. Rapid transit systems cannot survive without "feeder" links. The most successful modern systems have fast, frequent trains which serve closely-spaced stations.

The First Underground Railway

The very first "sub-railway" was proposed in 1835 in Britain. The plan was that it should link the two earliest mainline rail terminals on the outer edge of London with the city's central business districts. The scheme was abandoned as "altogether too novel". It was, however, sensible compared with some alternative remedies suggested for curing street congestion. One of the most bizarre was for a railway on suspension bridges slung between church towers.

Few people seriously considered the advantages of placing the railways *under* rather than over the roadways. One man who saw into the future was Charles Pearson, a British lawyer and member of parliament. His ideas were taken up and applied in the building of the world's first sub-surface (underground)

Courtesy, London Transport Museum

A London underground or "tube" train. The curved shape fits exactly into the tunnels. Much of the track outside central London, however, is above ground.

railway in 1860. It was opened by the Metropolitan Railway Company in London on 10 January 1863. The line, about 6 kilometres (3.7 miles) in length, linked Paddington mainline rail terminus with Farringdon Road in the City (London's business district). Construction was mainly by the "cut and cover" method, which involved digging a deep trench for the railway and then covering it over. The method is still used today.

The following year, Britain's parliament faced a flood of no less than 55 proposals for London railways. New lines were sanctioned and the underground network began to grow. The world's first "tube" railway was drilled deep under the River Thames near the Tower of London, using methods invented by the British engineer J. H. Greathead (1844–96) (see TUNNEL). It was opened in 1870 and worked temporarily by cable car. In 1886 Greathead started work on the 5-kilometre (3-mile) City and South London Railway. It included twin tunnels under the Thames and was opened on 18 December 1890. Apart from the use of electric motive power, the first "tube" had other striking features, including the small carriages with window slits (the vehicles were soon nicknamed "padded cells") and the foul smells which pervaded the tunnels.

This last difficulty was overcome on later lines by installing mechanical ventilation. The solution was engineered by Charles

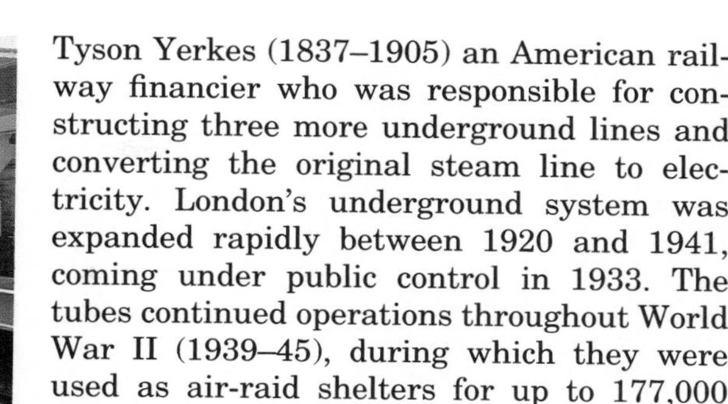

Tyson Yerkes (1837–1905) an American railway financier who was responsible for constructing three more underground lines and converting the original steam line to electricity. London's underground system was expanded rapidly between 1920 and 1941, coming under public control in 1933. The tubes continued operations throughout World War II (1939–45), during which they were used as air-raid shelters for up to 177,000 people each night.

London's first entirely new line for 50 years, the Victoria Line, was opened officially by Queen Elizabeth II in March 1969. Over 2.4 million passengers are carried daily on the present system, which comprises 408 kilometres (255 miles) of running lines, 273 stations, and 457 trains.

Underground Railways Worldwide

The first European underground was opened in Budapest, Hungary, in 1896. The Moscow Métro has a route length of 197 kilometres (123 miles), all but about 20 kilometres (12.5

Novosti

The stations on the Moscow Metro are elaborately decorated with marble and lit with glass chandeliers.

miles) in tunnels, and 123 stations. The system was built in the 1930s and was one of the first great achievements after the Communist revolution of 1917. It was designed intention-

The Hutchison Library

Inside a train on the New York subway.

ally as a proclamation of Soviet power and technical progress: public areas at the main stations are spectacular and spacious, with wide, island platforms and high concourses illuminated by chandeliers and decorated in the baroque style.

A similar approach was taken by the builders of the 192-kilometre (120-mile) Paris Métro, opened in 1900. Technology and art combined to provide a network noted not only for efficiency but the charm of decorative adornments in the *art nouveau* style prevalent between 1890 and 1910. The engineer was Fulgence Bienvenue. A modification of the cut-and-cover method was used. Side trenches were dug from vertical shafts and supports erected to hold up the streets above. Services on four of the Métro's 15 lines are operated by rubber-tyred trains which produce a quiet, smooth ride.

The New York City subway began operating in 1904 and is now the most intensively-used system of its kind in the world, with over 1,000 million passenger journeys made each year on its 23 lines, nearly all of which provide a 24-hour service. Total route length is 371 kilometres (231 miles) of which 220.5 kilometres (137 miles) is in tunnels, and 150.6 kilometres (94 miles) elevated. There are 456 stations. The network is managed by the New York Transit Authority, a subsidiary of the Metropolitan Transportation Authority, which operates the world's largest rapid transit system.

Modern Systems

Despite international rivalry for contracts to build new systems, and competition between the larger transport authorities to sell their expertise overseas, regular free exchange of information has resulted in a general uniformity of basic technologies and operating procedures of underground railways throughout the world.

Modern systems typically operate on direct current of 625–825 volts collected from a power rail that lies alongside the two running tracks (though some use 1.5 kV current picked up from overhead wires). In the most advanced systems, such as the Docklands Light Railway (DLR) opened in London in 1987, contact is made with the underside of the power rail instead of the top; this allows the top and sides of the rail to be insulated with a plastic cover for added safety and also reduces problems caused by ice and snow.

The DLR uses driverless, automatic trains each controlled by an on-board computer "masterminded" by a central computer, although a "train captain" is present on every train to assist passengers. On most rapid transit systems, trains are driver-operated.

Rolling stock must be strong, yet light enough to permit fast acceleration and low energy consumption. Cars are normally made of welded steel or steel and aluminium, with fire-resisting interior fittings. The cars are single or double units, sometimes linked by a two-axle bogie and known as "articulated". Motor units provide the "pulling power" through rotary electric motors that form part of their axles. Trailer units are not motorized. Motors are controlled electronically. Modern rolling-stock is fitted with two braking systems—disc, and rheostatic (which harnesses electromagnetic forces within the motors). Operating speeds vary between about 30 kilometres (18 miles) per hour and 80 kilometres (50 miles) per hour.

Safety Precautions

Safe operation is especially critical on rapid transit railways, as the "headway" (time/distance gap between trains) is often as short as one minute, compared with the usual minimum of four or five minutes on mainline railways. To ensure that trains respond to signals, wide use is made of automatic train control. This is achieved through updated versions of the track circuit, invented in the United States by William Robinson in 1872.

In basic track circuiting, an electric current is passed through the running rails and its circuit is completed through the wheels and axles of a train. If a train is in the section between two signals, it closes the circuit for the signals behind it so that these signals cannot show a "clear" to a following train. When no train is in the section, the current does not pass from one running rail to another and the signals in rear show the "clear" aspect. Modern systems use electric current in the form of coded impulses, and colour-light signals.

A further safeguard is the "trip", a trackside metal arm which is raised when a signal is at "danger". The arm strikes a lever on any train that tries to pass, the power is automatically turned off and the train brakes applied. Another common safety device is the "dead man's handle"; if anything happens to the driver—should he faint, for example—the pressure of his hand on a spring-loaded control lever is relaxed and the train comes to a halt.

Rapid progress is being made in the development of radiotelephone communications between trains and their controllers, as well as in automatic speed control and electronic interlocking of signals and points to prevent "clear" indications being given for two conflicting routes at the same time.

Modern Construction Methods

New technology is also applied in deep tunnel construction. The present equivalent of the picks, shovels, and explosives employed in the 19th century is the "drum digger" fitted with mechanical rotary cutters, moved forward by hydraulic rams. These huge tunnelling machines are kept on course by measurements taken at surface level, then transferred down working shafts by laser beam. Circular shields and hand-digging are still also used (see TUNNEL). If driven through rock, tunnels may be left unlined; if through soft soil, they are lined with precast iron, steel, or concrete rings or blocks. Prefabricated, continuous welded track, or short-length rails are then laid on a concrete trackbed or wooden sleepers, sometimes mounted in rubber "boots" to minimize noise and vibration.

In addition to achieving the highest standards of safety and engineering excellence, transit systems must be attractive to passengers, people who may have the choice of travelling by other kinds of transport. So the trend is towards clean, well-lit stations, television surveillance for security, comfortable seating, and bright decor inside air-conditioned cars.

UNDERWATER EXPLORATION see DIVING.

UNEMPLOYMENT see EMPLOYMENT.

UNIDENTIFIED FLYING OBJECT. An unidentified flying object, or UFO, is an unusual object or optical phenomenon observed in the sky, or somehow connected with the sky, and frequently thought by the observer to come from outer space. Most sightings can be explained in a more down-to-earth way.

The sighting of UFOs probably goes back to earliest times. The Bible relates the vision of the 6th-century prophet Ezekiel, who was said to have seen wheels and winged creatures in the air. The vision is probably a symbol or dream, but some people have taken it as evidence of UFO observations in antiquity.

UFOs are, however, generally regarded as a modern phenomenon. "Mystery airships" were first reported over the United States in 1896–97. During World War II (1939–45) pilots reported seeing strange metallic-looking objects "shadowing" their aircraft as if examining them.

People became more aware of UFOs following an incident that took place on 24 June 1947 over Washington, DC. A civilian pilot named Kenneth Arnold reported seeing on that date a fleet of nine circular objects flying across his aircraft's line of flight. Arnold said that they looked like "saucers skipping over water". From then onwards, the name "flying saucers" was popularly used to describe UFOs.

Since 1947 there have been UFO sightings in almost every country of the world. Some people have even claimed that they have had contact with beings from other worlds who have brought their "flying saucers" down to Earth and given human beings rides to other planets!

Forteau Picture Library/René Dahinden

Unidentified flying objects can often be confused with natural events or occurrences. These lens-shaped clouds over northern California, in 1980, could have been mistaken for flying saucers.

Most UFO sightings have been explained after investigation as astronomical effects or as events resulting from freak weather conditions. Some reported sightings are hallucinations, others are hoaxes. But about one in every ten sightings has never been satisfactorily explained.

From 1948 to 1969 the US Air Force regularly recorded UFO reports through its Project Blue Book. UFO observations were also investigated by the Central Intelligence Agency (CIA) in the 1950s. Following the findings of a commission set up in 1968, the US Air Force closed Project Blue Book, concluding that UFOs did not threaten US security and probably did not come from outer space. UFO reports continue, however. An opinion poll in 1973 revealed that 11 per cent of the adult population of the United States claimed to have seen what they believed was a UFO.

"Flying saucers" have figured in many science fiction stories and films. (See SCIENCE FICTION.)

UNION JACK see FLAG.

UNION OF SOVIET SOCIALIST REPUBLICS. The USSR, which is also known as the Soviet Union, is the world's largest country. It covers nearly one-seventh of the world's land area. The 15 republics of the USSR form one continuous land mass, larger than Canada, the United States, Mexico, and Central America together.

It has enormous agricultural wealth and about 285 million inhabitants. Its population is drawn from over 100 peoples, many of whom speak their own languages as well as the official Russian. The Russians are the largest group, and Russia is by far the largest of the 15 republics that make up the country. Until 1922 the whole country was simply known as Russia, or, after 1917, Soviet Russia.

The Soviet Union lies in both Europe and Asia. The European section contains about one-quarter of the area and three-quarters of the population. It stretches from the White Sea and Arctic Ocean in the north to the Black Sea and just north of the Caucasus Mountains in the south. The Caucasus and the lands adjoining the Turkish and Iranian borders are now included in Asiatic Russia and are known as Transcaucasia. (See BLACK SEA; CAUCASUS MOUNTAINS.) To the west, the Soviet Union is bounded by Norway, Finland, Poland, Czechoslovakia, Hungary, and Romania.

A low mountain range called the Ural Mountains forms the division between the European and Asiatic sections. This range is the only break in the vast central plains that make up most of the Soviet Union. (See URAL MOUNTAINS.) In Soviet central Asia, however, the Pamir and Tien Shan ranges include four peaks of over 6,700 metres (22,000 feet), one of which, Communism Peak at 7,495 metres

(24,590 feet) is the highest in the USSR. Siberia and the far east are more mountainous than the European part, with ranges reaching 4,000 metres (13,000 feet). The Caucasus includes Mount Elbrus 5,633 metres (18,480 feet) and several other peaks of over 5,000 metres (16,000 feet). However, these ranges, except for the low Ural Mountains, are all on the fringes of the USSR.

The Asiatic section of the USSR includes Siberia, Kazakhstan, the republics of Soviet central Asia, and Transcaucasia. Siberia stretches from the Urals to the Pacific Ocean (see SIBERIA). Soviet central Asia lies southwest of Siberia and is bounded on the east by China and Mongolia, on the south by Afghanistan and Iran, and on the west by the Caspian sea.

The rivers of the USSR form two main groups. Those of one group flow from the central part of the country northwards and those of the other flow southwards. Among the southward-flowing rivers are the shallow Ural, and the Volga, which is 3,700 kilometres (2,300 miles) long and the longest river in Europe (see VOLGA RIVER). Both flow into the Caspian Sea, and like all Soviet rivers, abound in fish. The Dniester, Bug, and Dnieper flow into the Black Sea (see DNIEPER RIVER). The Don flows into the Sea of Azov, a wide, shallow arm of the Black Sea.

In the northward-flowing group of rivers the most important are the Ob, Yenisei, and Lena in Siberia (on which there are separate articles), which flow into the Arctic. In central Asia the Amu Darya (Oxus) and Syr Darya (Jaxartes) flow northwestwards into the inland Aral Sea. Others, such as the Ili River, flow into Lake Balkhash or become lost in the deserts. The only important Soviet river flowing into the Pacific is the Amur, which for much of its 2,824-kilometre (1,755-mile) course forms the boundary between the USSR and China (see AMUR RIVER).

In addition to these rivers the Soviet Union

Greg Evans

The shimmering golden domes of the Cathedral of the Annunciation inside the walls of the Kremlin, Moscow.

Frank Spooner

Ship blocked by ice in Soviet Arctic waters.

has big lakes and two inland seas. Near the Baltic Sea are lakes Ladoga, Onega, and Peipus. The Aral Sea in Soviet central Asia is the fourth largest inland sea in the world. Lake Baikal in Siberia is the deepest lake in the world.

Climate

The landscape of the Soviet Union is extremely diverse, and so too is its climate, with extremes ranging from the bitter Arctic winters to the almost tropical heat of central Asia. Because the Soviet Union is such a huge land area it is little affected by ocean currents or sea winds and its climate therefore tends either to be very hot or very cold. Most of the places inland have hot summers and cold winters. Verkhoyansk and Oymyakon in northeast Siberia, with winter temperatures of down to −68°C (−90°F), are the coldest inhabited places in the world. In striking contrast is the suffocating heat of the Kara Kum Desert in Soviet central Asia, where the summer temperature rises above 49°C (120°F).

The rainfall varies with the region. There is more rain in a single cloudburst in the Caucasus area than falls in the entire year in the parched lands of Soviet central Asia. Parts of the Caucasus and Pacific coast have more than 1,500 millimetres (60 inches) of rain in a year. In the northwest, the yearly rainfall is about 450 millimetres (18 inches), decreasing towards the southeast, until in the sandy lands it is less than 125 millimetres (5 inches).

Plants and Animals

These extremes of climate and rainfall produce many different kinds of plant life. In the Arctic regions are the cold, treeless tundra plains, where the soil is always frozen below the surface. In the Asiatic part the tundras are dry and barren, but as the rainfall increases further west, mosses, lichens, dwarf shrubs, and a few flowers grow. (See TUNDRA.) South of the tundras begins the *taiga*, which is the great forest zone. It consists chiefly of conifer (cone-bearing) trees and stretches in an irregular line from the Gulf of Finland to the southern Urals and from there eastward to the

ZEFA

A frozen lake makes an excellent ice rink for these children in Siberia. This vast region has long severe winters and short summers. The coldest inhabited places in the world are in northeast Siberia.

Pacific. These forests cover about two-fifths of the Soviet Union (see also TAIGA).

Bogs, marshes, and shallow lakes are frequent among the northern woodlands. South of them, a narrower belt of rolling land is irregularly covered with forests of broad-leaved trees such as oak, ash, and hazel. Further south again are the vast treeless plains called the steppes (see STEPPE), which have a wealth of grasses and flowers in the uncultivated area. The fertile steppes form one of the most important grain-producing areas in the world.

John Massey Stewart

Sand dunes and wormwood trees in Repetek State Nature Reserve, a desert region rich in reptiles. The reserve occupies a part of the Kara Kum Desert of Turkmenistan, in the southern Soviet Union.

The animal life of the Soviet Union varies with the climate. In the Arctic regions are found seals, polar bears, the arctic fox, and reindeer. In the taiga, fur-bearing animals abound, including sables, foxes, ermines, minks, and squirrels, as well as wolves, bears, and wild pigs. In the central regions hares, marmots, jerboas, and other small animals are common, but most of the larger ones have been driven out by cultivation. Wild ducks, geese, and waterfowl of all kinds are found on the marshes. Fish are plentiful in the rivers and lakes.

Peoples of the Soviet Union

What is now the European part of the USSR was inhabited long before the 1st century AD. The inhabitants were mostly nomadic (wandering) people: Scythians at the time of the Greek Empire, Goths in the 3rd century AD, and Huns in the 4th century. By the 9th century, however, a more settled people called the Khazars had established towns on the lower stretches of the Volga and Don rivers. The forest regions to the north and west were inhabited by Finns, Lithuanians, and Slavs.

Slavic Peoples. The Slavs were closely related to the peoples of central Europe, especially to the Goths.

In the 6th century the Slavs began to spread southwards and by the 9th century they were settled in places as far apart as Novgorod in the north and near the Black Sea in the south. In their culture they lagged far behind the people of Europe, and lived mainly by hunting, having little settled agriculture.

With the opening up of the forest zone and the growth of trade came the establishment of cities, of which Kiev on the River Dnieper was the most important. The country round it was called Rus, the name given to the kingdom created there in the 9th century.

Throughout the 10th and 11th centuries the state of Kiev was constantly attacked from the east, and was defeated in 1068 by the Cumans, a Turkish people. Kiev then declined in importance and in 1169 it was sacked by Andrei Bogolyubsky, who transferred the capital to

Spectrum

Bread sellers dressed in eastern-style clothes in Samarkand, Uzbek SSR. Most of the USSR lies in Asia.

ZEFA

Ukrainians wander in the cloisters of the earliest centre of Russian Christianity, the Monastery of Caves in Kiev.

Vladimir, northeast of Moscow. After that the country was known as Russia.

In 1238 another eastern people, the Mongols, led by Genghis Khan's grandson Batu, sacked Vladimir and Kiev and turned Russia into a Mongol dependency. (See GENGHIS KHAN.) At the same time the Lithuanians seized much land in the north. Even under the Mongol rule, however, principalities such as Novgorod, and Muscovy (Moscow) continued to prosper. In 1380 Muscovy princes defeated the Tatars. By the end of the 16th century Russia had recovered complete independence and had won back all its lost lands.

Today, Russians make up just over 50 per cent of the Soviet population, while Ukrainians account for over 15 per cent.

Non-Slavic Peoples. These make up the remaining population. Among the non-Slavic peoples of the USSR the most numerous are the Turkic peoples of central Asia. These include the Uzbeks, Kazakhs, Kirgiz, and Turkmenians who, with the Tadzhiks (a people related to the Iranians), inhabit the area between the Caspian Sea and the Chinese border. Next come the peoples of the Caucasus: the Georgians, the Armenians, and the Azerbaijani, whose language is also Turkic. In the western part of the USSR live many non-Slavic peoples over whom Moscow has spread its rule. They include the Moldavians who are related to the Romanians; the peoples of the Baltic republics of Lithuania, Latvia, and Estonia; the Karelian (Finnish) peoples of the north; and some Poles and Greeks. There are also over two million Jews and a similar number of Germans scattered throughout the USSR.

Agriculture and Industries

Agriculture has always been a leading Russian occupation because of the large areas of land suitable for cultivation. In the southern part of the Soviet Union the steppes include the fertile "black earth" lands of the Ukraine and the Don and Kuban valleys. (See UKRAINE.) Wheat is the chief crop in the steppes, but large crops of rye, barley, oats, maize, sugar beet, soya beans, flax, hemp, and potatoes are also harvested. In the warm regions of the southern Crimea, parts of the Caucasus and Soviet central Asia, cotton, tea, tobacco, and fruits are grown. Both in Soviet Europe and central Asia cattle, pigs, sheep, goats, and horses are kept.

The great forest lands of the Soviet Union

are larger than the whole United States. They grow about one-third of the world's trees, and are a rich source of timber, much of which is sent abroad. Another valuable export is furs. Squirrel, white fox mink, and ermine skins are sent from the USSR all over the world. Fishing is another important industry. The Soviet Union's yearly catch represents nearly one-sixth of the world total.

The Soviet Union is also tremendously rich in mineral resources. Coal, iron, and oil were produced in increasing quantities until 1917 but production decreased for a short while after the Russian Revolution. This was because of the confusion and inefficiency caused at first by the introduction of state ownership and management of industry.

From 1928, however, the mining industry was pushed ahead rapidly by the government's programme of production. Besides coal, iron, natural gas, and oil, the Soviet Union has plentiful supplies of copper, tin, lead, nickel, chromium, mercury, bauxite (from which aluminium is obtained), and also gold. The output of Soviet industrial production is second only to that of the United States.

The traditional manufacturing areas in the USSR are Moscow and the surrounding district, Leningrad (see LENINGRAD; MOSCOW), and the region around the Krivoi Rog iron mines in the Ukraine. Their main products are textiles, steel, and machinery. All the newer industrial areas are in the Asiatic section of the Soviet Union. The largest is on the eastern slopes and foothills of the Ural Mountains, where the huge industrial centres of Sverdlovsk, Chelyabinsk, and Magnitogorsk have sprung up. The next area is based on the Kuznetsk coalfield in western Siberia, and includes the industrial towns of Novosibirsk (see NOVOSIBIRSK), Novokuznetsk, Kemerovo, Belovo, and Leninsk-Kuznetski. Other industries are to be found in Omsk (western Siberia) and Tashkent (central Asia).

Frank Spooner

A natural-gas-processing plant in Uzbekistan which is a leading gas-producing area of the Soviet Union.

FACTS ABOUT THE USSR

AREA: 22,402,200 square kilometres (8,649,500 square miles).

POPULATION: 285,428,000 (1988).

GOVERNMENT: Federal socialist republic.

CAPITAL: Moscow, 8,714,000.

GEOGRAPHY: Broadly speaking, the country consists of vast inner lowlands, open in the north to the Arctic and backed in the south, west, and east by high mountain regions. The European part of the country is divided from the Asian part by the Ural mountains. The highest peaks are in the Tien Shan and Pamir ranges on the borders of Afghanistan and China, and in the Caucasus mountains between the Black Sea and the Caspian Sea. The chief rivers are the Ob, Volga, Neva, Lena, Amur, Yenisei, Dnieper, and Don. Besides the Caspian Sea there are several very large lakes such as the Sea of Aral and lakes Baikal, Balkash, Ladoga, and Onega.

CITIES: Leningrad, 4,904,000; Kiev, 2,495,000; Tashkent, 2,077,000; Baku, 1,722,000; Kharkov, 1,567,000; Minsk, 1,510,000; Gorky, 1,409,000; Novosibirsk, 1,405,000; Sverdlovsk, 1,315,000; Kuybyshev, 1,267,000; Tbilisi, 1,174,000; Dnepropetrovsk, 1,166,000.

ECONOMY. Chief products and exports.

Agriculture, forestry and fishing: Potatoes, sugar beets, wheat, barley, vegetables, oats, rye, maize, flax fibre, cotton, grapes, sunflower seeds, rice, tobacco, sheep, cattle, pigs, goats, horses, poultry.

Mining: Iron ore, phosphate rock, salt, potash salts, bauxite, chromium ore, manganese, magnesite, asbestos, zinc, copper, lead, nickel.

Manufacturing: Crude steel, cement, pig iron, rolled steel, fertilizers, sulphuric acid, steel pipes, meat, sugar, paper, canned fish, resins and plastics.

Exports: Crude petroleum and petroleum products, machinery and transport equipment, mineral fuels and natural gas, chemical fertilizers and resins, wood and paper products.

EDUCATION: Children must go to school between the ages of 6 and 16.

The newest of the industrial areas is around Irkutsk in Siberia. Near here, huge dams across the Yenisei and Angara rivers supply one of the largest hydroelectric power stations in the world. The electric power is used for industries based on the supplies of coal, iron, bauxite, asbestos, mica, and other minerals in the surrounding country. The Soviet Union also has several nuclear power plants.

Communications and Transport

Transport and communications in the Soviet Union are still one of the weaknesses hampering its progress. The railways, which carry most of the heavy goods traffic, are insufficient for their task, although more lines are being built. East of the Yenisei River, passenger and freight traffic relies on the Trans-Siberian Railway to carry it to eastern Siberia and the Pacific coast (see TRANS-SIBERIAN RAILWAY), while the BAM railway stretches 3,200 kilometres (2,000 miles) from the Lena River to the Amur River region. The northern part of the Asiatic section of the USSR has few railways. The roads, too, are poor by modern standards although road building has speeded up, particularly in areas of recent industrial development. A network of highways runs from Moscow. Most large towns are linked by long-distance bus services.

The USSR is fortunate in possessing more than 100,000 kilometres (62,000 miles) of rivers that can be used by ships or by tugs and barges. Some of the European waterways are linked by a system of canals which makes it possible to travel by water from the Black and Caspian seas to the Baltic and White seas via the Baltic-Caspian waterway opened in 1965. Ships led by icebreakers can follow the Northern Sea Route – a narrow channel between the northern coast and the arctic pack ice – to ports near the mouths of the great Siberian rivers. Modern nuclear-powered icebreakers can keep the northern route open for 160 days each year. Air transport is increasingly important and internal air services link the major towns. Moscow is the centre of these services and the terminus for most international flights by the Russian state airline Aeroflot, the world's largest airline.

Before World War II (1939–45) the Soviet Union had few seaports. However, a number of new ports were obtained in 1940 and after the war, and these have made possible greater seaborne trade with other countries. In the Arctic, Pechenga (formerly Petsamo) and Murmansk are ice-free ports, as are most of the Soviet ports on the Baltic, except Leningrad. The most important of these Baltic ports are Tallinn, Riga, Klaipeda (formerly Memel), and Kaliningrad (formerly Königsberg). On the Asiatic coast, the port of Vladivostok-Nakhodka can only be kept open in winter by the use of ice-breakers (see VLADIVOSTOK). The Soviet ports on the Black Sea, of which Odessa and Batumi are the most important, provide access to the Mediterranean through the narrow straits of the Dardanelles and Bosporus.

Novosti

Chess is taught in Russian schools from an early age. It is thought to encourage healthy competition.

Pipelines for natural gas and oil are of great importance in the USSR. The pipeline from the Tuymazy oil fields near Kuybyshev stretches 6,500 kilometres (4,000 miles) eastwards to Irkutsk. The "Comecon" pipeline system carries Soviet oil from Brody in the Ukraine to Poland, the German Democratic

Republic, Czechoslovakia, and Hungary. The "Progress" pipeline from Yamburg in northwest Siberia to Uzhgorod on the Ukranian–Czechoslovakian frontier, 4,600 kilometres (2,900 miles) away, carries natural gas to Eastern and Western Europe.

Social Life

Education. Under the pre-1917 governments education was neglected, and in 1900 only about one-third of the people could read and write. By 1914 no more than a quarter of the children of school age were receiving regular education. Progress was still further hindered by the revolution of 1917 and new methods in which discipline and the authority of the teachers were relaxed.

In 1930, when the plans for a rapid spread of industry made it important to have educated workers, the government made primary education compulsory throughout the USSR and began to introduce a seven-year schooling system in towns. By 1939 a campaign to provide adult education had taken place, and about 90 per cent of the people were said to be able to read and write.

Today, education in the USSR is free and compulsory from the age of 6 to 16. Nursery schools and kindergartens are available for younger children. Modern Soviet schools lay stress on engineering and the sciences, although the arts, particularly music and ballet, are also important. The teaching of Soviet Communist ideas still plays an important part in education. Sport is also encouraged. Many people in the Soviet Union continue their education at technical colleges, and through evening and correspondence courses. The older universities of Moscow, Leningrad, and Kiev have been expanded and new ones established.

Religion. The official religion of Russia under the tsars was that of the Eastern Orthodox Church (see EASTERN ORTHODOX CHURCHES). After the revolution, the Bolsheviks separated the church from the state and persecuted the bishops and priests. They took away from the church its wealth and its places of worship, many of which were turned into museums or even used for "anti-God" exhibitions. Religious instruction was forbidden in the schools.

The Eastern Orthodox Church, although much reduced in size, is allowed to hold services and some of its church buildings have been restored. Other churches – such as the Roman Catholic Church, which once flourished in Lithuania, and the Protestant Church in Estonia – receive little encouragement but there is some toleration, and the same is true of the large following of the Muslim faith in Soviet central Asia. Soviet Jews too have been unfairly treated.

Food. The chief item of Soviet meals continues to be bread, which is usually of the "black" (actually very dark brown) kind. Other traditional dishes are *shchi*, which is

Novosti

The Hermitage Museum, Leningrad, founded by Catherine the Great in 1764, houses the priceless art treasures of the Russian tsars. It contains one of the finest art collections in the world.

Novosti

Above: A massive stainless steel sculpture, *Worker and Woman Collective Farmer* by Vera Mukhina (1937) celebrates Soviet achievements. **Top right**: *The Volga Bargemen* by Ilya Repin (*c.* 1870). **Right**: *Princess Davydov and Mademoiselle Rzhevskaya* by Dmitri Levitski (1776). **Far right**: *Portrait of an officer, Colonel Evgraf Davydov* by Orest Kiprenski (1809).

a cabbage soup, and *kasha*, a grain porridge. Specialities of Russian cooking are *pirozhki* (little meat pasties), *blini* (pancakes), *borsch* (beetroot soup), and various forms of sour milk and cream. The different regions of the USSR also have their own special local dishes. The delicacy caviar, which is the eggs or roe of sturgeon, mostly comes from the USSR.

Sport. Organized sport has received much encouragement in the USSR since the revolution, and Soviet athletes have frequently proved themselves Olympic and world champions. The state provides tracks, grounds, and indoor arenas for athletics and team games in most important cities and towns. The more popular sports are athletics, gymnastics, soccer, ice hockey, skiing and skating, basketball, and volleyball. Chess is popular, both as a pastime in parks and indoors, and as a world championship spectacle.

The Arts

Russian architecture shows best in its churches, which until the 17th century were by far the most important buildings in the country. The early churches were built of wood and something of the style of them descended to the later stone churches, with their square ground-plan, tent-like form, and onion-shaped domes. Novgorod, in particular, has many fine examples, and the multi-domed Cathedral of St. Basil in Moscow is world famous.

After the revolution, Russian architecture went through a period of experiments, called constructivism, using functional modern styles and man-made industrial materials. This was followed by a return to more ordinary buildings, although these were often highly decorated during the Stalin period. Since then, Soviet architects have adopted simpler designs and methods to deal quickly and cheaply with the great shortage of dwellings.

The Russian painting of the past is seen at its best in icons or sacred paintings, especially those of the 15th century. (See ICON.) The efforts of Peter the Great to introduce Western civilization brought to an end this Russian style of painting, and nearly all the later paintings by Russian artists are in the various styles that sprang up in the western European countries.

The Russians have a great wealth of traditional folk music, and the *balalaika*, a Russian stringed instrument, was used to play this music from the 18th century. However, it was not until the 19th century that a Russian composer, Mikhail Glinka (1804–57), began to compose truly Russian concert music. His opera *Ruslan and Lyudmila* marked the beginning of a new period. Other distinguished composers in the Russian tradition include Peter Tchaikovsky (1840–93); Mily Balakirev (1837–1910); Alexander Borodin (1833–87); Modest Mussorgsky (1839–81); and Nikolai Rimsky-Korsakov (1844–1908), all of whom wrote music that is still widely performed today.

Of composers writing in the 20th century the most important have been Sergey Rachmaninov (1873–1943); Igor Stravinsky (1882–1971), the most striking of the "modernist" school; and Sergey Prokofiev (1891–1953). The best-known of modern Russian composers is Dmitri Shostakovich (1906–75). Both Shostakovich and Prokofiev had difficulties with the Communist authorities. (There are separate articles on most of the famous Russian composers mentioned here.) Since the death of Stalin, however, there has been less of this ideological control (control of ideas) and the music of the two composers is generally approved by the authorities, as is much popular Western music.

The great Russian school of ballet was established under the tsars, and the Soviet government has continued to support it.

Novosti

Top: A ballet class at the Kharkov Palace of Pioneers.
Above: Ice hockey, an activity in which Soviets excel.

Among the great dancers produced by the Russians were Anna Pavlova (1882–1931); Vaslav Nijinsky (1890–1950), (there are separate articles on these two dancers); and Galina Ulanova (born 1910). The greatest creator of ballets was Serge Diaghilev (1872–1929), who brought together dancers, composers, painters, and singers into a brilliant whole. The Bolshoi ballet and theatre are world renowned. (See also BALLET.)

The first great Russian writer was Mikhail Lomonosov (1711–65), who created a language that would serve for literature. He did this by combining the spoken language of Russia with the language called Old Slavonic that until then had been used for books. The Russian prose style was further simplified and improved by the historian Nikolai Karamzin (1766–1826).

The golden age of Russian literature was the 19th century. The great poets of that time included Alexander Pushkin (1799–1837); Mikhail Lermontov (1814–41); and Fyodor Tyutchev (1803–73). Great playwrights were Alexander Gribodeyov (1795–1829); Nikolai Gogol (1809–52); Alexander Ostrovsky (1823–86); and, greatest of all, Anton Chekhov (1860–1904).

Ivan Krylov (1768–1844) wrote fables. Although Pushkin, Lermontov, and Gogol all wrote prose fiction, or novels, the first great Russian novelist to become famous outside Russia was Ivan Turgenev (1818–83). Ivan Goncharov (1812–91) was another great novelist, but the greatest were Leo Tolstoy (1828–1910), whose chief novels were *War and Peace* and *Anna Karenina*, and Fyodor Dostoyevsky (1821–81), whose best-known novels were *Crime and Punishment, The Idiot, The Possessed*, and *The Brothers Karamazov*.

Famous modern Russian writers include Maxim Gorky (1868–1936); Ilya Ehrenburg (1891–1967); Mikhail Sholokhov (1905–84); Osip Mandelstam (1891–1938); Boris Pasternak (1890–1960); Alexander Solzhenitsyn (born 1918); and the poets Anna Akhmatova (1889–1966), and Yevgeni Yevtushenko (born 1933). Many of these Russian writers have separate articles. Russian cinema, too, is world-famous, and popular in the Soviet Union. Sergey Eisenstein made classic films in the early 20th century, including *Battleship Potemkin* (1925).

Government of the Soviet Union

From its earliest history Russia was composed of many nationalities, with different languages, customs, and habits. They were held firmly together under the rule of the tsars, but many of them sought to become independent after the Revolution of 1917. Poland, Finland, and the three Baltic states of Estonia, Latvia, and Lithuania succeeded in obtaining independence. Separate governments were set up in Siberia, in the Ukraine, the Caucasus region, and elsewhere. Of the other peoples, many were at first unwilling to join the Soviet government because they feared that the Russians would dominate them. To quiet these fears the Soviet leaders drew up a constitution promising equality to all nationalities, races, and language groups. They also did away with the title Russia, which was hated by many of the other peoples, to whom it meant oppression by the Russians. In 1922 it was proclaimed that the new federation (group of states) would be known as the Union of Soviet Socialist Republics.

The union was begun in 1923 by the joining together of the four main republics that then existed: Russia, Belorussia, the Ukraine, and the Transcaucasian Republic. As time passed, other regions and neighbouring states were allowed to or forced to join the Soviet Union. There are now 15 of them and they are known as the constituent republics of the Soviet Union. The first and foremost among them is the Russian Soviet Federated Socialist Republic (RSFSR). The remaining 14 are described as Soviet Socialist Republics (SSR) and are (in alphabetical order) Armenia, Azerbaijan, Belorussia, Estonia, Georgia, Kazakhstan, Kirgizia, Latvia, Lithuania, Moldavia, Tadzhikistan, Turkmenistan, Ukraine, and Uzbekistan. (There are separate articles on all of them.)

Besides these 15 constituent republics, there are other autonomous republics as well as autonomous *oblasts* (districts) and *okrugs* (administrative areas). All these areas operate within a federal system of government (see GOVERNMENT), but under tight control from central government, governed by the Communist Party – the only political party in the USSR (see also COMMUNISM; POLITICAL PARTIES).

The Soviet parliament has two houses, the Congress of People's Deputies and the Supreme Soviet. The Congress has 1,500 members elected by the general public and 750 nominated by the Communist Party. It is chaired by the president of the Soviet Union and first met in 1989. The Supreme Soviet is elected by the Congress and has the power to pass new laws.

The most powerful body in the USSR is the Politburo of the Communist Party, which decides the policy of the country. It takes all the important political and economic decisions and is headed by the general secretary of the Communist Party, who is therefore the most powerful person in the country. The Council of Ministers is the arm of government that puts the policy into practice and administers the country. The present chairman of the Communist Party, Mikhail Gorbachev, is also the president of the country.

The 15 constituent republics have their own political systems much like the central system, with their own one-house Supreme Soviets. However, they are not independent units of government like the US states, which have law-making and tax-gathering powers. Government is directed by the central government filtering down through the bureaucracy.

The influence of the Communist Party starts at a very young age, from schools for the very young through to the Pioneers (9- to 14-year-olds) on to the Komsomol, which is the Communist Youth League for 14- to 28-year-olds. From here members will go on to the Communist Party, and positions of power. Only a small proportion of Soviet citizens actually belongs to the Communist Party, membership of which is regarded as an honour.

Early History

The first permanent settlements in what is now the USSR were those of the eastern Slavs who moved across from the Elbe River. North European and Middle Eastern merchants began to cross these lands in the late 8th century AD. At the same time the eastern Slavs had to fortify their settlements against raids by nomadic Asian tribes from the east.

In the 9th century, when the Norsemen were raiding and plundering western Europe, bands of Varangers, or Vikings, travelled southwards across the Baltic and down the rivers to the Black Sea. They sought not plunder but trade with Constantinople. The leaders of these armed bands of Scandinavian traders became the rulers of the eastern Slavs, and the land was known as Rus.

According to tradition the Varangian leader Rurik settled in Novgorod in AD 862. In 882 Rurik's brother Oleg occupied Kiev. Kiev was the chief centre of Russian trade and by the 11th century all the tribes of the eastern Slavs had submitted to the authority of the grand prince of Kiev.

Christianity reached Russia along this same trade-route. Vladimir, the grand prince of Kiev, became a Christian in 982 when he married the sister of the Emperor of Byzantium. (Byzantium was the old name for Constantinople; see BYZANTINE EMPIRE.) Vladimir firmly established Russian Christianity. Thus the eastern Slavs became members of the Eastern Orthodox Church and looked to Constantinople not only as the centre of their church but also as a centre of trade and culture. A lasting link was thus created between Russia and Constantinople, while the influence of Rome, which was the religious and cultural centre of western Europe, was shut out. In the 11th and 12th centuries Kiev took an active part in European affairs. The grand princes became united by marriage with many of the royal families of Europe. Kiev might have continued as a European capital had it not been for the Mongol conquests.

The Slav settlements centred on Kiev had long suffered from raids by Asian tribes. Early in the 13th century a new force, the Mongols, or Tatars, arose in eastern Asia. Led by Genghis Khan, they struck terror in Europe.

Society for Cultural Relations with the USSR

The building of Moscow in the 12th century. The original town was fortified by a strong wooden wall.

(See GENGHIS KHAN.) In 1238 under Batu Khan, Genghis Khan's grandson, they destroyed Kiev and occupied nearly the whole of Russia. The occupation lasted almost 300 years and when at last it ended Russia found itself not only cut off from Europe but backward by European standards.

By the end of the Mongol occupation Russia was united under the reigning prince of Muscovy (Moscow). The Mongols always encouraged the strongest princes in the lands they conquered, making them responsible for collecting the khan's tribute. (The tribute was the money paid by a conquered people to their conqueror.) The princes of Moscow early gained the Mongols' support and in 1353 the Mongols recognized Ivan II's rule over all the Russian princes. In this way Moscow, with all the advantages of its central geographical position, became the political capital. After the capture of Constantinople by the Turks in 1453, Moscow also became the religious centre of Russia.

Russia under the Tsars

Ivan III, called Ivan the Great, further strengthened Moscow's position by spreading its power over the surrounding regions. In 1480 he threw off Mongol rule and made Russia independent. Ivan IV came to the throne in 1533 and called himself *tsar* ("emperor") of all Russia. During his long reign, his cruel and violent rule earned him the title Ivan the Terrible. (See IVAN THE TERRIBLE.) During the early years of his reign, Ivan conquered Astrakhan and Kazan, making the important Volga River wholly Russian.

In 1598 the death of Ivan the Terrible's son Fyodor began a period known as the "time of troubles" which lasted for 15 years. Fyodor, a feeble-minded and weak ruler, died childless. Boris Godunov, who had been Fyodor's guardian and made decisions on his behalf, became tsar. He governed wisely but the noblemen were jealous of him, and in 1605 he was poisoned. His successor was the False Dmitri, who was so called because he claimed falsely to be the son of Ivan the Terrible. When Dmitri died Russia was torn by squabbles, and was invaded by the Poles and Swedes. Moscow was captured and burnt to the ground, but when this happened a wave of patriotic feeling suddenly united the Russians and they drove their enemies from the country. A national assembly with representatives from all classes of the population was called together in Moscow, and in 1613 Mikhail Romanov was elected tsar of Russia. He was the first of a long family line who held the throne until the revolution in 1917.

Peter I, who became known as Peter the Great and was tsar from 1682 to 1725, pushed Russia closer to Europe in all aspects of life. He also established Russia as a European power, and continued to build up an empire. The Russian defeat of Sweden under Charles XII after the long struggle called the Great Northern War was a chief factor in this rise to power.

Peter spent his reign reforming and developing Russia to make it as strong and advanced as other European nations. He built a new capital at St. Petersburg (now Leningrad) and formed a strong army and navy. He reorganized the country and brought in Western engineers and craftsmen to develop Russian industries and to train the people. During his long reign he brought about tremendous changes, but at the cost of many Russian lives. Also, the vast majority of the people remained as serfs, no better than slaves. (See PETER THE GREAT.)

The next important ruler of Russia was

Catherine II (1762–96). She too was known as "the Great". She was a German princess of great energy and ability who came to the Russian throne through marriage. She added further to Russian territory, mainly by taking land from Poland. Catherine also increased European influence, and particularly French influence, in Russia. She was attracted by French art and culture, but she did nothing to encourage in Russia the political ideas of the French Revolution, which began in 1789 (see FRENCH REVOLUTION). Instead she strengthened the power of the sovereign, making all the branches of government depend directly on her will. (See CATHERINE THE GREAT.)

During the reign of Alexander I (1801–25) Napoleon invaded Russia. He captured Moscow, but found only a city deserted and in great disorder. With no Russians to negotiate with, and facing a severe winter and food shortages, the French were forced to retreat with heavy losses. This defeat of Napoleon did much to arouse respect for Russia throughout the world. (See NAPOLEONIC WARS.)

Alexander I had many ideas about giving the people more freedom and when he came to the throne he promised reforms. He built schools and universities. He wished to set free the serfs, or peasants, who in those days were forbidden to leave the farms of the landowners. However, when in 1803 he finally approved the law that allowed landowners to free their serfs, only some 47,000 serfs, a small fraction of the total number, benefited.

Gradually revolutionary ideas spread in Russia and discontent increased. Secret societies to bring about reforms were founded, chiefly by educated members of the nobility. When Nicholas I came to the throne in 1825, these "radicals", as they were called, took the opportunity to stage a rebellion known as the Decembrist rising. It was put down by the new tsar but the ideas did not die.

Nicholas was a ruler who ignored the growing demands of his people for reform. Those who had been working with the Decembrists or were members of the secret societies, he sent to Siberia in exile. He did, however, improve the management of public affairs in Russia.

The reign of Nicholas I closed with the Crimean War (1853–56; see CRIMEAN WAR). Russia's defeat in this war increased the discontent in the country but Alexander II (1855–81) introduced a number of sweeping reforms. Of these the most important was the one by which the serfs were finally set free in 1861. It was a reform long overdue, and by the time it took effect the peasants were thinking not only about personal freedom but also about owning their own land. Alexander also intro-

Popperfoto

In a photograph taken before the revolution, a Russian peasant rocks his baby to sleep in a primitive cradle. Before the revolution many poor people laboured on the huge estates of the wealthy and lived in appalling conditions.

duced trial by jury, and a system by which the provinces governed themselves through *zemstva* or councils. He encouraged industrial development. During his reign Russia's industrial output was tripled, and many railways were built.

Despite these reforms the discontent continued to grow. The peasants now rebelled because they could not obtain enough land to support themselves. Many went to the cities where workers were needed in the new industries. The conditions in the factories were bad and the wages were barely enough for men to live on, but the landless peasants were forced to take this work or starve. Thus the rapid increase of industry, together with the freeing of the serfs, had the effect of creating another class of discontented people – the proletariat, or poor city labourers.

The period that followed these reforms was one of disorder and terror. The secret societies, seeking to start a revolution, began to use terrorist methods such as bombings and assassinations. Alexander II turned away from his reforms and became a supporter of those who were against change. In 1881 he was assassinated by a terrorist bomb and with him died any hopes of a democratic government being introduced.

His successor Alexander III (1881–94) boldly proclaimed his belief in the absolute rule and supreme power of the tsar. He was a strong-willed man who was determined to put an end to the disorder and terror in Russia. Unfortunately he followed a backward policy. He would not accept the progressive ideas that had made such headway during the previous 80 years and he firmly put down all groups and persons that opposed him. Jews and other groups were ruthlessly persecuted and political prisoners were exiled in thousands to Siberia. By the time of Alexander III's death, Russia was ripe for revolution.

Alexander III was a man of iron will, who chose his ministers carefully and watched closely over their work. His son, Nicholas II, who came to the throne in 1894, was a very different figure. He was well-meaning but weak, and without any real control over his government at a time when firmness was needed.

John Massey Stewart

Cossack soldiers on horseback admire the Trans-Siberian railway. It was begun in 1891.

In Nicholas II's reign the Trans-Siberian Railway was built and people were encouraged to settle in Siberia. On the Pacific coast Port Arthur, and Dalny (now the Chinese port of Luta) were opened. This spread of Russian power to the Pacific brought Russia into a clash with Japan. The Russo-Japanese War (1904–05) ended with the severe defeat of Russia and the almost complete destruction of the Russian navy.

Two Revolutions

The Russo-Japanese war had never been popular and the loss of it made people realize how bad things had become at home. Discontent increased when the tsar refused to grant the demands of the democratic political parties, and a series of strikes and riots including Bloody Sunday (see RUSSIAN REVOLUTION) developed into a revolution. Russian troops and sailors mutinied and there was a general strike; but eventually the revolt was put down.

Although the rising in 1905 was unsuccessful, it made Tsar Nicholas realize that he had to choose between a military dictatorship and giving way to the people's demands for reform. He chose the second course and issued the "October Manifesto", which was a written declaration that amounted to a grant of rights. It gave certain freedoms to the people such as freedom of speech and of conscience and the liberty to hold meetings. It also approved the election of an assembly called the Duma, which shared some of the tsar's law-making powers.

By changes in the methods of electing the Duma and by limiting its powers, the tsar and his ministers prevented it from becoming an effective parliament. Even so, the Duma did represent a small step towards democratic government, although most of the radicals regarded it as a complete failure.

Talk of revolution again became widespread. However, most of the Russian people preferred to wait for peaceful reforms. Thus, although there was discontent, there was no general support among the people for the overthrow of the tsarist rule, and that rule might not have collapsed had it not been for World War I, which began in 1914.

Russia joined the Allies against Germany in World War I. The Russian armies fought with magnificent bravery but, because they were so badly equipped and supplied they suffered heavy defeats, and over 1 million soldiers were killed. The inefficiency and neglect of the tsar's ministers and advisers were shown up all too plainly. The spirit of the people began to fail and the war became unpopular. The soldiers who had fought so bravely mutinied and deserted their regiments. Riots and strikes broke out in Petrograd (now Leningrad) and Moscow, and could not be put down. The revolution gathered force, led by Vladimir Ilich Lenin, and in March 1917 the tsar, lacking the support of his army, was forced to abdicate, or leave the throne. He and his family were shot by revolutionary troops on the night of 16–17 July 1918, in a villa at Ekaterinburg (now Sverdlovsk).

Popperfoto

A Russian battery overlooks the Manchurian front during the Russo-Japanese War of 1904–5.

A provisional (temporary) government was formed from members of the Duma and of the provincial councils but failed. Its authority was not recognized by a *soviet* ("council") in Petrograd composed of two Socialist groups. This soviet consisted of soldiers, workers, and peasants. Taking advantage of disagreements between the two groups, a third Socialist group called the Bolsheviks, which was better organized, took control of the Petrograd soviet and of those in other cities.

The Bolsheviks, who were extreme revolutionary Socialists led by Lenin, acquired their name at a meeting held in London in 1903. The word *bolshevik* comes from the Russian word meaning "majority", and was used for Lenin's party because he and his supporters outnumbered the others at the meeting. There is a separate article on Lenin, and on his fellow-leader Leon Trotsky (1879–1940). The Bolsheviks demanded that the government be handed over to the soviets, that peace be made, and that the land be distributed among the peasants. These ideas were very popular, especially among the soldiers. The provisional government was overthrown and most of its members were arrested. Towards the end of 1917 an assembly was elected. Although fewer than half of its members were Bolsheviks, they were to obtain complete control in a civil war (1918–20), and then form the Union of Soviet Socialist Republics.

The Soviet State

Lenin believed that the Russian Revolution was only the first of many that would overthrow the existing order in Europe and elsewhere. When, however, his hopes of further Communist revolutions in Europe were disappointed, Lenin had to turn all his efforts to improving the Soviet system in backward Russia. He changed the Communist Party into an organization with strict discipline, more like an army than a political party, through

Camera Press

Lenin (in the centre, flanked by supporters) founded the Russian Communist Party and led the revolution.

which he could govern the country and replace the central rule of the tsars. The party's main task, he said, was to change Russia from a largely agricultural country (and therefore a rather poor country) into a modern industrial power.

Communist ideas have their origin in the writings of the 19th-century philosopher Karl Marx. (See COMMUNISM; MARX, KARL.) He examined the working of Western industrial society and severely disapproved of it as unfair. Marx decided that this "capitalist" system would in the end collapse and would be replaced by socialism. The main idea of socialist theory, or Marxism, is that all the main sources of wealth in a country, such as its mines, factories, banks, and land, should be owned by the state, which must be under the control of the people so as to ensure fair shares for all. Marx called his idea of socialism "Communism".

Faced with the double task of governing the country and speeding up its industrial progress, Lenin developed the idea that between the revolution and full Communism, there must be a transition period. He believed that ordinary working people did not have the skill and knowledge to set up a Communist system themselves. During the transition period, a small group of educated people would be needed to guide them. In the USSR this group would be the Communist Party. Lenin's plan was that the party should rule until a full Communist system was established. During this period, too, people would work and be paid according to the two principles: "He who does not work shall not eat" and "From each according to his ability; to each according to his work". Once the power of the proletariat was secure and the country's wealth sufficient, society would be organized on the principles: "From each according to his ability; to each according to his *needs*". In this true Communist society there would be no need for the state, with its instruments of power such as the army and police, and it would disappear.

After the Revolution

Of the problems facing Lenin after the revolution, the most urgent was to make peace with Germany. German troops were already advancing into Russia. Lenin, whose Bolsheviks took the title of the All-Russian Communist Party in 1918, saw that he must have peace if Communist rule was to have a chance to establish itself. Against opposition from his own party he accepted the German terms and in May 1918 signed the Treaty of Brest-Litovsk. It was a harsh treaty which took away from Russia all the lands in the west that had been gained by Peter the Great and his successors, including the Baltic states. The Russians regarded these lands as the heritage of Peter the Great, and before long they were to recover them and control a good deal more.

After the revolution the various regions of Russia adopted the Soviet system, with the exception of the Ukraine and the Cossack lands on the Don and Volga rivers, and around the shores of the Black and Caspian seas. In the Ukrainian elections of November 1917 the Communists were heavily defeated and the Ukrainian people declared their independence from Moscow, which had long been their aim.

Germany recognized Ukrainian independence and by the Treaty of Brest-Litovsk, Soviet troops had to leave the Ukraine. However, after the defeat of Germany by the Allies in November 1918 the Soviet government declared that the Ukraine could no longer be recognized as independent. Later, the Ukraine became one of the republics forming the USSR.

Also opposing the Communists were the Cossacks. They were descended from Russian warrior horsemen whose task had been to defend the frontiers of Russia. They had been given lands, known as the Cossack lands, on condition that they fought for the tsars. But Communist forces drove them and the volunteer armies fighting with them from their positions on the Don River and in the Urals.

Then the Allies decided to take a hand in Russia. Their intention was partly to create a new fighting front against Germany, and in August 1918 Allied troops landed at Archangel, Murmansk, and Vladivostok. After the defeat of Germany, the Allied support for the opponents of the Communists increased. British ships entered the Black Sea with supplies for the White Army, as the main force against the Communists was called.

However, the Soviet government, which had introduced conscription (compulsory military service), sent Trotsky to reorganize the revolutionary, or Red, army, which he did brilliantly. The civil war lasted until the end of 1920. Gradually the leaders of the White forces began to differ and Allied support was withdrawn. The Communists were defeated in Poland, Finland, and in the Baltic provinces of Estonia, Latvia, and Lithuania, all of which became independent. Elsewhere, however, the Communists were successful.

During the civil war the Communists killed or imprisoned many who opposed them. Millions of people died, and the country was left starving and shattered. Unable in any other way to bring about its recovery, Lenin decided to move by easy stages. In 1921 he introduced

The Hutchison Library

Queuing for goods in Moscow's GUM department store. The elegant building dates from before the Russian Revolution.

a programme that brought back a certain amount of private ownership and management and also the customary methods of banking, taxation, wages, and payments. This programme, which was generally called the New Economic Policy (NEP) was halfway between Capitalism and Communism.

The period of the NEP, which lasted from 1921 until 1928, was, after Lenin's death, the period of rivalry between Leon Trotsky and Joseph Stalin within the Communist Party. Trotsky, the brilliant revolutionary, urged a policy of world revolution. Stalin wanted to make secure the achievements of the Russian Revolution before starting on world revolution. Stalin's ideas won the day. Trotsky was expelled from the party and in 1929 was driven from the country. (See STALIN, JOSEPH; TROTSKY, LEON.)

In 1928 Stalin, who by this time was firmly in control, began a policy of large-scale industrialization and of agricultural collectivization. "Industrialization" means the development of manufacturing industries. "Agricultural collectivization" came about as follows. When the Revolution took place in 1917 the peasants seized the land from the country squires and divided it among themselves. By Communist law, however, the land belonged to the state, and by Communist theory the peasants would produce more if they were made to work on large collective farms instead of on their own small plots. Stalin insisted on this "collectivization", although at first it caused a fall in agricultural production and even famine in some places. Instead of small plots for each family, the land was divided into huge *kolkhozy* (collective farms), each employing from 150 to 300 families. The produce was sold to the state, from which the *kolkhoz* rented the land and such machinery as tractors. Those resisting collectivization were deported to Siberia. Millions are believed to have died as a result.

By 1941, about 24 million people had left the land to work in the cities and new factories, and instead of 26 million small farms there were 242,000 *kolkhozy* occupying nearly all the land under cultivation. These were gradually combined to 44,000. There are also more than 7,000 *sovkhozy* (state farms).

Progress was planned by means of a number of "five-year plans" which laid down the task of each main industry and the "target" of output for it to aim at. The first five-year plan (1928–32) aimed chiefly at the development of heavy industries. It was a period of hardship and toil, but also one of great achievement. The second five-year plan (1933–37) continued the developments of the first, and the USSR began to become a great industrial country. One of the goals of the five-year plans was to build up the military strength of the Soviet Union.

In August 1939 the USSR and Germany signed a pact promising not to attack each other for ten years. This was Hitler's idea, to prevent Germany having to fight enemies to the west and east at the same time. World War II began with the German attack on Poland in September, and on 17 September Soviet troops invaded eastern Poland and seized it. The USSR then occupied Estonia, Latvia, and Lithuania, forcing them to become Soviet republics, and seized parts of Finland after a short war. This was done partly to form "buffer states" between the USSR and Germany.

Nevertheless, when the Germans attacked the USSR in June 1941 they quickly conquered most of the western part of the country. The Russians fought heroically. They were helped by supplies and equipment from the Western Allies, and also by a huge relocation effort in which they moved the machinery and workers from important factories to sites east of the Urals. Eventually the Red Army (as the Soviet armies were then called) drove back the invaders into Germany and overwhelmed them. The Russian war losses, however, were enormous. They were much heavier than those of any other nation. (See also WORLD WAR II.)

The chief task of the Soviet Union in its five-year plans after the war was reconstruction of the war damage. At the same time, the Soviet Union continued to keep up powerful armed forces. It had kept control over the states in eastern Europe liberated from German occupation by the Red Army. The armies of the

USSR and its satellites, or neighbouring Communist states, formed the strongest military force in the world.

Other tasks in the five-year plans were the development of the Soviet Arctic and the building of giant hydroelectric power stations to provide power for the new industries. In these tasks, the USSR made great use of forced labour. The forced-labour camps, which were believed at the time of the worst of Stalin's political "purges" to contain up to 15 million people, were kept full by the actions of the secret police who arrested innocent people without trial. Many people died in these purges.

Sovfoto

Russian soldiers practise shooting on skis. Winters in much of the USSR are long and extremely cold.

After Stalin's death in 1953, Nikita S. Khrushchev and Georgi Malenkov held power. Malenkov was succeeded by Nikolai Bulganin in 1955. However, by 1957 Khrushchev had become undisputed leader. Stalin was denounced as a traitor and statues of him removed. Under Khrushchev, central government ministries were abolished in favour of local management.

Although quite popular with the Soviet people, Khrushchev was unexpectedly dismissed in 1964. Leonid Brezhnev succeeded him as first secretary of the Communist Party and Aleksei Kosygin became chairman of the Council of Ministers. The power of the central ministries was re-established. Brezhnev became the country's most powerful leader, taking charge of both home and foreign affairs.

The USSR sent the first sputnik into orbit in 1957 and the first cosmonaut in 1961. Achievements in space were a cause of great pride in the USSR. The USSR began to play an active role in the Middle East, Africa, and Central America. Relations with China, once a staunch friend, became less friendly as the two countries pursued different forms of Communism. After World War II many international conflicts revolved around the two superpowers – the USSR and the USA – trying to gain or defend spheres of influence around the world. The Korean War (1950–53) and the Cuban missile crisis (1962) were examples of these conflicts, as was the Soviet military intervention in Afghanistan between 1979 and 1989 (see AFGHANISTAN).

Leonid Brezhnev died in 1982. His successor was Yury Andropov, who had been head of the KGB (the powerful secret police). Andropov unsuccessfully tried to end corruption and give the economy a boost. He died in 1984, by which time most of the Politburo (the leadership) were also very old. Konstantin Chernenko was already 73 when he succeeded as leader, and he died in 1985, allowing the succession of a more youthful leader, Mikhail Gorbachev, who was born in 1931 (see GORBACHEV, MIKHAIL). Gorbachev was determined to reform the Soviet system. He launched new policies under slogans that summed up his aims. The best known of these were *perestroika*, and *glasnost*. Perestroika means restructuring. It involved the reshaping of all aspects of Soviet life from industry and agri-

Popperfoto

The May Day Parade in Moscow's Red Square honours Soviet workers every year on 1 May.

culture to the theatre and respect for the environment. Glasnost, or openness, was designed to show up what was wrong with Soviet life and to look for solutions.

Gorbachev also wanted to see greater democracy in the Soviet system and to give the average person freedom to criticize officials and propose changes at work. Gorbachev planned to remove the Communist Party from the day-to-day running of Soviet economic life. He wished to see the local councils (the soviets) become more powerful and the central Communist Party with less influence at local level.

Gorbachev's approach to foreign policy, involving greater co-operation with the United States and other nations, led to the withdrawal of Soviet troops from Afghanistan, progress towards nuclear disarmament, and attempts to resolve the Middle East crisis.

UNITED ARAB EMIRATES is a union of seven emirates (states) in the Persian Gulf. Abu Dhabi (by far the largest territory), Dubai, Sharjah, Fujairah, Umm al-Qaiwain, and Ajman joined together in 1971, while Ras al-Khaimah joined the union in 1972.

The country is about 600 kilometres (375 miles) from Saudi Arabia on the west to the Gulf of Oman on the east. It extends only some 110 kilometres (70 miles) north along the Persian Gulf, to Saudi Arabia in the south. Most of the country is hot dry desert with little vegetation. Half the people are Arabs; the rest being Indians, Pakistanis, Iranians, and others. Many inhabitants are Sunni or Shiite Muslims (see Islam). Rich oil and natural gas deposits – among the world's largest – in Abu Dhabi and Dubai provide the country's wealth. Less than one per cent of the land can be farmed, and that has to be irrigated. There is a small fishing industry.

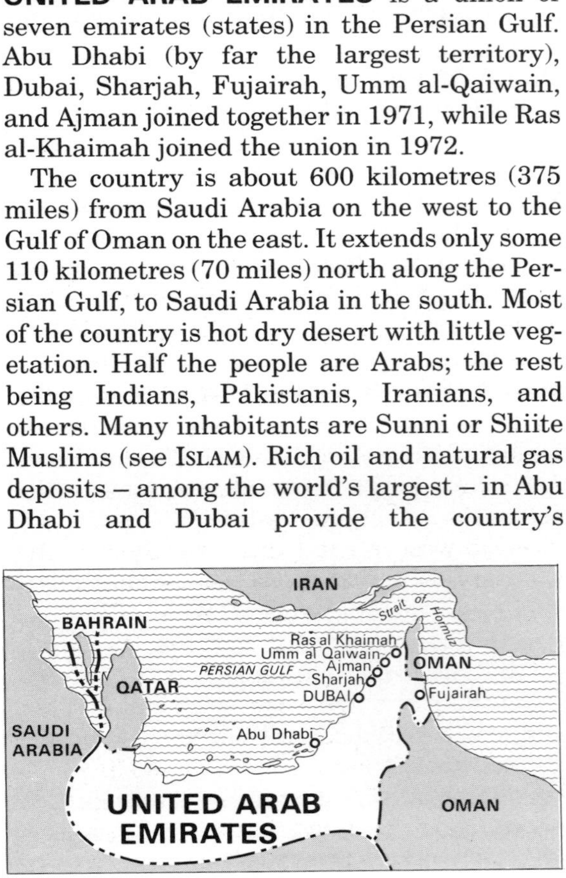

Each emirate is governed by its own sheikh (ruler) and each controls its own mineral rights, taxation, and police. The sheikhs sit on the governing council of the whole country, with one of their number as president. Any decision must be agreed by five of the rulers including those of Abu Dhabi and Dubai. Money from oil is shared between the emirates and is being spent on new schools, hospitals, roads, and factories. (See also Persian Gulf.)

FACTS ABOUT UNITED ARAB EMIRATES

AREA: 77,700 square kilometres (30,000 square miles).
POPULATION: 1,774,000 (1988).
GOVERNMENT: Monarchy. A federal union of seven states, each ruled by an emir.
CAPITAL: Abu Dhabi, 243,000.
GEOGRAPHY: Mainly low-lying desert.
CITIES: Dubai, 266,000; Sharjah, 125,000; al-'Ayn, 102,000; Ras al-Khaimah, 42,000.
EXPORTS: Crude petroleum.
EDUCATION: Children must attend school between the ages of 6 and 12.

History

Commercial and trading communities existed in the area as early as 3000 BC. The prophet Muhammad brought Islam to the region in the 1st century AD. Portuguese explorers first reached the coast at the beginning of the 16th century, and the British East India Company began trading there about 100 years later. By the end of the 19th century Britain had secured domination of the foreign affairs of the region, which became known as the Trucial States. When Britain left the region in 1971, most of the Trucial States joined together to form the United Arab Emirates.

UNITED KINGDOM. The United Kingdom of Great Britain and Northern Ireland (this is its full name) is made up of four parts: England, Scotland, Wales, and Northern Ireland. The Isle of Man and the Channel Islands belong to the British crown but are not part of the United Kingdom in the same way.

ZEFA

St. Ives, a fishing port and holiday resort on the north Cornish coast, has a thriving artists' community.

The United Kingdom occupies most of the British Isles, which lie on the north western seaboard of the European continent.

The Land

The United Kingdom occupies the greater part of the British Isles, a group of islands lying off the northwest coast of Europe. England, Scotland, and Wales occupy the largest island, Great Britain, which is about 950 kilometres (600 miles) from north to south, and 450 kilometres (280 miles) from east to west at its widest point. The northerly part of Great Britain, together with a number of islands—the Hebrides, Orkneys, and Shetlands—forms the kingdom of Scotland. Wales occupies the westerly portion of Britain that protrudes towards Ireland between the Bristol Channel and the Irish Sea. England, the largest of the three countries, occupies the remainder of Great Britain. Northern Ireland sits in the north-easterly corner of Ireland, with the Republic of Ireland to the south. The total area of the United Kingdom is 244,100 square kilometres (94,248 square miles).

To the west of the United Kingdom is the Atlantic Ocean. To the east lies the North Sea, and to the south is the English Channel. Between Britain and Ireland are the North Sea and St. George's Channel.

The country is most mountainous in Scotland, north of the central lowlands. Scotland has the highest point in the United Kingdom, Ben Nevis, at 1,343 metres (4,406 feet). A second large highland area, the Cambrian Mountains occurs in Wales. The highest point here is Mount Snowdon at 1,085 metres (3,560 feet). England's highest point is Scafell Pike, at 978 metres (3,210 feet). It is situated in the Lake District, in northwestern England. Other upland areas are the Pennines, which run north–south through the northern half of England; the hills of the southwestern peninsula of England; and the Southern Uplands of Scotland. The remainder of the country is lowland, gently undulating for the most part, but containing some distinct ranges of hills such as the Cotswolds and Chilterns in southern England, and the Campsie Fells and Ochil Hills in central Scotland. The flattest areas are found in the eastern counties of England—Cambridgeshire, Lincolnshire, Norfolk—and in parts of North Yorkshire. The land drops below sea-level near the large bay known as The Wash.

The largest river in the United Kingdom is the Severn, which rises in the Cambrian Mountains and flows through the west midlands of England, south to the Bristol Channel. Other lengthy rivers are the Thames, the Trent, and the Great Ouse, in England, and the Spey and Clyde in Scotland. The rivers Clyde, Tyne, and Mersey have become famous because of the big cities and industries that have grown up along their banks.

ZEFA

The Lake District in northwest England is a scenic region of mountains, lakes, and green valleys.

British Tourist Authority

The harbour of Portmadoc, northwest Wales, is formed from an inlet of Cardigan Bay, on the Irish Sea.

The climate of the United Kingdom is temperate. Average temperatures range from 4°C to 6°C (39°F to 43°F) in winter, and 12°C to 17°C (53°F to 63°F) in summer. The average annual rainfall is over 1,000 millimetres (40 inches).

The natural vegetation of the United Kingdom has been greatly altered by agriculture. Over most of the lowland, in the past, the vegetation was broad-leaved woodland dominated by oak. This has almost entirely disappeared and the woodland that exists today is mostly in the form of scattered patches, copses, and thickets, as well as plantations of coniferous trees. Heath and moorland cover about a third of the country; moorland is confined mainly to the wetter upland areas of the North of England and Scotland. Animal life has also been greatly affected by man, but, even so, there are many foxes, badgers, stoats, and weasels. Foxes are now quite common in suburban areas. Small mammals include mice, rats, squirrels, hedgehogs, moles, and shrews. The largest British mammal is the red deer, most numerous in Scotland.

The Economy

The United Kingdom is a small country yet rich in raw materials, such as coal, which is found in northern and central England, south Wales, and central Scotland. Beneath the North Sea, on its eastern side, lie valuable deposits of oil and natural gas. Although British farming is modern and efficient, with much use of machinery on most farms, not enough can be grown to feed the island's large population. So food has to be imported from overseas. Broadly speaking the emphasis is on dairy farming in the west of the country and arable in the east. The chief crops are barley, wheat, sugar beet, and potatoes. Sheep are kept on the Welsh and Scottish hills.

Celtic Picture Agency

South Wales is an area where large deposits of coal favoured the growth of industry.

The fact that the United Kingdom is an island country has played an important part in its history, for the sea and shipping have always occupied its people. So too have trade and industry, for only by making and selling goods abroad can the British earn money.

The United Kingdom is a crowded country. The most densely populated area is the south-east, around London. There are other large centres of population and industry in the midlands (Birmingham and Coventry), the northwest (Liverpool and Manchester), the north and northeast (the Yorkshire cities and Tyneside), Scotland (Glasgow), and Northern Ireland (Belfast). The total population of the United Kingdom is 56,628,000 (1985).

ZEFA

Mallaig on Scotland's West Coast, is a fishing port and steamer terminal for Skye and the Hebrides.

The French Emperor Napoleon said in the early 19th century that England was "a nation of shopkeepers". This is no more true of the United Kingdom today than it was of England then, for in Napoleon's time most people still worked on the land. This was before the Industrial Revolution which changed Britain from a farming country to one in which industries (mines, mills, factories, and engineering works) were of prime importance. (See INDUSTRIAL REVOLUTION.)

Out of every 100 people at work in Great Britain, fewer than 2 now work on the land (that is, in farming or forestry). Some 20 out of every 100 workers are employed in the manufacturing industries. These include chemicals, metals, textiles and clothing, engineering, food and drink, and others. Roughly 4 out of every 100 work in the building industries. Two out of every 100 work either in mining and quarrying, or in the gas, electricity, and water supply industries.

Shopkeeping does play quite a large part in British life, and 8 out of every 100 workers are involved in the retail trade, that is, in selling goods to the public. Transport and communications, too, are important, with roughly 5 out of every 100 workers, and so is national and local government service with about 6 out of every 100. That still leaves a large group, about a third of the total number of workers, who are to be found in the so-called "service" industries (leisure, travel, restaurants); in professions (such as law and medicine); in business (such as banking and insurance); and scientific work of one kind or another. Of the 21 million people in Britain who are employed, nearly 9 million are women. Another 2.6 million people are self-employed.

FACTS ABOUT THE UNITED KINGDOM

AREA: 244,100 square kilometres (94,248 square miles).
POPULATION: 56,751,000 (1987).
GOVERNMENT: Constitutional monarchy. Parliament consists of House of Commons and House of Lords.
CAPITAL: London (Edinburgh is the capital of Scotland, Cardiff is the capital of Wales, and Belfast is the capital of Northern Ireland).
GEOGRAPHICAL FEATURES: Generally speaking, Scotland and Wales are mountainous or hilly, whereas the greater part of England consists of much lower land—though not necessarily flat. The highest mountain is Ben Nevis in the western Highlands of Scotland; the longest river is the Severn, flowing into the Bristol Channel; the largest lake is Loch Lomond in west central Scotland.
CHIEF PRODUCTS: Manufactured goods, coal, iron, steel, natural gas, livestock, dairy produce, farm crops.
CHIEF EXPORTS: Machinery, commercial vehicles, aerospace equipment, chemicals, electrical and electronic equipment, oil, textiles and clothing.
CHIEF IMPORTS: Machinery, cars, manufactured goods, foodstuffs, raw materials (hides and skins, timber, wood pulp, rubber, wool, cotton, metal ores, and minerals), chemicals, metals.
IMPORTANT CITIES: London, Birmingham, Glasgow, Liverpool, Manchester, Leeds, Sheffield, Edinburgh, Bristol, Coventry, Nottingham, Hull, Bradford, Leicester, Stoke-on-Trent, Wolverhampton, Cardiff, Newcastle upon Tyne, Portsmouth, Plymouth, Derby, Southampton.
EDUCATION: Children must attend school between the ages of 5 and 16.

Unemployment, particularly among young school-leavers and in parts of the country with older industries (such as northeast England) has become a serious problem in recent years. One reason for this is the change that has been overtaking Britain's industries. Industries such as iron and steel, shipbuilding, and heavy engineering have declined. Newer industries, such as electronics and computers, have been set up but seldom need such large numbers of workers as the old industries.

Important manufacturing industries in Great Britain include metals, mechanical engineering, and metal goods; electrical and instrument engineering; motor vehicles and shipbuilding; chemicals, coal, and petroleum products; food and drink processing; and textiles and clothing. The older industries of iron and steel, shipbuilding, textiles, and heavy engineering, are still largely located in the traditional industrial areas of the west midlands, centred on Birmingham; the northwest, around Manchester and Liverpool; the northeast around Newcastle and Teeside; central Scotland, near Glasgow; south Wales; and Northern Ireland around Belfast. Other industries such as food processing, electronics, and light engineering are more widely distributed. London and the southeast of England is the country's leading industrial region; other centres are found around Bristol in the southwest, Southampton, on the south coast, and Aberdeen in northeast Scotland.

ZEFA

London's Tower Bridge spans the River Thames in the heart of the city.

Britain has a large and successful aerospace industry, making aircraft, aircraft engines, and space satellites. It is also an important producer of electronics, plastics, medicines, pottery, glass, books, and a wide range of metal goods ranging from costly jewellery to needles and pins.

England is the most densely populated part of the United Kingdom, with an average of roughly 361 people to every square kilometre of land. By contrast, Scotland has only 66 people on average to each square kilometre. Greater London is easily the largest city, with more than 6 million people. Other large cities include Birmingham, Glasgow, Leeds, Sheffield, Liverpool, Bradford, Manchester, Edinburgh, Bristol, Coventry, and Cardiff.

The railways form a network covering most of the country. Services operate over more than 16,000 kilometres (10,000 miles) of track. The United Kingdom has an extensive road system. Of 370,000 (230,000 miles) of public roads, about 3,000 kilometres (1,875 miles) are motorways. Over 20 million motor vehicles of all kinds crowd the roads.

In certain parts of Britain inland water transport is important. About 3,200 kilometres (2,000 miles) of canal are run by the British Waterways Board, though only 550 kilometres (340 miles) are used by freight barges. Canal improvement schemes are helping bring back traffic to the canals.

Britain has a number of busy ports, the busiest being the oil terminal at Sullom Voe in the Shetlands which handles oil and gas from the North Sea. Other chief ports are London, Milford Haven, Tees and Hartlepool, Forth, Grimsby, and Southampton.

London's Heathrow is the world's busiest airport for international traffic. London has a second large airport at Gatwick. Other airports include Manchester, Glasgow, Aberdeen, Luton, Birmingham, and Belfast.

Britain is part of the European Economic Community, with which much of its trade is conducted. Even so, it still has worldwide links with other members of the Commonwealth. (See EUROPEAN COMMUNITIES; COMMONWEALTH, THE.)

Government

England was united as a kingdom more than a thousand years ago. Wales became part of the kingdom during the Middle Ages. The thrones of England and Scotland were united in 1603 under James I, and from 1707 there was a single parliament of Great Britain with authority over England, Wales, and Scotland. In 1800 the Irish parliament was joined to that of Great Britain, completing the union of the United Kingdom. However, in 1922 the southern part of Ireland (now the Republic of Ireland) became a separate and self-governing country. The six counties of Northern Ireland chose to remain within the United Kingdom.

Government in the United Kingdom is carried on at three main levels. At the top is the sovereign, in whose name and on whose behalf all the important acts of government are carried out. Then comes the central government of the country under parliament. Central government is entrusted with the responsibilities that have to be handled on behalf of the United Kingdom as a whole. Lastly there is local government which provides a wide range of public services to regions, counties, and districts.

These different levels can most easily be explained by starting at the top; that is, with the monarch (Queen Elizabeth II). It is in her name that important acts of government are carried out. These acts of government include treaties (agreements) with other nations, new laws passed by parliament, and the punishment of offenders against the law. Nowadays, however, the Queen must not take part in politics, so government decisions are taken by her advisers instead. The chief of these advisers are the members of the cabinet, led by the prime minister with other ministers in charge of the main government departments (see CABINET; PRIME MINISTER).

Members of the cabinet belong to the dominant political party (see POLITICAL PARTIES) and the cabinet depends on the support of the House of Commons at Westminster, for it can govern the country only so long as it can obtain the majority vote of the House of Commons, that is, the support of most of the members, for any important question. When that support fails, the cabinet must resign and be replaced by another which is approved by parliament. Since a new House of Commons is elected at least once every five years, the cabinet of the day depends on the support of the people of the country. This is what is known as parliamentary democracy. (See DEMOCRACY; PARLIAMENT).

Defence, or preparing the country against the possibility of war, Commonwealth affairs, and foreign affairs are part of the duties of central government. So, too, are trade and agriculture, employment, health, pensions, and education. As money is needed for all this, central government is responsible for the government finance and taxation which provide it.

This broadly describes the central government of the United Kingdom and England. But differences exist in Northern Ireland, Scotland, and to a lesser degree Wales.

Northern Ireland. From 1921 to 1971 the duties of central government were divided between the parliament at Westminster, which includes members of parliament for Northern Ireland (Ulster), and a separate parliament in Belfast. Such matters as education, agriculture, insurance, and domestic subjects were settled by Northern Irish ministers and the parliament in Belfast, while others such as defence, foreign affairs, and postal and customs services were the responsibility of British ministers and the parliament at Westminster. Money raised by taxes was divided between Northern Ireland and the rest of the United Kingdom to pay for the duties performed by each.

Because of the violence in Northern Ireland, the Northern Ireland parliament was suspended in 1972. A secretary of state for Northern Ireland was appointed and Northern Ireland thus came under direct rule from Westminster. Northern Ireland has its own legal system and law courts.

Scotland has some measure of self-government but no parliament of its own. Scottish members of parliament sit at Westminster and Scotland has a secretary of state, a government minister who is a member of the cabinet. Five government departments in Edinburgh are known as the Scottish Office. They are: the Department of Agriculture and Fisheries, the Development Department, the Industry Department, the Education Department, and the Home and Health Department. Other government departments with particular Scottish responsibilities have offices in Scotland.

Scotland has its own system of courts and Scottish law is different from that of England. The two chief law officers for Scotland are the Lord Advocate and the Solicitor General for Scotland.

Wales has no separate parliament. Welsh members of parliament sit at Westminster, and the secretary of state for Wales is a member of the cabinet.

Local Government

Local government is conducted by locally elected councils employing paid officials to provide the services that people need at the local level. These services include housing, education, road maintenance, planning, and social services. The powers and duties of the local authority are decided by parliament and money to pay for the services is made available, in part, by grants from central government.

The organization of local government varies from one part of the United Kingdom to another. England and Wales are divided into counties that are in turn subdivided into districts. Scotland is divided into regions which are also subdivided into districts. Northern Ireland is divided into 26 districts; the county divisions were abolished in 1973.

In 1986 Greater London and the metropolitan counties of England, which contain the major centres of population, lost their local government status, and responsibility for local affairs was placed in the hands of the district councils. Some services such as police, fire fighting, and public transport, shared in common by these districts, are run by joint authorities.

See also the articles ELECTION; EUROPEAN COMMUNITIES; GOVERNMENT.

UNITED NATIONS. The United Nations is an organization of more than 150 countries who of their own free will have decided to work for world peace. It was set up officially on 24 October 1945. As well as trying to maintain peace and security in the world, the United Nations does what it can to develop friendly relations among all peoples and to see that any dispute is settled fairly. Because it encourages respect for other people's rights, the member states have agreed to work together to improve conditions for the poor or homeless, to combat disease, and to help the millions who cannot read or write.

The United Nations (often known simply as the UN) is not the first or the only organization that has been set up with these aims. However, because it includes a great many countries it is proving more successful than the League of Nations to which about 60 countries belonged between 1920 and 1946.

The constitution of the United Nations,that is, the way in which it is organized, is known as the UN Charter. It sets out the purposes of the United Nations, which can be described as follows:

To keep peace by settling quarrels or by taking steps to stop aggression;
To develop friendship among nations, based on respect for the equal rights of peoples and their own choice of government;
To bring about international co-operation in solving the world's problems;
To serve as a centre to help nations to combine in trying to achieve these aims.

To become a member of the United Nations, a country must say it wants peace, be willing to accept the aims of the UN Charter, and be judged by the UN as able to carry out these aims. The Security Council recommends new members and the General Assembly confirms the recommendation. There were 51 original members of the UN. Now there are more than 150, many of them ex-colonies which have become independent. Some of these newer states are very small, but all UN members have equal voting powers, regardless of size. So the original members have less power than formerly.

Naturally, with representatives from so many different countries working together and making speeches there are language problems. These are overcome by having interpreters who translate a speaker's words, as he talks, into six languages: English,

Popperfoto

US Secretary of State Edward R. Stettinus signs the UN Charter at San Francisco, California, in 1945. President Truman is second from the left.

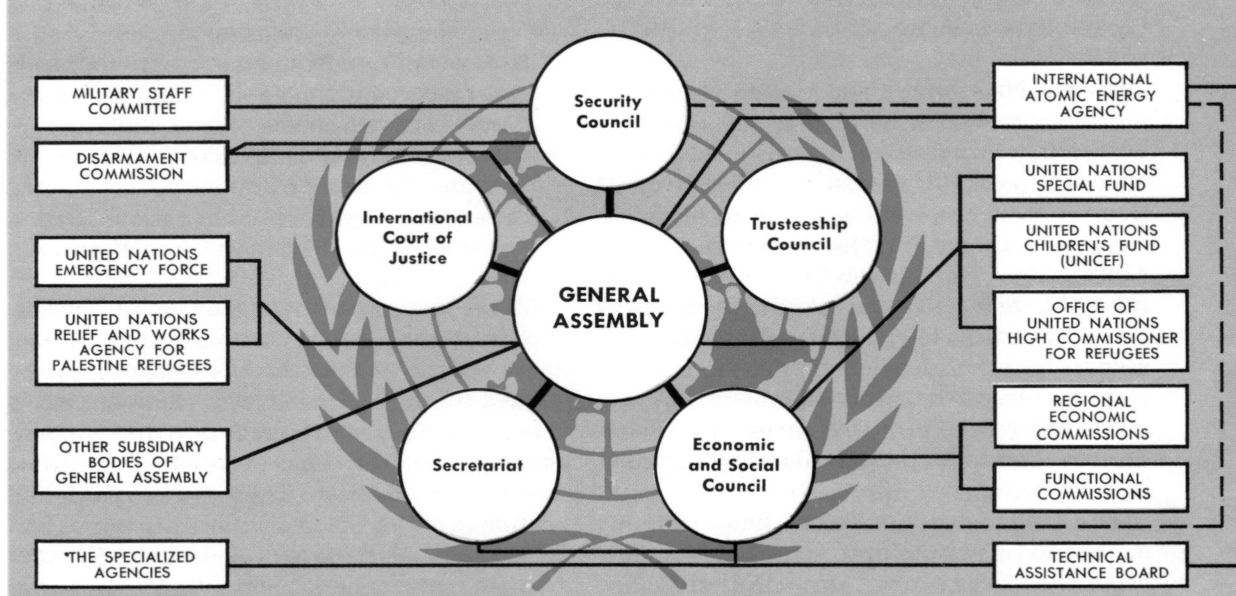

This shows the departments of the United Nations and how they are connected to the General Assembly.

French, Spanish, Russian, Arabic, and Chinese. Anyone who is present may listen to these translations through special earphones with six channels. Assembly documents are published in all six languages.

The Divisions of the United Nations

The United Nations is divided into six main working groups. These are the General Assembly, the Security Council, the Economic and Social Council, the Trusteeship Council, the International Court of Justice, and the Secretariat. The headquarters of the Secretariat is in New York. Most of the other groups usually meet in New York or Geneva in Switzerland, but the International Court sits at The Hague in The Netherlands. Meetings on specialized topics, such as drug abuse or the environment, often take place at UN offices in Vienna (Austria), Nairobi (Kenya), or other regional headquarters.

General Assembly. This is the main body of the UN and meets regularly near the end of the year. Sometimes it may hold special or emergency meetings. All UN members are represented in the General Assembly and each has only one vote, whether it is a large country or a small one. The Assembly is rather like a parliament and expresses the views of the world on the work of the UN and its various other agencies.

When an important question has to be settled by the General Assembly, such as one concerning money or the admission of a new member, at least two-thirds of the members present and voting must be in favour. Although each nation sends many representatives (known as delegates), there is one leader, often the country's foreign minister.

Security Council. This is chiefly responsible for international peace and security and consists of 15 members. Five of them (Great Britain, France, the United States, the Soviet Union, and China) always form part of the Security Council and are known as permanent members. The ten other members each serve for two years after being elected to the Security Council by the General Assembly.

Because the quarrels which come before the Security Council are generally political ones, the 15 nations do not always agree on a settlement. When they are voting to reach a decision any of the 15 members can say "no". When one of the permanent members says "no", this is known as the *veto*. The Security Council can take action only when nine of its members, including all the permanent ones, say "yes", although permanent members may abstain from voting without blocking action by the council. However, there are other ways in which the United Nations can act. For example, the General Assembly can be summoned for an emergency session to deal with a crisis.

When there is a dispute between nations, the Security Council may investigate it and call upon the nations to settle it peacefully. If this does not happen the Council may suggest ways of settling the dispute. If fighting has actually started, the Security Council may call for a cease-fire or for the cutting off of all trade and rail, sea, postal, air, and other means of communication. United Nations officials try to arrange peace talks. If a cease-fire is arranged, a UN peacekeeping force, consisting of troops from member countries, may be sent to the trouble spot.

Economic and Social Council. The United Nations has created a network of organizations to help the poor, the sick, and those who cannot read or write, whatever their race or religion. This work is carried out through the Economic and Social Council, which consists of 54 members who are elected for three years by the General Assembly.

There are a number of groups known as commissions working under the Council, and these specialize in subjects such as human rights, equality of women, trade, population, and drugs. One of these, the Commission on Human Rights, worked out the Universal Declaration of Human Rights which declares that all persons of all nations are entitled to the same rights.

Trusteeship Council. After World War I (1914–18), the colonies of Germany and Turkey were taken from them under a decision made by the League of Nations and were administered by other countries which looked after them until they were ready to rule themselves. The United Nations took over some of these *mandates*, as they were called, as well as some other areas after World War II (1939–45). Agreements known as trusteeship agreements were drawn up to say how the territories would be administered and which country was responsible for them. The agreements are looked after by the Trusteeship Council.

At the beginning, the Trusteeship Council, through the administering countries, looked after ten trust territories with 19 million people. All of them were in Africa or the Pacific Ocean. Most of them have become independent and have joined the United Nations as regular members.

International Court of Justice. This is the legal court of the United Nations and it considers disputes brought before it by countries, which in most cases agree to abide by the Court's decision. It also gives advice on any matters of international law which are placed before it. The Court is composed of 15 judges who are all from different countries and serve for nine years.

All questions before the World Court, as it is sometimes called, are settled by a majority of the judges present, and at least nine must be there. The judges are elected by the General Assembly and the Security Council. The Court may meet in other places besides The Hague.

Secretariat. The actual office staff of the United Nations make up the Secretariat, which prepares the work for the delegates and helps to carry out UN decisions. There are about 16,000 members of the Secretariat and they are from almost every member country. They have agreed to carry out the work of the United Nations, regardless of the country from which they come. Most of them work at the UN headquarters in New York, but others live throughout the world wherever they are needed. At the head of the Secretariat is the secretary-general. It is his job to bring before the United Nations any matter which threatens or breaks international peace and security, and to report each year on the work of the organization to the General Assembly.

The secretary-general played an important part when there was risk of war over Suez (1956) and Cuba (1962). So far there have been five secretaries-general of the United Nations: Trygve Lie (Norway), Dag Hammarskjöld (Sweden), U Thant (Burma), Kurt Waldheim (Austria), and Javier Pérez de Cuéllar (Peru).

Other special groups. As well as its many committees the United Nations has several branches which deal with special subjects.

The UN Children's Fund, generally called UNICEF, was set up after World War II to meet the emergency needs of children in Europe, but it is now permanent and helps many millions of mothers and children in the poorer parts of the world.

The UN High Commissioner for Refugees protects and helps more than 10 million refugees and displaced persons throughout the world and tries to assist those who are homeless in finding a new job and a new life in another country.

The United Nations also tries to help poor countries by sharing with them the knowledge and experience which some other countries have gained. This work, known as technical assistance, covers all sorts of activities, such as farming, engineering, health, railways, and fishing.

Organizations linked with the UN

Directly related to the United Nations are 16 special organizations which bring people throughout the world together to work on special problems which they all have in common. They are independent groups and may include some countries which do not belong to the United Nations. Most of them keep in contact with the UN through the Economic and Social Council.

The Food and Agriculture Organization of the United Nations (FAO) has the great task of trying to get supplies of food fairly distributed over the world. Because millions of people, particularly in the poorer parts of the world, do not have enough to eat, the experts of the

Popperfoto

The Chinese deputy foreign minister, Chiao Kuan-hua, speaking at the United Nations General Assembly, 1971.

FAO help governments to improve methods of farming, to fight animal and plant diseases, and to overcome waste of land and erosion (wearing away) of soil. The FAO has its headquarters in Rome.

The United Nations Educational, Scientific, and Cultural Organization (UNESCO) has its headquarters in Paris. It tries to educate the many millions of people, young and old, who cannot read or write and are able to use only very simple tools. This kind of education consists not only of book-learning but also of easy rules for health and simple methods of farming and industry. It aims at giving everyone the opportunity to go to school. UNESCO also spreads scientific knowledge so that people may live under better conditions.

The World Health Organization (WHO), with headquarters at Geneva, aims at fighting disease and improving the health of the minds and bodies of people everywhere. The WHO organizes worldwide campaigns against diseases such as malaria and tuberculosis which kill millions of people every year. It tries to prevent diseases from starting or spreading by looking after the health of babies, inoculating people, and teaching health workers how to use new drugs. The WHO also advises governments on many health matters, and it has special services to warn doctors about epidemics which may have started somewhere in the world.

Another of the specialized agencies is the

International Maritime Organization (IMO) which has its headquarters in London. It deals with the world's shipping and aims at improving safety at sea, and removing difficulties for users of ships.

The other nine agencies connected with the United Nations are just as important. The International Labour Organization (ILO), founded in 1919, tries to improve people's conditions of work. There are also the International Bank, the International Monetary Fund, the International Finance Corporation, the International Atomic Energy Agency, the Universal Postal Union, the World Meteorological Organization, the International Civil Aviation Organization, and the International Telecommunications Union.

How the United Nations was Formed

In October 1943, the United Kingdom, the USSR, the United States, and China agreed to set up an international organization to keep the peace. The same four countries had talks at Dumbarton Oaks, a large house in Washington, DC, during September 1944 to exchange ideas.

The difficult question of how to vote in the Security Council was settled at another meeting of statesmen at Yalta in the USSR in February 1945. It was also decided to hold a UN conference at San Francisco later in the year. This met from April to June 1945 and, after much work, the United Nations Charter was signed on 26 June and became effective on 24 October when the necessary number of countries ratified (confirmed) it.

The nations that met at San Francisco came with the purpose of setting up a permanent world organization which would save future generations from war and would have a broader programme of work than the League of Nations. None of them wanted to create a world government, which is why the UN does not pass laws. Each nation still keeps its own powers, and the UN Charter forbids interference in the local affairs of a member country. The United Nations cannot impose taxes of any kind. Each nation pays its share of the expenses of the UN.

UNITED STATES OF AMERICA.

One of the world's largest countries, the United States of America extends across the North American continent from the Atlantic Ocean on the east to the Pacific Ocean on the west. It is composed of 50 states and the District of Columbia. Forty-eight of the states lie between Canada on the north and Mexico and the Gulf of Mexico on the south. The 49th state, Alaska, lies northwest of Canada. The 50th state, Hawaii, is a group of islands in the Pacific Ocean.

The United States ranks fourth in both area and population among the nations of the world. It is the world's wealthiest country, having fertile lands, huge forests, and extensive mineral wealth. Great cities and industries have been built, and vast farmlands have been developed.

The people of the United States are generally called Americans. They include peoples of every nationality, race, and religion. Together, they form a highly uniform nation. Americans live under a democratic type of government that

Courtesy, The Library of Congress

Part of the original document of the Constitution of the United States of America, 17 September 1787.

Orville Andrews from National Audubon Society

A satellite photograph of the eastern coast of the United States. Chesapeake Bay and Albemarle Sound can be recognized.

gives them freedom and opportunity. They are well educated and have attained one of the highest standards of living in the world.

The Landscape

The *Atlantic Coastal Plain* extends from Cape Cod, Massachusetts, southward to Florida, and from there the *Gulf Coastal Plain* continues westward into Mexico. This region is mostly flat, seldom rising more than 150 metres (500 feet) above sea-level. Swamps, marshes, and lagoons occur in many places along the coasts of Virginia, North Carolina, Florida, and Louisiana. Sand dunes and offshore islands are common.

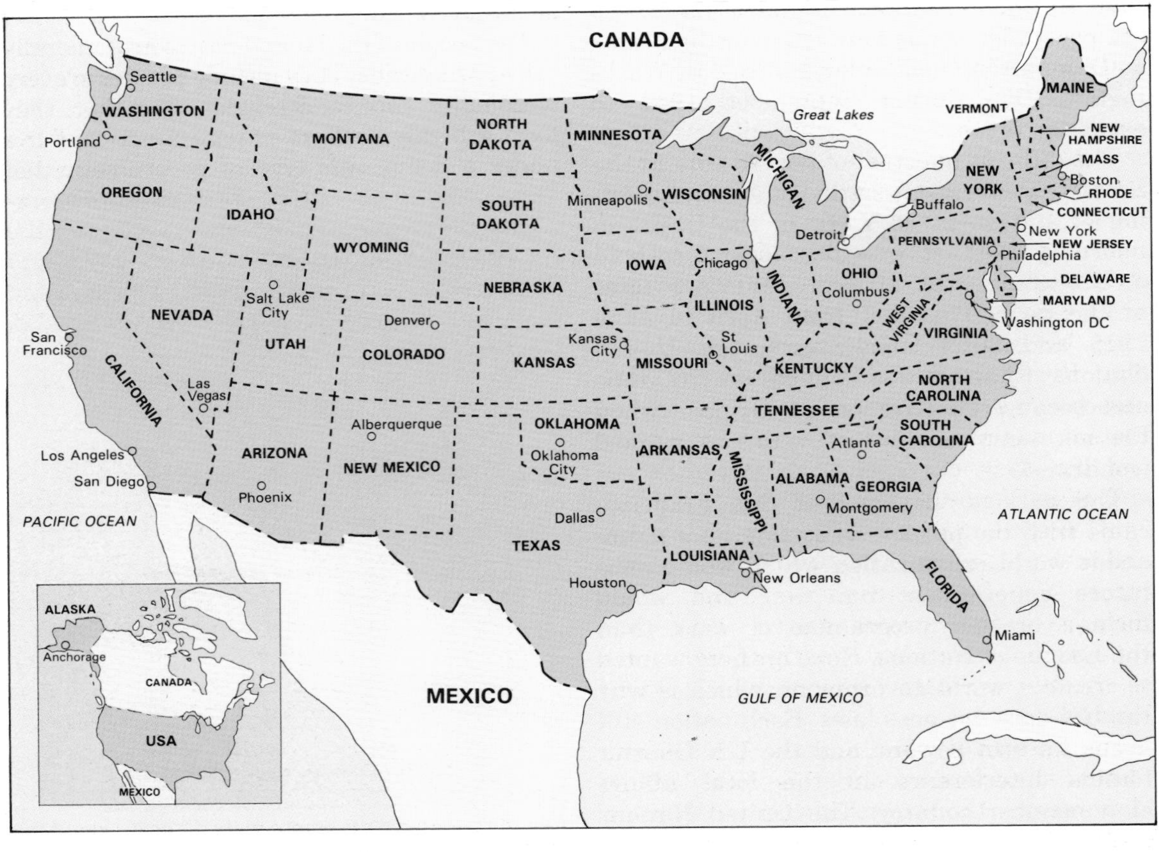

Between Cape Cod and New York City, the Coastal Plain is narrow and includes the islands of Nantucket, Martha's Vineyard, and Long Island. Between this lowland and the higher Piedmont Plateau is the fall line, so called because of falls or rapids that occur at the point the streams pass from the resistant rocks of the Piedmont to the softer material of the coastal plain, which is more easily worn down.

The *Appalachian Mountains* are composed of a wide belt of low mountains and plateaus that extend from northern New England southwestward to central Alabama. East of the Hudson River Valley are several areas of low, rounded mountain ranges, including the White Mountains of New Hampshire, the Green Mountains of Vermont, and the Berkshire Hills of Massachusetts. One of the highest peaks in the Appalachians is Mount Washington at 1,917 metres (6,288 feet), in the White Mountains of northern New Hampshire. (See APPALACHIAN MOUNTAINS.)

The northeast was once covered by great, slowly moving ice sheets, or glaciers. As the glaciers melted, they left many of the features that are common today. Among them are rounded hills, low ridges, hundreds of lakes, and countless large boulders.

West of the Hudson River are the Adirondack and Catskill mountains of New York, separated by the Mohawk River Valley. Mount Marcy rises to 1,629 metres (5,344 feet) and is the highest point in the state. Further to the southwest, the Appalachian Mountains are composed of many separate ridges, ranges, and plateaus, including the famous Blue Ridge Mountains of Virginia and North Carolina; the Great Smoky Mountains of Tennessee and North Carolina; the Cumberland Plateau, mainly in Kentucky and Tennessee; and the Allegheny Plateau of Pennsylvania and West Virginia. Mount Mitchell rises to 2,037 metres (6,684 feet) in North Carolina and is the highest peak in the eastern United States. Not all of this region is mountainous. Included in it are some gently rolling river valleys that provide useful farmland, such as the Shenandoah Valley of northwestern Virginia.

The Allegheny Plateau and Cumberland Plateau slope westward from the Appalachian Mountains to the Interior Plains and the Gulf Coastal Plain. Heights vary from about 1,200 down to less than 300 metres (4,000 to 1,000 feet). The plateaus are noted for their many caves, of which Mammoth Cave in Kentucky is among the world's largest.

Josef Muench

The cypress trees are covered with moss in this coastal swampland area of southern Louisiana.

The *Interior Plains* are the largest of the country's land regions, stretching from the Appalachians to the Rocky Mountains. Included are the Central Plains, which form the eastern part of the region, and the Great Plains, lying to the west. Elevations vary from sea-level to more than 1,500 metres (5,000 feet).

Courtesy, State of Connecticut Development Commission

Autumn countryside in Connecticut, on the eastern seaboard of the United States.

Far left: Mount Philo, Vermont. **Left:** The Mammoth Cave National Park in west central Kentucky is noted for its underground passageways. The cave's high, vaulted rooms are filled with unusual onyx and limestone formations.

Courtesy, Vermont Development Department

The easternmost part of the Central Plains merges gradually with the hilly lands of the Allegheny and Cumberland plateaus. The northern part was once covered by glaciers, which left layers of fertile soil when they melted. The glaciers also left other surface features, such as moraines, drumlins, eskers, lakes, and ponds (see GLACIER AND GLACIATION).

The Great Plains are an almost flat expanse of land between Canada on the north and Mexico on the south, rising gradually westward from the Mississippi River to the Rocky Mountains. The boundary between the Great and Central Plains is roughly the 500-millimetre (20-inch) rainfall line. The Great Plains, west of the line, generally receive less than 500 millimetres (20 inches) of rainfall annually; the Central Plains, east of the line, usually receive more. Rising above these plains are the Black Hills of South Dakota and Wyoming, which include the highest elevations east of the Rocky Mountains. Also within the region are the *Interior Highlands*, which lie mostly in southern Missouri and northern Arkansas. They include the Ozark, Boston, and Ouachita mountains. Here, elevations range from 150 to 885 metres (500 to 2,900 feet).

Bordering the northern Great Lakes is the *Superior Upland*, a region of low hills in northern Minnesota, Wisconsin, and Michigan. Among them is the famous iron-rich Mesabi Range of Minnesota, and the Porcupine and Huron mountains of Michigan. This forest-covered region, which extends northward as the Laurentian Upland of Canada, is rich in iron, copper, and other mineral deposits (see also CANADIAN SHIELD).

The *Rocky Mountains* form the eastern edge of a great highland area. They extend for more than 1,900 kilometres (1,200 miles) within the United States, from the Canadian border into Mexico. Many peaks rise more than 4,200 metres (14,000 feet) above sea-level. The Rockies consist of many ranges, basins, and valleys. The northern section is mostly in Idaho and Montana, with elevations up to 3,600 metres (12,000 feet). Among the major mountain groups are the Clearwater, Salmon River, Bitteroot and Lewis ranges. Included in the Middle Rockies are Yellowstone National Park, Grand Teton National Park, the Big Horn Mountains of Wyoming, and the Wasatch and Uinta mountains of Utah. This area is known for its spectacular scenery, such as Yellowstone's hot springs, geysers, and waterfalls (see YELLOWSTONE NATIONAL PARK). A cluster of broad flat areas within this region is known as the Wyoming Basin, which was used as a route of travel by many pioneer wagon trains. The Southern Rockies extend from southeastern Wyoming across Colorado into northern New Mexico. Fifty-three named peaks in Colorado are more than 4,200 metres (14,000 feet) high, hence early travellers generally avoided this region. Among the well-known sights of the region are Rocky Mountain National Park, Pikes Peak,

Mount Elbert, and the Garden of the Gods.

The *Interior Plateaus and Basins* lie between the Rockies on the east and the Sierra Nevada and Cascade Mountains to the West. This region, mostly dry and covered with desert vegetation, is composed of three large subdivisions: the Columbia Plateau, the Great Basin, and the Colorado Plateau.

The Columbia Plateau extends across eastern Washington and Oregon and southern Idaho. Much of the area is drained by the Columbia River and its tributaries. The rolling surface consists of many layers of volcanic lava, which flowed from volcanic cones and fissures thousands of years ago. The main rivers of the area have cut deep canyons through the lava and mountain ranges. The Snake River canyon is more than 1,500 metres (5,000 feet) deep in places, and Hell's Canyon reaches a depth of more than 2,400 metres (7,900 feet).

The Great Basin borders the Columbia Plateau on the south and includes most of Nevada and parts of California, Utah, Arizona, New Mexico, and Texas. It is mostly desert lowland, broken by widely separated mountain ranges. There are patches of irrigated land, which appear as rich oases. Included are the Salt Lake City area of Utah; the Colorado River Valley near Yuma, Arizona; and the Imperial Valley of southern California. Most streams in this region never reach the sea, but end in shallow salt lakes. In the north, basin elevations are more than a mile above sea-level. Towards the Mexican border, elevations are much lower. Death Valley and the Imperial Valley of California are mostly below sea-level.

The Colorado Plateau occupies much of eastern Utah, western Colorado, northern Arizona, and northwestern New Mexico. The Colorado River and its tributaries drain most

Montana Highway Commission (top left); Ray Manley-Shostal/EB Inc. (bottom left); Herb and Dorothy McLaughlin (above)

Top left: Bitterroot National Forest in western Montana contains many mountain lakes. It is one of 11 national forests in Montana. **Bottom left**: Mountainous region with glacier-filled valley, near Petersburg, Alaska. **Above**: Monument Valley, Arizona, contains striking rock formations created by erosion.

Alpha Photo Associates, Inc.

Woodland on Washington State's Pacific Coast.

of the region. The river flows southwestward from its source in the high Rockies, cutting deep canyons along its route (see COLORADO RIVER.) In northern Arizona it has carved the spectacular Grand Canyon (see GRAND CANYON). Other features include remarkable natural bridges in Utah and the petrified forest of Arizona.

The *Pacific Mountain region* extends along the Pacific Coast, including the high Sierra Nevada and Cascade Mountains, and the lower Coast Ranges and Klamath Mountains. The Sierra Nevada, in California, is known for its jagged peaks, high altitude lakes, deep canyons, and spectacular waterfalls. Mount Whitney reaches 4,418 metres (14,495 feet) above sea-level, the highest point in the United States, excluding Alaska (see also SIERRA NEVADA).

The Cascade Mountains are unusual in the United States because they include many volcanic peaks. They extend from northern California, through Oregon, to north central Washington. Mount Lassen, California, erupted in 1914 and displayed volcanic activity until 1921. The most recently active volcano is Mount St. Helens, Washington, which erupted violently in 1980. Within the Cascade Range, the highest peaks are Mount Rainier, Washington, at 4,392 metres (14,410 feet) and Mount Shasta, California, at 4,316 metres (14,162 feet). Ancient Mount Mazama, Oregon, has a 10-kilometre (6-mile) wide crater filled with water, called Crater Lake (see also CASCADE MOUNTAINS).

The Coast Ranges border the Pacific Ocean in Washington, Oregon, and California. Elevations are commonly between 600 and 1,200 metres (2,000 and 4,000 feet), although some peaks are higher. Two of the best natural harbours in the United States, Puget Sound and San Francisco Bay, are formed by breaks in these ranges.

Alaska is composed mainly of three regions: the Arctic Slope, the Central Plateau, and the Pacific Mountains. The Arctic Slope lies north of the Brooks Range. It is generally level, and is drained by rivers flowing northward to the Arctic Ocean. Alaska's largest land region is the Central Plateau, which is a rugged upland that reaches over 2,800 metres (9,200 feet) in the Brooks Range. The Pacific Mountains curve along the southern coast from the Aleutian Islands, to the Alaska Range, then southward in the Alaskan panhandle. Mount McKinley, rising to 6,194 metres (20,320 feet), in the Alaska Range, is the highest point in North America. (See also ALASKA.)

Hawaii is composed of eight large islands and many smaller ones. The eight main islands are part of a volcanic mountain chain that is mostly submerged. The highest peaks, both on the largest island, Hawaii, are Mauna Kea at 4,201 metres (13,784 feet), and Mauna Loa at 4,170 metres (13,680 feet). Kilauea, on the same island, has the largest active volcanic crater in the world. (See also HAWAII.)

The Sierra Nevada Range of California, seen from Glacier Point in Yosemite National Park. Half Dome, a glaciated bedrock knob, is on the left.

Josef Muench

The Climate

The climate of the United States is as varied as its landscape. However, the country may be divided into eight major climatic regions, in which the average weather conditions, such as temperature and rainfall, are similar.

The *humid continental* region includes all of the northeastern United States. Rainfall is highest towards the east. The Atlantic coast receives an average of 1,000 to 1,500 millimetres (40 to 60 inches) of precipitation (rain and melted snow) annually, while areas further westward receive 500 to 1,000 millimetres (20 to 40 inches). Fortunately, most of this region receives its heaviest precipitation during the growing season, which is that period between the last frost in the spring and the first frost in autumn. Places with a humid continental climate have a wide seasonal range of temperatures and a growing season of three to seven months. January temperatures usually average below 0°C (32°F) and it is not uncommon for daily temperatures to drop below −18°C (0°F). Summers are often hot and humid, with temperatures occasionally rising above 38°C (100°F).

A *humid subtropical* climate covers the southeastern part of the country. The average temperature of the coldest month is generally above freezing. Summers are long and warm. Rainfall is heaviest in the eastern part of the region, with an average of up to 1,500 millimetres (60 inches) in Florida and Louisiana, decreasing to 500 millimetres (20 inches) in central Texas. Snow is rare, except in the mountainous areas. The growing season varies from seven months in the north to almost a full year in Florida and southern Texas.

A *semi-arid* climate extends over most of the Great Plains and much of the Colorado and Columbia plateaus and the Wyoming Basin. Rainfall in this area generally varies from 250 to 500 millimetres (10 to 20 inches) per year, and there is a wide seasonal range of temperature. Winters are very cold, and summer temperatures above 38°C (100°F) are not unusual.

Desert climate covers the Great Basin of Nevada and neighbouring states. Rainfall is usually less than 250 millimetres (10 inches) per year. Summer temperatures may be extremely high; winter days are generally warm, but nights are cool. In the Imperial Valley, the growing season lasts the whole year round.

A *marine temperate* climate extends along the Pacific Coast from northern California almost to the Alaska Peninsula. This area has cool summers and mild winters. Frosts are rare. Rainfall is abundant and usually heavier in the winter months, with yearly averages from 750 to 3,800 millimetres (30 to 150 inches). Fog is common, and there are many cloudy days. The growing season ranges from three to eight months.

Subtropical dry, or Mediterranean, climate covers much of California. This region is noted for hot, dry summers and cool, moist winters. Almost no rain falls from May to October, but 400 to 500 millimetres (15 to 20 inches) occur during the remainder of the year. Snow is rare except in the Sierra Nevada. Summer temperatures are especially high in the Central Valley of California, and are much cooler along the coast. The growing season is from eight months to the whole year.

Charlie Ott from National Audubon Society

The tundra region of Alaska, where no trees grow.

The *Arctic and subarctic* climatic regions cover most of Alaska. The Arctic region is a small area along the northern coast, and its temperatures are moderated by the Arctic Ocean. The subarctic area has the widest range of temperatures in all of the United States. Summers are short and warm; winters are long and extremely cold. Most of the region has about 500 millimetres (20 inches) of rainfall annually. In the Arctic region, temperatures seldom rise above 10°C (50°F) in summer, while in the subarctic interior they may occasionally reach 32°C (90°F). Temperatures average below freezing for up to ten months per year.

Hawaii has a *tropical* climate, except at the higher elevations. Temperatures average about 24°C (75°F) year-round in the lowlands, but may drop to −6°C (20°F) in the mountains. Rainfall varies greatly over the islands. Honolulu, on Oahu, receives about 800 millimetres (32 inches) annually, while up to 11,887 millimetres (468 inches) have been recorded on the summit of Kauai Island.

Weather extremes. The hottest temperature ever recorded in the United States was 56.6°C (134°F), in July 1913, at Death Valley, California. The coldest temperature, −62°C (−80°F), was recorded in Alaska, in 1971. Death Valley is the driest area, averaging less than 50 millimetres (2 inches) of rainfall annually. The greatest snowfall occurs in the high mountains, with Paradise Inn, Washington, recording more than 15,240 millimetres (600 inches) per year. About 600 tornadoes strike the United States each year, mostly in the Great Plains states, and an annual average of four hurricanes strike the Atlantic or Gulf coasts.

Plant and Animal Life

The United States may be divided into four major regions based on plant and animal life: forest, grassland, desert, and tundra. Climate greatly affects the types of vegetation in any area. Trees will usually grow where rainfall is heaviest, and grasslands develop where the rainfall is lighter or highly seasonal. Where rainfall is below 250 milli-

Courtesy, Wyoming Travel Commission

American elk (wapiti), seen here in Montana, were once numerous but are now confined to the Rocky Mountains.

metres (10 inches), deserts may occur, while tundra vegetation grows at high altitudes and in the Arctic and subarctic regions of Alaska.

Forests once covered most of the eastern third of the nation, and small patches remain. Some of the trees, such as pine and hemlock, are evergreen and needle-leaved; others, such as oak, hickory, birch, and maple are broad-leaved and deciduous, shedding their leaves in winter. A third type, mainly in the South, is composed of evergreen broad-leaved trees. The white pine forests in Maine and in northern Michigan, Wisconsin, and Minnesota were the basis of an early timber industry. Now, forestry is more important in the southern states, where pine, oak, and walnut are used in the manufacture of paper, furniture, and other timber products. Many kinds of animal live in the eastern forest lands, including black bear, beaver, otter, deer, and squirrel. Moose, lynx, wolverine, and marten are found mostly in the northeast; possum, rabbit, fox, and raccoon are numerous in the South. Reptiles are also more common in the South, including the alligator and rattlesnake, copperhead, water moccasin, and coral snake.

Needle-leaved forests are extensive in the Rocky Mountains and parts of California, Oregon, and Washington. There are also patches of broad-leaved aspen and birch, plus some oak and maple. Tallest of all living plants are the giant redwoods of California, some more than 100 metres (350 feet) in height. Forests of the Pacific Northwest support the nation's leading lumbering activities. Animals living in these western forests include the black bear, grizzly bear, elk, deer, raccoon, and muskrat. Along the Pacific Coast are many seals and sea-lions.

The forests of Alaska are extensive along the Pacific Coast and on much of the Central Plateau. Trees common along the coast are spruce, hemlock, and cedar; on the plateau are mixed stands of spruce, birch, poplar, aspen, and cottonwood. Animals are abundant, including caribou, moose, elk, deer, bear, fox, wolf, and many smaller animals.

Hawaii's tropical trees are mostly evergreen, including coconut, mango, mulberry, and papaya. Animal life, while not abundant, includes deer, mongoose, lizards, and rodents.

Grasslands, before settlement, covered much of interior North America. On the Central Plains, wild grasses once grew as tall as a man. Towards the west, where there was less rainfall, the grasses became gradually shorter. Such tall grasses are often called prairie; short grasslands are referred to as steppe. Great herds of buffalo once grazed these areas, which today are devoted to wheat, barley, and cattle raising. Buffalo have almost disappeared; the coyote, prairie dog, and jackrabbit remain.

Deserts, in the United States, cover most of Nevada and parts of Utah, Arizona, California, and New Mexico. Sagebrush, yucca, and cactus are common, but are replaced by pine and juniper on the mountain ranges. One type of cactus, the saguaro, grows to a height of 15 metres (50 feet) in southern Arizona. Among the animals of the desert are the iguana, horned toad, Gila monster, and a variety of snakes.

Plants in the Arctic region of Alaska include mosses, lichens, and shrubs. The animal life of Alaska includes the caribou, walrus, musk-ox, seal, and polar bear.

Rivers and Lakes

The United States has some of the largest and the most useful rivers in the world. The Mississippi-Missouri river system is 6,210 kilometres (3,860 miles) long and with its tributaries, such as the Ohio, Illinois, Arkansas, and Platte, drains a large part of the Interior Plains. Other important rivers include the Hudson, Tennessee, Colorado, Columbia, and Rio Grande. The dividing line between the eastward- and westward-flowing rivers runs through the Rocky Mountains and is called the Continental Divide.

Fred Bond

The Mississippi River at Hannibal, Missouri. It is one of the world's longest rivers.

The Great Lakes form one of the world's most important inland waterways. They provide a transport route for iron ore, wheat, coal, and other products from Lakes Superior and Michigan on the west, to Lakes Huron, Erie, and Ontario on the east, and through the St. Lawrence Seaway to the Atlantic Ocean. Other large bodies of water include the Great Salt Lake of Utah, Lake of the Woods in northern Minnesota, Lake Okeechobee in Florida, and Lake Ponchartrain in Louisiana. (There are separate articles on most of these rivers and lakes.)

The People

The United States is often called a "melting pot", because many racial and nationality groups make up its population. Many traditions and ways of living have been mixed together. Most people emigrating to the United States were from Europe, but in recent years large numbers have come from Asia and Latin America.

The first European settlers found the land already inhabited by North American Indians, but the Indians were soon conquered or driven westward. Spaniards occupied Florida, the Southwest, and the West Coast. English settlers occupied the Atlantic Coast, along with others from Scotland, Ireland, Holland, France, and Germany.

Black Africans were imported as slaves, beginning in 1619, to work on plantations of indigo, tobacco, rice, and cotton. Immigration from Scandinavia and the Orient increased after the mid-19th century, followed by great numbers from Germany, Italy, eastern Europe, and Russia about 1900.

Beginning in 1790, the United States government has conducted a census of population every ten years. The census of 1980 indicated a total population of 226,504,825. The average increase of population is more than 2.3 million persons per year. The centre of population in 1790 was 37 kilometres (23 miles) east of Baltimore, Maryland; by 1980 it had moved more than 1,200 kilometres (750 miles) westward, into the state of Missouri.

During the same period, the population has become increasingly urban. By 1980, more than 160 cities had a population greater than 100,000. New York City, with more than 7 million inhabitants was the largest, followed by Los Angeles (California), Chicago (Illinois), Houston (Texas), Philadelphia (Pennsylvania), Detroit (Michigan), Dallas (Texas), San Diego (California), and Phoenix (Arizona). (There are separate articles on all these, and many other, American cities.)

Although the trend is towards larger cities, a few states remain chiefly rural. In Vermont, about 68 per cent of the people live in rural areas. Among other states that are largely rural are Mississippi, Alaska, West Virginia, South Dakota, North Dakota, and North Carolina. There are more town and city dwellers in the northeast, although California, Hawaii, and Texas, also have high populations.

The percentage of older people in the United States has increased steadily. Today, the average American citizen can expect to live to about 74 years of age. The average male marries when he is about 23 years old, the average female at age 21.

In 1980, about 83 per cent of the United States population was classified as white. Blacks accounted for 12 per cent, and the remaining 5 per cent was made up largely of Asians and North American Indians. About 9,600,000 foreign-born persons live in the United States. More than half of them came from the United Kingdom, Germany, Poland, the Soviet Union, Italy, Canada, Mexico, and Cuba.

Religion

The Constitution of the United States guarantees freedom of religious worship. This is because the original colonists included many people who came to America to escape religious persecution in other countries. Most of them belonged to some Christian group.

Today most Americans are members of a church group. About 54 per cent are Protestant, 37 per cent are Roman Catholic, and 4 per cent are of the Jewish faith. Protestants are divided into many subgroups, such as Episcopalians, Baptists, Methodists, Lutherans, Presbyterians, and Mormons. Other important religious groups include Buddhists, Muslims, and Hindus.

Language

The English, French, and Spanish all held territory during colonial times in what is now the United States. The English-speaking colonies expanded more rapidly, however, and English became the official language when the new nation was established.

The language spoken in the United States differs from that of England, since American English includes many words used by immigrants who mixed English with their own native languages. However, it maintains the same basic grammar and structure. Within the United States, spoken English varies from region to region. These variants are called dialects. Any dialect can usually be understood by any native speaker of American English.

The Economy

The United States is one of the world's leading countries in agricultural and industrial production. It, alone, produces more than one-fifth of the world's total output of goods and services. For many reasons, including an abundance of fertile land, fuel, mineral resources, and hydroelectric power, the United States became the leading commercial and industrial country. A free enterprise system also encouraged the growth of business and industry.

In colonial times most of the people earned a living from agriculture. Others were fur trappers, fishermen, lumbermen, traders, shipbuilders, and innkeepers. Families made many of the everyday things they needed, such as clothing and tools, and raised most of their own food.

As the population grew and transport improved, the fertile farmlands of the interior were settled. Maize became the chief crop of the northern plains, and cotton was dominant in the southeast. Improvements in farm machinery resulted in greater production with fewer workers. The expansion of railways after 1850 changed the course of the American economy from agriculture to industry. By the end of the century, the value of manufactured goods exceeded that of agricultural products for the first time.

Charles E. Rotkin, Photography for Industry

A lumber mill in Roseburg, Oregon: a pondman uses a pike pole to sort the logs being stored and to drive those to be sawn into the log chute.

The invention of the motor vehicle had a major impact on the American economy. Greatly increased motor vehicle manufacture, especially after 1920, increased the need for petroleum products. The oil industry grew to meet the demand. The related chemical industry also grew and created new synthetic materials, such as nylon, rayon, and Dacron for use in clothing. Factory output was stimulated greatly during World Wars I and II, which were especially important in development of the aircraft industry. Since then, most of the increase in employment has been through the manufacture of highly technical products, such as computers, and in the various service industries.

Manufacturing

The Northeast leads the country in manufacturing, followed closely by the Midwest. These two regions include more than half of all manufacturing plants and workers. Within the regions are many of the world's leading industrial cities, such as New York, Chicago, Detroit, Philadelphia, and Cleveland. The area has an excellent transport network, good sources of power, and an abundance of raw materials. The largest industries produce processed foods, primary metals, machinery, transport equipment, and clothing.

The *Food-Processing Industry* leads in the number of manufacturing plants and is among the leaders in the value of goods produced. This industry grew with the movement of people from rural areas to cities. With increased income per family, especially as more women entered the workforce, there has been a demand for a greater variety of foods and for foods that are easily prepared.

Meat processing was for many years centred in Chicago. Now, it has moved westward towards the major livestock raising areas, and Chicago is one of several important locations. Others include Omaha, Kansas City, Sioux City, St. Louis, Denver, and Fort Worth. Flour milling is important in Minneapolis, Minnesota and Buffalo, New York.

About half of the nation's sugar supply comes from sugar beets and sugar-cane grown within its boundaries. The rest is imported, largely from the Caribbean area, South America, and the Philippine Islands. Most of the beet-sugar factories are in Michigan and Ohio, the Rocky Mountain states, and California. Sugar-cane mills are in the producing areas of Hawaii, Louisiana, Florida, and Puerto Rico.

The *Metal Industries* include those that process ores directly from mines to those that roll, stretch, and shape various metals. From these primary stages, secondary processes turn the metals into finished products, such as motor vehicles, aircraft, appliances, and machinery. The most important metals are steel, aluminium, copper, lead, and zinc. Steel-making employs most of the primary metal workers, and the United States ranked third in world steel production in 1986. There are five major steel areas in the United States: eastern, Pittsburgh-Youngstown, Chicago-Gary, Birmingham, and western. About three-quarters of the iron ore comes from the northern Great Lakes states and most of the remainder is imported, primarily from South America and West Africa. Coal is provided almost entirely from domestic supplies.

Courtesy, Bethlehem Steel Corporation

Metal ore being refined and turned into finished metal at Bethlehem, Pennsylvania.

Until 1982, the United States led all nations in the production of refined copper, and since that year has been second only to Chile. Copper smelters are generally located near the mines in copper-producing states, such as Arizona, Utah, Montana, and New Mexico. The aluminium industry began in the 1880s, but there was little demand for the metal until it was used extensively in the aircraft industry during World War II (1939–45). Since then the demand for this light and durable metal has increased steadily.

Secondary metal industries include those that make products such as bolts, wire, hardware, transport equipment, and machinery. Most important of these is the motor vehicle industry, which is concentrated in southeastern Michigan but includes assembly plants in many other states. Aircraft manufacture is also spread across many states, although Washington and California provide half of the output by value. Many of the coastal states are engaged in shipbuilding or ship repair, while Pennsylvania and Illinois lead in the manufacture of railway equipment. Most other metal-product industries are concentrated in the Northeast or Midwestern states.

The *Textile and Clothing* industries turn out a variety of products made from cotton, wool, leather, and synthetic fibres. Among these, cotton is the most important in terms of both employment and value. The cotton textile industry began in New England in the late 18th century and flourished because of available water power and a humid climate favourable for spinning cotton thread. By the 1920s North Carolina replaced Massachusetts as the leader in cotton textile manufacture, and the industry had spread from Virginia to Georgia because of cheaper labour, new sources of electric power, air conditioning, and proximity to raw cotton. The South now dominates cotton textile production in the United States.

Woollen manufacturing also began in New England and continues to be of some importance in Boston and its surrounding area. How-

Boeing Co.

Assembly of jet airliners in a Seattle plant. Washington State is a leading producer of aircraft.

The Grand Coulee Dam in northeastern Washington is one of the world's largest man-made structures.

ever, woollen goods have especially suffered in competition with the newer synthetic fibres, such as nylon, acrylic, polyester, rayon, and acetate.

Clothing manufacture employs more people than does the textile industry and is concentrated mainly in a few large cities, such as New York, Chicago, Philadelphia, and Los Angeles. The New York City garment district is particularly famous.

The *Printing and Publishing* industry produces many millions of copies of newspapers, magazines, books, and other reading material each year. Most of the large companies have their headquarters in New York, Pennsylvania, New Jersey, or Illinois, but all other states are also involved significantly in printing and publishing.

Several million Americans work in *Other Industries*, such as those that produce electronic equipment, furniture, glass, cement, paper, rubber, tobacco products, and beverages. Most of these industries are scattered widely throughout the United States, although a few are concentrated in specific areas.

Energy and Power

The United States uses tremendous amounts of power in commerce and industry, and to provide heat and light for homes. Most of the power used in manufacturing comes from fuels such as petroleum, natural gas, and coal. In 1940, coal was the leading source of power, accounting for more than half of the total energy produced. By 1973, it was surpassed by petroleum and natural gas and supplied only one-sixth of the total. Water power accounted for just four per cent. Meanwhile, the first nuclear reactor was completed in 1957, and 71 reactors were in operation within the United States by 1978 for the generation of electricity. In the following year, however, an accident involving a reactor at Three Mile Island, near Harrisburg, Pennsylvania, caused much concern about nuclear radiation and human safety. The construction of nuclear power plants since that time has been greatly reduced, and in some cased discontinued. The electric utility industry remains the single largest consumer of coal in the country. Grand Coulee Dam, in the state of Washington, is the largest producer of water power.

Agriculture

Farms in the United States produce more food than the country can consume, and surplus agricultural products are therefore exported or are stored by the government. The increase in farm production has occurred while the number of farms and farm workers has declined. This is because of an increased use of machinery and fertilizers, and the merging of small farms into larger land holdings. On the modern farm, tractors, combine harvesters, maize and cotton pickers, trucks, hay balers, milking machines, and other equipment have replaced much of the hand labour and animal power of earlier days. The average farm size has increased steadily in recent decades, to about 160 hectares (400 acres), as small farms are abandoned and large farms are increasingly mechanized.

The most important single crop grown in the country is maize, known locally as corn. It is produced in almost every state, but the leading ones are those of the Corn Belt, especially Iowa, Illinois, Indiana, Nebraska, Minnesota, Ohio, and Missouri. The United States produces about as much of this crop as the rest of the world combined.

Wheat is the second most important grain and Kansas is the leading wheat state. North Dakota, Montana, Oklahoma, Illinois, Washington, and Nebraska are also major wheat producers. Oats are grown in the northern Great Lakes states; barley in the Dakotas, Montana, and California; and rice in Texas, Louisiana, and California.

Some crops, such as soya beans, cotton, and tobacco, are called industrial crops because they are used extensively in manufactured products. Soya beans are used for vegetable oil, livestock feed, paints, and plastics. Illinois, Iowa, and Indiana are the leading soya bean states. Cotton also ranks high in value. Texas is by far the leading cotton-producing state, followed by Mississippi, California, and Arkansas.

North Carolina and Kentucky produce more than half of the tobacco crop, but South Carolina, Tennessee, Virginia, and Georgia are also important producers. Peanuts are grown extensively in Georgia, North Carolina, Alabama, Virginia, and Texas.

Large quantities of sugar are produced, both from beets and from cane, but half the sugar consumed in the United States must be imported. Sugar-cane grows best in the warm, humid climates of Hawaii, Louisiana, and Florida; sugar beets do well in the cooler, drier climates.

The cultivation of fruit and vegetables depends largely on markets and climate. Vegetable growing is widespread, but major producing areas are usually near large cities or where the growing season is almost year round. The leading vegetables are white potatoes, tomatoes, lettuce, sweet corn, and beans.

Grapes are the leading fruit by value and are grown mainly in California. Much of the grape crop goes into wine-making, which has expanded rapidly since 1960. The United States also grows huge quantities of citrus fruit and apples, plus peaches, plums, pears,

Courtesy, Iconographic Collection, State Historical Society of Wisconsin

Beginning in the 19th century, several machines were invented that made harvesting easier and quicker. Cyrus McCormick's reaper was one of the first successful machines for harvesting grain. The reaper greatly increased the amount of grain farmers could harvest and helped make the Midwest an important agricultural region.

Courtesy, US Soil Conservation Service, photo by Herrin F. Culver

Contour-planted forest on steep land prevents topsoil from being washed away. This is one method adopted by the US Department of Agriculture to prevent the occurrence of erosion.

and various kinds of melons and berries. Other tree crops, such as walnuts, almonds, pecans, and dates, also yield considerable farm income.

Livestock raising is one of the leading forms of agriculture in the United States. Although the number of dairy cattle has decreased drastically since the 1940s, milk production remains the highest of any country in the world. The breeds of cow have been improved and they are better fed, and in this way milk production per cow has increased steadily. The leading beef-producing state is Texas, but beef cattle are also raised in almost every other state. Pigs are most numerous in the Corn Belt, sheep in the Great Plains and western desert country, and poultry in the Southeast, the Midwest, and near large urban markets.

Mining

The history of mining is similar to that of agriculture, in that production has increased greatly while the number of mines has steadily decreased. A major cause for concern is that the nation's mineral wealth is being rapidly exhausted and its economy is increasingly dependent upon mineral imports.

The petroleum industry began in the United States when Colonel E. L. Drake drilled a successful well near Titusville, Pennsylvania, in 1859. At first the most desired product was kerosene for burning in lamps. The industry did not really boom until the arrival of the mass-produced motor vehicle created a demand for petrol, lubricating oils, and greases.

The major areas of petroleum production have shifted southwestward from Pennsylvania to the Gulf Coast of Texas and Louisiana, then to the Great Plains from Oklahoma to North Dakota, and westward to California. Texas is the leading state in production; Alaska's Prudhoe Bay field, discovered in 1968, is believed to contain the nation's largest oil reserve. The United States is one of the few countries in which natural gas is a major fuel, most of which comes from Texas and Louisiana.

The United States has huge coal resources and is one of the world's leading producers. About 90 per cent of the coal production is in the eastern part of the country, while more than half of the reserves are in the West. West Virginia and Kentucky lead in coal output, but Pennsylvania, Illinois, Ohio, and Virginia are also important.

Iron ore is the most important metal mined in the country. Iron and steel, made from iron ore, are used by many of the most important industries. About three-quarters of the total production comes from the Lake Superior area, especially from the Mesabi Range of Minnesota.

Among the other important metal ores mined in large quantities are copper, lead, zinc, bauxite (for aluminium), and uranium. Ferro-alloys, such as molybdenum and manganese are also significant. Gold and silver mining have long been important in many of the western states.

Non-metallic minerals are especially important to the chemical and construction industries. Florida produces more than 80 per cent of the nation's phosphate, while New Mexico leads in potash. These minerals, along with nitrates extracted from the air, are the basic ingredients of chemical fertilizers to improve crop yields. Sulphur, mainly from the Gulf Coast of Texas and Louisiana, is also produced in great quantities. Salt is pumped from deep wells as brine, mined from deposits of rock salt, or evaporated from sea-water. Tremendous quantities of sand, gravel, and stone, used in cement, concrete, and other building materials, are obtained from quarries throughout the nation.

Forestry and Fishing

The forests of the United States are among the country's most valuable resources. In addition to providing timber, pulp, and paper, and many other wood products, they help to prevent soil erosion and contribute to the beauty of the landscape. More than 80 per cent of the timber is classified as softwood. It comes mostly from such needle-leaf evergreens as the Douglas fir, white pine, and western yellow pine of the Pacific Northwest and Rocky Mountain states, and the southern yellow pine of the South. Naval stores, such as turpentine and rosin, are obtained mainly from southern pines, which are also a major source of cordwood for the manufacture of pulp and paper. Even so, large quantities of wood products must be imported from other countries, especially newsprint from Canada.

The fishing industry has been important since colonial times. All of the coastal areas of the United States have significant fishing industries. California, Texas, Alaska, Louisiana, and Florida are the leading states by value of catch. Menhaden is the fish caught in greatest numbers. It is used mostly for fish oil, fertilizer, and animal feed. More valuable is seafood used for human consumption, such as shrimps, salmon, tuna, oysters, and lobsters.

Transport and Communication

Transport is highly developed in the United States. An era of river canals, in the early 19th century, was followed by the construction of railways throughout the country. However, passenger transport by railways is now only a small part of total passenger movement, and the shipment of freight by railway has also decreased rapidly in recent decades. Private motor vehicles carry about 87 per cent of the inter-city passenger traffic and airlines about 10 per cent. The United States has more motor vehicles, and more miles of road, than any other country in the world.

Pipelines transport more than one-fifth of all inter-city freight, mostly in the form of natural gas, petroleum, and petroleum products. More than 354,000 kilometres (220,000 miles) of pipeline carry oil and gas throughout the nation from the southwestern petroleum fields. Construction of a trans-Alaska pipeline was completed in 1977. Inland waterways carry about one-sixth of the total freight, especially bulky, low-value commodities. Major waterways include the Great Lakes, the Mississippi-Missouri river system, and the New York State Barge Canal.

Communication is mainly by radio, television, telephone, and publications. Newspaper circulation averages more than one paper per family per day, and most families own at least one radio and a television set. Magazine circulation averages more than two issues per person per year, and about 1,000 million books are sold annually. More than 40 per cent of the world's telephones are in the United States. These, along with telegraph, radio, and cable services help to maintain communication both domestically and with foreign countries. More than 31,000 government-owned post offices distribute the mail.

The United States leads all other nations in volume of foreign trade. The main export is machinery of all types, followed by wheat, cotton, tobacco, and other agricultural goods. Coal and coke are also exported. Imports include petroleum, tropical crops, iron and other metal ores, rubber, newsprint, and motor vehicles. Most of the foreign trade is with Canada, Latin America, Western Europe, and Japan. Leading seaports include New York, Baltimore, Miami, Los Angeles, San Francisco, and Seattle. Since the St. Lawrence Seaway was opened in 1959,

Chicago and Detroit have also become centres of foreign trade.

Education

The administration of public (state) education in the United States is largely carried out by state and city governments, although various forms of support are received from the federal government. The Constitution provides for a separation of church and state, hence religious education may not be taught in the publicly run schools. Public education usually includes eight years at the primary level, then four years of high (secondary) school. It is generally free at high school, and attendance is compulsory from ages 7 to 16. Almost one-quarter of the nation's population is enrolled in some type of school. About 90 per cent of the elementary and high school students are in public, tax-supported schools, while the remainder are mostly in Roman Catholic institutions. More than 3,000 colleges and universities offer advanced levels of training, with state-supported institutions having three-quarters of the total enrolment. More federal and local tax money is spent on education than on any other item except national defence.

Government

The government of the United States is organized as laid down in the Constitution of the United States, drawn up in 1787 and ratified (accepted) by all 13 states in 1789. It sets out a federal system in which power is divided between the central federal government and the individual state governments. The Constitution defines the rights and responsibilities of federal and state government, and limits the powers of the federal government by laying down a system of checks and balances designed to ensure that no branch of government can exceed its authority (see CONSTITUTION OF THE UNITED STATES). The Constitution divides government into three branches: the legislative, the executive, and the judiciary.

The legislative, or law-making, branch is the Congress of the United States. It has two elected chambers and all states of the Union are represented in each. In the upper house, the Senate, members are elected for six years. In the lower house, the House of Representatives, members are elected for two-year terms.

Congress makes the laws for the country as a whole. The Constitution forbids it to pass any laws on matters that are the sole concern of individual states. Its powers are limited by the right of the United States president to veto, or forbid legislation (see CONGRESS OF THE UNITED STATES).

The executive is the branch that administers the country according to the laws passed by Congress. It is headed by the president of the United States, who is sometimes called the chief executive. There are 13 departments, whose heads are appointed by the president and act as his cabinet. There are also many other bureaus. The executive does not just passively accept congressional rulings but can influence legislation itself. The president can recommend laws and the Constitution allows him to share with the Senate the power to decide foreign policy. He holds office for four years and can be re-elected for a second term, but no more. Should he be seen to be acting beyond the scope set out by the Constitution or against the law of the land, the president can be impeached (tried) by Congress and removed from office if found at fault (see IMPEACHMENT; PRESIDENT).

The judiciary is the branch responsible for the federal court system. It is responsible for interpreting laws made by Congress and seeing that they are correctly applied. The Supreme Court of the United States is the highest court in the country. It consists of a chief justice and eight associate justices, all of whom are nominated by the president of the United States and appointed after approval by the Senate. Generally, the court deals with cases in which laws are believed to disagree with the Constitution or when it is believed that an error of law has been made by a lower court.

Most cases tried in the federal court system are first heard in the district courts. There are 89 district courts in the 50 states, one in the

District of Columbia, and one in Puerto Rico. Together, they have more than 475 judges. There is one court of appeals in each of the 11 judicial circuits into which the United States and its territories are divided.

FACTS ABOUT THE UNITED STATES OF AMERICA

AREA (excluding territories and possessions): 9,529,063 square kilometres (3,679,192 square miles).
POPULATION: 243,785,000 (1987).
GOVERNMENT: Independent federal republic composed of 50 states.
CAPITAL: Washington (District of Columbia).
GEOGRAPHICAL FEATURES: One-third of the country is covered by the western highlands, which include the Sierra Nevada and the Rocky Mountains. In the east are lower highlands, the main range being the Appalachians. The broad central plains, sloping southwards and eastwards, are drained by the Missouri-Mississippi river systems. Bordering the Atlantic and the Gulf of Mexico is a lowland belt. The highest mountain is Mount McKinley 6194 metres (20,321 feet) in the Alaska Range (Alaska); the longest river is the Mississippi-Missouri 6,212 kilometres (3,860 miles); the largest lake is Lake Michigan 58,016 square kilometres (22,400 square miles).
CHIEF PRODUCTS: Maize, wheat, barley, soya beans, groundnuts, tobacco, citrus fruits, cotton, livestock, timber, petroleum, coal, natural gas, iron, copper, lead, zinc, bauxite, gold, silver, uranium.
LEADING INDUSTRIES: Iron and steel, machinery, motor vehicles, aircraft, electronic equipment, computers, foodstuffs, chemicals, plastics, textiles, printing and publishing, paper, timber products.
IMPORTANT CITIES (over 500,000 inhabitants): Baltimore, Boston, Chicago, Cleveland, Columbus, Dallas, Denver, Detroit, Honolulu, Houston, Los Angeles, Memphis, Milwaukee, New Orleans, New York, Philadelphia, Phoenix, San Antonio, San Diego, San Francisco, San José, Washington.
EDUCATION: In most states children must attend school between the ages of 7 and 16, but school age varies (from 6-8 to 16-18).

The United States is a member of many international organizations. Among these are the United Nations, based in New York City; the North Atlantic Treaty Organization (NATO), based in Brussels, Belgium; and the Organization of American States, with headquarters in Washington, DC.

UNITED STATES OF AMERICA, HISTORY OF. The ancestors of most of the people who live in the United States today came from the British Isles, Europe, and Africa. When the first settlers arrived in the 16th century, the land was sparsely inhabited by peoples who came to be called Indians. It was Christopher Columbus who in 1492 first used the name Indian for the native American people. He did so because he thought that he had arrived in the East Indies. (See INDIANS, AMERICAN.)

When the king and queen of Spain were informed that Columbus had actually discovered a new world, they lost little time in laying claim to it. They established colonies on the West Indies islands and in Mexico and Central America. They claimed all of South America except Brazil (claimed by Portugal).

In 1513, Juan Ponce de Leon, a Spanish explorer, landed on the east coast of what is now the state of Florida and claimed it for Spain. In 1539 another Spanish explorer, Hernando de Soto, landed on the west coast of Florida with a large company of men. They explored the land to the north and west and were the first white men to see the Mississippi River. A year later another Spaniard, Francisco de Coronado, led an exploration from Mexico into what is now the southwestern United States. On the basis of these various explorations Spain claimed nearly all the land that now forms the southern half of the United States. (See PONCE DE LEON, JUAN; CORONADO, FRANCISCO.)

Meanwhile, other countries were also becoming interested in the new land. In 1497 and 1498 John Cabot explored the northeast coast of North America. It was upon these voyages that England based her claim to America. (See CABOT, JOHN AND SEBASTIAN.)

In 1524 a French expedition commanded by Giovanni de Verrazano explored the coast of North America from the Carolinas northward. Ten years later another French expedition led by Jacques Cartier sailed up the St. Lawrence River. On a later voyage Cartier went up this river to a high point which he named *Mont Réal*, meaning "mount royal". This is how the city of Montreal, Canada, got its name. (See CARTIER, JACQUES.)

The First Colonies

England made several unsuccessful attempts to establish settlements in North America near the close of the 16th century, but by the mid-18th century had founded a chain of colonies along the Atlantic coast from Maine to Florida. The first permanent settlement by Englishmen was made at Jamestown, Virginia, in 1607. (See VIRGINIA; SMITH, CAPTAIN JOHN.) Jamestown was founded for commercial reasons by a group of merchants called the Virginia Company of London. They hoped that the settlers would find gold and send it and other valuable products back to England. But no gold was found. Food supplies ran short. The settlement was on a low-lying, unhealthy site, and many colonists fell ill and died.

Within a few years, however, the development of tobacco growing put the colony on its feet, and in 1619 the company gave the colonists the right to share in making the laws for the colony. A representative assembly called the House of Burgesses was formed, the first of its kind on American soil. Also in 1619 the first women settlers arrived, as did the first black men. The blacks were not slaves but indentured servants who were bound to work for a master for a certain number of years.

In 1620 a group of Pilgrims established a settlement at Plymouth, Massachusetts. The Pilgrims were English Protestants who objected to some of the beliefs and practices of the Church of England. Some of them had gone first to live in the Netherlands.

The *Mayflower*, the ship in which the first Pilgrims sailed across the ocean, was to have landed in northern Virginia. It ran off course, however, and dropped anchor in the shelter of Cape Cod in Massachusetts. The leaders of the group decided to settle on the nearby shore. They first drew up a notable agreement called the Mayflower Compact. By signing this document they agreed to form a government of their own and to obey its rules and regulations. (See MAYFLOWER.)

The Puritans, like the Pilgrims, were English Protestants who also objected to the practices of the Church of England. They did not want to separate from it, however, but thought that by remaining in the Church they could reform, or purify, it. (See PURITANS.) They decided to form a company and go to America where they could organize their Church as they pleased. The Massachusetts Bay Company, which they formed, was granted land between the Charles and Merrimac rivers in Massachusetts. By 1630 nearly 1,000 Puritans had come to the new colony, and it soon prospered and grew strong.

The Massachusetts Bay Colony has been called the "mother of colonies". Thomas Hooker led a group of settlers from Massachusetts to the upper Connecticut River valley to form a new settlement. Other people from Massachusetts settled in the lower Connecticut valley. In 1662 the settlements of Hartford and New Haven combined to become the colony of Connecticut. Roger Williams and Anne Hutchinson disagreed with the Puritans and were forced to leave Massachusetts. They and their friends made settlements which in 1644 became the colony of Rhode Island. Massachusetts laid claim to settlements which were made in New Hampshire and Maine. New Hampshire became a separate colony in 1679, but Maine remained a part of Massachusetts until it achieved statehood in 1820.

Maryland was settled in 1634 by the second Lord Baltimore. The land for this colony had been granted to Lord Baltimore's father by the king. Lord Baltimore was the sole proprietor of the colony, but he granted the settlers a representative assembly. Although he and his father were Roman Catholic, the assembly passed the Act of Toleration, which permitted any Christian to settle in Maryland.

In 1609 Henry Hudson, in command of a Dutch ship, the *Half Moon*, sailed into New York Bay and up the river that later was to be named in his honour. (See HUDSON, HENRY.) The Dutch claimed this region, and in 1624 they sent a shipload of settlers. They called their colony New Netherland.

New York was a busy port city in the middle of the 18th century. Shown above is the old part built by the Dutch. The newer part (below) was built by the English.

The Bettman Archive

The English colonists in New England and Virginia looked upon the Dutch as intruders. After a long period of conflict, an English fleet appeared in New York Bay in 1664 and seized the Dutch colony. The king of England gave the colony to the duke of York and changed its name to New York.

Later Colonies

Pennsylvania was founded in 1681 by William Penn. King Charles II granted Penn a large tract of land west of the Delaware River in settlement of a debt which he owed Penn's father. William Penn, who had become a Quaker, wished to found a colony where every man could worship God in his own way. (See PENN, WILLIAM; FRIENDS, SOCIETY OF.)

Penn believed that the Indians should be treated fairly and should be paid for their land. He drew up a plan of government for his colony and allowed the people to make their own laws. Philadelphia, known as the "city of brotherly love", became the largest city in the colonies. Penn invited many people to come to his colony. Englishmen, many of whom were Quakers, settled in Philadelphia and along the Delaware River. Later, Germans came to the colony in large numbers and settled in the region extending westward to the Susquehanna River. Still later, Scots-Irish settled in western Pennsylvania.

In 1702 the settlements of East and West Jersey were joined together to form New Jersey. The settlements made by the Swedes and the Dutch on the lower Delaware were controlled by Pennsylvania, but after 1704 Delaware was considered a separate colony.

In 1663 King Charles II granted a large tract

of land along the Carolina coast to eight of his friends. Within a few years, two areas were settled: one in the north and another in the south. Later the colony was divided into North and South Carolina.

Georgia was the last of the English colonies to be founded in the land that was to become the United States. It was settled in 1732 by James Oglethorpe.

Colonial Government and Economy

The government of each colony was modelled on the government of England. In the proprietary colonies, such as Maryland and Pennsylvania, the governor was appointed by the proprietor (the man to whom the king had given the colony). In some of the colonies the governor was appointed by the king. Only in Connecticut and Rhode Island was the governor elected by the people. Representative assemblies, resembling the English parliament, were established in most of the colonies. Only citizens who owned property or paid taxes, however, were allowed to hold office or vote for members of the assembly.

In New England, where most of the people lived in villages and towns, local government was conducted by the town meeting. In the South, where most people lived on large farms and plantations, the county was the basis for local government.

The first settlers who came to live in the colonies were confronted with difficulties and hardships. They had brought only a few supplies with them. To exist they had to build homes, clear land, and plant crops. If friendly relations with the Indians were not established, the settlers had to protect their homes and families from attack.

Most of the early colonists were farmers because they had to produce their own food. In time, however, the living patterns of the colonists began to change. In New England, for example, where the soil generally was not suited to farming, the people turned to lumbering, shipbuilding, and fishing. The southern colonies found their soil and climate well suited to growing tobacco, rice, and indigo. Many southerners owned only small farms, but others established large plantations worked by slaves. They sent their crops to England in exchange for goods that were needed in their homes. The colonists of New York, New Jersey, and Pennsylvania found grain and stock farming profitable. They not only raised enough for themselves but also produced wheat, flour, beef, and pork to sell to other colonies.

Trade was an important part of colonial life. The colonies traded with each other and also with England, the continent of Europe, and the West Indies. The colonial towns of Boston, New York, Philadelphia, and Charleston grew into busy commercial cities.

The colonists did not neglect learning. In 1647 a Massachusetts law required every town of 50 families or more to provide schooling for its children. Harvard College was founded in Massachusetts in 1636, the College of William and Mary in Virginia in 1693, and Yale College in Connecticut in 1701. The first printing press was set up in Massachusetts in 1638. Postriders began carrying mail from one colony to another, and stagecoach lines were established between the colonial cities.

By 1750 the population of the colonies had reached 1,200,000. Some settlers had gone to live in the sheltered valleys of the Appalachian Mountains. The colonies became interested in the land that lay west of these mountains, but they were blocked by the French and the Indians.

In 1608, only one year after the settlement of Jamestown, the French had founded Quebec, the first permanent French settlement in North America. Frenchmen explored the upper St. Lawrence River, the Great Lakes region, and the Mississippi River valley. One of them, Robert La Salle, planted a cross and the French flag at the mouth of the Mississippi River in 1682 and claimed all of the land drained by the river for France. (See CANADA; LA SALLE, ROBERT.)

Both the French and the British built forts in western Pennsylvania to protect their claims to the upper Ohio valley. In 1754 fighting began in this region between the French and British forces. The French and Indian War, as this conflict was called, ended in 1763 with the defeat of France and its Indian allies. The victory gave Britain control over all of French Canada and the territory between the Appalachian Mountains and the Mississippi River.

The American Revolution

At the end of the French and Indian War, Britain faced new problems in America. The British government decided to exercise firmer control over colonial trade. The colonies were told that they should help pay for the cost of the war and for their future defence. The British parliament passed laws to regulate colonial trade with Britain and other countries. A stamp tax was adopted, and taxes were levied on certain imports into the colonies. (See AMERICAN REVOLUTION.)

Even though some of these laws were for the benefit of the colonies as well as of Britain, the colonists objected to them. They argued that since they were not represented in the British parliament they should not be taxed by it. More important was the fact that the colonists had come to feel self-sufficient by this time. They had had experience in governing themselves through their own assemblies and in fighting during the French and Indian War. Many of the people who lived in the colonies at that time had been born in America and considered it their home.

The First Continental Congress, made up of representatives from the 13 colonies, met in Philadelphia in 1774 to try to improve colonial relations with Britain. This effort failed, and fighting broke out in Massachusetts between British troops and the colonial Minutemen. The battles of Lexington and Concord marked the opening of the American Revolution in April 1775. The Second Continental Congress then met and chose George Washington to command the colonial troops.

Many of the colonists opposed taking up arms against Britain, but others such as Samuel Adams in Massachusetts, Benjamin Franklin in Pennsylvania, and Thomas Jefferson and Patrick Henry in Virginia believed the colonies should assert their rights (see FRANKLIN, BENJAMIN; HENRY, PATRICK; JEFFERSON, THOMAS). Jefferson, with the aid of a committee, drafted a statement declaring that, "these United Colonies are, and of Right ought to be Free and Independent States". On 4 July 1776 this statement, called the Declaration of Independence, was adopted by the Second Continental Congress. (See DECLARATION OF INDEPENDENCE.)

The Signing of the Declaration of Independence, by John Trumbull, at Independence Hall, Philadelphia.

IN CONGRESS. JULY 4, 1776.

The unanimous Declaration of the thirteen united States of America.

The Declaration of Independence.

The war for independence did not go well for the colonists at first. General Washington barely managed to keep his small army together because of defeats and lack of supplies. Finally the tide turned in the colonists' favour in 1777, when a British army under General John Burgoyne was defeated at the Battle of Saratoga. After that victory, France decided to help the colonies in their war against Britain. The fighting ended in 1781 with the surrender of the British forces at Yorktown, Virginia. By the Treaty of Paris in 1783, Britain recognized the independence of the American colonies. The area extended from Maine to Florida and westward to the Mississippi River.

Before the war ended, the Second Continental Congress drafted the Articles of Confederation under which the newly independent states agreed to co-operate in certain matters. The Articles, adopted in 1781, provided for a loose union of states and reserved most of the powers of government for the states. Congress could not tax the people directly. It could not levy tariffs on imported goods or regulate trade among the states. The Articles made no provision for strong executive or law-enforcing branches of government. It soon became apparent that the union formed by the states was not strong. (See ARTICLES OF CONFEDERATION.)

The Constitution

George Washington, Alexander Hamilton, James Madison, and other leaders became dissatisfied with the Articles of Confederation (see MADISON, JAMES). A convention, therefore, was called to meet in Philadelphia in 1787 to amend them. After the delegates assembled they decided to set the Articles aside and draft an entirely new constitution. When the new constitution was ratified by the states, it became the supreme law of the land. The Constitution provided for a federal type of government: a union of states under a strong central government. It gave the federal government power to levy taxes and to regulate commerce. It stated clearly what powers the federal government had and what powers were reserved for the states or to the people.

The Constitution provided for three branches of government: legislative, executive, and judicial. The law-making body was to consist of a Senate, in which each state was to have two members, and a House of Representatives, in which each state was to have a number of representatives based on its population.

Some people objected to the Constitution because it made no provision for the protection of individual liberties. Fortunately provision had been made for amending the Constitution. When the first Congress assembled, a number of amendments guaranteeing individual rights and liberties were drawn up. After being ratified by the states, ten amendments were added to the Constitution. They are called the Bill of Rights. (See BILL OF RIGHTS.)

The new government under the Constitution was organized in New York City in 1789 with George Washington as the first president. Congress proceeded to exercise some of the powers that were granted to it by the Constitution. (See WASHINGTON, GEORGE.)

Alexander Hamilton, secretary of the treas-

Pioneers usually travelled in groups for protection.

Culver Pictures, Inc.

ury, and others among the merchant class believed that a strong central government should exercise the powers the Constitution gave it. These people came to be called Federalists. Thomas Jefferson and his followers, who included many labouring men and farmers, feared that the national government might exercise too much power. These people came to be called Anti-Federalists, or Republicans. It was in this way that political parties came into being. (See HAMILTON, ALEXANDER; POLITICAL PARTIES.)

Westward Expansion

After the country became independent, it was expected that many people would move into the region between the Appalachian Mountains and the Mississippi River. In 1785 the Continental Congress had passed a law providing for the survey of the land north of the Ohio River and for its sale to land companies and to individuals. Two years later the Ordinance of 1787 was passed. It organized this region as a territory and provided that in the future new states would be formed within the territory.

Settlers followed traders and explorers into the region west of the Appalachian Mountains. In 1792 Kentucky was admitted to the Union as a state. In 1796 Tennessee became a state. Kentucky and Tennessee were the first states to be created west of the Appalachian Mountains.

Most of the people who settled in the West became farmers. They raised their own food and within a few years produced flour and salt pork for sale. They shipped these and other products on flatboats down the Ohio and Mississippi rivers to New Orleans, where they were transferred to ocean-going ships.

Difficulties soon arose over shipping at New Orleans. The land on both sides of the Mississippi River at that point belonged to Spain. Later, this region as well as the land along the west side of the Mississippi was transferred to France. Neither country was pleased to see United States citizens settle in the Mississippi valley. (See WESTWARD MOVEMENT.)

In 1803 Thomas Jefferson, who had been elected president in 1800, decided that the United States should buy New Orleans and the land along the lower Mississippi from France. To everyone's surprise, France offered to sell to the United States all of her territory west of the Mississippi. The offer was accepted and with the payment of $15 million the United States received the entire territory of Louisiana. It almost doubled the size of the country.

In 1804 Meriwether Lewis and William Clark set out from St. Louis to explore the Louisiana Territory. They and their men

Brown Brothers

Courtesy, Nebraska State Historical Society

1 Where trees were plentiful, log cabins were built.
2 Where there were no trees, the settlers built sod huts.

ascended the Missouri River, crossed the Rocky Mountains, and followed the Columbia River to the Pacific Ocean (See LEWIS AND CLARK EXPEDITION.) Two years later Zebulon Pike crossed the Louisiana Territory and followed the upper Arkansas River into the Rocky Mountains. The United States also expanded to the south. In 1819 Spain signed a treaty ceding Florida to the United States.

The New Country's Foreign Policies

In 1789, the year in which the new United States government was organized, a revolution began in France. The French people rose against the king and set up a representative government. This civil war alarmed Austria, Prussia, and Britain. Within a short time, France was at war with her European neighbours and Britain in a war that was to drag on under the leadership of Napoleon I for 15 years. (See FRENCH REVOLUTION; NAPOLEON (EMPERORS OF FRANCE).)

During the Napoleonic Wars, when Britain and France were fighting, the United States tried to remain neutral. However, it could not carry on trade with either France or Britain without running into trouble with the other. To make matters worse, the British began stopping United States ships and searching them for British seamen who had deserted. Sometimes they forced United States sailors into their naval service. People who lived on the western frontier accused the British of supplying the Indians with arms. Finally, in 1812, the United States Congress declared war on Britain.

Several United States ships won battles at sea, but on land the war did not go well. A British force landed near Washington, DC, in 1814 and set fire to several public buildings in the city. The British were repelled in their attacks on Baltimore and New Orleans, but United States forces failed to drive them out of Canada. The war ended with the Treaty of Ghent. (See WAR OF 1812.)

During the early 19th century, Spain's colonies in Central and South America declared themselves independent. Later, Spain attempted to regain control over her colonies and it appeared that some European powers might help her do so. Under these circumstances, President James Monroe in 1823 issued a statement that has since become famous as the Monroe Doctrine. It stated that North and South America were no longer open to colonization and that any attempts by European countries to interfere with independent American governments would be regarded as unfriendly acts.

Trade and Industrial Growth

In the 1790s the first textile mills for spinning yarn and weaving cloth were built in the United States. In 1793 Eli Whitney invented the cotton gin, which speeded up the separation of seeds from cotton fibres. The growing of cotton spread throughout the southern states, and the number of cotton mills in both the United States and Britain grew rapidly. The invention of the sewing machine by Elias Howe in 1846 completed the process by which cotton and wool could be made into finished garments by the use of factory machines. (See COTTON; WHITNEY, ELI.)

Other inventions helped the farmer. Cast-iron ploughs slowly replaced clumsy wooden ones. In 1831 Cyrus McCormick invented a horse-drawn reaper for harvesting grain. Horse-drawn harrows, drills, and mowers were invented, as well as a horse-powered threshing machine. These improvements helped grain farmers of the North as much as the cotton gin helped cotton farmers of the South.

The manufacture of factory machines and farm tools created a greater demand for iron. Blast furnaces fired by charcoal had been built in the colonies. The discovery of coal in Pennsylvania led to the use of coke in blast furnaces. Ironworks were set up for the manufacture of household utensils, farm implements, factory machines, and steam engines.

The shipment of goods from factories to farms and from farms to towns and cities made better means of transport necessary. The first hard-surfaced road was built from Philadelphia to Lancaster in Pennsylvania in the 1790s. It was built by the Lancaster Turnpike Road Company and people who used it were required to pay tolls. Many other companies were formed to build roads.

Several canals were built in the early 19th century. For example, the Erie Canal, completed in 1825, crossed the state of New York, connecting Lake Erie with the Hudson River. Canals were also built in the West.

The invention and improvement of the steam engine led to even more important developments in transport and trade. The first successful steamboat, the *Clermont*, was built by Robert Fulton (see FULTON, ROBERT). It made its maiden voyage on the Hudson River in 1807. The early 1830s saw the birth of United States railways. Steam locomotives made successful runs on the Baltimore and Ohio Railroad in Maryland, the Charleston and Hamburg Railroad in South Carolina, and the Mohawk and Hudson Railroad in New York. Within the next 20 years these railways were extended and others were built in the East, South, and West. By 1850 there were more than 14,500 kilometres (9,000 miles) of railways in the United States. (See RAILWAY.)

Improvements in transport encouraged the growth of mining, manufacturing, and trade. By 1840 the country's population had grown to more than 17 million. A third of the people lived in the West, and most of the western territories had been organized into states. Many people had gone beyond the western borders in search of fortune and adventure. Fur traders penetrated the Rocky Mountains and the Pacific Northwest, and southern farmers moved into Texas.

Texas had declared itself independent of Mexico in 1836. In 1845 it was admitted into the United States. This led to a boundary dispute and a war between the United States and Mexico. When the war ended in 1848, the United States gained control of the entire Southwest except for the Gadsden Territory, which it purchased from Mexico in 1853. In 1846 the United States and Britain agreed to divide the Oregon Country between them at the 49th parallel. By 1848 the United States had expanded to the Pacific Ocean. Thousands of pioneers followed the Oregon Trail to establish new homes in the Northwest. Thousands more adventurers set out to seek their fortunes in the goldfields of California.

Reform and Controversy

One of the purposes of the Constitution was to "promote the general welfare". During the period from 1820 to 1860 many people proposed reforms of United States laws for the benefit of the people. In 1787 only men who owned land and paid taxes were permitted to vote. By 1820 there were many men, such as traders and factory workers, who owned no land of their own but felt they should have the right to vote. State after state passed laws that extended the right to vote to all male citizens, regardless of property ownership.

Women began to demand the same rights. In many states women were granted the right to own property and to attend college, but they had to wait many years before gaining the right to vote and hold office.

In earlier times schools were thought necessary only for those who were to become ministers, lawyers, and teachers. Now people began to think that all children should receive an elementary education and that higher schools should be provided for those who wished to continue their education. Horace Mann of Massachusetts and De Witt Clinton of New York persuaded their states to support free public (state) elementary and secondary schools.

Factory workers began to form trade unions. They demanded safer working conditions, shorter work days, higher wages, and free schools for their children. In the 1840s national and state laws were passed limiting the working day to ten hours for certain kinds of work.

A notable political event of this era was the election of Andrew Jackson to the presidency in 1828 (see JACKSON, ANDREW). Jackson lived in Tennessee and was the first man from the West to be elected president. He believed that any man of average ability could hold a government job and that such jobs should be given to those who helped their party win the elections. This practice came to be called the "spoils system". While Jackson did not originate the spoils system, he was severely criticized for his use of it. (See JACKSON, ANDREW.)

Dissension in the Union

Other problems were leading to heated and violent debates. These disagreements revealed a growing split between the East and West and especially between the North and the South.

The greatest problem confronting the country at this time was slavery. When the first census was taken in 1790 there were more than 700,000 slaves in the United States. Most of them were in southern states where they worked in tobacco and cotton fields. Some people in both the North and in the South began to feel that slavery was evil and should be abolished. The Northwest Ordinance of 1787 had prohibited slavery in the region north of the Ohio River. By 1804 all of the northern states had abolished slavery, and in 1808 the importation of slaves was prohibited. (See BLACK AMERICANS; SLAVERY.)

The invention of the cotton gin in 1793 and the expansion of cotton plantations had greatly increased the demand for slaves in the South. When Missouri applied for admission to the Union as a slave state, the northern states objected. A compromise was reached in 1820. It provided that Maine should come in as a free state and Missouri as a slave state, but that slavery should be prohibited in the rest of the Louisiana Territory north of parallel 36° 30′.

During the 1830s and 1840s the debate over slavery continued. In 1848 a new crisis arose when the territory acquired from Mexico was to be organized. After heated debates in Congress another compromise was reached in 1850. California, where gold had been discovered in 1848, was admitted as a free state. The people who lived in the rest of this territory were to decide for themselves whether they should have slavery. The slave trade was abolished in the District of Columbia.

Many people thought the Compromise of 1850 had settled the matter for good, but two years later the book *Uncle Tom's Cabin* by Harriet Beecher Stowe appeared. It aroused intense feeling in the North against slavery. In 1854 Congress passed the Kansas-Nebraska Act, which permitted people of these two territories—both north of the Missouri Compromise line—to decide whether they should have slavery. People from both the North and South rushed into Kansas to help decide the issue. Fighting raged in "Bleeding Kansas". Three years later the United States Supreme Court, in the Dred Scott case, declared the Missouri Compromise unconstitutional.

Courtesy, The Library of Congress

Northern troops laid seige to Petersburg, Virginia, in 1864. When the beseiged Confederate forces withdrew after a year, the way was open for the capture of Richmond, the southern capital.

As the date for the 1860 presidential election approached, the debate over slavery became the main campaign issue. Two of the candidates, Abraham Lincoln and Stephen Douglas, both from Illinois, had debated the issues in 1858. Lincoln was chosen as the candidate of the Republican party. (See LINCOLN, ABRAHAM.)

The Country Divided

Shortly after the election of Abraham Lincoln as president in 1860, the southern states began to secede (withdraw) from the Union. They formed the Confederate States of America and elected Jefferson Davis of Mississippi as their president. (See CONFEDERATE STATES OF AMERICA; DAVIS, JEFFERSON.)

In his inaugural address Lincoln declared that he intended to preserve the Union and that he would hold and protect government property. When Confederate forces fired on Fort Sumter in Charleston harbour, Lincoln called for 75,000 volunteers, and the Civil War, sometimes called the War Between the States, began. The war lasted four years and took a terrible toll in lives lost and in the devastation of the land and disruption of society. (See CIVIL WAR, AMERICAN for a full account.)

Neither side was prepared for war, but the North had more ships, railways, men, and supplies, and was able to carry the war into the South. Northern ships blockaded southern ports and northern armies gained control over the border states. Fierce battles were fought in both the east and the west. In 1863 Lincoln issued a proclamation which freed the slaves in the southern states that were at war. In that same year the Battle of Gettysburg was fought in Pennsylvania, which a Confederate army had invaded. (See GETTYSBURG, BATTLE OF.) Although this battle marked the turning point of the war, fighting continued for another year and a half. The war ended in April of 1865 at Appomattox Court House in Virginia when General Robert E. Lee surrendered to General Ulysses S. Grant. (See GRANT, ULYSSES S; LEE, ROBERT E.)

The Civil War settled two important points: that all people in the United States were to be free, and that no state could withdraw from the Union. In his second inaugural address, a few weeks before the end of the war, Lincoln said, "Let us strive . . . to bind up the nation's wounds . . . to do all which may achieve and cherish a just and lasting peace among ourselves and with all nations". Lincoln had drawn up a plan for the restoration of the Union. Then, only a few days after the close of the war, he was assassinated. The reins of the government fell into the hands of the vice-president, Andrew Johnson, and new plans for the restoration of the Union were drafted and put into effect by Congress.

The Country Reunited

At the close of the war the South lay in ruins, for most of the fighting had occurred there. In the last year of the war all of the slaves had been freed by the adoption of the Thirteenth Amendment to the Constitution. Many of the former slaves roamed about in search of work. Few were able to make a living.

Radical Republicans, who were in control of Congress after the war, wished not only to keep the Republican party in power but also to punish the South for having started the war. The South was placed under military rule. New state constitutions were drawn up, and new state governments were formed. Men who had taken the side of the Confederacy were denied the right to vote and hold office. The new state governments were made to ratify the Fourteenth Amendment to the Constitution, which gave citizenship to all freed men (former slaves). These years were known as the Reconstruction Period.

Within ten years after the end of the Civil War, new economic systems developed in the South. Plantation farming by slaves was replaced by tenant farming and sharecropping. Railways were rebuilt and extended. Lumbering flourished and textile mills were built. Birmingham, Alabama, became the centre of a thriving iron and steel industry.

The discovery of gold in Colorado, Nevada, Idaho, Montana, and the Dakotas attracted fortune seekers from both the North and the South. The extension of the railway to Kansas enabled Texas cattlemen to drive their herds to Kansas and then ship them by rail to eastern markets. The Homestead Act of 1862 offered free land to people who settled in the West. New western states were admitted to the Union when they had a large enough population. Minnesota was admitted in 1858, Oregon in 1859, Kansas in 1861, Nevada in 1864, Nebraska in 1867, and Colorado in 1876.

New means of communication and transport between the East and the Far West were established. In 1858 a stagecoach line, the Overland Mail, was opened between Missouri and California. In 1860 the pony express (see PONY EXPRESS) operated by a chain of relay riders, began carrying mail between Missouri and California. A year later a telegraph line connected New York City and San Francisco, a distance of 5,600 kilometres (3,500 miles).

In 1862 Congress chartered two companies to build the first transcontinental railway in the United States. The Union Pacific was to build its railway westwards from Omaha, Nebraska, and the Central Pacific was to build its railway eastwards from Sacramento, California. In 1869 the lines were joined at Promontory, Utah.

Economic Growth

In 1864 the United States was the fourth most productive manufacturing country in the world. Thirty years later, in 1894, it ranked first. This came about through development of natural resources, the rise of big business, improvements in transport, and an increasing demand for manufactured goods.

The introduction of the Bessemer process for making steel and the discovery of rich iron-ore deposits in Alabama and in the Mesabi Range of Minnesota led to a rapid increase in the production of steel. The discovery of oil in Pennsylvania in 1859 foreshadowed the coming of the petrol engine, which led to the development of the motor car and of the aeroplane. In 1879 Thomas A. Edison invented the electric light. (See EDISON, THOMAS ALVA.)

By 1893 the Duryea brothers had made the first successful petrol-driven motor car in the United States. Within another ten years Henry Ford, Elwood Haynes, George Selden, and Ransom Olds developed other models and built factories to manufacture cars. (See FORD, HENRY; MOTOR VEHICLE.) In 1903 Orville and Wilbur Wright made the first successful flight in an aircraft. The production of aircraft had just started when World War I began in 1914. (See AIRCRAFT; WRIGHT, ORVILLE AND WILBUR.)

Andrew Carnegie and John D. Rockefeller were among the first men in the United States to organize business on a large scale. After establishing a steel mill in Pittsburgh, Pennsylvania, Carnegie leased iron-ore lands in the Lake Superior region and bought ships to carry the ore across the lakes. Then he bought a railway which ran from Lake Erie to Pittsburgh and acquired his own coal mines in Pennsylvania. (See CARNEGIE, ANDREW.) When Rockefeller began the refining of petroleum, he leased oil lands and drilled oil wells. He gained control over certain railways and pipelines for shipping at low rates. (See ROCKEFELLER FAMILY.)

The growth of big manufacturing corporations made necessary the hiring of a large force of workers. Each worker was trained to do only one step in the manufacturing process. The assembly-line method of making cars was introduced by Henry Ford in 1913. Large-scale industrial organization, division of labour, and the assembly line resulted in mass production.

By the beginning of the 20th century, factories were producing all sorts of goods, from locomotives and farm machinery to household utensils, in great quantities. Through developments in transport and merchandising, a great variety of goods and services was becoming available to almost everyone.

Immigration

From 1840 to 1890 many immigrants came to the United States from Great Britain, Ireland, Germany, and the Scandinavian countries. Some of these people found jobs in eastern cities. Some helped build canals and railways. Many of the German immigrants settled in midwestern cities, and the Scandinavian immigrants took up farmlands in the upper Mississippi valley. Immigrants from China and other parts of Asia found jobs in California and other western states.

After 1900 more than 1 million immigrants of all nationalities arrived every year. Some of

The Granger Collection

In the late 19th and early 20th centuries, thousands of European families emigrated to the US every year.

these people returned to their homelands after a few years, but the great majority remained in the United States. Most of them settled in big cities such as Boston, New York City, Philadelphia, and Chicago.

Towards the close of the 19th century some citizens felt that too many aliens were coming to the United States. In 1882 Congress passed a law prohibiting the immigration of insane persons, criminals, and paupers. This law also barred all labourers from China. In 1907 an agreement was reached with Japan whereby Japanese labourers were prohibited from migrating to the United States. In 1921 a new immigration law set up a quota system which allowed only a certain number of immigrants to come from each country.

Labour and Farm Movements

The growth of big business made it difficult for the individual worker to seek his own advancement. It was to deal with this situation that labour unions were organized. Unions for special types of workers, such as shoemakers and printers, had been formed in some cities before 1800. National unions, however, did not appear until after the Civil War. The first national labour organization to achieve lasting success was the American

Federation of Labor (AFL), organized in 1886. It was a federation of craft and trade unions (such as the carpenters' union and plumbers' union) and therefore included mostly skilled workers. The AFL advocated the eight-hour day, the six-day week, and the abolition of child labour.

Some labour leaders believed that all workers in such basic industries as steel-making, mining, and motor-vehicle manufacturing, rather than in specific trades, should have their own unions. In 1935 the Committee for Industrial Organization (CIO) was formed and began the organization of such unions. By 1939 the CIO (renamed Congress of Industrial Organizations) had organized a number of industrial unions and had a membership as large as that of the AFL. (See TRADE UNION.)

United States farmers also came to see the need for an organization to promote their interests. In 1867 a group of farmers formed the National Grange of the Patrons of Husbandry. The Grangers advocated improvement of farm life, agricultural education, co-operative selling, and fair railway rates.

As a result of the farmers' complaints, Congress passed the Interstate Commerce Act in 1887. It created the Interstate Commerce Commission and made it responsible for regulating railway rates. In 1906 the powers of the Commission were strengthened, and four years later its powers were extended to the regulation of cable, telegraph, and telephone companies.

In the late 19th century some large corporations gained monopolies in certain industries. This was done by obtaining control over competing firms or by driving them out of business. An industrial organization which controlled many or most of the companies within a single industry was called a trust. Such an organization was in a position to control production within an industry and to set high prices for its goods.

Many people, including small businessmen, farmers, working men, and merchants, protested against this practice. In 1890 Congress passed the Sherman Anti-Trust Act, which declared that certain monopolistic practices by trusts were illegal. In 1914 Congress created a Federal Trade Commission and gave it the power to prevent unfair methods of business competition.

Administrative Reform

During the early years of the country's history, voting was done in public and bystanders could tell how each person voted. Today the secret ballot, known as the Australian ballot, is in use throughout the United States.

For many years candidates for political offices were chosen by party leaders at nominating conventions. The voters often were not satisfied with the people who were nominated. In 1903 Wisconsin passed a direct primary law which provided that an election, called a primary election, should be held so that the voters within each political party could choose a candidate for the Senate. Since that time the use of primary elections to choose candidates for local, state, and national offices has become widespread. In keeping with this development the Seventeenth Amendment to the Constitution, which provides that senators shall be elected by the people instead of by the state legislatures, was adopted and added to the Constitution in 1913.

Two more amendments were added to the Constitution after World War I. The Eighteenth Amendment, adopted in 1919 (repealed in 1933), prohibited the manufacture and sale of intoxicating liquors. The Nineteenth Amendment, adopted the next year, gave women the right to vote.

The period between 1870 and 1920 was an age of growth and reform. It was a period of change in the relationship of government to business. Laws were passed to regulate industry, transport, banking, and trade in order to protect the interests of working people, farmers, and the general public. People demanded an end to corruption in politics and business, greater safeguards for the country's health, better schools, and improved opportunities for people in all walks of life.

Razzmatazz has long been a part of US presidential campaigns. This wood engraving from an 1876 newspaper shows a massive procession staged in New York City for Samuel J. Tilden.

The Granger Collection

New Territories

As early as 1783 Russia had established fur-trading posts in Alaska. After fur trading became less profitable, Russia sold Alaska to the United States in 1867 for $7,200,000. (See ALASKA.)

Near the close of the 19th century the United States came into possession of territories which lay far beyond its borders. One of these was the Hawaiian Islands in the Pacific Ocean. For many years United States ships on their way to Asia had stopped at the islands to take on supplies and to trade. The United States government and United States businessmen had great influence in the affairs of the islands. In 1898 Congress annexed the islands and later organized them as a territory. (See HAWAII.)

In 1898 the United States and Spain went to war because of a dispute over Cuba. At the close of the war the United States gained control over Puerto Rico, the Philippines, and the island of Guam. Spain was paid $20 million, and Cuba was granted independence. (See SPANISH-AMERICAN WAR.)

During the Spanish-American War it required two months for the battleship *Oregon* to sail from the Pacific Ocean to the Atlantic Ocean. It had to steam all the way around South America. The incident showed the need for a canal across the isthmus of Panama as a short cut between the two oceans. A French company had tried to build such a canal but had failed. The United States then bought the company's rights to the canal.

At that time Panama belonged to Colombia. When Colombia objected to the building of a canal by the United States, Panama declared its independence from Colombia. The United States at once recognized Panama as an independent country and bought a strip of land 16 kilometres (10 miles) wide across Panama through which the canal was to be built. It also agreed to pay Panama a sum of money each year. In 1904 United States engineers began work on the canal. It

The Granger Collection

Theodore Roosevelt inspects a steam shovel during work on the Panama Canal which began during the term of his presidency.

The United States joined World War I in 1917 and sent thousands of troops by sea to Europe.

The Bettman Archive

took eight years to build and cost $300 million. In 1914 it was opened to the ships of the world. (See PANAMA CANAL.)

World War I

Just a few days before the first ship passed through the Panama Canal a war began in Europe. It resulted from a conflict of policies between two groups of European countries. Germany, Austria-Hungary, Turkey, and Bulgaria formed one group called the Central Powers. Great Britain, France, and Russia formed the other group called the Allied Powers. Although Italy had treaty agreements with the Central Powers, it joined the Allies.

The United States tried to remain neutral and succeeded in staying out of the war from 1914 to 1917. In 1916 President Woodrow Wilson was re-elected, in part because "he kept us out of war". The United States position, however, became more and more difficult. The Allied Powers needed to buy United States goods, and the Central Powers were determined to stop this trade. German submarines destroyed Allied ships. United States citizens travelling on these ships lost their lives. The United States protested, but the war at sea went on. In April 1917 Congress declared war upon the Central Powers and thus the United States entered the war.

United States troop and supply ships, convoyed by the navy, crossed the Atlantic Ocean in great numbers. Two million men of the American Expeditionary Forces joined the soldiers of Britain, France, and the other Allied countries. They helped to turn Allied defeats into victories on the battlefields of Europe. The United States navy helped to drive German submarines and destroyers from the Atlantic Ocean. In November 1918 Germany finally asked for peace. On 11 November an armistice was signed and the war was over. (See WORLD WAR I.)

Before the war ended, many Allied leaders had begun to draw up plans for the peace treaty. In 1919 these men met at Versailles, France, where treaties between the countries engaged in the war were drafted and signed. Among the many agreements was one that President Wilson insisted upon. It was the provision that a League of Nations be established to maintain peace among the countries of the world in the future.

When the Treaty of Versailles, including the proposal to create a League of Nations, was put before the Senate, there was a heated debate. President Wilson set out on a speaking tour to persuade the people to support the treaty and the League of Nations. While he was in Colorado, he suffered a stroke that left him partly paralysed. He lived to see the Senate reject the Treaty of Versailles and refuse to participate in the

League of Nations. In 1920 the Republican party came into power again with the election of Warren G. Harding as president. (See WILSON, WOODROW.)

From Prosperity to Depression

Although the decade of the 1920s was to be one of the most prosperous periods in the history of the United States, it got off to a bad start. A minor depression occurred after the end of the war while the country was adjusting to a peacetime economy. During the presidency of Harding a number of scandals rocked the country.

Despite the postwar depression, political scandals, and a wave of industrial strikes, the economy improved in the early 1920s. High tariff laws were passed to protect United States industries and farmers from foreign competitors. Income and corporation taxes levied during the war were reduced. The government began reducing the national debt by redeeming the bonds that people had purchased during the war.

Factories boosted their output during the 1920s. The number of private motor cars increased from 8 million to 23 million. The new film industry grew so rapidly that by 1930 more than 20,000 cinemas had been built. The expansion of existing industries and the establishment of new ones provided many jobs at good wages. Consumers demanded an endless variety of goods: refrigerators, vacuum cleaners, radios, and other appliances for the home; better clothes to wear; cars for business and pleasure; and finer homes to live in.

The 1920s were years of speculation. Everyone wanted to get rich quickly. Banks loaned money freely to farmers and businessmen to buy land and machinery. Many people bought land in California and Florida, intending either to sell it for a profit or to live on it after they retired. Millions of people began speculating in stocks and bonds. As security prices rose the investors borrowed money from banks and mortgaged their homes in order to buy more stocks and bonds.

Many people began to think that prosperity had come to stay and that unemployment and depressions were things of the past. Others saw danger signals. Foreign trade began to fall off when other countries raised their tariffs in retaliation against high United States tariffs. There was excessive instalment buying and borrowing of money for speculation. Banks became less willing to make loans to people for these purposes. By 1929 the building boom came to a halt. Unemployment increased. In October 1929 a financial panic occurred when prices on the New York Stock Exchange collapsed. The prices of stocks tumbled as thousands of stockholders tried to sell their stocks. The stock market crash marked the beginning of the worldwide Great Depression of the 1930s.

Herbert Hoover, who had been elected president in 1928, urged employers to maintain their wage rates and avoid laying off workers. Congress created the Reconstruction Finance Corporation (RFC) to make loans to industries, railways, and banks. Other measures were taken to help businessmen, farmers, and workers. When the presidential election year of 1932 arrived, millions of United States workers were still without jobs. Farmers were losing their farms through mortgage foreclosures. Banks, unable to collect the loans they had made, were closing their doors. State and local governments were complaining that they were no longer able to provide relief payments to the unemployed. The Democratic candidate Franklin D. Roosevelt was elected president, promising a "New Deal" in the United States.

The New Deal

The New Deal began as soon as Roosevelt was inaugurated on 4 March 1933. (See ROOSEVELT, FRANKLIN.) The new president called Congress into special session and announced a four-day "bank holiday" during which all banks were closed. Congress started on a "hundred days" programme of emergency legislation. New banking laws were quickly passed to help banks that were in distress and to reopen closed banks. Other laws were passed to create agencies to provide relief for the unemployed and to improve social conditions generally. Other measures were passed to help business. The Federal Housing Administration (FHA) was created to encourage the construction industry, and the Agricultural Adjustment Act (AAA) was passed to control the production of livestock and farm crops and help increase farm income. Farmers who co-operated in the programme were given cash payments as well.

The National Labor Relations Act (Wagner Act) upheld the right of workers to organize unions and to bargain collectively with their employers. In 1938 another labour law, the Fair Labor Standards Act, was passed. It established minimum wages and maximum working hours for certain industries.

Another New Deal act that helped millions of people was the Social Security Act, passed in 1935. It provided assistance to people of retirement age, to the blind, and to mothers and dependent children. It also set up a system of unemployment insurance. The law has been amended many times so that farmers, domestic workers, self-employed workers, and others—in addition to industrial workers—are covered by it.

By 1940 the country had made some progress towards recovering from the depression. Factory production had increased and more men were back at work. Farmers were enjoying better incomes. Yet at the very moment when people were feeling relief from the depression, another war broke out in Europe.

World War II

As early as the 1920s, events began to pave the way for the war that broke out in Europe in 1939. In Italy the Fascist party gained control and its leader Benito Mussolini set himself up as dictator. He set out to build a new Italian empire. (See FASCISM.) In Germany the Nazi party led by Adolf Hitler denounced the Treaty of Versailles and began to build a strong Germany. (See HILTER, ADOLF; NAZISM.) In Asia the government of Japan fell into the hands of military forces preparing for war.

In 1931 Japanese forces attacked Manchuria, a province of China. Four years later Italy attacked Ethiopia in Africa. In 1937 Japan launched a full-scale attack on China. In 1938 German forces marched into Austria and united that country with Germany. A year later Germany invaded and occupied Czechoslovakia, a country with which the United States, Great Britain, and France had many close ties. In 1939 Hitler's forces launched a lightning attack on Poland. Soviet forces crossed Poland's eastern border at the same time and within a few days Poland was conquered and its territory divided between Germany and the USSR. When Germany invaded Poland, both Britain and France declared war on Germany, and World War II had begun.

During the winter of 1939–40 German military forces remained idle while the USSR attacked Finland and took a slice of its territory. The German army and air force went into action again in the spring and quickly conquered Denmark, Norway, the Netherlands, and Belgium. France fell after a few days' resistance. Germany and Italy formed an alliance called the Rome-Berlin Axis. Only Britain was left in the fight and through the long winter of 1940–41 its cities felt the full fury of attacks by German bombers.

The United States government tried to remain neutral, though the feelings of most of its people were on the side of Britain. By the autumn of 1940 the United States had begun to extend military aid to Britain. At the same time it began to strengthen its army and navy for defence in case of attack.

In September 1940 Congress passed a law drafting young men for military service. Billions of dollars were appropriated for armaments. In 1940 Roosevelt was elected for a third term and thus became the first United States president to be elected more than twice.

The United States at War

In March 1941 Congress passed the Lend-Lease Act, which permitted the president to turn over military supplies to countries fighting against Fascism. In June, Hitler launched a surprise attack on the USSR. Then on Sunday, 7 December, Japanese planes launched from aircraft carriers attacked the United States naval base at Pearl Harbor, Hawaii. The attack came as a surprise and seriously crippled the United States fleet. The United States declared war on Japan the next day, and within a few days Germany and Italy declared war on the United States.

Efforts to strengthen the United States armed forces moved into high gear at once. Millions of men were taken from civilian life and trained to be soldiers. Industry was expanded to produce ships, tanks, planes, and other war supplies. By 1944 United States factories were producing twice as much as all the factories of Germany, Italy, and Japan combined. Through price control and the rationing of scarce consumer goods the country was put on a wartime economy.

After attacking Pearl Harbor, Japan took advantage of the fact that the United States was unprepared to carry the war immediately across the wide Pacific. Japan overran China and Southeast Asia. In the spring of 1942 the United States was forced to surrender the Philippines to Japan. Soon, however, United States and Allied naval forces were ready to take the offensive in the Pacific. In June 1942 they defeated the Japanese fleet in the Battle of Midway, the turning point of the war in the Pacific.

Meanwhile, in Europe, United States fliers had joined British pilots in air raids over Europe. They helped to destroy railways, factories, oil refineries, and air and naval bases. The United States sent supplies to the USSR to help the Russians fight the invading German armies.

In the autumn of 1942 United States and British troops landed in North Africa. With the aid of French troops stationed there, the German and Italian forces in North Africa were defeated. This opened the way for an allied invasion of Europe by way of Sicily and Italy. Italy surrendered in September 1943, leaving Germany to fight alone in Europe. In June 1944 Rome fell to the Allies. Meanwhile, a powerful Allied force had gathered in England. On 6 June 1944 this force, commanded by United States General Dwight D. Eisenhower, crossed the English Channel and invaded France. The final phase of the war in Europe had begun. Also in 1944, forces led by General Douglas MacArthur recaptured the

The Bettman Archive

During World War II the United States sent men and equipment to battle areas around the world. US troops are here landing at Iwo Jima in the Pacific in 1945.

Philippine Islands and cut Japan off from her oil, rubber, and tin supplies.

From October 1944 to April 1945 Germany fought a losing battle against advancing Soviet armies on the east and Allied armies on the west. Mussolini was killed by his own countrymen, and Hitler died, probably by his own hand. On 7 May 1945 Germany surrendered and the war in Europe ended.

Early in 1945 United States Marines captured the islands of Iwo Jima and Okinawa, which were within striking distance of Japan. On 6 August 1945, a United States plane dropped a new kind of bomb on the Japanese city of Hiroshima. This one atomic bomb was so powerful that it destroyed nearly the whole city. Within a few days a second atomic bomb was dropped on Nagasaki, a Japanese shipbuilding centre. On 14 August 1945, Japan surrendered. (See also WORLD WAR II.)

World War II was the most destructive war in history. Over 10 million Allied soldiers were killed in battle. Millions of civilians were killed or injured, mostly during bombing raids. People throughout the world were determined that it should be the last world war.

At the end of the war the United States quickly demobilized its armed forces. The country was the leading industrial power of the world. Its territory had not been ravaged by war. It was for this reason, in part, that other countries looked to the United States for leadership in the establishment of peace.

Postwar Prosperity

Even before the war ended, leaders of the Allied powers had taken steps to ensure the future peace of the world. In April 1945, delegates representing 50 countries met in San Francisco to plan the organization of the United Nations (UN). The purpose of the UN was to promote peaceful relations among the countries and to advance the social, economic, and political progress of all peoples of the world. (See UNITED NATIONS.)

In 1947 the United States formulated two new foreign policies. One was called the "Truman Doctrine", named after Harry S. Truman, who became president upon the death of Roosevelt in 1945. Its purpose was to provide economic and military aid to countries that were threatened by Communist aggression (see TRUMAN, HARRY S.) The other was the "Marshall Plan" named after secretary of state George C. Marshall. It offered economic help to the countries of Europe so that they might recover from the war. In 1949 the United States joined Canada and ten European countries in forming the North Atlantic Treaty Organization (NATO) as a defence against possible attack.

David Douglas Duncan, Life © Time Inc.

Members of the first Marine brigade to reach Korea advance during the defence of the Pusan perimeter.

In 1950 war broke out in Asia. Communist forces of North Korea invaded South Korea in an attempt to unite all Korea under their control. The UN Security Council immediately voted to send help to South Korea. President Truman ordered United States troops stationed in Japan to go to the aid of South Korea. They were soon joined by small contingents sent by other UN members. Chinese

Communist troops, posing as volunteers, went to the aid of North Korea. The war ended in 1953 with the establishment of a neutral zone between North and South Korea.

In 1952 Dwight D. Eisenhower was elected president, the first Republican to be elected to that office since 1928. He was re-elected in 1956. One of Eisenhower's first acts was to persuade Congress to create a new cabinet post, the Department of Health, Education, and Welfare (see EISENHOWER, DWIGHT).

In 1954 the United States Supreme Court handed down an important decision about blacks in public (state) schools. It said that white and black children should not be segregated, that is, required to go to different schools. Segregation was the rule in most southern states, and many southerners denounced the Court's decision. During the 1950s and into the 1960s, blacks protested against racial discrimination and demanded equal rights. (See BLACK AMERICANS.)

Two important steps were taken by the United States government in the 1950s to improve transport. One was the National Highway Program, passed by Congress in 1955, to build new and improved highways in all parts of the country. The other step was an agreement with Canada, signed in 1954, to build the St. Lawrence Seaway, which made it possible for ocean-going ships to reach the Great Lakes.

The USSR launched the world's first artificial Earth satellite, Sputnik 1 on 4 October 1957. It was followed on 31 January 1958 by the first United States satellite, Explorer 1. These events were hailed as the beginning of a new Space Age. Ten years later the United States landed the first man on the moon. (See SPACE EXPLORATION.)

Alaska became the 49th state and Hawaii became the 50th state in 1959.

In 1960 John F. Kennedy was elected president. He was the first Roman Catholic president as well as the youngest man ever elected to the office. He called his programme for change in the United States the "New Frontier" (See KENNEDY, JOHN F.).

In foreign affairs, Kennedy sought to develop a new image for the United States. He created the Peace Corps, an organization of volunteers to help people of developing countries; and the Alliance for Progress, a programme involving co-operation between the United States and Latin America to solve Latin America's economic problems. Kennedy also achieved a step towards a disarmament treaty. In 1963 the United States, Great Britain, and the USSR signed a treaty which banned all nuclear tests except those made underground.

Little progress was made in settling other issues between the United States and the USSR. In 1962 Kennedy learned that Soviet missiles capable of attacking the United States had been installed in Cuba and demanded that the missiles be removed. The Soviet government complied, easing the threat of a nuclear confrontation.

On 22 November 1963, in Dallas, Texas, Kennedy was assassinated. Vice-President Lyndon B. Johnson became the 36th president. Johnson successfully urged Congress to pass two Kennedy measures: a tax cut and a civil rights bill opening up all public accommodation to blacks and guaranteeing equal job opportunities. He proposed a "war on poverty" in the United States. He also continued the policy of giving aid to South Vietnam in its fight against the rebel Vietcong and North Vietnam.

In 1964 Johnson was elected president in a landslide vote over his Republican opponent Senator Barry Goldwater. During his full term, Congress passed much of Johnson's legislative programme. It included continuing the war on poverty, increasing federal aid to education, a civil rights bill, and Medicare.

The 1960s was a period of civil unrest and, often, violence on the part of black Americans and other minorities. (See CIVIL RIGHTS, UNITED STATES for detailed events; see also KING, MARTIN LUTHER, JR.)

The chief problem faced by Johnson during his administrations was the war in Vietnam, where the United States role had gradually changed from one that was largely supportive and advisory to one of active combat. By the end of 1967 almost half a million United States troops were in South Vietnam. The mounting costs and casualties of the war caused great controversy. Pressure for ending the war increased. In 1968 peace talks began in Paris.

President Johnson, losing popularity because of the Vietnam War, did not run for re-election in 1968. Former Vice-President Richard M. Nixon, a Republican, became the 37th president, defeating Democrat Hubert H. Humphrey. Nixon began withdrawing United States troops from Vietnam, but continuing aerial bombardment brought increasing protests. Finally, in January 1973, a peace treaty was signed. (See VIETNAM WAR.) Early in 1972 Nixon visited the People's Republic of China, and as a result the United States established official, though limited, relations with mainland China.

At home inflation was a serious problem during the early 1970s, despite wage and price controls. In the 1972 election Nixon had overwhelmingly defeated Democrat George S. McGovern. But the unfolding Watergate scandal, which implicated the president in illegal activities to win the election, weakened his support. In August 1974, facing almost certain impeachment, Nixon resigned and Vice-President Gerald R. Ford became the 38th president.

Under the Ford administration, inflation, and other domestic problems continued. By the election year of 1976 there was slight improvement in the economy. Nevertheless, Democrat Jimmy Carter, former Georgia governor, defeated Ford in the election.

There were energy shortages during the first three years of Carter's presidency. A series of energy programmes raised prices and encouraged conservation. Inflation and unemployment remained high, and credit restrictions adopted in 1980 and high interest rates caused a severe slowdown in the housing and car industries.

In 1978 the Senate ratified treaties to give up United States control of the Panama Canal by 1999. In 1979 the United States and China normalized relations and signed a trade pact. The United States broke off formal relations with Taiwan.

In November 1979 militant Iranians captured the United States embassy in Teheran and took its occupants hostage. Iran continued to hold most of the hostages despite economic reprisals and worldwide condemnation of the act. The final 52 hostages were not released until January 1981.

In the 1980 election the Republican Ronald W. Reagan defeated Carter in an electoral landslide to become the 40th president. Republicans won control of the Senate for the first time since 1954. On 30 March 1981 Reagan was shot in an assassination attempt, but he recovered. Reagan concentrated his efforts on economic recovery, and during his first term inflation declined sharply. In foreign affairs his administration was concerned with finding means to deal with political terrorism. Later in his presidency economic difficulties arose from the country importing much more than it was exporting. In 1989 Reagan was succeeded by his vice president, George Bush.

UNIVERSE. All the things that exist – stars and cities, planets and people, quasars and quarks – make up what we call the Universe. Everything we know (and everything we do not know) is contained within its vastness. Questions about the physical Universe – What is it made of? How big is it? How and when did it form and what will happen to it? – have fascinated astronomers for centuries. Other questions – Why does the Universe exist and what is the human race's place in it? – are of more interest to philosophers. Many civilizations have stories and myths concerning the creation of the Universe. (See ASTRONOMY; MYTH AND LEGEND; PHILOSOPHY.)

The word Universe comes from two Latin words, *unum*, meaning "one", and *versum* (from *vertere*), meaning "turn". The word perhaps originally meant everything that could be seen in one complete turn of the head. In time the Latin word *universum* came to mean "total" and was used as a translation of the Greek *kosmos*, meaning "the whole orderly world". This word is the origin of the English words *cosmos* and *cosmic*, and *cosmos* and *Universe* now mean the same thing: the whole of ordered creation.

Scientists who study the physical Universe as a whole are called cosmologists. Cosmology is closely connected with physics and astronomy (see ASTRONOMY; PHYSICS) which provide the facts on which it is based. Cosmologists construct "models" of the Universe in order to account for the things they observe in it. Over the centuries, however, cosmological models have had to be changed many times, and much of our present opinions about the Universe were formed only in the 20th century.

Changing Views of the Universe

In ancient times all but a few scientists and philosophers believed that the Earth was the centre of the Universe and that the Sun, Moon, and stars revolved around it. The stars appeared to be fixed on the inside of a crystal sphere. But the Sun and Moon, together with five "wandering stars", or planets (from the Greek *planetes*, "wanderer"), moved independently against the background of the fixed stars. Everything moved around the Earth in an orderly fashion as if driven by a sort of machine. Ancient astronomers worked out complicated schemes that accounted for the motions of planets and the daily revolutions of the Sun and stars.

The most influential of these ancient astronomers was Ptolemy of Alexandria, whose great work the *Almagest*, written in the 2nd century AD, set forth the complex motions of the heavenly bodies in a theory that stood unchallenged for about 1,400 years. It was not until the 16th, 17th, and 18th centuries that our modern idea of a Sun-centred Solar System floating in the vast, black emptiness of space amid a galaxy of stars similar to the Sun began to take shape. Nicolaus Copernicus, Galileo Galilei, and Johannes Kepler showed that the Earth and the other planets went round the Sun; Sir Isaac Newton discovered the existence of the force of gravity, which holds them in their orbits; and at the end of the 18th century Sir William Herschel and his successors studied the Milky Way and investigated many of the misty patches of light called nebulae and discovered them to be galaxies beyond the Milky Way.

As the 19th century advanced, astronomers realised that the Universe was unimaginably immense, far bigger than anyone could have dreamed. An indication of just how large the Universe is came in 1838, when the great German astronomer Friedrich Wilhelm Bessel accurately measured the distance from the Sun to the nearby star 61 Cygni by means of parallax (see STAR). This was the first such measurement made, and Bessel's result proved staggering. He worked out that 61 Cygni lies 97,432,493 million kilometres (60,543,400 million miles) from the Sun. Such a vast distance for a close star obviously meant that conventional measurements in millions of kilometres or miles were unwieldy and ultimately meaningless. It was easier and less cumbersome to express such a distance in terms of how long something very fast would take to cover it. The fastest thing known is light. A ray of light moving at a constant velocity of nearly 300,000 kilometres (186,000 miles) per second travels a distance of nearly 10 million million kilometres (6 million million miles) in a year. Such a distance is called a light-year (see STAR). By this reckoning, 61 Cygni is 10.3 light-years away: just a short walk down the street in astronomical terms. (Modern estimates in fact put it at a distance of 11.2 light years.) Our next-door neighbour among the stars is Proxima Centauri—only 4.3 light-years away.

During the 19th century the distances of other stars were discovered, and in 1912 the discovery that the intrinsic brightness and the period of Cepheid variable stars were linked allowed their distances to be worked out accurately. (For an explanation of Cepheid variables, see STAR). From 1914 the American astronomer Harlow Shapley mapped the structure of the Milky Way Galaxy. He deduced that the Sun and its family of planets lie about 30,000 light-years from the centre of the Galaxy. Shapley's work laid the foundation for an accurate measurement of the Galaxy's dimensions. It is now generally accepted that the Galaxy is a flattened disc 100,000 light-years across, with a central bulge surrounded by a halo of older stars above and below the disc and with spiral arms extending from the disc and consisting of young stars and the gas and dust from which they are born. Astronomers have worked out the distances to other galaxies after finding Cepheid variables in them. (See GALAXY.)

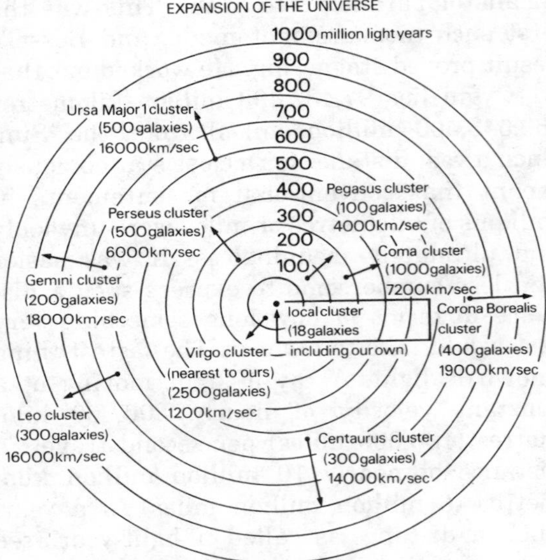

The Universe is expanding. This diagram shows the speed at which the major clusters of galaxies are moving away from the neighbourhood of our own galaxy.

Current Cosmological Models

The galaxies are not regularly arranged in space. The majority of them, like our own Milky Way system, belong to clusters. The clusters are moving through space relative to one another. In 1929, the American astronomer Edwin Hubble discovered that the distant galaxies are moving away from us and from each other at speeds directly proportional to their distances. That is, the further away they are, the faster they seem to be moving. This so-called *recession* of the galaxies is due to the fact that the Universe, immense as it is, is expanding. This expansion had been predicted in 1922 by the Russian mathematician Alexander Friedmann, using Albert Einstein's general theory of relativity (See RELATIVITY).

Two modern theories, which have been developed during the 20th century, describe the way the Universe behaves. The "steady state" theory says that the Universe looks the same everywhere, and at all times in the past and future. As it expands, new material is continually created to fill up the gaps. The other theory is called the "big bang" theory. It says that the Universe has evolved to its present state from a state of "singularity", where everything was packed closely together. At some point in the past, this intensely dense, hot material exploded and was hurled into space. As it cooled, bits of it were drawn together by the mutual pull of gravity to form the first stars and galaxies. According to the "big bang" theory, the Universe is about 10,000 million to 20,000 million years old. (The Earth is about 4,600 million years old.) Cosmologists now believe that the "big bang" theory is the correct one, because the Universe was evidently hotter and denser in the past than it is now.

Because light takes so much time to get to the Earth, we can never see any part of the Universe as it is now but only as it was in the past. The further away an object such as a distant galaxy is, the nearer it is, as it appears to us, to the time of the "big bang" and the start of the Universe. Measuring the speeds and distances of receding galaxies allows us to estimate the age of the Universe. But we do not know if any matter existed before its creation.

Matter and Energy

Although the Universe appears complicated to us, it really only consists of two things: matter and energy (see ENERGY; MATTER). Matter is anything made up of molecules, atoms, or other particles—our own bodies, the world we live in, all the planets, stars, galaxies, and nebulae we observe in space. Energy is the power locked up in matter by means of which the matter can perform an action. For example, for a piece of matter to move or to attract another piece of matter energy is needed. Even gravity can be thought of as a form of energy. Albert Einstein found that matter and energy are interchangeable and that a tiny amount of matter can be turned into an enormous amount of energy. This process is at the heart of nuclear reactions (see NUCLEAR ENERGY). Matter itself can be considered as a form of energy. The total energy of a system is conserved. That is, in any closed system, or throughout the Universe itself, the total amount of energy remains the same.

Most of the energy in the Universe is in the form of electromagnetic radiation (see RADIATION). Thermonuclear fusion reactions deep inside stars release the heat and light that make them shine. Stars also send out infra-red and ultraviolet radiation and radio waves. Radio waves have been of particular importance to astronomers; they can penetrate clouds of interstellar dust that absorb light. Thus radio astronomers have been able to examine such areas of space as the central region of the Milky Way, which is shrouded in dust and therefore obscure to optical telescopes. Other sources of radio waves include clouds of ionized gas such as those that make up certain types of nebulae; clouds of neutral (non-ionized) hydrogen, which radiate electromagnetic energy at an average wavelength of 21 centimetres (8.2 inches) and have been detected throughout the space between the stars; and quasars, the strange, very distant objects on the edge of the Universe that have the size of a solar system and the energy output of 100 galaxies or more (see QUASAR).

Other forms of electromagnetic energy detectable in the Universe include X-rays (see X-RAY). Several X-ray sources have been detected by instruments carried into space aboard rockets and satellites. X-ray sources so far detected include supernova remnants such as the Crab Nebula and Cassiopeia A, and the strange objects Cygnus X-1 and Scorpio X-1. The Cygnus source may be connected with a black hole (see BLACK HOLE). Other X-ray sources are not linked to visible objects, and astronomers are not fully aware of their origin and nature.

Throughout the Universe astronomers have detected faint background radiation. This is thought to have a number of causes. Some of it is perhaps the trace of the vast amount of energy that was released at the start of the Universe—a sort of "echo" of the "big bang". Most of the rest seems to be caused by the passage of cosmic rays through interstellar and intergalactic space. Cosmic rays are tiny particles, mostly protons, shot out from stars at very high speeds. An enormous number of cosmic-ray particles strike the Earth every day and can be detected by the effects they have on the atmosphere and on sensitive instruments. A Geiger counter can count cosmic-ray particles passing through it because each particle interacts with the gas in the instrument to produce a burst of electric current. Supernovae in the Milky Way and other galaxies pour out vast streams of cosmic-ray particles that spiral through space. If they encounter a magnetic field they are accelerated to velocities approaching that of light and are made to produce what is called "synchrotron" radiation. This is emitted at wavelengths ranging from those of radio waves to the X-rays.

The End of the Universe

The laws of physics as we understand them at present suggest that the universe can never be at rest. It will either expand for ever until all the stars have used up all their fuel and end as black holes or cold dark globes, or else it will reach a maximum limit and begin to contract under the influence of gravity until all the matter and energy in it is once more concentrated into a singularity. After this has happened there may be another "big bang", and the Universe will start expanding again. Perhaps the Universe has been through several "big bangs" already.

Other Solar Systems

Are there other systems of planets like our Solar System? It used to be believed that planetary systems were very rare in the Universe. However, most modern cosmologists think they may be fairly common. A star quite close to Earth, known as Barnard's Star, is noted for having a large motion of its own, which may be due to the presence of a giant planet larger than Jupiter. Infra-red astronomy has shown that some stars have "grains" travelling around them. These may be small planets or planetary systems in the process of formation. Some experts think that there may well be other planets, possibly with intelligent life on them. (See PLANET.)

UNIVERSITY AND COLLEGE. After secondary school the next step on the educational ladder is a university or college. These are places where courses in higher education may be followed, successful completion of the course being marked by the award of a degree (graduation). Higher degrees may be obtained by those who continue their studies with post-graduate research in a chosen field of learning.

The modern university has its roots centuries ago, in the Middle Ages. The universities of those days were merely societies of scholars or teachers formed for mutual protection, and there were no permanent buildings. These institutions grew, and eventually buildings were bought for the housing and teaching of the scholars; certain legal rights and privileges were obtained, and universities became permanent bodies. The first medieval university was at Salerno, Italy; in the 9th century it became known throughout Europe as a school of medicine, although it was only formally made a university in 1231.

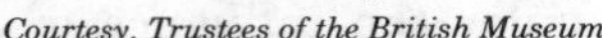
Courtesy, Trustees of the British Museum

A 17th-century view of Cambridge University, England, an engraving from *Cantabrigia Illustrata* (1670).

ZEFA

With more than 30,000 students, the University of Istanbul is the largest, and the oldest, in Turkey.

Towards the end of the 11th century, another Italian university developed at Bologna. Salerno was exclusively a medical school, but Bologna taught other subjects as well. It first earned a reputation as a school of law, and over the years faculties (departments) of medicine, arts, and theology were added. The teachers, following the example of the students, formed themselves into guilds, or "colleges". The certificates or licences to teach that were required for admission to the instructors' guilds became the earliest form of academic degree. Students, regardless of their future calling, finally came to seek the professor's licence or degree as an indication of a good education.

The University of Paris, most famous of the medieval schools of higher learning, was officially organized in the second half of the 12th century. Like other early universities of northern Europe, it grew out of a school attached to a cathedral. It was attached to the Cathedral of Nôtre Dame and was famous as a centre of theological (religious) learning. Over a period, faculties of canon (church) law, medicine, and the arts, were added. The University of Paris became the model for all the later universities of northern Europe.

Paris also served as the model for the first English universities, Oxford and Cambridge. Legally recognized by the 13th century, both universities consisted of a number of self-

ZEFA

Clare College, Cambridge, founded in the 14th century, is one of 31 residential colleges of the university.

governing colleges. The college system still exists today in Oxford and Cambridge. Each college provides lodgings and instruction for its members, while examinations are set and degrees given by the university.

American Universities and Colleges

Much confusion exists in the United States concerning the nature of a university, as opposed to a college, and the term is often misused. The word "college" has generally come to mean an institution attended after high school, usually for general rather than specialized training. Specifically, a college is an institution of higher education which consists of only one faculty and offers only a single course of studies. The course of studies is usually in the liberal arts (including social studies, humanities, and the natural sciences). There is a great number of liberal arts colleges in the United States and they form a basic element in the American system of higher education. A university, in addition to a liberal arts college, also includes other special colleges or schools. These special schools train students for the professions such as law, medicine, engineering, and the like. Most universities also have a graduate school for advanced study in various fields. Colleges sometimes prepare students for graduate work in a university.

Higher Education in the New World. Before the American Revolution, the colonists had founded ten colleges. The number has steadily increased, and today there are about 3,000 institutions of higher learning in the United States.

The first college in the United States was Harvard College, founded at Cambridge, Massachusetts, in 1636, and named after its first benefactor, John Harvard. Originally very small, its students all pursued the same course of study, which concentrated on Greek, Latin, and mathematics (like Oxford and Cambridge in England, on which it was modelled). Modern science was only taught from the 19th century. Next followed William and Mary College in Williamsburg, Virginia (1693); Yale in New Haven, Connecticut (1701); Princeton, New Jersey (1746); and Columbia, New York (1754). Except for William and Mary College, all these are now universities. They are "endowed" universities meaning that they are maintained by invested funds, student fees, and the gifts of benefactors. Many endowed colleges received their original endowment from religious groups. Other noted endowed institutions in the United States are Cornell (New York), Stanford (California); Duke (North Carolina), Dartmouth (New Hampshire), New York

The Granger Collection

Harvard College at Cambridge, Massachusetts, in *c.*1725, from an engraving by William Brugis (1740).

University; Johns Hopkins (Maryland); Clark (Massachusetts); and the University of Chicago.

The American universities changed radically after the American Civil War. A wider choice of subjects was offered, and graduate training was introduced. Over the years, the curriculum (course of study) became more democratic, and the teaching of Latin and Greek all but disappeared. Some of the pressure to change came from farmers, who demanded that colleges should offer a more practically oriented education. A new "land-grant college" was introduced, teaching agriculture, veterinary science, journalism, engineering, and so on. One of the original land-grant colleges was Cornell (Ithaca, New York), founded in 1865. It is the only privately-funded land-grant college.

McGill University in Montreal is one of Canada's best-known universities.

State Universities. Besides the endowed institutions, there are many state universities, such as the universities of Michigan at Ann Arbor, California at Berkeley and other centres, and Wisconsin at Madison. One of the earliest was established in Virginia by Thomas Jefferson in 1819. These are mostly supported by state taxes. Some of them are very large and combine undergraduate training and graduate professional schools. Almost every state has its own university, and the students of the state receive an education there at very little cost. Municipal universities, such as the University of Cincinnati in Ohio, are modelled on the state institutions.

Women's Colleges. The opportunities for women in university education have increased. State institutions are coeducational (open to both men and women). Nowadays, almost all endowed institutions admit women. There are also colleges that are devoted exclusively to the education of women, the oldest of which is Mount Holyoke, Massachusetts, founded in 1837. It was only during the latter part of the 20th century that many traditional men's and women's colleges became coeducational.

Junior Colleges. The junior or community college is a modern development and usually provides two-year courses beyond secondary school. The main purpose of such colleges is the extension of opportunity for higher education to all members of the community. Many of them offer correspondence courses, lecture classes off the campus, and home study programmes.

Universities and Colleges in Britain

Following Oxford and Cambridge, established in the 12th and 13th centuries, the Scottish universities of St. Andrew's, Glasgow, Aberdeen, and Edinburgh were created from the 15th to the 17th centuries. Much later, during the 19th century, came the civic (city) universities, such as London, Birmingham, and Manchester. These offered an education in the sciences, technological fields, the fine arts, and the humanities (Latin and Greek classics). During the 1960s, many new universities were founded (for example, Sussex, Essex, Warwick). Today there are 46 universities in Britain.

Since 1967, 30 polytechnics have been established. They are distinguished by their emphasis on technical subjects and by having much closer links with commerce and industry than do the universities. A graduating student is awarded a degree, which is equivalent to a university degree.

Ninety per cent of higher education in Brit-

Coventry Evening Telegraph
A graduation ceremony at a British university is a formal occasion, at which all participants wear gowns.

ish universities is state-funded, although the universities themselves are completely independent. They appoint their own staffs, and decide what and how their students should be taught.

Oxford and Cambridge have residential colleges in which students live during term time, but not all British universities are residential. Most are in large towns, and many of their students come from the local area and live at home. In recent years, however, universities have provided more hostels and halls of residence.

A first degree (undergraduate course) at a British university usually takes three years of full-time study, although some specialist courses, such as medicine, take longer. Unlike American universities and colleges, where standards may vary dramatically from one institution to another, the standard throughout Britain is fairly uniform. Thus a first-class degree at Manchester, for example, is equivalent to a first-class degree at Oxford. This uniformity in standard is partly achieved by the practice of having external examiners from other universities marking all examination papers.

The word "college" in Britain refers to a variety of educational training institutes, most of which are not of the same academic standing as a university. There are, for example, technical colleges, colleges of agriculture, art and music, commerce, building, religious instruction, and teacher training.

An important new development in higher education commenced in 1971 with the Open University, based at Milton Keynes in Buckinghamshire, England. This offered degree courses to all, based on correspondence, televised lectures, and residential courses held at various centres throughout the country.

Australia, New Zealand, and Canada

Australian and New Zealand universities, the oldest of which date from the 19th century, are all modelled on the English system. The first Australian university was established at Sydney in 1850. The University of Otago (1869) was the first in New Zealand. Today there are 19 universities in Australia and six in New Zealand. Postgraduate education in both countries has expanded since World War II, and there has been a greater emphasis on research. Universities in both countries are publicly supported.

Canada's earliest universities, modelled on European universities, had religious connections. There are today 65 publicly supported universities in Canada. Among the leading Canadian universities are McGill University, Montreal, founded in 1821; the University of Toronto (1827); Queen's University, Ontario (1841); the French-language Laval University, Quebec (1852); and the University of British Columbia, Vancouver (1908).

ZEFA

Entrance to the University of Adelaide, founded in 1874. It is Australia's third oldest university.

URAL MOUNTAINS. Stretching some 2,000 kilometres (1,250 miles) southwards across the Soviet Union from the icy Kara Sea almost to the Caspian Sea are the Ural Mountains. The eastern slopes form the boundary between Europe and Asia. Although in some places they reach heights of more than 1,500 metres (5,000 feet), and the highest mountain Mount Narodnaya is 1,894 metres (6,214 feet), there are many valley ways across them, particularly at Sverdlovsk through which passes the Trans-Siberian Railway. The slopes of the Urals, especially on the western side, are quite gentle.

The Urals are important for their great mineral wealth. They have long been one of the main sources of the rare metal platinum, and the deposits of iron, copper, chromium, and bauxite are very large. Gold and silver, gems and precious stones, coal, and asbestos are also found. On the west of the range is the largest oil field in the Soviet Union. Pipelines carry oil from here to the chief industrial towns and bring natural gas from central Asia. The iron and steel and chemical industries are most important in the district, among whose chief cities are Perm, Sverdlovsk, Chelyabinsk, and Magnitogorsk.

URANIUM is a rare whitish metal that looks rather like bright steel but is nearly two-and-a-half times as heavy. It had very few uses until 1940, when a method of obtaining energy from it was discovered.

Uranium was discovered in 1789 by the German chemist Martin Heinrich Klaproth (1743–1817), who obtained the new substance from the rock called pitchblende. He named it uranium in honour of Sir William Herschel's discovery of the planet Uranus in 1781. Klaproth thought he had obtained an element, or pure substance, but in 1841 the French scientist Eugène-Melchior Péligot (1811–90) showed that what Klaproth had really obtained was uranium oxide, a compound of uranium and oxygen. In 1842 Péligot was the first to prepare metallic uranium.

In 1896 the French scientist Antoine Becquerel (1852–1908) showed that uranium compounds give off rays which, although they cannot be seen, behave like rays of light in that they darken a photographic plate or film, even if it is wrapped up. This property, called radioactivity, was examined by Pierre Curie and his wife Marie (see CURIE, MARIE AND PIERRE). They discovered an even more powerfully radioactive element, which was called radium.

Courtesy, National Film Board of Canada

A uranium mine near Blind River, Ontario, Canada. Canada is one of the world's major uranium producers.

It was shown that radioactive substances do not stay the same, but change (decay) into other elements. Radioactive decay occurs because the nuclei of radioactive atoms are heavy and unstable. They break up at a fixed average rate to form other atoms, at the same time giving off particles or rays. Uranium decays to form radium, which in turn decays, and so on, until (millions of years later) a stable form of lead is formed. (See ATOM; NEUTRON; RADIOACTIVITY.)

The method by which energy is obtained from uranium is explained in the article NUCLEAR ENERGY. The energy is produced in the form of heat. Weight for weight, several million times more energy can be produced from uranium than from the burning of fossil fuels such as coal and oil.

Uranium is therefore an extremely valuable substance. Before 1914 most of it was obtained from Joachimsthal in south Germany (now

Jachymov in northwest Czechoslovakia), but from 1924 the deposits in Katanga, in the Belgian Congo (now Zaire), became the main source of supply. After World War II (1939–45) uranium was discovered in Canada—in the Great Bear Lake area and later in the province of Ontario. It was also found in the United States on the Colorado plateau and, in far greater quantities, in the Ambrosia Lake district of New Mexico. Considerable quantities are obtained from the gold-bearing rock mined in the Witwatersrand region of South Africa. Uranium is also mined in Australia, France, China, and the Soviet Union.

Uranium occurs in nature as a mixture of two main forms, or isotopes: uranium-238 (which accounts for more than 99 per cent) and uranium-235 (which accounts for less than 1 per cent). Uranium is never found in the pure state because it is a substance that combines with others very readily. The extraction of uranium from the ores (rock and earth) containing it is complicated, for there are generally other metals mingled with it. Usually the ore is ground into powder and treated with strong acid or alkali which is allowed to soak through it. Afterwards the uranium is recovered (usually in the form of uranium oxide) from the liquid. The manufacture of uranium metal from uranium oxide is always done under very strict control, because unless great care is taken at every stage the process or the product may become dangerous.

URANUS is the seventh planet out from the Sun in the Solar System and the first planet to be discovered following the invention of the telescope. This discovery was made accidentally by the German-born English astronomer William Herschel in 1781 during a routine sky survey at his observatory in Bath (See HERSCHEL, SIR WILLIAM). On 13 March in that year he came across an object that looked decidedly unstarlike in appearance, and an observation made a few nights later showed that its position against the background stars had altered. This led Herschel to believe, initially, that he had discovered a comet, but prolonged observation of its orbital motion brought astronomers to the conclusion that the object was in fact a planet. The name Uranus, in honour of the ancient sky god who in Greco-Roman mythology was the father of Saturn, was suggested by the German astronomer J. E. Bode.

When favourably positioned Uranus can actually become visible to the unaided eye. In view of this it is surprising that its discovery was not announced earlier. In fact, the planet had actually been observed many times before 1781, although in each case it was mistaken for a star and was even catalogued as one.

Uranus is a strange greenish-blue world a little larger than the planet Neptune, which it resembles closely (see NEPTUNE). Like Jupiter, Saturn, and Neptune, Uranus is classed as one of the giant planets. As far as we know, it is a low-density world and consists of a rocky core surrounded by water and shrouded in a deep, dense atmosphere made up of hydrogen and helium. The top of this atmosphere looks remarkably featureless and has none of the belts and zones visible on Jupiter and Saturn. It seems to consist of a cloud layer of frozen methane gas. The methane absorbs red light and reflects the rest, which accounts for the greenish-blue colour of Uranus. Infra-red measurements taken from Earth-based observatories indicate that the temperature at the top of the planet's atmosphere is a bitterly cold −213°C(−351°F).

Uranus is some 51,000 kilometres (31,700 miles) in diameter, almost four times the size of the Earth. It takes almost exactly 84 years to travel once around the Sun, orbiting it at an average distance of nearly 2,870 million kilometres (1,783 million miles). This puts Uranus twice as far away from the Sun as Saturn is.

A curious and unique aspect of Uranus is the fact that its axis of rotation is tilted at an angle of almost 98°. (That of the Earth is only 23½°.) This means that Uranus is travelling around the Sun on its side. Thus at one point in its orbit the south pole of the planet faces the Sun while the north pole is in darkness and at the opposite point the north pole faces the Sun while the south pole is in darkness.

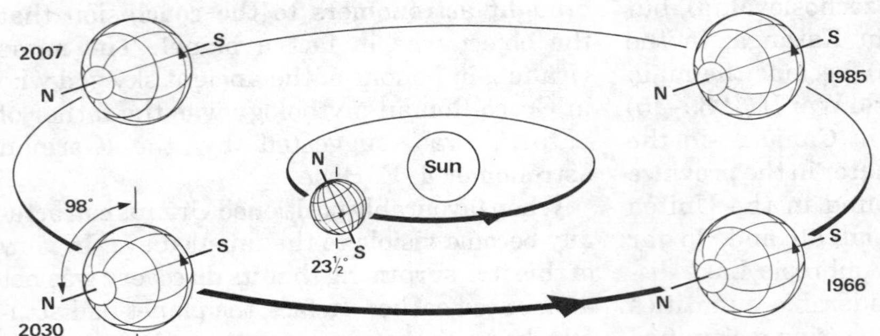

Uranus is unique among the planets of the Solar System because its axis of rotation is tilted at an angle of 98°. The Earth's axis, by comparison, is only tilted at 23½°. Because Uranus orbits the sun on its side the poles of Uranus each experience a prolonged period of day followed by an equally lengthy period of night. It takes Uranus 84 years to complete an orbit.

On 10 March 1977 astronomers were able to study a rare event when Uranus passed in front of a faint star known by the catalogue number SAO 158687. As Uranus approached the line of sight to the star, the star appeared to "wink" five times. The same thing happened after Uranus had crossed in front of the star. From these "winkings" observers deduced that Uranus has a system of at least five rings surrounding it. Later findings have shown that the number of rings is in fact ten (see below).

Before 1986 everything we knew about Uranus had been learned from observations made from the Earth. But on 23 January of that year the American spaceprobe Voyager 2, which had been launched in August 1977, flew past the planet at a distance of about 81,000 kilometres (50,000 miles). It took photographs and measurements that added enormously to our knowledge of Uranus. But the Voyager 2 mission presented some unexpected results.

Voyager 2 detected a magnetic field on Uranus. The source of the field, however, is not at the planet's centre but at a point about halfway between the equator and the north pole. Like the Earth, Jupiter, and Saturn, Uranus is surrounded by an area of magnetic influence known as a magnetosphere. But because the magnetic field is "off centre", the magnetosphere seems to wobble. Charged particles trapped in the magnetosphere are speeded up near Uranus's magnetic poles, producing radio waves that regularly vary in strength as Uranus rotates on its axis. Thus Voyager 2 was able to provide the first accurate measurement of Uranus's "day" based on these signals—about 17¼ hours.

Before the Voyager 2 encounter, Uranus was known to have five faint satellites. Two of these, Titania and Oberon, were discovered by William Herschel in 1787. The others—Miranda, Ariel, and Umbriel—were discovered in the 19th and 20th centuries. Voyager found another ten moons, all of them much smaller than the five already known. Voyager's photographs of the five largest moons revealed that each was different. Oberon shows many large craters probably made not long after the satellite was formed. There is also a mountain about 20 kilometres (12 miles) high. Titania, the largest of the Uranian satellites, has few old large craters; its surface is covered with smaller and much younger craters and deep cracks. Umbriel's surface shows only large ancient craters, suggesting that it has changed little since it was formed; yet it should be peppered with small impact craters of more recent times. Ariel, similar in size to Umbriel, reflects twice as much light as its twin. The surface has cracked in Ariel's recent history, and a lava-like material has flowed out from the interior to cover some of its large, old craters. The smallest and innermost of the five large satellites, Miranda, surprisingly has the most varied terrain. It consists of rugged highland areas and grooved or ridged lowland regions. In one place a crack in the surface has created a cliff 20 kilometres (12 miles) high.

Voyager confirmed the presence of ten rings, all of which are narrow and very faint, reflecting very little of the sunlight that falls on them. The rings seem to be regions of

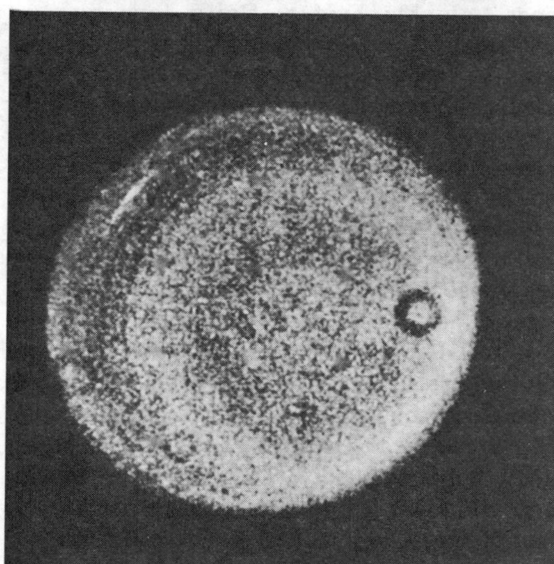

Science Photo Library

Voyager 2 passed by Uranus in 1986. It photographed the planet's rings (top) lit by the Sun. A computer-processed image of Uranus's whole disc shows a white streak of cloud at the top left of the picture.

concentrations of particles within a sort of "doughnut" of very thin material surrounding Uranus. The particles may be methane ice that has been changed into a black organic compound by the effects of radiation. Several of the ten small satellites discovered by Voyager 2 appear to be acting as "shepherds", using their gravitational influence to keep the rings from breaking up. All the rings and satellites are in the same plane as Uranus's equator, that is, at right angles to the planet's orbital path.

URUGUAY, the smallest of the ten South American republics, is only 500 kilometres (310 miles) from north to south, and 470 kilometres (290 miles) from east to west. It lies in the southeastern part of the continent, on the north bank of the Rio de la Plata estuary on the Atlantic Ocean. Its neighbours are Brazil to the north and Argentina to the west.

Uruguay has no mountains but is a fairly hilly country, with many streams and rivers. It takes its name from its largest river, the Rio Uruguay, which forms the western boundary with Argentina. The word Uruguay is Guarani Indian and means "the water where birds and shellfish abound". The biggest tributary of the Rio Uruguay is the Rio Negro, which crosses the country diagonally from northeast to southwest. In the west, streams from the hills flow through wooded valleys, but most of Uruguay consists of rolling pasture land.

The Atlantic coast is about 190 kilometres (120 miles) long with sandy beaches all the way from the Brazilian boundary to the Uruguayan capital, Montevideo. The climate is pleasant and healthy, and cooler than that of southern Brazil. However, the sudden storms which now and then sweep across the pampas (plains) in Argentina also occur in Uruguay.

The local trees are willow, acacia, rosemary, myrtle, laurel, and mimosa. Early Spanish settlers introduced poplars, peaches, and many

Popperfoto

Left: The holiday town of Punta del Este. **Right**: A herd of Hereford cattle. Beef is one of Uruguay's main exports.

other fruit trees. Eucalyptus and fir trees have been planted among the sand dunes along the coast. The pampas are bright with scarlet and white verbenas and other brilliant wild flowers.

Most of the wild animals of Uruguay have been killed off. The rhea, or South American ostrich, is seldom seen, although a few are kept in a half-tamed state. A few pumas and jaguars live on the wooded islets and banks of the larger rivers, and there are *carpinchos*, or water hogs, and a kind of small armadillo called the *mulita*. The birds include vultures, parakeets, hummingbirds, bright-plumaged cardinals, herons, and large flocks of lapwings. The *horneros* (oven birds) build their oven-shaped nests on telegraph posts, and a common sight on the pampas are burrowing owls perched on fence-posts.

In 1603 the Spanish governor of Paraguay, to the north, sent 100 cattle and 100 horses to Uruguay, then still uncolonized. The animals were left to run wild on the pastures. The herds increased, and when about 100 years later Spanish settlers arrived along the northern bank of the Rio de la Plata, they found many thousands of wild cattle roaming over the Uruguayan hills and plains.

The settlers became *gauchos* (cowboys of the pampas, usually of mixed Spanish and Indian origin), rounding up the cattle. They sold the hides to merchants, who sent them abroad. Sheep- and cattle-rearing are the most important occupations today and wool is Uruguay's most valuable export. Dairy farming and agriculture are increasing, but production is usually sufficient only for local needs. The main crops are wheat, maize, oats, and rice. Peanuts are used for making vegetable oil; grapes are made into wine.

Industries and People

In the towns the most important industries are those to do with freezing and packing meat. There are also large textile mills and flour mills. Sugar and petroleum brought from abroad are refined (purified) in Uruguay to meet local needs, and other factories make tyres, chemicals, clothing, furniture, cigarettes, wine, and beer. Tourists, from Argentina and Brazil, make up another important source of income.

FACTS ABOUT URUGUAY

AREA: 176,215 square kilometres (68,037 square miles).
POPULATION: 3,058,000 (1987).
GOVERNMENT: Independent republic.
CAPITAL: Montevideo.
GEOGRAPHICAL FEATURES: The country forms part of the pampas region of South America, and consists of a low, rolling plain, with some higher ground in the north. It is bounded in the west by the Rio Uruguay and in the south by the Rio de la Plata.
CHIEF PRODUCTS: Cattle, sheep, wheat, maize, oats, oilseeds, potatoes, grapes.
IMPORTANT TOWNS: Montevideo, Paysandu, Salto.
EDUCATION: Children must attend school, which is free, between the ages of 6 and 14.

Uruguay has no coal or oil, so hydroelectric power is important. The Rio Negro has been dammed to supply water power. Minerals are scarce and belong to the state, as do many industries. Quarries in the hills provide granite and marble.

The building of railways began in the 1860s, and by 1911 Uruguay had a greater length of lines in proportion to its size than any other South American country. The railways, like the chief roads, fan out from Montevideo, which is the chief port. There are regular air services between the chief towns and Carrasco airport outside Montevideo.

The Uruguayans are not a seafaring people and have few large ships. Many river craft, however, ply up and down the Rio de la Plata, the Rio Uruguay, and the Rio Negro. Small steamers can reach Salto, Uruguay's second largest city, on the Rio Uruguay.

The people of Uruguay are mostly of European descent, chiefly from Spain and Italy. The American Indians who lived in the country before the Spaniards came have died out, but there are families of mixed Spanish and Indian blood in the country districts.

About one-third of the population lives in the southeastern part of Uruguay, in and around Montevideo, which is the only large city (see MONTEVIDEO). Paysandu, the third city of the republic, is the centre of the meat-packing industry. The chief area for cultivation is in the south, stretching along the shore of the Rio de la Plata. This area, however, is only a very small part of the whole country.

The language of Uruguay is Spanish, and most of the people are Roman Catholic. Although there are not enough schools and teachers in the country districts, education in Uruguay is very advanced compared with other South American countries.

Among a number of notable writers, Uruguay has produced one of South America's foremost playwrights, Florencio Sanchez (1875–1910), and the short-story writer, Horacio Quiroga (1878–1937).

History

Indian tribes inhabited the area before the arrival of the first European explorers in the early 16th century. The Spanish did not begin to colonize Uruguay until the 18th century. As the land had no precious metals and was far from the route between the port of Buenos Aires and the gold and silver mines of Peru, the Spanish colonists passed it by. At that time they called it the *Banda Oriental*, meaning "eastern shore", as it lay on the east bank of the Rio Uruguay. Today the full official title of the country is *Republica Oriental del Uruguay* ("Oriental Republic of

Top: On Uruguay's plains, gauchos (cowboys) round up cattle for shipment to market. **Centre**: A sea-lion colony on Lobos Island, off the Uruguayan coast. **Bottom**: Huge sheep herds graze on extensive Uruguayan pastureland. Sheep form the basis for Uruguay's important wool industry.

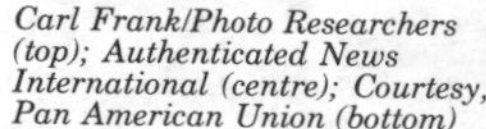

Carl Frank/Photo Researchers (top); Authenticated News International (centre); Courtesy, Pan American Union (bottom)

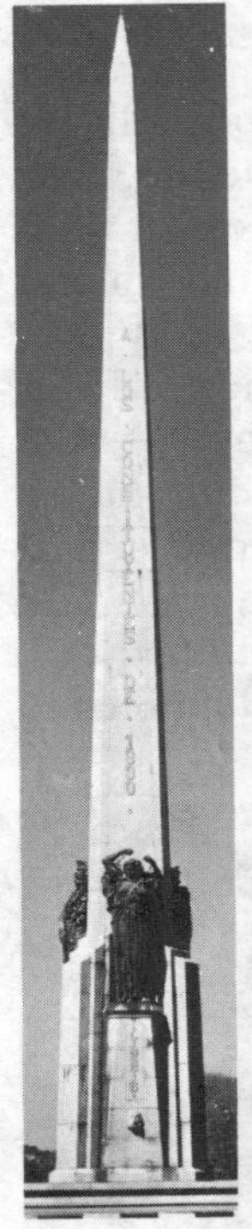

In Montevideo the Obelisk (left) honours the patriots of independence. In Plaza Independencia (below right) stands a statue of Jose Artigas, a national hero. Sandy beaches (bottom) line the city's waterfront.

J. Allan Cash/Rapho Guillumette (left); Carl Frank/Photo Researchers (below right); Authenticated News International (bottom)

Uruguay"), and the people still call themselves Orientales.

During the 17th century the herds of cattle increased in the Banda Oriental and some horsemen crossed the river from Buenos Aires to get hides. However, it was the Portuguese from Brazil who made the earliest attempt at large scale settlement. In 1680 a Portuguese expedition reached the Rio de la Plata and camped where the town of Colonia now is. The Spanish on the south bank were determined not to allow the Portuguese to establish themselves in the Plata estuary, so they attacked and defeated them. In 1726 to help in thrusting back further advances from Brazil the Spanish built a fort where Montevideo now stands. That was the beginning of a struggle between Buenos Aires and Brazil that lasted for more than 100 years.

Until the early part of the 19th century, the Banda Oriental was part of the Spanish province of La Plata. The fight for independence from Spain was led by a *gaucho* named José Gervasio Artigas (1774–1850), who became the national hero. However, Artigas was driven into exile in Paraguay in 1816, when the Portuguese invaded and overran the Banda Oriental. After his fall, the Banda was taken over by Brazil. Meanwhile the people of Buenos Aires had declared their own independence from Spain. They felt that as the Banda Oriental had formerly been Spanish it now belonged to Buenos Aires, not to the Portuguese. The struggle for Montevideo therefore began again.

In 1825, 33 Uruguayan patriots—now known as "The Immortal Thirty-Three"—who had been in exile, set out to free their land from the Portuguese. They were helped by forces from Buenos Aires. In 1828 the Buenos Aires government and Brazil signed a treaty giving up their claims to the Banda Oriental and recognizing Uruguay as an independent republic.

Peace did not come with independence. Quarrels between local politicians, some of whom were supported by Buenos Aires and others by Brazil, led to civil war. In 1865 Uruguay was drawn into a war on the side of Brazil and Argentina against Paraguay. Confusion and disorder continued in Uruguay until 1906.

In 1903 a remarkable statesman and social reformer named José Batlle y Ordonez (1856–1929) became president. Under his wise direction Uruguay developed into a peaceful and democratic country, recognized as a pioneer nation in social and political reforms. The eight-hour working day was established in Uruguay long before any other South American republic, or even the United States, passed such a law.

President Batlle y Ordonez believed that state ownership was in the people's interest, and that the money for the public services and the industries should come from the Uruguayans themselves and not be borrowed from abroad. So in Uruguay the state owns the railways, buses, electric plants, telephones and postal services, several banks and the port of Montevideo. It also controls the nation's television and radio.

In 1952 the posts of President and Vice-President were abolished, and Uruguay was then governed by a nine-man national council elected for four years. However, the economy of Uruguay suffered because of a world slump in wool, beef, and hides, and in 1966 the Uruguayans voted to restore the old presidential system. A socialist revolutionary group, the Tupamaro National Liberation Front, began a guerrilla war against the government, kidnapping and killing some politicians. The Tupamaros were eventually defeated by the army, which in the 1970s played an increasingly important part in government. From 1973, Congress was dissolved, and the President ruled directly, with the advice of the army and a council of state. In 1984 Uruguay returned to democratic civilian rule.

UTAH. The state of Utah in the United States was founded in July 1847 by a group of 143 Mormons, led by Brigham Young. The Mormon Church, the Church of Jesus Christ of the Latter-Day Saints, was founded in Fayette County, New York, in 1830. Because it disassociated itself from the traditional Christian denominations, it quickly found itself the object of persecution. The Mormons moved westward along the American frontier to find places to live and worship as they chose. From New York they went to Ohio, then to Jackson County, Missouri, and then to Nauvoo, Illinois. Even at Nauvoo, a community they had built up from nothing, they were attacked by violent mobs in 1846. They fled across Iowa to Council Bluffs, and finally decided that only in the unoccupied Far West could they find peace.

At the foot of the Wasatch Mountains they founded Salt Lake City to be the capital of the State of Deseret. As founded, Deseret included all of what is now Utah and Nevada, along with portions of Idaho, Oregon, Colorado, New Mexico, Arizona, and California. The US Congress eventually whittled away this vast territory until it became today's Utah.

ZEFA

The Mormon temple in Salt Lake City, state capital of Utah, and Mormon capital of the world.

While it existed, Deseret was the most successful attempt to combine church and state since the Puritans had settled Massachusetts in the 17th century. The Mormons made a desert bloom into a rich agricultural region. They prospered under the strict discipline of Young and his successors. The Mormons still exert a strong, and sometimes decisive influence, on the social, political, and economic climate of the state. (See also MORMONS.)

The Land

Utah is a state of mountains, deserts, and high plateaus. It is bounded on the north by Idaho and Wyoming, on the east by Colorado, on the south by Arizona, and on the west by Nevada. At its southeast corner it meets New Mexico at what is called the Four Corners, the only place in the United States where four states touch forming perfect 90° angles.

Utah has three natural regions: the

These unusual rock features in Monument Valley, Utah, were formed by wind erosion.

Courtesy, Utah Tourist and Publicity Council

Colorado Plateau, the Great Basin, and the Rocky Mountains. The Colorado Plateau covers a little more than half the state in the southeast. It is a region of high mesas (table-shaped hills) and brightly coloured canyons. The great Colorado River passes through on its way to Arizona. Many of the streams that join the Colorado have cut steep canyons across the plateau.

Courtesy, Salt Lake City Chamber of Commerce

Alta, in the Wasatch Mountains, is a popular ski resort.

The Great Basin region, covering about one third of Utah, has small mountain ranges separated by flat valleys. The Great Salt Lake is located in the northern section of the basin. To the west of the lake is the Great Salt Lake Desert, which includes the Bonneville Salt Flats, an area made famous by several land-speed record attempts. The whole region was once part of the huge Lake Bonneville, a body of water as large as today's Lake Michigan.

The Rocky Mountain region contains two major ranges, the Wasatch and the Uinta. Of the two, the Uinta has the higher peaks, some reaching more than 4,000 metres (13,000 feet). The Uinta is the only significant mountain range in the United States running east to west instead of north to south.

Utah has four distinct seasons, an unusual feature for a desert region. It has a continental climate, with hot summers and cold winters. Rainfall is slight, averaging only 330 millimetres (13 inches). Most of the agriculture, therefore, depends on irrigation. The growing season along the southern border is about 200 days, while in the northern mountain areas it is less than 60 days.

The lack of human settlement in so much of Utah leaves abundant room for wildlife. Among the large animals in the highlands are mule, deer, elk, antelope, bobcats, cougars, coyotes, and bighorn sheep. There are still small herds of buffalo on the Colorado Plateau. Smaller animals include porcupine, beavers, minks, lizards, horned toads, rattlesnakes, and prairie dogs.

Millions of migratory birds stop annually to feed at sanctuaries near Great Salt Lake. Birds native to the highlands are vultures, wild turkeys, pheasants, eagles, partridges, and hawks.

The People

The earliest known inhabitants of Utah were the cliff-dwelling Anasazi Indians (see also CLIFF DWELLERS). When European explorers arrived they found tribes of Utes, Shoshones, and Paiutes. Today the population is overwhelmingly of European descent, particularly from several Mormon migrations, with about five per cent made up of other groups.

More than three-quarters of the state's population lives in a narrow belt stretching from Ogden in the north, through the Salt Lake City area, south to Provo, a distance of about 145 kilometres (90 miles). Salt Lake City, the state capital, has the largest population, followed by Provo, Ogden, and Sandy City.

The Economy

The year 1869 was a dividing line in the state's history. Until then the Mormons had lived in relative seclusion, developing an economy based on agriculture, handicrafts, and small industry. In 1869 the last spike was driven in the ground to complete the first transcontinental railway. Utah immediately became more accessible to emigrants from the East. Many of the new arrivals went into mining, a type of work the Mormons had avoided. After statehood in 1896 the resources of the state were increasingly exploited by corporations and enterprising individuals from outside Utah.

The present economy is quite diverse. Mining is the chief industry. Utah ranks 21st in the United States mineral production. The state is the world's leading producer of beryllium (a metallic element) and is among the top five US states in production of gold, silver, lead, uranium, and molybdenum. Other minerals contributing to the state's prosperity are coal, copper, gilsonite (asphaltite), and petroleum. The Great Salt Lake contains valuable minerals, and several chemical industries are located on its shores.

Most of the farmland is used to graze livestock, including beef and dairy cattle, sheep, pigs, and poultry. Field crops grown on irrigated land include sugar beets, wheat, barley, corn, oats, hay, potatoes, peas, and tomatoes. Fruit crops include cherries, melons, apricots, apples, peaches, and pears.

Courtesy, Utah Department of Publicity and Industrial Development/Clyde Anderson Photo

Aerial view of the Bingham open-pit copper mine. This area of north-central Utah is rich in minerals.

Tourism brings in a good deal of money annually. Utah is well known for its winter sports facilities. There are also three national parks: Bryce Canyon, Zion, and Canyonlands.

Education

The Mormons established their own schools beginning in 1847. The public (state) school system was started by the territorial government in 1860, but no school was opened for six years. Tax-supported high schools were authorized by the legislature in 1910.

The University of Utah was founded in 1855 as the University of Deseret in Salt Lake City. The leading Mormon institution of higher edu-

Courtesy, United States Steel Corporation

The steelworks at Geneva, on the outskirts of Provo, Utah, are the largest in the United States West.

cation is Brigham Young University, located at Provo.

History

The first wagon train of Mormons arrived in 1847 to found a settlement and to prepare the way for further migrations. By October 1847 more than 2,000 Mormons had arrived. They set about building irrigation projects, laying out their city, and establishing schools. In 1848 the colonists planned their civil government, and the following year they drew up their constitution for the State of Deseret. Brigham Young became the first governor, and remained in office until 1857.

FACTS AND FIGURES

Area: 219,887 square kilometres (84,899 square miles).
POPULATION: 1,665,000 (1986).
MOUNTAIN RANGES: Wasatch and Uinta; highest peaks: King's Peak, 4,123 metres (13,528 feet); Hayden Peak, 3,802 metres (12,473 feet); Marsh Peak, 3,731 metres (12,240 feet); Nebo, 3,620 metres (11,877 feet).
RIVERS: Colorado, Green, San Rafael, Virgin, Sevier, Bear, Provo, Weber, and San Juan.
CITIES: Salt Lake City, 163,033; Provo, 74,378; Ogden, 64,407; Orem, 52,399; Sandy City, 50,546.

By 1850 the United States had won the Mexican War and claimed the whole Southwest. Deseret, cut down from its original vast size, became the Utah Territory. By 1860 there were more than 150 self-sufficient Mormon communities.

Conflict with the Indians was kept to a minimum. The Mormons decided it was cheaper and easier to feed the Indians than to fight them. The Mormons were not so fortunate with the United States government. Mormon practices differed from those of most other religious groups. Polygamy, having more than one wife, was not accepted at all by the rest of the nation. The Mormons had to abandon polygamy before being accepted into the Union. On 4 January 1896, Utah was admitted as the 45th state.

By the early 20th century there was a substantial non-Mormon population engaged in mining and livestock raising. The first ore to be processed in large amounts was copper, from a mining claim that had first been registered in 1863. Smelting plants built at Magna, Tooele, Garfield, and Murray made Utah one of the world's leading smelting regions.

World War II brought the need for many metals to fill war needs. The Geneva Steel plant was built in 1943 as part of the war effort. Manufacturing and mining continued to expand after the war, and Utah became the site of several large defence installations. Industries specialising in rocketry, aircraft, computers, and other electronic devices have been established in the state.

UZBEKISTAN. The Uzbek Soviet Socialist Republic is the fourth largest in the Soviet Union, covering an area of 447,400 square kilometres (172,700 square miles). It is located in Soviet Central Asia and is the principal cotton-producing area in the Soviet Union, and the third largest in the world. It is bordered by the Kazakh Soviet Socialist Republic to the north and west, the Turkmen SSR and Afghanistan to the south, and the Tadzhik SSR and Kirghiz SSR to the east. It is also called Uzbekistan.

Most of the region is a sandy desert lowland. The part west of the Aral Sea rises to the Ust-Urt Plateau, and in the east it extends into the foothills and valleys of the Tien Shan and Alaj mountains. The streams that flow from these mountains provide water for the irrigation of desert land. They include the Amu-Darya, Syr-Darya, and Zeravshan rivers and their tributaries. There are many fertile oases.

Irrigation agriculture is the most important activity in Uzbekistan. The long, hot summers are exceptionally favourable for growing cotton, rice, and the mulberry trees that are necessary for the production of silk. Farmers in Uzbekistan also produce wheat, and raise cattle, and Karakul sheep.

Industrial plants in various Uzbekistan cities process the locally produced cotton, silk, and other agricultural products and ship them to all parts of the Soviet Union. Tashkent, the capital and largest city, manufactures agricultural and other heavy machinery. It is also a major Soviet cultural, educational, and transport centre for Central Asia. Samarkand and Bukhara are educational and textile centres. The Uzbek republic has a well developed railway system that connects all the important inhabited areas. Tashkent is the principal air centre of Soviet Central Asia. Most of the inhabitants are Uzbeks, a Muslim group of Turkic people and the republic is a centre for Muslim culture. Russians are the second largest group.

Uzbekistan has a history that dates back to the pre-Christian era. Samarkand was a thriving capital city when captured by Alexander the Great in the 4th century BC. It was later invaded and ruled by various Asian groups, including the Arabs, Turks, and Mongols. It reached its height of glory as the capital of Tamerlane, or Timur, in the 14th century. (See TAMERLANE.) At that time the city became a world famous cultural centre with schools, a college, and an astronomical observatory. Many of the beautifully decorated buildings that were built during the period are still preserved. Among the most famous are several Muslim mosques and the tomb of Tamerlane.

Bukhara early became a trading centre for caravan routes from distant areas of Asia. Bukhara, Kokand, and Khiva became the capital cities of three separate Muslim states. These states were forced to become part of the Russian Empire in the second half of the 19th century. In 1924, the Soviet government established the Uzbek area as one of the union republics of the USSR. The population is 17,496,000 (1984).

ZEFA

Futuristic fountains stand in front of the imposing town hall in Lenin Square, Tashkent.

VACCINATION AND INOCULATION are methods of protecting people against a serious illness by giving them a mild form of it so that they do not catch the serious form later in life.

Until the end of the 18th century, one of the most dreaded diseases was smallpox, which killed many people and disfigured many more. Inoculation against smallpox using the contents of the actual "pocks" (the spots on the skin) was carried on to a certain extent in the East, but it was not very successful mainly because serious disease often resulted.

Vaccination, which proved to be the best method of preventing smallpox, was discovered by Dr. Edward Jenner in 1796 (see JENNER, EDWARD). Jenner believed that cowpox, a mild disease transmitted by cows, was caused by the same virus that caused smallpox, but that the disease was weakened when it passed through the cow. To prove this, he inoculated a boy with the contents of cowpox spots, then with smallpox germs. The boy remained healthy. Jenner's methods were accepted and vaccination programmes were started in many countries. Thanks to a worldwide effort smallpox has now been wiped out.

"Inoculation" and "vaccination" are often confused. To *inoculate* is to put into the body the microbes that will cause a mild case of a disease. After the body suffers this mild attack, it is then resistant to the more serious forms of the disease. "Inoculation" also means introducing germs or other microbes into

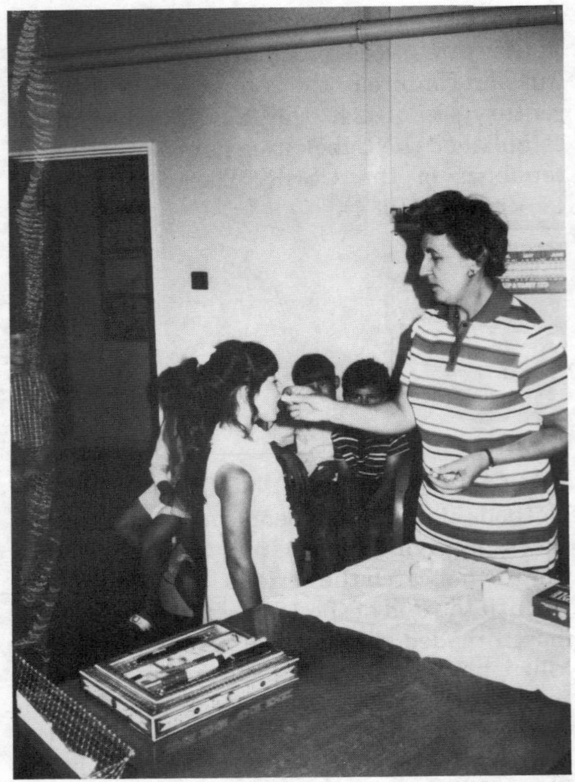

Picturepoint

Although most vaccinations are better done by injection, polio vaccine is one of the few that can be effectively given by mouth.

something. For example, a laboratory worker may *inoculate* a culture dish with bacteria, using a needle and syringe or a fine tube.

Vaccination originally meant to protect against smallpox only, by inoculating with cowpox germs ("vaccinia") as Jenner did. However, Louis Pasteur suggested that, in honour of Jenner, the term be applied to any infection where weakened or changed living germs were used to give protection against similar, more dangerous ones. So now *vaccination* applies to any infectious disease where this is done. The substance containing the germs, which are usually weakened or disabled by heat or chemicals, is called the *vaccine*.

Many germs are destroyed in the digestive system if they are swallowed. So vaccination is usually done through a break in the skin or by an injection into the blood.

Once in the body, the germs are attacked by the body's immune system and killed off. The mild case of the disease is over. Next time similar germs enter, the immune system will recognize them at once and destroy them before they have time to multiply and cause disease. Producing protection, or immunity, using a vaccine in this way is called *immunization* (see IMMUNITY.)

Immunization is carried out against many diseases, including diphtheria, tetanus, whooping cough (pertussis), measles, polio, cholera, tuberculosis, yellow fever, rabies, typhoid, and influenza (flu). Different countries have different rules about which diseases are protected against, and at which ages. Usually injections are given during infancy or childhood, to give protection as early as possible. In some cases, to lessen side-effects, the vaccinations are given at intervals. For protection against certain diseases, such as tetanus, you need a booster dose every few years.

In some countries, vaccination against certain diseases is compulsory. Others prefer a voluntary arrangement. Some countries do not allow visitors to enter unless they have proof that they have been vaccinated against certain infections. Even after a disease has died out in a region, if a proportion of people are not vaccinated and an infected person comes in, the disease can take hold once again.

Vaccination has brought enormous benefits, but there are arguments against it. Some people see it as an infringement of their personal freedom—something being done to their bodies that they might not agree with. Also, vaccination is never completely 100 per cent effective, a few people may catch the infection later. And in some instances, such as whooping cough, vaccination has caused severe illness and even brain damage and mental disability. Some people argue that it is wrong to vaccinate a healthy child, with a risk of injury, when there is a chance of avoiding the disease naturally. In the case of whooping cough, however, the risk of someone dying from the infection when not vaccinated is many times greater than the risk of damage caused by the vaccination itself.

VACUUM. The word vacuum comes from the Latin *vacuus*, meaning empty. A total vacuum would be an empty space from which all forms of matter—solid, liquid, or gas—had been removed (see MATTER). Such a total vacuum has never been created; outer space was at one time thought to be a true vacuum, but it is now known to contain minute amounts of gases, notably hydrogen, and sometimes particles of dust.

Special vacuum pumps can be used to create partial vacuums which are classified as soft, or low (when a relatively small percentage of gas is removed from a space), and hard, or high (when a high percentage of gas is removed leaving a space in which pressure is considerably less than atmospheric pressure).

Vacuums are created and used for a variety of purposes. There are separate articles on VACUUM CLEANER and VACUUM FLASK. Electric-light bulbs contain a partial vacuum so that the filament does not burn up in the oxygen of air. Vacuum tubes are essential components of much modern electronic and scientific equipment including television sets, particle accelerators, and electron microscopes.

Vacuums are also important in the food, drink, and medical industries. Liquids under vacuum boil at lower temperatures than at atmospheric pressure. Vacuum evaporation is useful for concentrating solutions such as milk, fruit, and vegetable juices without destroying the taste or quality of the product. Many processed foods and some medicines are vacuum-packed so that they keep fresh longer.

VACUUM CLEANER is an electric machine for removing dust from carpets, furniture, floors, and walls.

Before the days of vacuum cleaners or carpet sweepers the only way to clean a carpet or upholstered furniture was to brush or beat it. The dust filled the air and much of it then settled back on the furniture and carpet. A vacuum cleaner sucks the dust straight into a bag without spreading it about and removes it more effectively than a brush can.

A vacuum cleaner contains an electric motor which drives a fan. This creates a vacuum—an empty space (see VACUUM)—into which air rushes. The loosened dirt goes through with the air and is trapped in a bag. The air continues through the machine, thus maintaining the suction.

Vacuum cleaners are of either the upright

Mary Evans Picture Library

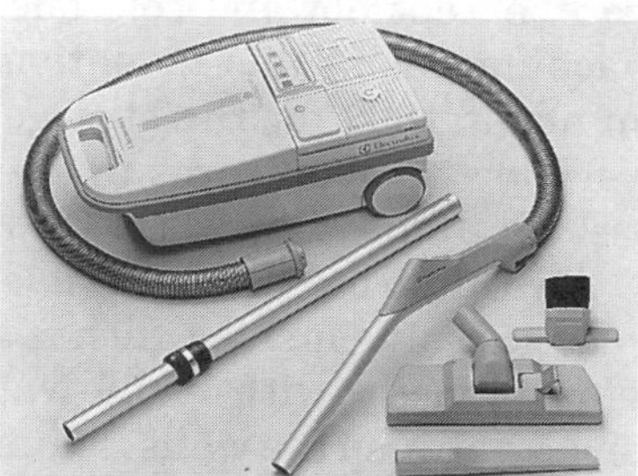

Courtesy, Electrolux

Far left: A hand-operated vacuum cleaner as used in 1903. Supported by a belt round the operator's waist, the bellows sucked in dust when compressed and released. **Left**: A modern upright vacuum cleaner for use on carpets. **Above**: A canister vacuum cleaner with a variety of attachments for cleaning all kinds of surface.

type or the canister type. An upright cleaner consists of a long handle with the motor and fan at the end closest to the ground. There are revolving brushes underneath operated by pushing the cleaner backwards and forwards. The bag is attached to the handle. The canister cleaner contains the motor, fan, and bag in a cylindrical or spherical canister on to which a tube is fixed with the brush at the end. There is usually a selection of brushes or other attachments for cleaning different sorts of surface. In the older vacuum cleaners the dust bag is made of fabric and must be emptied when full. More modern cleaners have disposable paper dustbags.

The earliest vacuum cleaners appeared in the 1850s with fans or bellows worked by hand. The earliest electric cleaners could not be moved and were only used to clean the floors of large buildings. In the United States, James Murray Spangler developed a portable electric vacuum cleaner and he sold the idea to William Henry Hoover, the manufacturer who first mass produced them and whose name has been famous for vacuum cleaners ever since.

VACUUM FLASK or BOTTLE. Hot drinks can be kept hot and cold ones kept cold in a vacuum flask. This invention was developed in about 1892 for the storage of liquid air at very low temperatures by the Scottish scientist Sir James Dewar (1842–1923).

A vacuum or "Thermos" flask has a metal or plastic casing inside which is a bottle, made of glass or metal, with double walls. The air in the space between the walls is pumped out, leaving a vacuum (see VACUUM). As explained in the article HEAT, heat can be transferred in only three ways: by conduction, by convection, or by radiation. As the space between the walls of the vacuum flask is empty, heat cannot travel across it by conduction or by convection. Radiation of heat from one wall to the other is reduced by silvering the outside of the inner wall and the inside of the outer wall. Bright surfaces are poor radiators but good reflectors of heat, so hardly any radiant heat crosses the vacuum. (See CONDUCTION; CONVECTION; RADIATION; REFLECTION AND REFRACTION.)

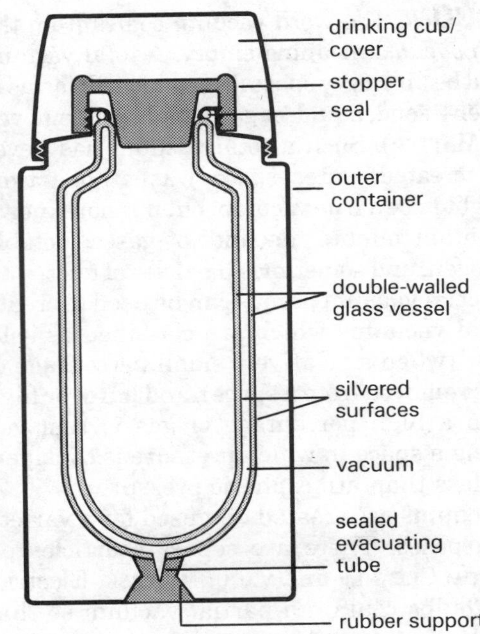

The construction of a modern vacuum flask. Special glass must be used for the vessel to prevent it from cracking when hot or cold liquids are poured in.

The bottle stands on cork in its casing and is packed round with some substance such as crinkled cardboard or cork which is a poor conductor of heat. The mouth of the bottle is closed with a cork or plastic stopper and the casing has a screw-top which can be used as a cup. The use of poor conductors such as cork reduces the passage of heat between the bottle and the casing. Some heat does pass, mostly through the stopper, but a well-made flask stores hot or cold liquids for a long time with little change in temperature. There are also vacuum flasks designed to store hot or cold food.

VALVE. To control the flow of fluids, that is, of liquids and gases, valves are used. A simple form of valve is a gas tap. Its tapered plug can be turned in the shell so that the hole through it is either in line with the pipe, allowing the gas to flow, or across the pipe, thereby preventing the flow.

Screw-down valve. The plug type of valve is suitable only for low pressures. For higher pressures a screw-down valve is used. A simple form is the ordinary water tap, in which a disc covered with leather or rubber is pressed against a flat metal seat, through which the water flows, by means of a screwed spindle. For still higher pressures an all-metal valve is used against a tapered metal seating.

Non-return valves are used where the fluid must flow in one direction only, as in the valve of a bicycle tyre. The valve is forced open by the pressure of the fluid but if that pressure becomes less, the backward pressure from beyond the valve closes the valve against its seating, preventing a return flow.

Safety valves are used to prevent pressures from increasing beyond safe limits, as for example in the boiler of a steam engine. The valve is ordinarily held in the closed position by a strong spring, so that a certain pressure must be reached before the valve is forced open. The steam then escapes until the pressure inside the boiler falls to the safe amount, when the spring closes the valve again. In the boilers of stationary (fixed) engines, weights may be used instead of springs.

Sluice valves and *gate valves* can be used to control large flows of liquid. The valve slides across the pipe rather like a sliding door, and when open allows an uninterrupted flow.

Reducing valves are used to lower the pressure of a fluid. Valves of this kind are fitted to the oxygen cylinders used by welders (see WELDING) to reduce the high pressure of the gas inside the cylinder to the lower value needed for the welding torch. They may also be used to reduce the pressure of the mains water supply (see WATER SUPPLY) to prevent damage to appliances such as washing machines.

Poppet valves in motor-car engines are worked by the engine itself so as to admit mixed air and petrol gas to the cylinder and to allow the burnt gases to leave it. (See INTERNAL COMBUSTION ENGINE.)

The devices used in radio and electronic mechanisms for controlling the flow of electrons (which is the same thing as an electric current) are also called valves in Great Britain, although they are generally called tubes in the United States and Canada. The smallest modern electronic valves are of transistor type. (See ELECTRONICS and RADIO.)

VAN ALLEN BELTS. The Van Allen belts are doughnut-shaped radiation belts or regions surrounding the Earth. They are shaped by the Earth's magnetic field, which "traps" electrically charged particles into zones marked out by the magnetic field lines. (See MAGNETISM.) The field lines emerge at the North Pole, sweep out huge arcs around the Earth, and re-enter the Earth at the South Pole. Most of the charged particles are trapped in two fat belts running parallel to the

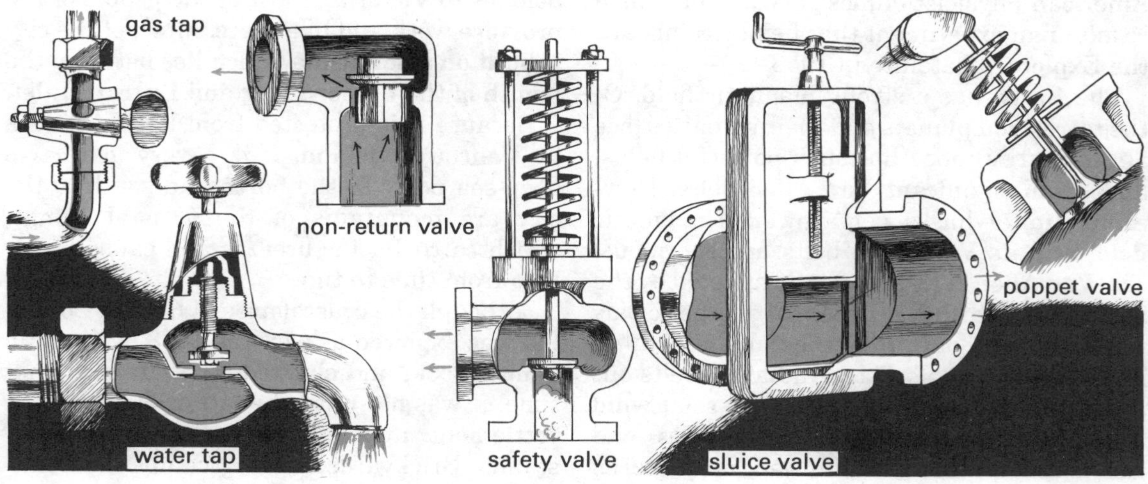

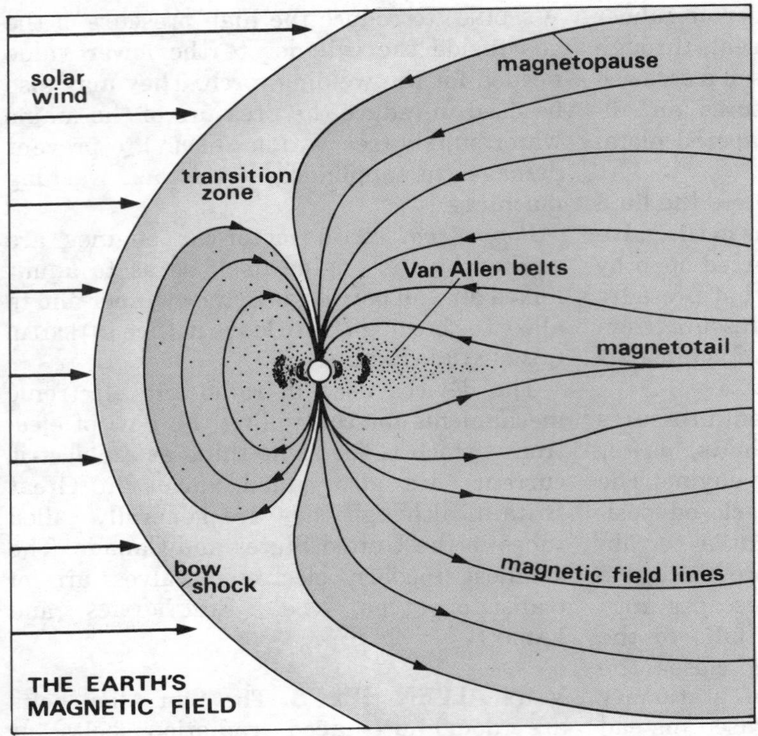

The charged particles that reach the Earth from the Sun are trapped by the Earth's magnetic field into two zones running parallel with the equator. These are the Van Allen Belts, which protect the Earth from cosmic rays and other dangerous energetic particles coming from space. The belts are part of the Earth's magnetosphere.

equator, 5,500 kilometres (3,420 miles) and 14,000 kilometres (8,700 miles) above the Earth's surface. The Van Allen belts shield the Earth from energetic particles coming from outer space. At the poles, where the belts are weakest, energetic particles strike the atmosphere and cause the Aurora Borealis and Aurora Australis (see NORTHERN AND SOUTHERN LIGHTS). They were first discovered by the American physicist James A. Van Allen, as a result of an experiment that he placed aboard the Explorer I satellite in 1958.

The Earth has a strong magnetic field. Of the terrestrial planets and their satellites (see SOLAR SYSTEM) none has such powerful fields, and so no significant Van Allen belts. However, Jupiter has a very powerful magnetic field, and its Van Allen belts are enormous. The Van Allen belts are greatly affected by the solar wind, which is a stream of energetic particles "blown" out from the Sun (see SUN). These particles "blow" the radiation belts out away from the Sun. Changes in the solar wind affect the shielding ability of the belts, and this is thought to affect the weather patterns on Earth. The regions around the Earth in which the charged particles of the solar wind interact with the Earth's magnetic field make up what scientists call the magnetosphere.

VANCOUVER is the third largest city in Canada and the most important in the west of that nation. Although it is not the capital of the province of British Columbia (that honour belongs to Victoria), most of the people of the province work and live there. Much of the city is built on a peninsula which lies between the mouth of the Fraser River and Burrard Inlet.

Because it is protected from Pacific storms by Vancouver Island, it is a very attractive deep-sea port. To the north and south of the city are mountains of the Coastal Range, which catch Pacific breezes and cause heavy rain from time to time.

Although the coastal area of British Columbia was explored as early as 1778 by Captain James Cook, and claimed for Britain at that time, it was not until the late 1860s that any settlement appeared where the city now stands. Brickyards, logging camps, and sawmills were among the earliest businesses established on the peninsula. Following the completion of the Canadian Pacific Railway in 1885, the company president, Sir William Van Horne, decided to extend the line 30 kilometres (18 miles) west, in order to arrive at a better place to build a port. He was given a huge area of land by the provincial government. In 1886 Vancouver became a city, and was named after the English navigator George Vancouver, who surveyed the west coast of North America in 1792. From that modest beginning, the city developed slowly until the end of World War II in 1945. After that the growth of trade with Japan, Korea, China, Southeast Asia, Australia, and New Zealand made it possible for Vancouver to grow too. Timber, plywood, and other products from British Columbia's forests, minerals from the mines, grain and meat from the prairies, and manufactured goods pass through the city to other countries bordering the Pacific Ocean. Products from the Orient, destined for all parts of Canada, flow in through the port of Vancouver. The harbour extends within a great arm of the coastal mountains and is one of the finest in the world. Across the harbour entrance (the Narrows) is the Lions Gate bridge, a fine suspension bridge linking the city with the suburbs of North and West Vancouver. One of the most attractive recreational features of the city is Stanley Park on the city side of the bridge.

ZEFA

Vancouver, commercial centre of British Columbia, occupies a superb site facing sea and mountains.

The city itself is bright and modern. Huge skyscrapers tell of its importance to business and trade. In 1986, Vancouver was the site of a world's fair, Expo 86, which attracted millions of visitors to the city.

A maritime museum, art galleries, a planetarium, an opera house, the Vancouver Symphony Orchestra, and many small theatres contribute to the cultural life of the city. The University of British Columbia (founded 1908) and Simon Fraser University (1963), and several colleges of applied arts and technology are found in and around Vancouver. A domed stadium, "BC Place", and the Pacific Coliseum provide facilities for sporting events.

The population of the metropolitan area is 1,331,000 (1984).

VANDALS. The Vandals were one of the several groups of Germanic tribes who took part in the general migration of peoples from central Europe that eventually led to the destruction of the Roman Empire. They came originally from the basin of the Oder, in what is now East Germany. Racially connected with the Goths and Lombards, the Vandals nevertheless came into conflict with them. In the time of Constantine I (early 4th century AD) they were defeated by the Goths. The Vandals were allowed by the Romans to settle as a subject people in Pannonia, a region which included the northeastern part of present-day Austria and the western part of Hungary.

They remained in Pannonia for about 60 years. Then, coming under pressure from the Huns, they emigrated to Gaul. The Franks defeated them and in AD 409 the Vandals, under the leadership of their king, Gunderic, crossed the Pyrenees into Spain. The Silingian Vandals settled in Andalusia, and the Asdingians in Galicia. The Silingians were wiped out by the Goths and the armies of the Roman Empire. The Asdingians prospered, and finally marched across Spain to Andalusia.

In 428 or 429 Bonifacius, the count of Africa, who had quarrelled with his government at Rome, invited the Vandals to settle in his province. More than 80,000 of them went over to

Africa under their king Gaiseric. Bonifacius soon found that his guests were more to be feared than the Romans, and asked them to return to Spain, but it was too late. The Vandals proceeded to conquer northern Africa for themselves. By 430 only the cities of Carthage, Hippo, and Cirta were holding out against them. In 435 they made a treaty with Rome under which Carthage and the surrounding province were to remain Roman. The Vandals were to occupy the other six provinces.

Gaiseric did not observe the treaty. In 439 he seized Carthage and reigned over all Roman Africa. He was more interested in robbery than he was in making conquests. An Arian Christian himself, he persecuted the Catholic Christians, looted and burned their churches, and tortured the priests until they revealed the hiding places of the church treasures. In 455 Eudoxia, widow of the Emperor Valentinian, made the same mistake as Bonifacius. She invited Gaiseric to give her his support at Rome. Gaiseric occupied the city, and looted it for 14 days. There was no resistance, so he did not burn the city or harm the buildings. He took back to Africa vast amounts of booty, including Eudoxia and her daughters. This exploit had much to do with making the term "vandal" mean one who destroys precious things he is too uncivilized to appreciate—even though the Vandals were no more guilty of this than any other invading barbarians of the period.

In 477 Gaiseric was succeeded by his son Hunneric. Hilderic, who became king in 523, was a Catholic, and restored the bishops to their churches. But he was unpopular, and his warlike cousin Gelimer deposed and imprisoned him. This gave the Emperor Justinian a chance to intervene. His general Belisarius landed in Africa at the head of a Byzantine army in 533. One Vandal army was away in Sardinia, but Belisarius defeated the other and entered Carthage. When the Sardinian army returned, the Vandals met him with their full strength at Tricameron. After a stubborn battle they too were defeated, and Gelimer took to flight, surrendering in 534. Many of the Vandals were taken into the Byzantine army and the rest disappeared from history.

VANDERBILT FAMILY. The Vanderbilts, one of America's most prominent and richest families, made a huge fortune in the early days of steamboat and railway transport. Much of their wealth was used to support universities, art galleries, and other educational and cultural establishments.

Cornelius Vanderbilt (1794–1877) was the son of a poor farmer and boatman. At the age of 16 he bought a sailing boat which he used as a ferry from Staten Island, New York, to New York City. He gradually enlarged his fleet of ships until by 1846 he was a millionaire. He became known as "the Commodore". At the age of 50 he began to purchase the stock of the New York and Harlem Railway, and by about 1864 he withdrew his capital from the steamship lines and made a second fortune in railways. His companies included the New York Central and the Hudson River Railroad and the Lake Shore and Michigan Southern Railroad. He opened the Grand Central terminus in New York City, providing many people with employment. Near the end of his life he gave $1 million to Vanderbilt University, Nashville, Tennessee. When he died, most of his money was divided between his son and four grandsons, only a small amount going to his wife and eight daughters.

William Henry Vanderbilt (1821–85) was the son of Cornelius. His father set him up as a farmer on Staten Island and he was soon running a profitable business. In 1857 his father made him receiver of the bankrupt Staten Island Railroad and he quickly cleared the debts. He succeeded his father as president of the New York Central and added several more railway companies to the family business. He also made gifts to Vanderbilt University and other colleges. He amassed a private art collection and made gifts to the Metropolitan Museum of Art, New York City.

Cornelius Vanderbilt II (1843–99) was the eldest son of William Henry. He too went into the railway business and was director of more than 30 railway companies. He continued the family's gifts to charitable and cultural organizations.

William Kissam Vanderbilt (1849–1920) was the second son of William Henry. He was less interested in business and preferred the arts and sport. He collected paintings and other works of art and was involved with the Metropolitan Opera in New York City. He also enjoyed sailing and in 1895 retained the America's Cup for the United States with his yacht *Defender*.

BBC Hulton Picture Library

William Kissam Vanderbilt (1878–1944) photographed with his son (right).

George Washington Vanderbilt (1862–1914) was the third son of William Henry. He presented many gifts to literary and arts institutions, including Columbia University. He created Biltmore, North Carolina, a huge estate where experiments in forestry and agriculture were carried out.

Cornelius Vanderbilt III (1873–1942) was the son of Cornelius Vanderbilt II. He was a financier and was a colonel of the US Army engineers. His brothers Alfred Gwynne Vanderbilt (1877–1915) and Reginald Claypoole Vanderbilt (1880–1925) were both interested in show horses. Reginald Claypoole's daughter was **Gloria Morgan Vanderbilt**, born in 1924.

William Kissam Vanderbilt (1878–1944) and **Harold Stirling Vanderbilt** (1884–1970), William Kissam's two sons, were both associated with the New York Central Railroad. Harold Stirling invented the game of contract bridge and won the America's Cup three times.

Cornelius Vanderbilt, Jr. (1898–1974) was the son of Cornelius Vanderbilt III and founded a chain of newspapers.

VAN DYCK, Sir Anthony (1599–1641). The Flemish artist, Sir Anthony Van Dyck, was one of the world's greatest portrait painters, and, after Rubens, the greatest Flemish painter in the 17th century. (See RUBENS, PETER PAUL.) He mostly painted portraits of European aristocracy, dressed in beautiful costumes and draped with jewels; but he also did some religious, historical, and mythological paintings.

Van Dyck, the seventh of 12 children, was born in Antwerp (now in Belgium), where his father was a wealthy silk merchant. When he was just ten, he was apprenticed to a local painter; by 18, he was a full member of the Antwerp guild of painters. He worked for a few years with Rubens, who influenced his style and helped him find patrons, although later on their relationship became strained. Then, in 1621, after a few months in England, Van Dyck travelled to Italy where he spent the greater part of the next five years, mostly in Genoa. There he painted the same aristocrats whom Rubens had painted 14 years earlier. He travelled widely in Italy and learnt from the great Italian painters, especially the Venetian, Titian (see TITIAN).

In 1627 Van Dyck returned to Antwerp and during the next five years produced some of his finest religious paintings, as well as many portraits. Then, in 1632, at the invitation of King Charles I, he went to England again. There he became court painter, for which he received an annual salary of £200, and was knighted. He painted many portraits of the king and his family, and of English noble men and women. The portrait called *King Charles on Horseback*, completed in 1638, is in the National Gallery, London, and is one of his finest works. Van Dyck became a wealthy man but his extravagant way of life led him into

Courtesy, the Cleveland Museum of Art, John L. Severance Collection

Portrait of Sir Thomas Hammer, cupbearer to Charles I, by Anthony Van Dyck, painter to the King.

debt. He died in London, aged 42, and was buried in St. Paul's Cathedral.

In his use of colour, his elegance, and the ease with which he painted, Van Dyck was a master. He ranks next to Titian as a portrait painter. As a painter of refinement, polish, and distinction, and as a master of dress, furniture, and decoration, he was unmatched.

Van Dyck's paintings are in galleries all over the world. They include *Self-Portrait* (c.1621), Metropolitan Museum of Art, New York City; *Giovanni Vicenzo Imperiale* (1626), National Gallery of Art, Washington, DC; and *Charles I and Henrietta Maria with their Children* (completed 1638), Royal Art Collection, Windsor.

VAN GOGH, Vincent (1853–90). Vincent van Gogh was one of the great Dutch painters. Although his painting career lasted only ten years, he produced about 800 oil-paintings and 700 drawings. During his troubled lifetime, beset with mental illness, only his brother Theo believed in his painting and helped him, but now his name and his pictures are famous throughout the world.

Vincent van Gogh was born at Groot Zundert in the Netherlands, where his father was a Protestant minister. He began work in a firm of art dealers, but when he was 24 he decided to devote his life to religion and worked as a preacher among coal miners in Belgium. After a time he realized that he was not the right kind of person to do this work, and it was then that he turned to painting. After studying in Brussels, he lived with his father, painting scenes of the lives of the working people of the village, and of the moorland around. One picture was called *The Potato Eaters* (1885, now in the Rijksmuseum Vincent van Gogh, Amsterdam). Van Gogh explained: "I have tried to make it clear how these people, eating their potatoes under the lamplight, have dug the earth with those very hands they put in the dish... and honestly earned their food."

In 1886 van Gogh went to stay with Theo in Paris, and the Impressionist artists whom he

Musée Rodin, Paris/Bridgeman

Portrait of Père Tanguy (1888), an example of Van Gogh's mature style, is considered a masterpiece.

met there encouraged him to paint in much brighter and clearer colours than before. Pure, blazing colours are the most wonderful thing about the famous paintings on which he worked after this time, many of them done at Arles, in the south of France, where, thanks to Theo's help he finally went to live. At Arles he painted the blossoming fruit trees, the fields bathed in sunlight, cypress trees and sunflowers, his simple room, and his village neighbours.

During the last three years of his life he suffered from terrible fits of depression, and in 1890 he committed suicide. In between his depressions, however, he went on painting, and produced some of his finest pictures in his last years. These included *The Chair and the Pipe* (1888–89), Tate Gallery, London; *The Starry Night* (1889), Museum of Modern Art, New York City; and *Self Portrait* (1890), Louvre, Paris.

VANILLA. The vanilla plant is a member of the orchid family. There are several species, or kinds, the one from which vanilla flavouring comes being called *Vanilla planifolia*. The bell-shaped flowers are greenish-yellow and the leaves are broad. The slender yellow pods or beans, which grow 20 centimetres (8 inches) long, contain an oily black pulp full of tiny black seeds.

The vanilla plant grows in lowland regions where the air is damp and hot and the soil is loose. Its home is Mexico and Central America, but it is also grown in Madagascar, Java, and other tropical islands. Another species which grows wild in Oceania is *Vanilla tahitenis*, Tahiti vanilla. Vanilla plants twine round posts or trees and are kept carefully pruned. Often the plants live for 50 years.

Vanilla essence is extracted in the following way. Just before the beans are ripe they are cut from the plant and cured by being heated in large oven rooms, exposed to sun and air, and then put into tightly closed places to sweat. This treatment makes the beans shrink and turn brown. Then they are chopped and mixed with alcohol, which gradually absorbs their flavour.

Flower heads, pods, and leaves of the vanilla plant.

Vanilla is used for flavouring sweet foods and drinks and for scenting soap and perfume. It was used by the Aztecs to flavour *xocoatl*, the drink they made from cocoa. However, vanilla beans are costly to produce and so vanillin, a substance which resembles the oil of the vanilla bean but is less good, is either manufactured artificially or obtained from the tonka bean which comes from another South American tree. Vanilla from vanilla beans is now seldom used.

VANUATU (formerly the New Hebrides). Vanuatu is a republic in the southwest Pacific Ocean, some 800 kilometres (500 miles) west of Fiji, and 1,700 kilometres (1,100 miles) east of Australia. It is made up of 12 main islands, the largest of which are Espiritu Santo, Malekula, Efate, Ambrym, Aoba, and Tanna, and some 60 smaller islands. They form a chain about 800 kilometres (500 miles) in length. The total area of the islands is 12,189 square kilometres (4,706 square miles).

The islands are volcanic, the soil is rich and deep, and the land is densely wooded. Most of the rainfall comes in summer, from November to April. Mud and malaria-bearing mosquitoes make the rainy season unpleasant. The fertile soil produces crops such as breadfruit, sago-palm, bananas, sugar-cane, yam, taro, arrowroot, oranges, pineapples, and sandalwood. Many of the people make their living from selling copra (the oil-yielding kernel of the coconut), coffee, and cocoa. Fishing and tourism are also major industries.

Most of the population is Melanesian (see RACE), but there are also some of European, Chinese, and Polynesian ancestry. Schools and hospitals are run by the government and by missionaries. Both French and English are spoken, a legacy of the two countries' joint rule from 1906–80, as well as a local language called Bislama. The main town and capital of the islands is Vila, on Efate Island.

The Vanuatu group of islands was sighted in 1606 by a Portuguese navigator, but most of the islands were only charted when Captain James Cook explored them in 1774.

When Captain Cook visited the New Hebrides there were probably about 1 million inhabitants, but European diseases such as measles and influenza later killed enormous numbers and reduced the population to about 96,000. Early in the 19th century British traders visited the islands for sandalwood. Later in the 19th century cotton planters arrived forcing the inhabitants to work on the plantations. Others were forced to work on the sugar plantations in Queensland and Fiji.

The republic, which is a member of the Commonwealth, has a parliamentary system of government, led by the prime minister. The total population of Vanuatu is about 145,000 (1987).

VARANASI (also called Benares or Banaras) in India, is the holy city of the Hindus, who believe that their souls will be saved if their bodies are burned beside the nearby Ganges River. (See HINDU AND HINDUISM.)

Varanasi stands on the high outer bank of a long curve of the Ganges. The bank is steep and terrace upon terrace of temples and palaces rise from the water's edge. Along the water front, which is walled with stone, are quays of carved masonry. The landing places and flights of steps up the terraced river bank are known as ghats. On some of the ghats funeral pyres are built, like bonfires. Every year hundreds of thousands of Hindu pilgrims come to Varanasi to wash away their sins in the sacred river.

The streets that lead upward from the ghats into the city are so narrow that a cart cannot pass through them. The houses are often painted deep red and covered with designs of gods, men, and beasts. They are taller than the little Hindu temples, of which there are about 1,500 in Varanasi, some of them housing the sacred monkeys. The Golden Temple is regarded by the Hindus as their holiest shrine but the largest building in the city is the Muslim mosque of Aurangzeb (who was one of the Mogul emperors). Varanasi is a city of learning and has a Sanskrit University and also the chief university of India, the Banaras Hindi University, which has a women's college.

Popperfoto

The Manikarna ghat, or landing place, at Varanasi. Many Hindu pilgrims come here to bathe in the sacred River Ganges.

The city's brasswork is still famous, but the chief industries are those producing silk brocade, gold and silver thread, and lacquered toys. Varanasi has a population of 708,647 (1981).

See also the article GANGES, RIVER.

VATICAN CITY is the name of a tiny independent state which lies on the right bank of the River Tiber within the city of Rome itself. Its area is only 1 square kilometre (less than half a square mile) and it has only about 800 inhabitants, yet by millions of Roman Catholics throughout the world it is revered above all cities. The reason for this is that the Vatican City is the headquarters of the Roman Catholic Church and is ruled over by the Pope, who is himself the Bishop of Rome. (See the

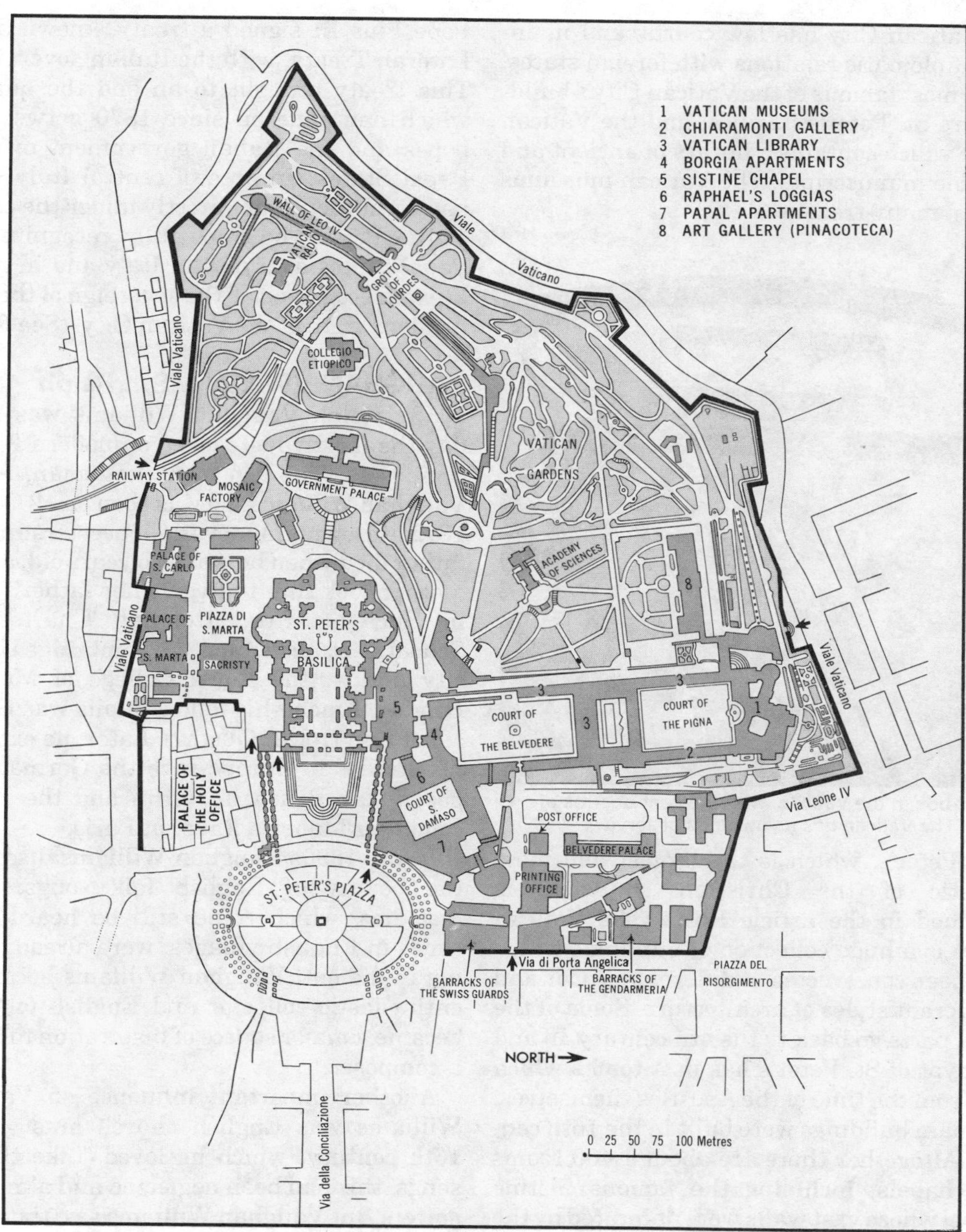

Map of the Vatican showing the principal buildings. Dark arrows indicate the main entrances.

separate articles POPE; ROMAN CATHOLIC CHURCH.)

The Vatican City is a complete state in miniature. It is administered by a governor who is appointed by the Pope. It has its own flag, postal facilities, telephone system, and a powerful radio station capable of worldwide broadcasts. It has its own banking system, and by agreement with the Italian government, the coins of the Vatican City are allowed to circulate in Italy itself. The state also has an official newspaper which is published daily.

The Vatican City has law courts, and maintains diplomatic relations with foreign states.

The most famous of the Vatican City's buildings are St. Peter's Basilica, and the Vatican palace which contains a library of ancient and valuable manuscripts. The Vatican museums contain many treasures.

Camera Press

A letter-box in the Vatican, with the coat of arms of Pius X. The Vatican has its own postal service.

St. Peter's, which is the largest and most majestic of the Christian churches, is described in the article ROME. The Vatican palace is a huge collection of buildings which have been constructed at different periods and in different styles of architecture. Some of the oldest parts go back to the 4th century AD and the crypt of St. Peter's has in it tombs which date from the time of the Apostles themselves. The main buildings were built in the 16th century. Altogether there are about 1,400 rooms and chapels, including the famous Sistine Chapel whose vast walls were decorated by the great artist Michelangelo. One of the features of the Vatican City is the Swiss Guard, who are the Pope's personal bodyguard. They make a splendid sight in their picturesque uniforms which were designed by Michelangelo in the 16th century.

The Vatican City did not come into existence as a separate state until 1929. In that year Pope Pius XI signed a treaty, known as the Lateran Treaty, with the Italian government. This treaty brought to an end the quarrels which had gone on since 1870 between the popes and the Italian government over the Papal States, an area of central Italy which had until then been directly under the control of the Pope. The Pope fully recognized the Papal States as a part of Italy and in return he was recognized as the sovereign of the independent state of the Vatican City. (See ROME.)

VAUGHAN WILLIAMS, Ralph (1872–1958). Ralph Vaughan Williams was in his day the most widely loved of modern English composers. The son of a clergyman, Arthur Vaughan Williams, he was born on 12 October 1872 at Down Ampney in Gloucestershire. His father died when he was two years old, and his mother took him to live at her father's home in Surrey. After attending Charterhouse School he studied music at Cambridge University and at the Royal College of Music in London. Among his fellow pupils was Gustav Holst (see HOLST, GUSTAV). Later, he extended his studies in Europe with the German composer Max Bruch in Berlin and the French composer Maurice Ravel in Paris.

In the 1890s Vaughan Williams discovered the beauty of English folk songs. These melodies, which could still be heard sometimes in English villages, were already starting to die out. Vaughan Williams became an enthusiastic collector and English folk song became a major source of inspiration to him as a composer.

Another important influence on Vaughan Williams was English church music of the 16th century, which he loved. Like the folk songs, this had been neglected and almost forgotten. But Vaughan Williams saw the beauty in it. In 1904–06 he edited a new Church of England hymn book called *The English Hymnal*. For this book he revived old tunes, both religious and non-religious, and contributed many of his own, including his stirring setting of "For all the Saints". He recalled directly the beauty and power of Tudor church music in his *Fantasia on a Theme of Thomas*

Tallis (1909), a work for strings; and his *Mass in G minor* (1923), for unaccompanied choir.

After military service during World War I, Vaughan Williams became professor of composition at the Royal College of Music. He lectured both in Britain and abroad and encouraged many younger English composers.

BBC Hulton Picture Library

Ralph Vaughan Williams, photographed in 1951 after completing his opera *The Pilgrim's Progress*.

Vaughan Williams wrote a considerable amount of great music. His orchestral works include nine symphonies. Among these are *A Sea Symphony* (1910), for choir and orchestra; *A London Symphony* (1914, revised 1920); and the *Pastoral Symphony* (1922). His songs are some of the finest in English music and include the cycle (series) *On Wenlock Edge* (1909) and the ever-popular *Linden Lea*, written about 1900.

Late in life Vaughan Williams began writing music for films, and the music he wrote for *Scott of the Antarctic* became his *Seventh Symphony* (1953), also called *Sinfonia Antarctica*. Some of his best music was inspired by English poetry, particularly that of Shakespeare, John Milton, John Bunyan, and William Blake.

For many years Vaughan Williams lived quietly at his home in Surrey and he regularly conducted the choir at the Leith Hill Musical Festival until he was over 80. He died on 26 August 1958, and was buried in Westminster Abbey in London.

VEGA, Lope de (1562–1635). The great Spanish poet and dramatist Lope de Vega was brilliant and prolific in his writings. An embroiderer's son from Madrid, he was in no way attracted to his father's humble craft, and after receiving a Jesuit education, he was encouraged by a rich patron to enter the priesthood. However, his youthful instinct for adventure soon made him turn from a religious life. He began writing poems and plays and was already becoming a famous writer by his early twenties.

Lope's life was a colourful one. In 1588 he sailed with the Armada against England, returning safely. He had many passionate love affairs, and his many love poems are addressed to a number of women who were his mistresses. For the last 30 years of his life he was confidential secretary to the Duke of Sessa, a man who treated him shamefully, and immorally turned him away from a second attempt to become a priest.

Lope de Vega is supposed to have written 1,800 plays and hundreds of shorter dramatic works and poems. Of his dramas, nearly 500 plays and shorter pieces survive. They cover a wide range of subjects. There are dramas of intrigue and chivalry, plays about peasant life, sacred and Biblical dramas, and pastoral romances. His poems include an epic attacking the great English admiral Sir Francis Drake. He also wrote an autobiographical novel, *La Dorotea*. Lope de Vega is regarded as the founder of Spanish drama and both his plays and his poetry greatly influenced later literature, not only in Spain but also in Europe generally.

VEGETABLES come from a variety of plants which have been cultivated by man for centuries. Although cereal crops such as wheat and rice are more important to the diet, vegetables give variety and are rich in minerals, especially calcium and iron, and vitamins, especially A and C.

Various parts of vegetables are eaten. In the case of the carrot, parsnip, and beetroot it is the root, where plant food, mainly starch is stored. Most root crops, as they are called, are dug up in the autumn, for if they are left in the soil the plant will use the food to make flowers and seeds.

In other vegetables it is the underground stem, or tuber, not the root, which becomes swollen with food. The potato is the best example of this kind of vegetable. What we call eyes are really young buds, and when potatoes are kept long enough to sprout it is these buds that grow into long shoots. So each potato, besides containing a good store of food, is capable of growing into a new plant.

The buds of cabbages and Brussels sprouts are eaten, so are the stems of asparagus and the leaves of spinach and lettuce. Cauliflowers and broccoli are really young flower heads swollen with food.

A number of fruits and seeds are commonly called vegetables. The most obvious examples of these are tomatoes, marrows, and cucumbers. Examples of seeds that are eaten as vegetables are peas and beans. In some kinds, such as French beans, the pods and seeds are both eaten.

There are separate articles on most of the vegetables mentioned here.

Food Value and Cooking

Many vegetables contain a great deal of water—as much as 96 per cent in the case of lettuce—but they also have important food substances such as carbohydrates, proteins, fats, minerals, and vitamins. Carbohydrates, fats, proteins, and minerals are needed by the living body and so must be included in a balanced, or correct, diet. Vitamins are needed only in very small quantities, but if they are absent, diseases such as scurvy occur. (See VITAMIN.) Vegetables also provide what is known as roughage, which gives bulk to the food and lets the digestive juices mix with it.

A potato, contains roughly 80 per cent water, 16 per cent starch (carbohydrates), 2 per cent protein, 1 per cent minerals, 1 per cent roughage and vitamins, and a trace of fats.

The vitamins and minerals may be lost by canning vegetables, but if they are dried or frozen they may keep them. A diet rich in minerals, vitamins, and roughage is provided by a regular supply of fresh vegetables. The best way of eating them uncooked is in salads, where they are generally cut up and mixed with oil or dressing.

Vegetables are generally more digestible if they are cooked, but cooking can easily be overdone. Minerals are quickly boiled out and vitamins can be destroyed by heat. Usually it is necessary to boil vegetables only long enough to make them soft, and a better way of cooking them is by steaming or baking. In this way the minerals and vitamins remain and the flavour is often improved. (See also COOKING.)

Growing Vegetables

Most vegetables have been cultivated in some form since very early times. But for several thousands of years they were only known to the people in the part of the world in which they originated. Potatoes, tomatoes, peppers, and sweet corn were native to the continent of America and were unknown in Europe until the end of the 15th century. Onions and turnips probably originated in the Middle East and Asia, whereas carrots, cabbage, and celery were known in Europe for thousands of years. There is more about what sorts of food are eaten in different countries in the article FOOD.

Many vegetables that we know today are different from the wild ancestors from which they have been produced through centuries of selective breeding.

Until the 19th century, when large industrial cities grew up, most people grew their own vegetables or bought them in local markets. The only vegetables available were those grown in the climate and conditions of the place where they were consumed. In the spring and summer there would be plenty of fresh green vegetables available if the weather was good, but in the winter there would only be the vegetables that could be successfully stored, such as root crops, or preserved by drying or pickling. Beans, peas, and lentils are easy to dry and still form the basis of nourishing winter soups in many countries. Cabbage is pickled and fermented in the form of sauerkraut. Red cabbage is also a popular vegetable for pickling, as are small cucumbers, peppers, and mixtures of chopped vegetables.

Now, with fast, reliable air, road, and rail transport it is possible in developed countries to buy all sorts of fresh vegetables almost all the year round. Of course, if they have had to be brought thousands of miles to the consumer they will probably be expensive. However, many vegetables are now available at all times of the year, more cheaply, frozen, canned, or freeze-dried (see FOOD PROCESSING).

ZEFA

Beans must be supported by poles, which they naturally twine round. Hoeing kills the weeds that grow between the rows of plants.

In many countries of the world, mainly Africa, Asia, and Central America, people still rely to a large extent on what they can grow themselves. Any surpluses may be sold in a local market. In industrialized countries also many people grow their own vegetables for pleasure or to save money. If there is only a limited space available, they may concentrate on growing something special that is expensive to buy in shops and markets. However, most people have to rely on vegetables grown by someone else.

There are two main types of vegetable growers: the market gardener and the vegetable grower who produces a crop in bulk for processing (that is, not for sale fresh, but for freezing or canning). Market gardeners produce a variety of vegetables for a local market. Often they "force" vegetables, that is, produce them out of the normal season by growing them in greenhouses.

The grower who produces vegetables for processing, cultivates huge quantities of one kind which must all be ready at the same time. Since they will be immediately frozen, canned, or dried, the appearance of the vegetables is not as important as it is for vegetables that are sold fresh in a market or shop. When the crop is ready, it is harvested as quickly as possible by machinery, often working continuously through the night.

VEGETARIAN. A vegetarian is someone who avoids eating the flesh of animals (meat, poultry, or fish, including shellfish). Most vegetarians will also not eat eggs or cheeses made with animal rennet, or use cosmetics or toiletries which contain animal ingredients or are tested on animals. *Lacto-vegetarians* will eat milk and cheese but not eggs; *ovo-vegetarians* eat eggs but no dairy products; *vegans* are very strict vegetarians who avoid all animal products, even milk, eggs, and honey. The word "vegetarian", coined around 1842, comes not from "vegetable" but from the Latin word *vegetus* meaning "whole, fresh, full of life".

People are vegetarians for a number of reasons. Some think that it is wrong to keep and kill animals for use as food and in other products. Others choose to be vegetarians because they believe that a vegetarian diet is healthier than a diet that includes meat. Indeed, a vegetarian diet fits in very well with modern medical advice to cut down on fat, salt, and sugar, and to eat more fibre and fresh vegetables. It is also cheaper than meat. Some people are vegetarian because of their religious beliefs. Most Buddhists, Hindus, and Jains are vegetarians, as are members of a number of Christian religious sects. Some people have chosen to be vegetarian for ecological reasons. They argue that the growing of vegetables takes up much less valuable space than the raising of livestock; moreover, it is easier to provide food for all the people on Earth by growing vegetables for food rather than raising vegetable-eating animals.

Is a Vegetarian Diet Healthy?

Some people worry that a vegetarian diet will be short of protein, but this is not the case. Plenty of protein can be obtained from the great variety of nuts, seeds, pulses, cereals, and soya products (such as tofu) which are now widely available, and from eggs and milk products. It was once thought that plant proteins were inferior to animal proteins, being deficient in some amino acids. It is now known that a mixture of plant proteins complement one another. For example, a shortage of an amino acid in one plant food, such as pulses, is counterbalanced by an excess of that amino acid in a different plant food, such as a cereal. Protein combinations such as beans on toast, rice and lentils, bean stew with pot barley, oats and nuts (as in muesli), provide very high quality protein. (See NUTRITION; PROTEIN.)

All other nutrients are present in adequate quantities in the lacto-vegetarian diet. If dairy products are not eaten, a supplement of vitamin B_{12} becomes essential. Many vegetarian foods are fortified with this vitamin (yeast extracts, some soya milks, some breakfast cereals, and so on). Vegetarians obtain iron from dried fruit, leafy green vegetables, wholemeal flour, pulses, oats, nuts, and brown rice. They obtain calcium from cheese, nuts, sesame seeds, leafy green vegetables, and soya.

Vegetarians have been responsible for the invention of foods such as peanut butter, cornflakes, muesli, and high-protein vegetable foods made to taste like meat.

VELAZQUEZ (1599–1660). Diego Rodriguez de Silva Velazquez was a Spanish artist, and one of the great painters of his time. For many years of his life he lived at the court of King Philip IV of Spain, and some of his most famous pictures are portraits of the king, his family, and members of the court, including the dwarfs and jesters.

Velazquez was born in Seville, where his father was a lawyer. He became a pupil of a well-known artist of the city, whose daughter he later married. At first Velazquez was interested in painting everyday things, such as the fish, fruit, and flowers of the market place. In order to study the human face and all its expressions, he engaged a peasant boy as his servant and made sketches of him in every mood.

Alinari

As court painter to Philip IV, Velazquez painted this charming portrait of Princess Marguerite in 1653.

In 1622 Velazquez set out for a visit to Madrid and in the following year he was summoned to Madrid again by the chief minister of the young King Philip, to paint a portrait of the king on horseback. The friendship between the king and Velazquez which started then continued for the rest of the artist's life. He and his family settled in Madrid, and soon he became known as the finest painter in Spain. The king rewarded him with various official posts, but Velazquez never allowed honours and riches to spoil his serious work of painting.

Another great artist, the Flemish painter Peter Paul Rubens, visited Madrid in 1628 and persuaded Velazquez, who had been appointed to show him the art treasures of Spain, to go Italy to study the paintings there. This Velazquez did, and the ideas he gained helped to improve his own painting. On his return to Spain he painted portraits of members of the Spanish court, including a full-length one of the king which is now in the National Gallery in London. At times, however, his days were taken up by other duties for the king, such as going to Italy again to buy works of art for the royal palace. It was on this second visit in 1650 that Velazquez painted Pope Innocent X's portrait, which the English painter Sir Joshua Reynolds described as the "most beautiful picture in Rome". In 1660, just after making the arrangements for the grand scenic displays to be held in honour of the Spanish princess's marriage, Velazquez caught a fever and died.

One of Velazquez's great paintings is *The Surrender of Breda* (1634–45; Prado, Madrid), in which a courteous and noble Spanish general is being presented with the keys of a city defeated in battle. It was painted for the throne room of the Buen Retiro palace and is Velazquez's only historical painting. In the background are the fires and confusion of war. Other famous paintings by Velazquez are *The Lady with a Fan* (*c.*1638–39), Wallace Collection, London; and *Philip IV in Military Dress* (1644), Frick Collection, New York City.

VELOCITY is a word that comes from the Latin *velox*, meaning "swift". It is sometimes used to mean speed alone, that is, distance covered in a given time, but correctly speaking the velocity of an object is its speed *in a particular direction.*

If a motor car is said to be going at 100 kilometres an hour, this means that if it travelled for one hour it would cover a distance of 100 kilometres. However, cars do not usually travel far without some change of speed. So if we say that a car that covered 200 kilometres in 4 hours had an *average* speed of 50 kilometres an hour, it was sometimes travelling faster than 50 kilometres an hour, and at other times slower. If a moving object has a steady speed, its speed is said to be *uniform.*

Speed is the rate at which distance is covered, but velocity, or speed in a particular direction, is the rate of change of position in that direction. If a model train is running round a circular track at uniform (steady) speed, its velocity is not uniform because its direction is constantly changing.

An object has uniform velocity only if it travels in a straight line. Uniform velocity seldom continues for any long period. A stone dropped from a height, although it falls vertically, does not have uniform velocity. Its speed increases by 9.75 metres (32 feet) a second every second of its fall (see GRAVITY).

The rate at which the speed of an object increases is called *acceleration.* In the case of the falling stone, it is 9.75 metres (32 feet) a second each second. Note that if the stone is thrown upwards its vertical speed *decreases* at 9.75 metres a second each second while it is rising; this is called *deceleration*, or, sometimes, *negative acceleration.* Scientists use the word acceleration to mean rate of change of velocity. Thus, if a car travelling northwards along a straight road changes its speed in 30 seconds from 20 kilometres an hour to 50 kilometres an hour, its average acceleration during that period of 30 seconds is 1 kilometre an hour per second northwards. (See ACCELERATION.)

An aircraft or a boat can have two velocities at the same time, one caused by the engines or other source of power driving it and the other caused by the wind or current. It moves, in consequence, with what is called a *resultant velocity*, which is obtained by putting together the two velocities. For example, an aircraft flying northwards at an air speed of 900 kilometres an hour in a wind blowing from the north (that is, dead against it) at 50 kilometres an hour, travels over the Earth's surface with a velocity of only 850 kilometres an hour northwards. If a boat is rowed eastwards at 2 kilometres an hour across a river flowing southwards at 2 kilometres an hour the resultant velocity of the boat can be found by representing the three velocities in the

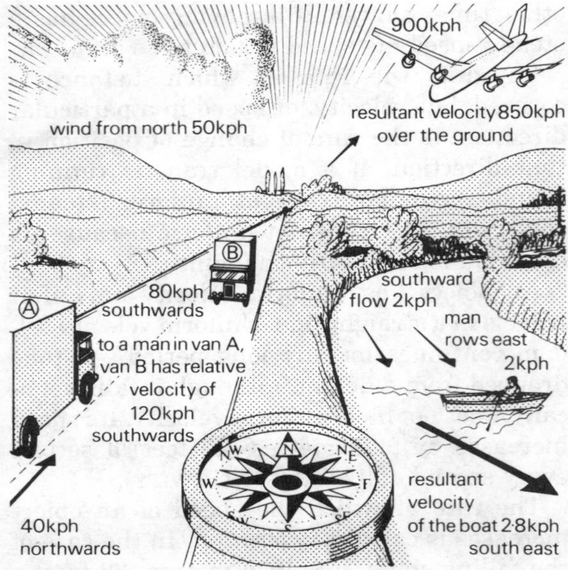

The diagram shows some examples of resultant velocities as explained in the text.

form of a right-angled triangle. The two sides that form the right angle represent the speed and direction of the boat and the current. The third side opposite the right angle (the hypotenuse) represents the resultant velocity of the boat. Its value is found by applying Pythagoras's theorem, which states that the square of the length of the hypotenuse is equal to the sum of the squares of the lengths of the other two sides (see MATHEMATICS; PYTHAGORAS). In this example, $2^2+2^2=8$. The square root of 8 is about 2.8, so the boat travels at 2.8 kilometres an hour in a south-easterly direction.

When two objects are moving, one has a velocity relative to the other. For example, although raindrops may be falling vertically they appear to have a slanting motion to some-one in a moving train or motor car, and their *relative* motion is at an angle inclined to the vertical. The relative velocity of a car travelling at 80 kilometres an hour south to one travelling at 40 kilometres an hour north is 120 kilometres an hour south. That is, to a person in the second car, the first one appears to be travelling south at 120 kilometres an hour. All the velocities measured by an observer are, strictly speaking, *relative*, except for the velocity of light which is always constant. You can read more about this in the article RELATIVITY.

VENEERING. The practice of veneering means glueing a very thin layer of finely marked wood over a base of plain but more solid wood. The ancient Egyptians used veneer on mummy cases about 6,000 years ago. The craft was revived in Europe in the 17th century where French furniture makers developed the craft and adapted it with other techniques, such as marquetry (see below). Much of the furniture made in Britain in the 18th and 19th centuries by craftsmen such as Hepplewhite and Chippendale was veneered so that the wood underneath was hidden (see FURNITURE).

Nowadays veneer is in great demand as plywood, in which plain woods are used for the inside layers, or plies, and more decorative ones for the surface. By using veneers hardboard, blockboard, and synthetic boards may be made to look like the very best hardwoods. Since veneers are very thin, it can be seen that one log of a rare and beautiful wood will provide many sheets of veneer. These thin sheets are obtained by sawing, slicing, or rotary-cutting, the last being by far the most economical method. In rotary-cutting the log is "turned", as in a lathe, against the sharp edge of a very long knife which peels off the wood in a huge shaving like a roll of paper. This roll is then cut up into suitable sizes (see also TIMBER).

Marquetry is the name given to a design (usually based on flowers, fruit, and natural forms) which is worked in coloured veneers, each piece being inlaid (cut) into the background. Marquetry was a very popular decoration in France at the time of Louis XVI. In *Parquetry*, patterns are formed by veneers cut into geometrical shapes or strips and fixed so that their grains run in opposite directions. This is where the term "parquet" flooring comes from. The use of coloured and grained veneers to form pictures, for example, landscapes, is called *Intarsia*. It began in Italy in the 14th century but is still very popular today as a home craft. *Inlay* is where a piece of decorative wood or other material, such as metal or mother-of-pearl, is set into a cavity in the main structure of the piece being decorated.

VENEZUELA is a republic in the northern part of the South American continent. It is bounded on the north by the Caribbean Sea and has a coastline 3,000 kilometres (1,865 miles) long, with many islands. To the west is Colombia, to the east Guyana, and to the south Brazil.

Venezuela has high mountains, tropical rain-forests, and hundreds of rivers. The great Orinoco River rises in the south and makes a wide curve to flow through the centre of the country. It is joined by many tributaries and flows out to the Atlantic Ocean through several swampy mouths. (See ORINOCO RIVER.) In the area north of the Apure River and part of the Orinoco, are grassy plains called *llanos*, where great numbers of cattle are raised. In the southeast of the country are the Guiana Highlands, which are covered with forests and are little explored. Also in the Guiana Highlands are the Angel Falls, a great waterfall 979 metres (3,212 feet) high on the River Carrao. They are the highest falls in the world.

Although Venezuela is only just north of the equator, parts of it are high in the mountains and the height makes their climate very much cooler. In the wooded parts of Venezuela live jaguars, pumas, ocelots, monkeys, and snakes.

The people are mainly of mixed Spanish and Indian descent. Italian, Portuguese, German, and Arab immigrants have settled in Venezuela, and there are also people of African origin, living mainly along the coasts. Most of the people are Roman Catholic and they speak Spanish. Caracas, situated some 900 metres (3,000 feet) in the mountains, is the capital. It lies 10 kilometres (6 miles) from the sea and is

Camera Press

Caracas, capital of Venezuela, lies at 900 m (3,000 ft) in a valley of the central highlands.

Herds of cattle graze on the Llanos in Venezuela's plains region. Venezuelan cowboys, or llaneros, are like the gauchos of the Argentinian pampas.

Courtesy, Creole Petroleum Corporation from Pan American Union

connected to Maracaibo, the country's second city and chief port, by road. Maracaibo is the centre of the oil industry.

FACTS ABOUT VENEZUELA

AREA: 912,050 square kilometres (352,164 square miles).
POPULATION: 18,272,000 (1987).
GOVERNMENT: Independent republic.
CAPITAL: Caracas.
GEOGRAPHICAL FEATURES: There are four main regions: (1) the Maracaibo lowlands, round Lake Maracaibo in the northwest; (2) the Merida mountains, a spur of the Andes, to the south and east of Lake Maracaibo; (3) the Orinoco River Basin with its grassland plains or *llanos* and forests; (4) the Guiana Highlands south of the Orinoco.
CHIEF PRODUCTS: Coffee, cocoa, sugar, tobacco, cotton, maize, livestock, petroleum, natural gas, iron and steel, petrochemicals, gold, diamonds, paper, textiles, clothing.
IMPORTANT TOWNS: Caracas, Maracaibo, Barquisimeto, Valencia, Maracay.
EDUCATION: Chldren must attend school between the ages of 7 and 13.

Agriculture and Industry

About a fifth of the people work on the land, growing maize, rice, coffee, cocoa, tobacco, sesame, and fruit. Cotton and sugar-cane are grown on the narrow coastal plain. However, most of Venezuela's wealth is from petroleum. The main oilfields are in the northwest, on the shores of Lake Maracaibo. Venezuela is one of the world's largest oil producers. Rich deposits of iron ore are mined, as well as gold, diamonds, coal, and salt. The "Iron Mountain" of Cerro Bolivar rises on the uplands beside the Orinoco River. The main industries include petrochemicals, iron and steel, paper, textiles, clothing, motor vehicles, cement, and aluminium. Beer, cigarettes, chocolates, and shoes are also made, but most of the manufactured goods Venezuela needs are imported from abroad.

No railways join Venezuela with neighbouring countries and there are few railways inside the country. Most of the railways and roads are near the towns along the coast. Travel by boat on the Orinoco and its tributaries is still the only means of transport for many people. The river-port of Ciudad Bolivar is the commercial centre for an enormous part of the

Courtesy, Standard Oil (NJ) from Pan American Union

Oil derricks dot the surface of Lake Maracaibo. The rocks of the region contain oil that is Venezuela's greatest source of wealth.

interior of Venezuela. The bridges across the Orinoco at Ciudad Bolivar and across the mouth of Lake Maracaibo greatly improved communications.

History

Christopher Columbus discovered the coast of what is now Venezuela in 1498 and the following year Alonso de Ojeda landed near the mouths of the Orinoco River. An Indian village built on piles (posts) above the swamps reminded his party of the European city of Venice so they named this village Venezuela, or "Little Venice".

Venezuela was one of the first parts of the South American Spanish Empire to revolt against Spain, and a Venezuelan revolutionary leader, Francisco de Miranda, is known as the father of South American independence. In 1811 Venezuela declared itself independent from Spain, although Spain did not recognize its independence until many years later. Another Venezuelan, Simon Bolivar (see BOLIVAR, SIMON), then became the leader of an army that gradually freed the whole of the northwestern part of South America from Spain. Bolivar combined Ecuador, Colombia, Venezuela, and Panama into a single state called Gran (Great) Colombia but this union fell apart and Venezuela became a separate country in 1830. After this it went through a series of civil wars and was often ruled by dictators.

Venezuela is a democracy with a president who is elected for five years at a time. The congress (parliament) consists of the Senate and the Chamber of Deputies.

VENICE is an Italian city and seaport at the northwestern end of the Adriatic Sea. It is one of the most beautiful cities in the world and seems to rise straight out of the water. In fact, Venice is built on about 120 low islands in the Lagoon of Venice, protected from the open sea by strips of land. Motor vehicles are not allowed in the old city, and people travel by boat on the 170 or so canals.

A causeway just over 4 kilometres (2.5 miles) long connects Venice with the mainland of Italy and carries a railway and a motor road. Coming out of the station, travellers can take a motor ferry-boat through the heart of the city, along the Grand Canal, which curves in the shape of a reversed letter "S". The Grand Canal is busy with other boats, including the elegant black *gondolas* for which Venice is famous. They are flat-bottomed, with raised bows and stern, and are often about 9 metres (30 feet) long. They are usually propelled by one oarsman, the gondolier, who stands at the stern.

As the ferry-boat zigzags from stop to stop on the canal, the city unfolds, revealing palaces, churches, and fascinating glimpses down side canals. Beautiful palaces follow one another, the water lapping against their walls. The Ca' d'Oro (house of gold) is especially magnificent, with its richly decorated front. It was built by a wealthy merchant of the 15th century and is now a museum. The boat passes under the Rialto Bridge, one of Venice's 400 bridges, which has a row of tiny shops along each side. Next comes the Accademia delle Belle Arti, the city's art gallery. Near the end of the Grand Canal the domed church of Santa Maria della Salute slides into view. (The name in English is St. Mary of Health; this church was built to commemorate the ending of the Plague in 1630.)

Then, facing open water, comes the finest part of Venice, where the Ducal Palace stands. This is where the *doge*, or head of the Venetian state, used to live. Its upper part is faced with cream and pink stones in a pattern of light and delicate colour. It contains magnificent rooms with painted ceilings. From the palace an enclosed bridge, the Bridge of Sighs, leads across a small canal to the old prisons. About the front of the palace a wide quayside stretches away eastwards. Here big ships can anchor.

A short distance away from the eastern tip of Venice, across the lagoon, lies the strip of the Lido, a fashionable bathing resort with a broad sandy beach.

Beside the Ducal palace is the *Piazzetta* ("little square"), which leads into St. Mark's Square, the *Piazza San Marco*. At this end of the great square stands the five-domed Byzan-

Above: Venice is a city of canals. Gondolas, which are flat-bottomed boats, are the traditional means of transport. **Right**: St. Mark's Square, famous for its pigeons. The domed church of St. Mark is in the background and the Ducal palace on the right.

Fritze Henle/Photo Researchers
J. Allan Cash from Rapho Guillumette

tine church of St. Mark. Its vast dim interior gleams with mosaics and coloured marble. Its dazzling altar screen is covered with gold and precious stones.

St. Mark's Square is surrounded on most of the other three sides by dignified, arcaded buildings. Cafés set their tables out in the square and people meet there, listening to the cafe orchestras. The campanile, or bell-tower, stands 98 metres (320 feet) high above the square. The *Merceria*, Venice's busiest shopping street, leads out of the square.

Many of the Venetian streets lead into *campi*, or small squares. Often these have a carved stone well-head in the centre around which children play. Along the many alleys there are churches, some of them big and imposing, others tiny and hidden away.

In the lagoon to the northeast of Venice small islands lie. The most important of these are Murano, famous for the glass its people make; Burano, a lace-making centre and the home of fishermen; and Torcello, which was once the rival of Venice but is now a quiet village.

The Grand Canal and the buildings that flank it have changed little since medieval times. The Rialto Bridge, which is lined with shops, has spanned the canal since the 16th century.

Authenticated News

Although Venice now receives much of its income from the tourist trade, it has other industries too. Furniture, glass, lace, and jewellery are made and there are factories. The main industrial area of Venice is Porto Marghera, on the mainland. It has many works connected with engineering, a shipbuilding yard, chemical works, paint factories, flour mills, and factories where food is canned. Marghera is also a thriving port.

Venice itself is growing old. The problem of how to protect the foundations of buildings has become serious. This is especially true of the buildings on the Grand Canal, where the wash of motor boats causes damage. The city is also subject to floods, as its foundations are gradually sinking, and many of the famous buildings and statues have been damaged by pollution.

Venetian History

Venice was once a great republic and was called *La Serenissima*, "the most serene". Its beginnings were humble. From the 5th century AD, when the mainland of Italy was continually being invaded by barbarians, some of the mainland people took refuge on the islands of the Lagoon of Venice. There were already small settlements of hardy fisherfolk on the islands and gradually the settlements drew together and in 697 they elected their first doge. In the very early 9th century the people of the islands decided that their capital should be in the place where Venice now stands. This decision was a wise one, for the complicated channels in this part of the lagoon made it easier to defend than the other cities. However, the people had to ram thousands of logs into the mud to make it firm, and on these shaky foundations Venice still rests.

As time went by, the republic built up its trade and became prosperous. At first the ordinary people had a say in their government, but the noble families gained more and more power. In 1297 they drew up the Golden Book of Nobility and decreed that only the sons of those families recorded in it should belong to the Great Council, which elected all officers of state from its members. Thus ordinary citizens lost their say in government forever. Later, the dreaded Council of Ten was set up to prevent conspiracy and to punish crimes against the state. Spies and secret police worked for it pitilessly and no rebellion or plot succeeded.

From early days the Venetians were sailors and traded by sea. They had to protect their merchant ships and their sea routes. Thus Venetian history is often a story of war at sea. Venice provided the ships to carry the men and horses of the Fourth Crusade (see CRUSADES). When the Crusaders attacked Constantinople, Venice gained enormous spoils. It obtained islands and trading posts throughout the eastern Mediterranean and became one of the great states of Europe. This led to conflict with Genoa, another seafaring republic in the Mediterranean. Bitter wars followed. They lasted until Venice's final victory in 1380. Genoa was not ruined, but Venice was left in control of the eastern Mediterranean trade. During the 15th century Venice also won territory on the mainland of Italy. This had its drawbacks, for it involved Venice in conflicts in Europe just when the Ottoman Turks were pushing westwards. (See OTTOMAN EMPIRE.) Practically alone, Venice fought against the Turks for about 250 years, and in 1571 the Venetian fleet played a big part in defeating the Turkish fleet in the Gulf of Lepanto (now the Gulf of Corinth) off the shores of Greece. However, Venice kept on losing territory and slowly became exhausted, not only because of the Turkish wars.

Trade in the Mediterranean was greatly reduced after the Portuguese discovered the sea route to India round the southern tip of Africa. (See EXPLORATION.) Previously, goods being sent to and from the East had been carried partly by sea and partly by land, and they had gone through ports in the eastern Mediterranean. When it became possible for goods to be sent by sea the whole way, without touching the Mediterranean at all, the trade of Venice was badly affected. The opening up of the New World—the West Indies and the continents of North and South America—also took trade away from the Mediterranean and thus from Venice.

By the 18th century Venice had lost its great position and most of its possessions in the eastern Mediterranean. Finally in 1797 the French seized the city and gave it to the Austrians in return for Milan. Although the Venetians revolted in 1848, Venice remained Austrian until 1866, when it became part of the new kingdom of Italy.

You can read about famous Venetian artists in the article PAINTERS AND PAINTING; and about Marco Polo, the 13th-century Venetian merchant who travelled to China, in the article POLO, MARCO. (See also ADRIATIC SEA.)

The population of Venice is about 377,670 (1985).

VENTILATION see HEATING AND AIR CONDITIONING

VENTRILOQUISM is the art of speaking without appearing to. The ventriloquist produces his or her voice in such a way that the sounds seem to come from some other source. The word "ventriloquism" comes from the Latin *venter* ("belly") and *loqui* ("to speak"): the Roman performers thought that words were formed in the belly.

Actually, the ventriloquist forms his words in the normal manner, but allows the breath to escape slowly and muffles the tones by narrowing the glottis, or opening between the vocal cords. He opens his mouth as little as possible, drawing back his tongue and using only the tip of it, while he tries to keep his lips still. This last, of course, is particularly difficult with consonants such as "b", "m" and "p".

Until the late 19th century a ventriloquist talked to imaginary persons in the roof or up the chimney, after, of course, attracting attention to the spot. The modern ventriloquist generally uses a dummy in the shape of a doll with movable head and lips which looks as though it is talking.

Considering that everyone in the audience knows very well that the dummy cannot speak, the success of the act is really astonishing. However, in order to achieve this, the ventriloquist has to build up a strong character and personality for the dummy, while keeping a flat, quiet, and colourless tone of voice and manner for himself or herself. When the two of them have a conversation, the dummy nearly always turns out to have a louder voice and gets the better of the arguments. All this is designed to turn the attention of the audience away from the ventriloquist's mouth. Dummies have had their own television and radio series, in which the ventriloquist apparently plays only a small part!

The ancient Eygptians and Greeks knew about ventriloquism. It is possible that their priests and priestesses used ventriloquism to create sounds such as the "voices" which came from the oracles (see ORACLE). The Zulus, Maoris, and Eskimos are among the peoples who are often expert ventriloquists.

Some birds that mimic other birds and human voices (such as parrots and budgerigars) may be said to practise a form of ventriloquism.

VENUS, the name the Romans gave to Aphrodite, the Greek goddess of love, see APHRODITE.

VENUS, in astronomy, is the second planet in outward succession from the Sun, orbiting it at an average distance of 107.5 million kilometres (66.6 million miles) along a path that is very nearly circular. In size Venus is very much like the Earth. Its diameter is about 12,103 kilometres (7,520 miles), 0.95 times that of Earth; its density is 5.24 grams per cubic centimetre, as against Earth's 5.52; and its mass is 0.81 times that of our planet. But although in dimensions, and probably in internal structure too, the Earth and Venus are sisters, Venus is in most other respects a world almost totally unlike our own.

Because Venus's path around the Sun lies within that of the Earth, the planet appears to us as a morning or evening star, rising just before or setting just after the Sun. In some parts of the world Venus may rise as much as three hours before dawn or set three hours after sunset. Venus is the most conspicuous of the planets and is in fact the brightest object in the night sky after the Moon. When the Greeks observed Venus as a morning star they called it Phosphorus; as an evening star it was known as Hesperus. Ancient peoples, struck by the beauty of its pearly light, connected it with the goddess of love and beauty, who in Greece was called Aphrodite and in Rome, Venus.

As an *inferior* planet, that is, one whose orbit lies within that of the Earth, Venus shows shape changes, or phases, like the Moon and Mercury. When the Italian astronomer Galileo discovered this fact in the early 17th century, it provided convincing proof to the scientific world that the old Earth-centred idea of the Universe was wrong and that Copernicus's suggestion, that the Earth went around the Sun, was more likely to be correct. Another 17th-century astronomer, the Dutchman Christiaan Huygens, noted the complete lack of permanent visible markings on the Venusian disc and was one of the first to suggest that its surface was perhaps hidden by a thick atmosphere. We now know that Huygens's speculation was right.

NASA/Science Photo Library

A close-up of the cloud-covered planet Venus taken from a distance of 65,000 km (40,000 miles) by the US Pioneer-Venus spacecraft in February 1979.

Venus's dense atmosphere held back knowledge of the planet until the 20th century. Now the use of scientific techniques such as spectroscopy and radar have helped unravel some of the mysteries surrounding Venus. In addition, unmanned spaceprobes of the Soviet Venera series and the American Mariner and Pioneer series, launched during the 1960s and 1970s, have studied Venus directly and allowed us at least to glimpse its surface.

In our modern view of Venus we must put aside all thoughts of beauty. Venus has one of the most hostile environments in the Solar System. Its dense atmosphere contains more than 96 per cent carbon dioxide, 3 per cent nitrogen, and traces of water vapour, argon, and neon. The top layer of the atmosphere consists of a 100 per cent covering made up of clouds of concentrated sulphuric acid, beneath which lie other dense clouds of sulphur dioxide and liquid and solid sulphur. Chemical reactions here produce lightning and other electrical disturbances. The carbon dioxide traps the Sun's heat by the "greenhouse effect" (see Carbon Dioxide and Monoxide). Thus the temperature on the surface of Venus is about 460°C (860°F), a raging inferno!

FACTS ABOUT VENUS

AVERAGE DISTANCE FROM THE SUN: 107.5 million kilometres (66.6 miles).
LENGTH OF YEAR: 224.7 Earth days.
PERIOD OF AXIAL ROTATION: 243 Earth days. (retrograde, or backwards).
LENGTH OF VENUSIAN "DAY": 118 Earth days.
DIAMETER: 12,103 kilometres (7,520 miles).
MASS: 0.81 (Earth=1).
DENSITY: 5.245 (water=1).
AVERAGE SURFACE GRAVITY: 0.904 (Earth=1).
ATMOSPHERIC COMPOSITION: Carbon dioxide 96%; nitrogen 3.5%; water vapour 0.002%; traces of carbon monoxide, oxygen, sulphur dioxide, hydrochloric acid. Upper cloud layers composed of sulphuric acid, sulphur dioxide, and free sulphur.
ATMOSPHERIC PRESSURE: 94 bars (Earth=1 bar).
AVERAGE SURFACE TEMPERATURE: 460°C (860°F).

Pictures sent back by the Soviet probes Venera 9 and Venera 10 in 1975 revealed that Venus's surface was a rough desert plain strewn with both jagged and rounded rocks, some the size of boulders. Radar mapping of the surface by means of Earth-based radio telescopes and the American spacecraft Pioneer Venus 2 (1978) revealed high isolated mountain ranges and deep basins. The highest mountain so far known on Venus is Mount Maxwell, standing 11,000 metres (36,000 feet) above the planet's surface. Venus's gravity is about nine-tenths that of Earth, but no human being could live on Venus because its dense poisonous atmosphere produces a pressure more than 94 times as great as normal air-pressure at sea-level on our planet. Add to this the fact that the rocks may become hot enough to glow red, and one can fairly imagine Venus as being very close to our vision of Hell.

Venus's axis is tilted only about 3° from the plane of its orbit around the Sun, which means that it experiences no seasonal changes like those on Earth or Mars. Venus takes 225 Earth days to make one circuit of the Sun and 584 Earth days to complete one cycle of phases. But it takes no less than 243 Earth days to complete one rotation on its axis. Another remarkable fact is that, compared with the other planets in the Solar System, Venus rotates backwards, that is, from east to west. A "day" on Venus, from one noon to the next, lasts 118 Earth days. A curious feature of Venus's rotation concerns the part played in it by the Earth. Of all the planets in the Solar System, Venus comes closest to the Earth, approaching to within 42 million kilometres (26 million miles) of it. Strangely, whenever Venus reaches this point in its orbit, it always has the same face turned towards the Earth. This is probably due to our planet's gravitational effects on Venus.

VERACRUZ. On the hot and humid Gulf of Mexico, 425 kilometres (264 miles) east of Mexico City, is the most important seaport in Mexico. It is an interesting combination of old and new. Modern buildings and docking facilities contrast with Spanish colonial buildings. A great lighthouse overlooks the breakwater which protects the docks from the storms. The city has modern facilities and many fine homes set on wide avenues. Railways and roads connect Veracruz with Mexico City and the interior highlands.

The most important products shipped from Veracruz are vanilla, sugar, coffee, and chilies. Machinery, chemicals, and wheat from other countries enter Mexico here. In addition to its shipping, Veracruz is important for the manufacture of cigars, shoes, rum, beer, and chocolate. Fishing is an important occupation.

Veracruz was the first Spanish settlement

in Mexico. It was founded by Hernan Cortes in 1519. The present port city, dating from 1599, has had an exciting history. In the 17th and 18th centuries pirates attacked and captured it. The French seized the city twice, in 1838 and 1861. It fell to the United States in the Mexican War, and again in 1914.

The population of Veracruz is 284,822 (1980).

VERB. In every sentence there are two parts, a subject and a predicate: in the sentence "John walked quickly down the winding road" for example, "John" is the subject and all the other words are the predicate. The chief word in the predicate of any sentence is always a verb and you can see how important it is by trying to leave it out. ("John quickly down the winding road" does not make proper sense at all.) The work a verb does is to tell what the subject of a sentence *does* or what it *is* or what *is done to* it; for example, "The lion *escaped*", "The day *is* fine", "The cat *was killed*".

Every verb has several different parts and sometimes it changes its spelling or adds on endings. For instance, the words *walk*, *walks*, *walking*, *walked* are all parts of one verb, and *break*, *breaks*, *breaking*, *broke*, *broken* are parts of another. *Swim* changes to *swam* and *swum*, *go* changes to *went* and *gone*. Some changes are made by using an extra auxiliary (helping) verb, such as *is* or *have*: "I *have seen* him", or "the rain *is stopping*". The different parts of verbs and the reasons for the various changes are explained in the rest of this article.

Infinitive and Participles. The part of the verb that we usually use when we talk about it is the *infinitive*. We say, for instance, that *walk*, *walks*, *walking*, and *walked* are all parts of the verb "to walk"; *broken* is a part of the verb "to break". The infinitive is made by putting "to" in front of the verb.

Two other special parts of the verb are called the *participles*: the *present participle* and the *past participle*. The present participle is made by adding the ending *-ing* to the verb; for example, *build*, *building*; *go*, *going*; *run*, *running*; *take*, *taking*. (There are some rules of spelling that have to be learnt about this, such as that the *n* is doubled in *running* and the *e* is left out in *taking*.) The present participle is what is called a verbal adjective. This means that as well as being part of a verb it can also do the work of an adjective; for example, "the boy is *running* away" (verb) and "the *running* brook is never silent" (adjective).

The part of the verb that ends with *ing* can also be used as a verbal noun or *gerund*. Then it is part of a verb but does the work of a noun; for example, "*running* is fun".

The past participle of many verbs is made by adding on the ending *ed*, *-d*, or *t*. For example, *wreck*, *wrecked*; *stare*, *stared*; *burn*, *burnt*. However, there are many other verbs which make their past participles not by adding anything on but by changing the spelling in some way. Sometimes just the vowel is changed: *swim*, *swum*; *spin*, *spun*; *stride*, *strode*. Sometimes the letter *n* is added at the end: *see*, *seen*; *drive*, *driven*; *give*, *given*. Sometimes the vowel is changed and *en* is added as well: *break*, *broken*; *speak*, *spoken*. A few verbs change in other ways.

The past participle is a verbal adjective, just as the present participle is. For example, "I *have broken* the vase" (verb) and "the *broken* vase cannot be mended" (adjective).

Person and Number. In grammar, every verb is described as being in either the first person, or second person, or third person, according to what its subject is. If the subject of a verb is the person who is speaking—"*I* sing, "*we* laughed"—the verb is in the first person. If the subject is the person or persons *spoken to*—"*you* sing", "*you* were all laughing"—the verb is in the second person. If the subject is the person or persons, or thing or things, *spoken about*—"*the bird* sings", "*they* laughed"—the verb is in the third person.

Verbs also have the same *number* as their subjects. If the subject is one person or thing, such as *I* or *the bird*, the verb is *singular*. If the subject is more than one person or thing, such as *we*, *they*, or *the soldiers*, the verb is *plural*.

The verb sometimes changes according to the number and person of its subject: I *walk*, but she *walks*; we *sing*, they *sing* but the bird *sings*. In nearly every verb an *s* is added on for the third person singular of the present tense. (Tenses are explained in the next paragraph.) The verb "to be" is an exception to the general rule, and has complete changes:

	Singular	*Plural*
1st person	I am	we are
2nd person	you are	you are
3rd person	he, she, or it is	they are

Tense. Verbs also change to show the different times at which the action they express takes place. In English there are three main "times" or *tenses* of verbs: *present*, *past*, and *future*.

	Present	
	Singular	*Plural*
1st person	I walk	we walk
2nd person	you walk	you walk
3rd person	he, she, or it walks	they walk

	Past	
	Singular	*Plural*
1st person	I walked	we walked
2nd person	you walked	you walked
3rd person	he, she, or it walked	they walked

	Future	
	Singular	*Plural*
1st person	I shall walk	we shall walk
2nd person	you will walk	you will walk
3rd person	he, she, or it will walk	they will walk

Many verbs make their past tense like this one, by adding the ending *-ed*. However, many others make their past tense, as they do their past participles, by changing their spelling in some other way. For example, I *sit* changes to I *sat*; *I fall* to *I fell*; *I think* to *I thought*; *I buy* to *I bought*.

Besides these three main tenses there are also *continuous tenses* and *perfect tenses*. These are described in the article TENSES.

Transitive and Intransitive Verbs. Verbs are called transitive when they can have a direct object, that is, when they express an action which is *done* to someone or something, or "passes over" to someone or something. For example, "the dog *killed* the rat", "Mary *will bite* the apple"; "rat" is the object of "killed", "apple" is the object of "will bite".

Intransitive verbs have no direct object of their action. For example, "the audience *giggled*", "the dog *ran away*".

Active and Passive Voice. When a verb tells us what the subject does, it is described as in the *active voice*. When a verb tells what the subject *has done to it*, it is in the *passive voice*. The passive voice is made by adding some part of the auxiliary verb "to be" to the past participle of the main verb. For example, "He *was gored* by the bull", "The orange *was eaten* by Mary". Intransitive verbs can never be put in the passive voice.

Mood. As well as telling what the subject *does or has done to it* or what it *is*, a verb can sometimes give a command or express a wish. These differences are called the *moods* of the verbs. Verbs that tell what the subject does or is are in the *indicative* mood: "The deer *leapt*", "The dog *is* black". Verbs that give a command are in the *imperative* mood: "*Bring* it here!" "*Be* quiet!" Verbs that express wishes are in the subjunctive mood: "God *save* the Queen!", "If only he *were* here". The subjunctive mood is not much used in English nowadays, but sometimes comes in sentences after *if:* "If I *were you*, I would go home".

VERDI, Giuseppe (1813–1901). Giuseppe Fortunino Francesco Verdi was the greatest of the Italian opera composers of the 19th century. He was born at Le Roncole, near Busseto in northern Italy, on 10 October 1813. His father was a poor innkeeper and Verdi's childhood was hard. However, he learned to sing and play the organ and at about the age of 13 he began composing music of various kinds, much of it for the church and for the local music society in Busseto. When he was 18 Verdi applied to enter the Milan Conservatory (music school) but was rejected because he was too old. However, Antonio Barezzi, a merchant of Busseto who had long taken an interest in Verdi's musical development, paid for him to study privately in Milan.

Verdi composed his first opera *Oberto, Conte di San Bonifacio*, in 1836. Its successful

BBC Hulton Picture Library

Giuseppe Verdi, composer and conductor.

production at La Scala, Milan's great opera house, led an opera promoter to commission a second one from the young composer. This one, staged in 1840, failed so badly that Verdi almost gave up writing operas. But in 1842 he was given the libretto (words) of *Nabucco*, the story of the Biblical king Nebuchadnezzar. The work attracted him greatly, and his setting of the chorus of patriotic prayer sung by the Hebrew slaves held captive in Babylon is one of the most moving pieces of music ever written. *Nabucco* was followed by *I Lombardi* (1843); *Ernani* (1844); *Macbeth* (1847); and *Luisa Miller* (1849).

When he was 37 Verdi wrote the first of the operas by which he is known everywhere today. This was *Rigoletto* (1851). Then came *Il Trovatore* (1853), which was a great success, and *La Traviata* (also 1853). (The story of these operas is told in the article OPERA.)

Others followed in the next few years, including *Simon Boccanegra* (1857, revised 1881); *Un ballo in maschera* (A Masked Ball) and *La forza del destino* (1859); The Force of Destiny (1862). Altogether Verdi wrote 27 operas.

Verdi lived at a time when the various parts of Italy—some independent states, others ruled by foreign countries—were struggling to unite themselves into one nation. He took an active part in this struggle and in 1860 was elected to the first Italian parliament. But two years later he resigned his seat and carried on composing. He wrote *Don Carlos*, an opera about the son of King Philip II of Spain, which was produced in Paris in 1867. *Aida*, with its Egyptian story (see OPERA) was very popular when it was produced in 1871 at a new opera house in Cairo, Egypt, to celebrate the opening of the Suez Canal, and it is still one of Verdi's most popular operas.

In 1868, following the death of the great composer Rossini (see ROSSINI, GIOACCHINO), Verdi suggested the composition of a requiem in his memory, to be written jointly by himself and other leading Italian composers. But the idea came to nothing. Six years later, Verdi completed a magnificent *Requiem* on his own, very dramatic in style. It was written in memory of Alessandro Manzoni, a great Italian writer who had just died.

By this time Verdi was getting on in years and as he had enough money he decided to live in the country and spent much of his wealth helping the poor. People took it for granted that he would write no more. But then, when he was over 70, he surprised the world with the greatest of all his works—the opera *Otello*, based on Shakespeare's play *Othello*, which had been adapted by his friend Arrigo Boito, one of Italy's greatest authors. It was produced at La Scala in 1887, and as Verdi left at the end of the performance, the crowds were so enthusiastic that they unharnessed the horses from his carriage and pulled it themselves to his hotel. Six years later when Verdi was nearly 80 his last opera, *Falstaff*, based again by Boita on several historical plays of Shakespeare, was given at La Scala. His very last work was his *Four Sacred Pieces* (1898) for choir and orchestra. He lived on to the age of 87 and died in Milan on 27 January 1901.

VERMEER, Jan (1632–75). Jan Vermeer (Jan van der Meer van Delft) was, after Rembrandt, the greatest of Dutch painters. He lovingly recorded middle-class life in Holland following the long struggle for independence from Spain.

He was born and died in the town of Delft in Holland, but little else is known about his life. His father was a silk weaver and dealer in paintings, a business which Vermeer himself later carried on. He seems never to have left Holland. He became a member of the local guild of painters in 1653, several times acted as one of its officials, was married, and had eight children. He worked slowly and fewer than 40 of his paintings survive.

Vermeer's earliest paintings were of religious and mythological subjects and were larger in scale than his later works. His mature paintings are almost all of domestic interiors and of people engaged in everyday tasks. A girl reads a letter, or a servant pours milk from a jug, a scene rendered with subtlety and truth. The paintings, although full of detail, are in no sense photographic. Vermeer's calm perception and colour sense give them a timeless quality.

Courtesy, Trustees of the National Gallery

Young Woman Seated at a Virginal (*c.*1670), is one of Jan Vermeer's lavish, detailed domestic interiors.

Vermeer died heavily in debt. His widow had to sell two paintings to pay a baker's bill. After his death his paintings were considered of little value and it was not until the middle of the 19th century that their extraordinary merit was recognized. They are now among the most valuable paintings in the world. His best-known works include *A View of Delft* (*c.*1660), Mauritshuis, The Hague; *Maidservant Pouring Milk* (*c.*1658), Rijksmuseum, Amsterdam; *The Lacemaker* (*c.*1665), Louvre, Paris; and *Woman with a Water Jug* (*c.*1664–65), Metropolitan Museum of Art, New York.

VERMONT, located in the northeast corner of the United States, is one of the New England states. Its name means the Green Mountain state and comes from the French words, *vert*, meaning green, and *mont*, meaning mountain. The range of that name runs through the state from north to south like a spinal column of stone, varying in width from 32 to 58 kilometres (20 to 36 miles). There are so many mountainous regions in the state that virtually all of it sits on a bedrock of granite and other minerals. Farming has always been a precarious undertaking because of the thin soil and boulder-strewn landscape. However, granite, marble, and other kinds of stone have been successfully quarried since colonial days.

Vermont combines the atmosphere of 19th-century New England with a prosperous 20th-century economy based on manufacturing. The rural population consists largely of descendants from the Puritan colonial Yankees, while the cities have proved to be a haven for later immigrants from Ireland, southern Europe, and French Canada. It is a small state, less than 145 kilometres (90 miles) at its widest point. Its cities, too, are small. Burlington is the largest; yet it had fewer than 40,000 inhabitants in the mid-1980s. In total population, only Alaska and Wyoming have fewer people.

If the resident population is small, the annual tourist population is enormous. Millions of people visit Vermont to enjoy the

ZEFA

The Capitol at Montpelier, which is Vermont's state capital. It is named after a city in southern France.

breathtaking scenery, fish in the rivers and lakes, or spend time on the ski slopes at Stowe, the Mad River Valley, and other resort areas.

The Land

Vermont is bordered on the north by the Quebec province of Canada; on the east by New Hampshire, just across the Connecticut River; on the south by Massachusetts; and on the west by New York. About 180 kilometres (112 miles) of the New York border is taken up with Lake Champlain. Vermont's greatest north-to-south length is 256 kilometres (159 miles), and its width varies from 143 kilometres (89 miles) in the north to 60 kilometres (37 miles) in the south.

There are three major land regions: the Green Mountains, the Champlain Lowland, and the New England Upland. Of the three, the Green Mountains form the largest segment, running as they do from Quebec to Massachusetts. The mountains are part of the Appalachian Highland, which covers so much of the eastern United States (see APPALACHIAN MOUNTAINS). The Green Mountain region averages about 610 metres (2,000 feet) above sea-level. The state's highest peak, Mont Mansfield, is in this range.

The Champlain Lowland covers most of the area between the Green Mountains and Lake Champlain. It is a tableland good for growing crops. At the southern end of the lowland, however, is a range of smaller mountains, the Taconics. Along the eastern slopes of this range is the narrow Valley of Vermont, about 136 kilometres (85 miles) long.

Between the Green Mountains and the Connecticut River is the New England Upland, or the Vermont Piedmont. This region, too, runs the length of the state north to south. Within it, in the northeast corner, are the White Mountains, a lower range than the Green Mountains.

Being inland from the sea, Vermont has a continental climate. The summers are short and warm, while the winters can be long and quite cold. Autumn is the most pleasant time of year, and the changing colours of the leaves are an annual tourist magnet. Snow falls in the highlands as early as October, while it does not usually appear at lower elevations until December. Annual rainfall averages 820 millimetres (32 inches) at lower elevations and 1,270 millimetres (50 inches) in the mountains. The ski resort areas may have more than 2,540 millimetres (100 inches) of snow every winter. The growing season in the western lowlands is from 130 to 150 days. In the rest of the state it ranges from 100 to 130 days.

The People

The first settlers to arrive in Vermont, in the 1760s, were Puritan New Englanders, descendants of immigrants from England and Scotland. The population today is overwhelmingly white, made up of descendants of the original stock and of later immigrants from the British Isles, Ireland, Canada, Sweden, Italy, Poland, Greece, and other nations. Less than one per cent of the population are black Americans.

Most of the population continues to live in rural areas, although the region around Burlington has grown markedly since 1970 because of the increase in manufacturing jobs. About 40 per cent of the total population is concentrated around Burlington. In the southern end of the state there has been a significant growth because of its ski areas and easy access from the much larger out-of-state urban areas

ZEFA

The striking colour of the trees in autumn is a feature of the Vermont countryside.

to the south. Many out-of-state residents have built second homes in Vermont.

The Economy

Since the period of the American Revolution, Vermont's economy has gone through cycles of prosperity and decline. It has been a farming state from the beginning, in spite of the difficulties the land poses for agriculture. Dairying has always been the chief form of agriculture; consequently hay for cattle feed has been the main crop. In recent decades the number of farms has been declining as smaller units have been combined for the sake of efficiency. The primary farming areas are in the Champlain Lowland and in the Connecticut Valley. Apart from cattle and hay, the farms also produce potatoes, oats, maize, market-garden crops, and apples. Other livestock include turkeys, sheep, chickens, and pigs. Vermont is a leading state in the production of maple syrup and maple sugar.

Quarrying has contributed to the economy since the first granite and marble were dug in 1785. Vermont stone has been used in many notable public buildings in the United States. Among them are the Supreme Court building in Washington, DC, and the United Nations building in New York City. Besides marble and granite, Vermont also produces sand, gravel, asbestos, talc, mica, slate, and limestone.

Lumbering became a significant industry quite early. Farmers cleared their land of trees, burnt the wood, and shipped it out to be sold as potash. Huge areas of the state are commercial forestland. Today, instead of burning the trees, the timber is used for many wood products, including paper, furniture, baseball bats, hockey sticks, flooring, boat oars and paddles, trailers, and toothpicks. There are sawmills and woodworking shops in almost every part of the state.

Most of Vermont's workforce is engaged in some form of manufacturing. Textile mills once formed a thriving industry, as they did in much of New England. Most of the firms have closed or moved out of state. Current industries manufacture non-electrical machinery, machine tools, computers and other electronic devices, optical glass, plastics, scales, cereals, roofing paper, and food products. Printing and publishing are also a large part of the economy.

Education

Vermont has been strongly committed to public (state) education since its constitution of 1777 provided for building a school in every town, and a state university. Locally elected boards govern school policy for primary and secondary schools. The state, however, provides much of the funding, especially for teacher training and for special education programmes.

ZEFA

A dairy farm near Pomfret in Vermont, which is one of the leading dairy states in the United States.

Vermont has some of the finest colleges in the United States. Middlebury College, Goddard College, and Marlboro College have earned national reputations as coeducational institutions; and Bennington College is an outstanding school for women. The state supports the University of Vermont, at Burlington, which was chartered in 1791.

FACTS AND FIGURES

AREA: 24,900 square kilometres (9,614 square miles).
POPULATION: 541,000 (1987).
MOUNTAIN RANGES: Green Mountains. Highest peaks: Mansfield, 1,339 metres (4,393 feet); Killington Peak, 1,293 metres (4,242 feet); Ellen, 1,260 metres (4,135 feet); Camel's Hump, 1,244 metres (4,081 feet); and Cutts Peak, 1,225 metres (4,020 feet).
RIVERS: Connecticut, Lamoille, Winooski, Otter Creek, White, and West.
CITIES (1980): Burlington, 37,712; Rutland, 18,436; Bennington, 15,815; Essex, 14,392; Montpelier, 8,241.

History

The first European to visit Vermont was the French explorer Samuel de Champlain in 1609 (see CHAMPLAIN, SAMUEL DE). No permanent settlement was made until the French established themselves on Isle La Motte in Lake Champlain in 1666. Meanwhile, the territory that is now Vermont had been claimed by England. Massachusetts, New Hampshire, and New York laid claim to parts of Vermont. New York and New Hampshire nearly went to war over Vermont, an event prevented by the onset of the American Revolution. Under cover of this war, Vermont declared itself an independent republic in 1777.

Vermont remained independent until January 1791, when it adopted the United States Constitution and joined the Union. It was the first new state after the original 13. Montpelier was selected as the capital in 1805.

The state grew and prospered in the decades before the American Civil War. Its commercial connections were improved by the building of the Champlain Canal in 1823, and the arrival of the railway in 1848. After the Civil War the population began shifting westward in search of more open land. Farming became less profitable, but immigrants arrived to work in lumbering and quarrying.

Vermont's economy remained fairly static until after World War II (1939–45). Since then industrialization has expanded and the tourist trade has mushroomed, especially the winter-sports business. Since 1970 the state's population has increased at a rate higher than the national average.

VERNE, Jules (1828–1905). The French writer Jules Verne is sometimes called the "father of science fiction". His life spanned a period full of scientific discovery and the development of many ideas of great scientific importance. These discoveries and ideas formed a background for a series of tales that proved to be among the most imaginative and exciting stories ever written.

Verne was born in Nantes in France, and studied law in Paris before turning to writing both plays and stories. In 1863 he published in a magazine the first of his *Voyages extraordinaires*, which was entitled (in English) *Five Weeks in a Balloon*. It was an immediate success and was the first of many exciting stories of fantasy.

Although his stories had fantastic settings, Verne was careful to put in a good deal of realistic detail, so making the story more convincing. His careful attention to detail was combined with a remarkable imagination. In *Twenty Thousand Leagues under the Sea*

The Walt Disney Company

Ned Land (played by Kirk Douglas) tackles a giant squid in the 1954 film version of Jules Verne's novel *Twenty Thousand Leagues under the Sea.*

(1870) he wrote about submarines and aqualungs (neither of which had then been invented), and in *From the Earth to the Moon* (1865) he predicted the birth of space travel. His other books include *A Journey to the Centre of the Earth* (1864), *The Mysterious Island* (1874), and *Around the World in Eighty Days* (1873). First published as a serial, this last book turned out to be one of Verne's most popular stories. It tells how an Englishman called Phileas Fogg attempts a round-the-world journey to win a bet.

Many of Jules Verne's novels were turned into exciting films. Among the best were the Walt Disney version of *Twenty Thousand Leagues under the Sea* (1954), and *Around the World in Eighty Days* (1965).

See also SCIENCE FICTION.

VERSAILLES. The French town of Versailles is about 18 kilometres (11 miles) southwest of Paris and is the capital of the department of Yvelines. However, when people speak of Versailles they more often mean the great 17th-century palace of Versailles than the town itself. The palace was the main residence of the kings of France, and seat of government, for over 100 years.

King Louis XIV built this palace. (See the article LOUIS, KINGS OF FRANCE.) His father Louis XIII (1601–43), who loved hunting in the woods around what was then the village of Versailles, had built a small hunting-lodge there. However, Louis XIV wanted a palace that would be finer than any in France and he chose to build it at Versailles, keeping his father's hunting-lodge as part of the new palace. Work was started in 1661 under the architect Louis Le Vau. After he died Jules Mansart followed him as architect. However, the king himself took a great interest in his new palace and had a hand in all the plans. In 1682 he moved his court and his ministers from Paris to Versailles.

The enormous palace with its magnificent rooms, richly furnished, enabled the king to live in greater splendour than any other European monarch and pleased him greatly. Its grounds were designed by André Le Nôtre and were equally magnificent, with artificial lakes, elegant fountains, and many statues.

The palace has witnessed many important events in French history, and ranks as one of France's greatest national heritages. Some of the first scenes of the French Revolution took place there (see FRENCH REVOLUTION). Some 80 years later, while France and Prussia were at war (1870–71), the Prussians captured Versailles and made it their headquarters. On 18 January 1871, King William of Prussia was proclaimed emperor of Germany in the famous Hall of Mirrors in the palace. On 28 June 1919, after France, Britain, and their allies had

ZEFA

The palace of Versailles was believed to house some 5,000 persons attached to the French royal court.

defeated Germany in World War I, the Treaty of Versailles was signed in the same room. After 1871 it was the custom for the president of the French Republic to be elected at Versailles.

The palace is now a museum and, together with its ornate gardens, attracts tourists from all over the world.

VERSE see POETRY.

VERTEBRATE. There are two main groups of animals: those without backbones, called the *invertebrates*, and those with backbones, called the *vertebrates*. The vertebrates are in general more complicated than the invertebrates, and grow to a bigger size. Fish, amphibians, reptiles, birds, and mammals are all vertebrates, whereas insects, molluscs, and crustaceans are not. See the article ANIMAL, as well as the articles FISH; AMPHIBIAN; REPTILE; BIRD; MAMMAL.

The word vertebrate comes from the Latin term for the individual bones of the spine or backbone, the *vertebrae*. The first vertebrates were the first fishes, which evolved about 510 million years ago. It is thought that the backbone gave them an advantage because it formed a flexible support to the body which could be swung to and fro by muscles, to produce fast swimming movements. The backbone also formed a protective tube around the fragile spinal cord, a vital part of the nervous system.

In recent times the term vertebrate has been replaced in zoology by chordate. A chordate is an animal that has a semi-stiff rod of tissue down its back, called a notochord, at some stage in its development. The notochord is thought to be the forerunner of the backbone. Animals such as the lancelet or amphioxus, a small eel-like creature, and sea-squirts (in their larval form) have a notochord, but not a backbone. All vertebrates have a notochord early in their development.

Any creature with a notochord belongs to the major group, or phylum, called Chordata. Within the Chordata are the subgroups, or subphyla, Urochordata (such as sea-squirts), Cephalochordata (including lancelets), and Vertebrata (the vertebrates).

See also ZOOLOGY.

VESPUCCI, Amerigo (1454–1512), was an Italian merchant and explorer-navigator after whom the continents of America were named. Vespucci was born in Florence, Italy. He worked for the Medici family and was sent by them to Spain in 1492 (see MEDICI FAMILY). There he helped to prepare ships for Columbus's second trip to the New World in 1493.

The early voyages of Columbus had reached only the West Indian Islands. Vespucci claimed that he was the first European to reach the mainland of South America. This was on 16 June 1497, eight days before John Cabot reached Nova Scotia. Whether Vespucci actually sailed around the Gulf of Mexico, Florida, and up to Chesapeake Bay in this 1497 voyage remains unresolved. Some authorities think that Vespucci's voyage was not made until 1499. (See also COLUMBUS, CHRISTOPHER.)

Vespucci made several other voyages from Spain and Portugal. On a trip in 1501 he sailed

BBC Hulton Picture Library

Amerigo Vespucci, after whom the continents of North and South America are named.

along the coast of South America to what later became Argentina. He was the first European to visit the River Plata. Other explorers thought that they were near Asia, but Vespucci realized that he was off the coast of a new continent. He wrote this in letters that were later published. His information was used by a German map-maker who drew one of the first maps of the New World, and used the name America, which is a Latin form of Amerigo, for the new continent.

Vespucci became a Spanish citizen in 1505, and in 1508 he was appointed chief pilot, or navigator, of Spain. He was placed in charge of preparing maps of the newly discovered territory and planning routes to the New World.

VETCH. Among the plants of the pea family are the vetches, climbing plants very closely related to the broad bean. Like other leguminous plants, vetches enrich the soil and they are also used as food for cattle (see LEGUMINOUS PLANTS). There are many different kinds of vetch and the flowers may be blue, purple, yellow or white. The leaves are divided into many little leaflets. The plant climbs by means of some of the leaf-stalks called tendrils which, instead of bearing leaves, curl round other plants and so enable the weak stem, often 1.2 metres (4 feet) long, to reach up into the light and air. The fruit, like that of other leguminous plants, is a pod containing two or more seeds.

NHPA/G. J. Cambridge

Meadow vetchling is a European grassland plant.

Vetches grow by roadsides and in fields and woods all over Europe and North America. Another name for them is tares. The parable of the tares in the New Testament of the Bible tells how wheat was planted in a field and the sower's enemy planted tares among it by night. At the time of harvest the wheat was gathered into the barn and the tares were burned. The wheat stands for the people who do good in the world and the tares for those who do evil.

VETERINARY MEDICINE. Medicine is the prevention, diagnosis, and treatment of diseases and ill-health in people. Veterinary medicine is concerned with animals. In many countries, people can only call themselves a vet (veterinary surgeon or veterinarian) if they have undergone several years of special training and passed exams to obtain a qualification in veterinary medicine. In some countries the same doctors treat animals and people.

For centuries the care of sick animals was in the hands of farmers, shepherds, farriers, grooms, and others who were acquainted with animal-keeping. Their knowledge came from serving as apprentices, from folklore, and from their daily experiences with the animals.

In the second half of the 18th century veterinary medicine began to develop as a science, with the establishment of veterinary colleges. The first were in Europe, and those at Lyons (the first), Hanover, Stockholm, and Bologna are more than 200 years old. The Royal Veterinary College at London's University College was founded in 1791. Nowadays there are veterinary colleges in most countries.

Training to be a Vet

People who wish to become vets must want to care for animals and get on well with them. They usually have to pass several higher exams at school, especially in science subjects such as biology, chemistry, physics, and mathematics. Courses at veterinary colleges are very popular and there are not usually enough places for everyone who applies.

Courtesy, PDSA

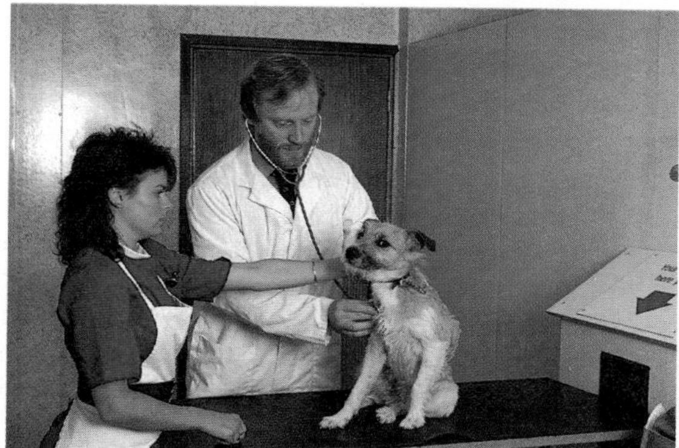

A vet listens to a dog's heartbeat with a stethoscope for any irregular sounds that would indicate disease.

The training lasts several years (five in Britain, seven in the United States). Students learn about anatomy (the structure of the body) and physiology (the workings of the body), in domesticated animals such as horses, oxen, pigs, sheep, dogs, cats, and chickens. They study pathology and microbiology (diseases and their causes), together with the feeding and care of animals. As they progress, they learn about medicines and operations for sick animals, and they may study more unusual creatures such as zoo animals and fish. Towards the end of the course the students work with sick animals brought to the college, or to animal hospitals, and they usually spend some time with a qualified vet to gain day-to-day experience. Studying to be a vet is one of the most difficult trainings for any profession.

After Qualification

Most new vets become assistants to established practitioners. They work in general practice, dealing with the public and their animals, and being paid for each job they do. Some specialize in caring for farm animals, others in unusual or zoo animals, and some in household pets in a small-animal practice.

There are many other possibilities. Some vets take up a career in teaching at a veterinary college. Others work for a commercial organization such as a drug company or foodstuffs producer: vets are needed anywhere that animals are kept and used. Most countries have a national organization which employs vets to help control diseases in farm animals. Their tasks include the prevention of the spread of dangerous diseases, such as rabies and foot-and-mouth disease. Other vets find careers in research, working on new veterinary or medical products. Some travel to developing countries to help and advise on animal care. Most branches of the armed forces and the police employ vets, for example to look after horses and dogs.

Zoological Society of London

A vet at London Zoo listens to the breathing of a young deer for signs of congestion.

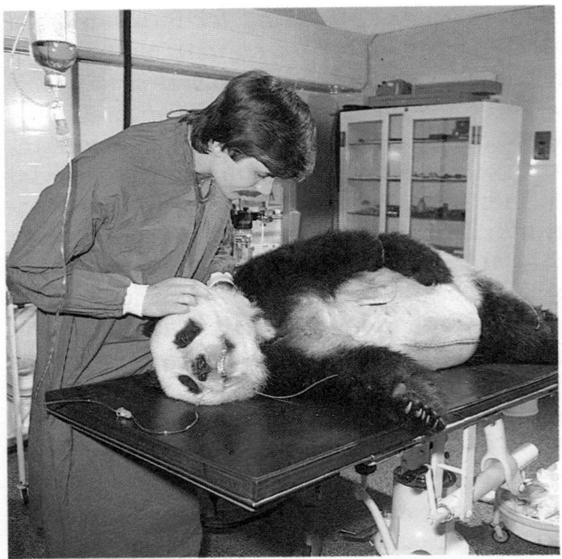

Zoological Society of London

A giant panda receiving a drip feed in London Zoo. These animals are difficult to keep healthy.

The Daily Work of a Vet

In general practice, vets work in much the same way as doctors. They have a surgery where pets are brought for health checks and treatment. Often several vets work together in a group practice, where each may have a speciality, such as dogs or horses. The practice may have assistants, trainees, receptionists, and specially-trained veterinary nurses. The vets make house or farm calls to attend to sick animals. Some of the drugs and equipment they use are similar to those used in human medicine. They may X-ray an injured animal to see if it has any broken bones, sew up a wound, neuter a pet whose owners do not want it to breed, or any one of a hundred other tasks.

Courtesy, PDSA

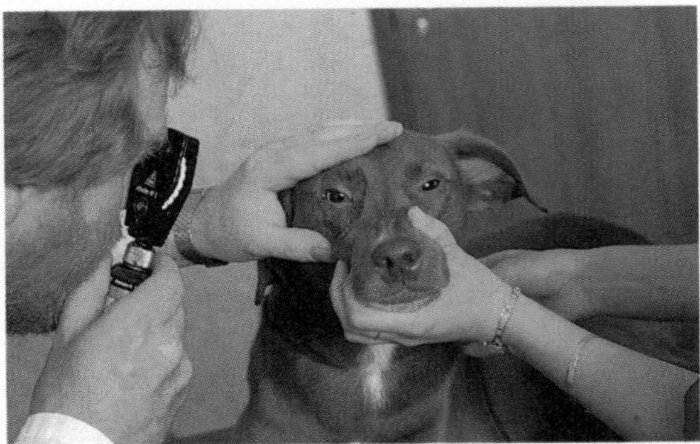

A nurse holds still a dog's head while the vet looks at the retina of its eye through an ophthalmoscope.

They may attend to a dog injured in a road accident or travel to a remote farm to assist a cow which is giving birth. A zoo vet might have to fly halfway round the world to treat a rare animal such as a panda or tiger. A vet may be asked to attend to an animal that has been ill-treated, and in some cases he or she may have to destroy it, painlessly, if the animal is too old or too sick to recover.

Apart from prescribing drugs and carrying out operations, vets give advice to owners about keeping their animals healthy and protecting them from serious diseases. This is called preventive veterinary medicine. For example, puppies are given injections to immunize them against distemper and leptospirosis, diseases which used to cause considerable suffering. Similarly, horses are protected against tetanus and influenza, and sheep from diseases that otherwise could quickly spread through an entire flock. Health problems sometimes arise on farms where the animals are not fed or housed properly, and this may involve the vets in a lot of work and careful discussion to improve matters.

VIBURNUM is the name of 200 species of flowering shrubs of the honeysuckle family. Most grow in Asia and North America, with some European species.

Many are garden favourites for their showy flowers, fruit, and autumn foliage. The American wayfaring tree or hobblebush (*Viburnum alnifolium*) has white flower clusters and red berries that turn purple-black. It grows up to 3 metres (10 feet) high. The similar European wayfaring tree (*Viburnum lantana*) grows slightly taller. The Japanese snowball (*Viburnum plicatum*) is another popular garden plant with clusters of large, white, ball-shaped flower heads. *Viburnum carlesii*, from Korea, has beautiful sweet-smelling pink flowers opening to white.

Some viburnums, such as the European guelder rose (*Viburnum opulus*), have small fruit-producing flowers surrounded by a circle

NHPA/Stephen Dalton

White flowers of the European guelder rose (*Viburnum opulus*) develop into clusters of bright red berries.

of much larger flowers that are sterile (unproductive).

Viburnums like a deep, rich soil with plenty of humus, in a sunny position.

VICTORIA (1819–1901). The longest reign, nearly 64 years, of any British sovereign was that of Queen Victoria. She was born in London, at Kensington Palace, on 24 May 1819. Her father was Edward, duke of Kent, the fourth son of George III, and her mother was a German princess, also called Victoria. At her birth Alexandrina Victoria, as the princess was called, was fifth in succession to the throne (George III was still alive). Before her came the king's sons: the Prince Regent (later George IV), the duke of York, the duke of Clarence (later William IV), and her own father. When she was eight months old, however, her father died.

Victoria, known in her childhood as Drina, was brought up in Kensington Palace, closely guarded by her mother and Baroness Lehzen, her German governess. Baroness Lehzen became a more important person to Victoria than her own mother. Her father's place was taken by her uncle Leopold, the duchess of Kent's brother, who was the widower of princess Charlotte, George IV's daughter. In 1831 Leopold became the first king of the new country of Belgium, and he and Victoria continued to write affectionate letters to each other until Leopold's death in 1865.

Victoria became queen on 20 June 1837, when she was 18. The archbishop of Canterbury and the lord chamberlain hurried to Kensington Palace in the early morning to tell her that William IV was dead. Lehzen roused her to hear the news and she came downstairs in her dressing-gown and slippers with her hair hanging loose. Both the lord chamberlain and the archbishop knelt before her and kissed her hand as they saluted her as queen.

The people of Britain were delighted to have a young queen after a succession of elderly and rather disreputable kings. Victoria handled affairs of state with great dignity and grace. She was guided by the prime minister Lord Melbourne, who was devoted to her. Enjoying her freedom after her strict upbringing, Victoria kept her mother out of political affairs, although Lehzen advised her on matters connected with the running of the court.

Victoria was crowned on 28 June 1838. There was a great procession through London and a splendid ceremony at Westminster Abbey, but it had not been properly rehearsed and several mistakes were made. For one thing, the archbishop of Canterbury forced the coronation ring on to the wrong finger causing her a good deal of pain.

For a time Victoria went through a period of unpopularity, partly owing to her fondness for gaiety and dancing. All this was changed when she married her cousin Prince Albert, the nephew of her uncle Leopold. Leopold, determined to bring the marriage about, had sent his friend Baron Stockmar, a very able man, to prepare Albert for his future position. Victoria, in spite of having many European princes as suitors, did not particularly want to get married. However, when Albert visited her in 1839 she fell in love with him almost at once and, as it was not possible for anyone to ask the queen to marry him, she proposed to him herself. They were married on 10 February 1840, in the Chapel Royal at St. James's Palace.

The Bettman Archive

Queen Victoria, Britain's longest reigning monarch, surrounded in old age by her children and grandchildren.

Although he was too shy and solemn to be immediately popular with the British people, Albert was a very intelligent man with a good deal of character, and gradually he became the queen's adviser and partner in political questions. She gave up the lightheartedness of her early reign and devoted herself to family life and public duties. Between 1841 and 1857 she had nine children, four sons and five daughters.

Victoria was extremely fond of the highlands of Scotland and she and Albert spent many holidays at the new royal residence which they built at Balmoral in Aberdeenshire. They also built a new home at Osborne in the Isle of Wight. These years were the happiest of the queen's life, in spite of many quarrels with the foreign secretary Lord Palmerston, a strong-minded man who did not pay the queen the respect she thought was due to her. She described Palmerston in a letter to her uncle Leopold as a "dreadful old man".

The greatest grief of Queen Victoria's life came when Prince Albert died in her presence on 14 December 1861. He was only 42, but he had overworked ever since his marriage. Victoria's grief was overwhelming. She took to wearing the deepest black and refused to live any more in London, shutting herself up at Windsor and her other country homes. Above all she liked to be at Balmoral in the company of a few faithful highlanders, especially John Brown, a rugged, blunt-speaking man who was her servant until he died in 1883.

As Victoria was seldom seen in public and there were hardly any royal occasions, she began to become unpopular. There were criticisms of her in the newspapers and a handful of members of parliament began to speak in favour of a republic. The queen was very resentful at these remarks, for she felt that she was devoting herself so much to political work that her health would break down if she also had to appear in public. Much as she missed Albert's help, she would not allow anyone to take his place, certainly not her eldest son Albert Edward (later Edward VII), who was not enough like his father to please her.

In 1874, when Benjamin Disraeli became prime minister, the queen's life became much happier. Disraeli was a Conservative, and although Victoria as a young woman had preferred the Whigs (who were the opposite party), she became very enthusiastic about Disraeli's policy of expanding the British empire. In particular, she was delighted when he proclaimed her empress of India in 1876. More important, Disraeli pleased her by his courtly manners, wit, and flattery. By contrast, his opponent the Liberal leader W. E. Gladstone appeared solemn and pompous, respecting the institution of monarchy rather than the queen herself, and Victoria grew to dislike him strongly. She complained that he spoke to her as if she were a public meeting. (See DISRAELI, BENJAMIN; GLADSTONE, WILLIAM.)

In 1887 Victoria completed 50 years as queen, and a great jubilee was held for her. Wearing a black dress, with the ribbon of the Order of the Garter and a white feather in her bonnet, she drove through the streets of London cheered by her subjects, who had forgotten their grievances against her. They saw her not only as their own queen but also as the head of a great and expanding empire. Ten years later, in 1897, another jubilee was held to celebrate 60 years of her reign.

Even when she was an old woman Victoria remained interested in what was going on in the world. In 1900, when she was over 80, she paid a visit to Ireland to show her gratitude to the Irish for the way in which they had fought in the Boer War in South Africa.

Later that year her health began to fail and she moved to Osborne. She drove out for the last time on 15 January 1901, and on 22 January she died, in the presence of several members of her family. She was buried in St. George's Chapel, Windsor, on 1 February, but as she wished to be buried with Prince Albert the coffin was lifted three days later and taken to his tomb at Frogmore near by.

In many ways Queen Victoria was stern, especially with her children, who were all rather frightened of her. She shared some of the characteristics of what is now called the Victorian Age: its primness, strictness, and extreme social formality. Her sternness can perhaps best be shown by considering the well-known remark she made about something she did not approve of: "We are not amused". But she also had a sense of humour. She showed great courage and a wish to help her subjects in trouble, this is seen in her support of Florence Nightingale's work for soldiers in the Crimean War. She was an interesting and lively writer and from girlhood until her death she kept a diary, underlining many words for emphasis and putting in some fine illustrations, for she drew beautifully.

VICTORIA is one of the states of Australia. It is situated in the southeast corner of Australia and, after Tasmania, is the smallest of the states. It covers an area of 227,600 square kilometres (87,900 square miles). However, it contains more than one-quarter of all the people in Australia. Melbourne is the capital of Victoria, the chief port, and in every other way the most important city in the state. (See MELBOURNE.) Apart from the cities of Geelong, Ballarat, and Bendigo, the other cities and towns in the state are relatively small.

Much of the northern boundary of Victoria follows the Murray River (see MURRAY-DARLING RIVER SYSTEM). Along the greater part of the Murray are rolling plains broken up by low ridges. Across most of the centre part of the state there is high land, much higher in the east than in the west, for in the east are several mountains more than 1,800 metres (6,000 feet) high. South of this are plains again and then more areas of high land, but these

Ten of the Twelve Apostles (rock sea-stacks) along the coast of Port Campbell National Park, Victoria.

ZEFA

southern plains and southern uplands do not cover nearly such a large area as those to the north. The coastline, which is the southern boundary of the state, is about 1,600 kilometres (1,000 miles) long.

The climate of Victoria is not the same in all parts of the state. North of the central mountains there is much hot dry weather but south of the mountains it is cooler and wetter. Except in the very high part, most summers everywhere include a few days when the temperature exceeds 35°C (95°F). Drought and bush fires are not uncommon and sometimes do great damage to livestock, pastures, and other vegetation. The climate in the mountains varies according to their height, but only in the higher parts in the east is snow regularly seen in winter.

Much of the natural vegetation of Victoria consists of eucalyptus trees of one kind or another, small and scattered in the dry areas, and larger and closer together in the wetter areas. In the mountains there are grasslands which can be used for pasture in the summer.

Agriculture and Industry

Sheep are reared mainly on the plains of southwestern and central Victoria. (Wool is by far Victoria's most valuable export.) Beef cattle are found in much the same areas, but dairy cattle need the rich grass of the wetter southern plains. Wheat is grown in the northwestern part of the state and so are oats and barley, but in smaller amounts. Fruit growing is carried on round Melbourne and in the far northwest round the town of Mildura, where it has been made possible by great irrigation works along the Murray River.

Many new industries have been started in recent years. Aluminium smelting, electronics, motor-vehicle manufacturing, engineering, textiles, clothing, and foodstuffs are the major industries. Most of the new factories have been built in the neighbourhood of Melbourne but in some cases the government has persuaded factory owners to set up businesses in country towns. Victoria has no commercial black coal but in the southeast are great quantities of brown coal (see COAL). There are natural gas and oil fields offshore in the Gippsland basin. Melbourne uses only natural gas and the offshore oil fields are in full production, making Australia nearly 80 per cent self-sufficient in oil and petroleum products.

Some of the dry lands along the Murray River have been irrigated since the 19th century, and irrigation schemes are constantly being increased so that more land can be made fertile. In the eastern mountains the waters of several rivers are being used both for irrigation and for making electricity. Scientists have greatly helped the farmers by discovering which fertilizers are most suitable for the particular types of soil in Victoria. Sheep farmers used to lose a great deal of money every year because Australia had an enormous population of rabbits, which ate the grass that would otherwise have fed sheep. Since the rabbits have been killed off by a disease called myxomatosis the farmers have been able to increase their numbers of sheep.

ZEFA

Mount Buffalo National Park, Victoria, is a mountain plateau reserve in the Great Dividing Range. It lies 320 km (200 m) northeast of Melbourne.

Victoria has good road and railway connections. Victorians can spend a holiday among the mountain snows, or surf-riding and fishing on the southeast coast, or on a fruit or wheat farm in the north. A wide variety of sports is played, and Victoria is the home of "Australian Rules" football, a very fast, high-scoring game in which players can use both hands and feet. (See AUSTRALIAN RULES FOOTBALL.)

Victoria's History

The first permanent settlements in this part of Australia were made in the 1830s when people from the island of Tasmania and from the settled parts to the northeast discovered that there was excellent sheep country in what is now Victoria. These "squatters" (men who occupied land without paying for it) developed wool-growing and made themselves and the colony rich. By 1840 Melbourne had 4,000 inhabitants and was growing rapidly.

Two important events happened in 1851. Victoria became a separate colony and gold was discovered there. Until 1851 what is now Victoria was part of New South Wales (see NEW SOUTH WALES), but the British parliament passed an act in 1850 which made it a separate colony, with its own government. It was named after Queen Victoria. Gold was discovered about June 1851. Within four months 23,000 gold-seekers had flocked into Victoria from other parts of Australia and everybody was talking about Ballarat, Bendigo, Castlemaine, and Buninyong, the places where the richest finds were made. By 1852 Europeans were also arriving to seek their fortune and within about six years the population of Victoria rose to nearly 500,000. Some people thought that the miners would cause great outbreaks of lawlessness, but there was only one clash between them and the government. This is explained in the article EUREKA STOCKADE.

From about 1860 the gold-workings were becoming exhausted and many miners found themselves without work or money. However, by that time Victoria was being opened up as a great farming and sheep-rearing area, so some of them turned to agricultural work. At the same time railways were being built. These both helped the farmers to move their goods and provided many jobs.

Melbourne was already the home of several important writers: Rolf Boldrewood (whose real name was Thomas Alexander Browne), the author of *Robbery Under Arms*, Marcus Clarke, and Adam Lindsay Gordon. The first really good painters of Australian sights and scenery did their best work in Victoria during the 1880s and 1890s. In political affairs Victoria strongly supported the idea that the various Australian colonies ought to federate, or unite together. When they did this in 1901 they ceased to be known as colonies and became states. (See AUSTRALIAN HISTORY.)

The 1890s were hard years for Victoria partly because the price of wool and wheat, its main exports, fell sharply. There was great unemployment and unrest, and the government took over transport, roads, water supply, and electricity. By the 1920s Victoria had a greater variety of industries and if one failed people could find work in another. Then in the 1930s world trade became disorganized and Victoria once more went through bad times.

Since the mid-20th century the state has made rapid progress. Its population has risen faster than that of any other Australian state and reached 4,141,200 (1986).

Famous Victorians

Only a few famous Victorians can be mentioned here. Sir Isaac Isaacs (1856–1948), who was a lawyer by profession, became a politician, then a judge, and was the first Australian to be made Governor-General of Australia. Sir John Monash (1865–1931) achieved fame during World War I as a brilliant general, and he was also an engineer of great skill. Seven Australian Prime Ministers have been Victorians: Alfred Deakin (1856–1919), James Henry Scullin (1876–1953), Stanley Melbourne Bruce (Viscount Bruce) (1883–1967), John Joseph Curtin (1885–1945), Robert Gordon Menzies (1894–1978), Harold Holt (1908–1967), and John Grey Gorton (born 1911). The best-known Australian novel, *The Fortunes of Richard Mahony*, is set in Victoria, where its author was born. She wrote under the name of Henry Handel Richardson but was actually Mrs J. G. Robertson. In 1960 the distinguished physician Sir Frank Macfarlane Burnet was awarded the Nobel prize for medicine.

VICTORIA, LAKE which is also called Victoria Nyanza, is Africa's largest lake. It lies mainly in Tanzania and Uganda, with a small part in Kenya. With an area of 69,484 square kilometres (26,828 square miles) it is the world's second largest freshwater lake. Lake Superior in North America is the largest. Lake Victoria occupies a shallow depression in the East African plateau, and its greatest depth is only 80 metres (262 feet).

The lake is the chief source of the White Nile. It is fed by several rivers, one of which, the Kagera, is regarded as the furthest source of the Nile. The Lake's only outlet is in the north, near the town of Jinja, Uganda. Here it drains into the Victoria Nile through the Owen Falls Dam. This dam and its hydroelectric power station were completed in 1954, submerging a former waterfall.

In 1858, the British explorer John Hanning Speke reached the lake, which was known to the Arabs as Ukerewe. He named it after Queen Victoria. Densely populated lowlands surround the lake. The largest of its many islands is Ukerewe in the southeast. Cities and towns on or near the lakeshore include Kampala, Entebbe, and Jinja in Uganda, Bukoba and Mwanza in Tanzania, and Kisumu in Kenya. Fishing is a major activity in Lake Victoria. Steamer ships provide goods and passenger transport across the lake.

VICTORIA FALLS. On the boundary between Zambia and Zimbabwe, the Zambezi River plunges into a great gorge 108 metres (355 feet) deep and forms the Victoria Falls. The Victoria Falls are twice as deep and twice

ZEFA

Fine spray thrown up by the Victoria Falls creates a rainbow in the sunlight, and keeps the surrounding area lush and green throughout the year.

as wide as Niagara Falls. At the widest point they are 1,675 metres (5,500 feet) across. Fine spray is flung up from the Falls, and in sunlight or even moonlight rainbows gleam among the tiny drops. The smoky appearance of the spray and the roar of the falling waters give the falls their African name of *Mosi-oa-tunya*, or "the smoke that thunders". The spray leaps up over 300 metres (1,000 feet), and is visible 65 kilometres (40 miles) away.

The Victoria Falls were discovered by David Livingstone in 1855. A hydroelectric power station serves the town of Haramba in Zambia. The railway from Cape Town passes close by the Falls and is carried across the gorge on the magnificent Falls Bridge, from which can be seen the whirlpool and rapids below the Falls. On the northern shore in Zambia is a game park. Victoria Falls is also the name of a nearby township.

VIDEO RECORDING. The idea of recording pictures from television was first proposed in the late 1920s by John Logie Baird (see BAIRD, JOHN LOGIE), the inventor of television itself, who used an ordinary "78" record to store still pictures for showing on his television set. Then the idea was forgotten, and for years the only practical way of storing television pictures was on film. Videotape came into use in the 1960s.

Most modern video recordings are made on magnetic tape which registers all the sounds and colours in the television picture in the form of electronic signals which can then be "read" by a video playback unit and turned back into pictures (see SOUND RECORDING AND REPRODUCTION). Video recording on tape first came into use in the 1960s when it proved popular for "playing back" television pictures (as in the instant replay of an incident during a televised sporting event), but it only became freely available to the general public in the 1970s. Since then it has changed the way in which many of us use television.

A video recorder can be thought of as a television set which has a tape recorder instead of a screen. A viewer can watch one programme on a television set while the video recorder tapes another programme from a different channel. The tape can then be rewound and the programme can be replayed at the viewer's convenience. Using a timer on the recorder it is also possible to tape a programme whilst the viewer is out of the house or away on holiday. This is known as "time shifting", and has now become sufficiently refined to allow the recording of a series of programmes without having to return and reprogramme the video recorder.

Although the first use of video recorders was simply for time shifting, they are currently used more commonly to view prerecorded tapes. These tapes may be purchased or hired from companies which specialize in making the latest "movies" available before they have been sold to the television stations for broadcasting.

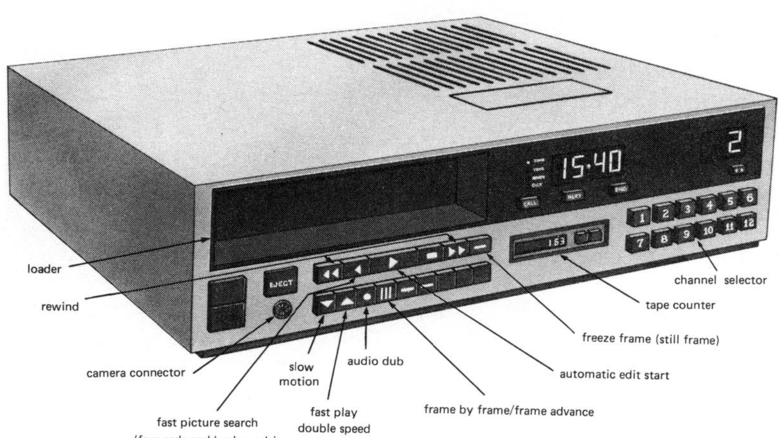

Video cassette recorders (VCRs) like this one are now found in many homes. Most owners use them to watch commercially recorded programmes and films, or television programmes that they have recorded themselves. A VCR usually has a timer, allowing TV programmes to be recorded in the owner's absence.

Videos are now so popular that a new crime has appeared: video "piracy". This is when someone copies a film or video tape without the permission of the copyright owner (see COPYRIGHT). Some commercial video recordings incorporate electronic devices which prevent such illegal copying.

Video tapes are sold in cassette form, and the size of the cassette has given rise to a number of video-recorder systems. The two most commonly used systems are the VHS system and the Sony-derived Betamax system, although various smaller format systems are available for use with portable video cameras and recorders. Cassettes containing enough tape for up to four hours are freely available, and with a "half-speed" recording facility on the video recorder up to eight hours of television may be recorded for later viewing.

Videodiscs

Videodiscs look rather like long-playing (LP) records (vinyl discs). Unlike a tape, a disc cannot be erased (rubbed clean) or recorded over. The disc is covered with millions of tiny pits. These are computer-produced representations of sound and pictures. Their messages are "decoded" by the playback unit's electronic apparatus so that we can see them on the screen as a normal television picture.

Unlike an LP record, a videodisc has no grooves. Its information is hidden beneath a smooth plastic coating that protects the pits on the inner surface of the disc. Also, a videodisc spins much more quickly than an LP record, as much as 30 times a second. Most discs are "read" or decoded by a laser beam travelling across the pits; others have a stylus similar to the kind used on a record player.

Videodiscs cannot be used for home recording. But they last far longer than videotapes. A videotape starts to wear out after about 100 plays as the oxide coating falls off the tape. A disc, especially the laser-played kind, is not worn at all, even after thousands of plays. Videodiscs are also better at showing still pictures. To find a particular part of a tape programme, you must search through the whole tape. On a disc, the laser or stylus can find and play the part you want in a split second. So a disc makes an ideal "information store", in which to look up information. Books and old films stored on videodiscs should last for thousands of years.

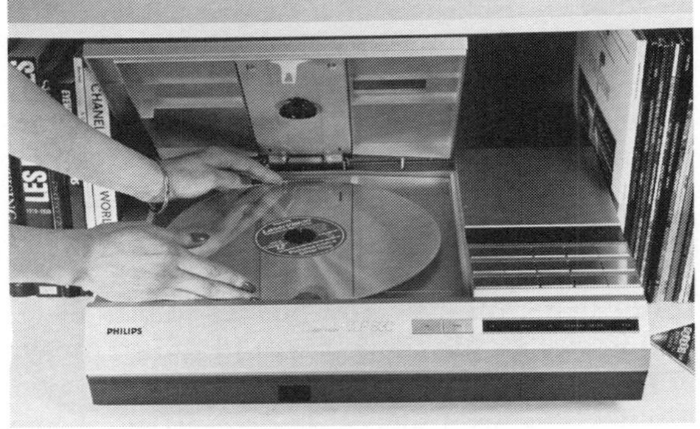

Courtesy, Philips Laser Vision

A videodisc looks like an LP record with a plastic coating. It has no grooves and is read by a laser.

VIENNA is the capital of Austria and at the same time a federal province in its own right. It is situated in the east of the country, surrounded on all sides by the province of Lower Austria, only 65 kilometres (40 miles) from the borders of Hungary and Czechoslovakia (see AUSTRIA).

ZEFA

The centre of Vienna has many baroque buildings and monuments. Outdoor cafes are popular in summer.

Vienna is renowned as a centre of music and is associated with many of the greatest names in music: Haydn, Mozart, Beethoven, Brahms, Bruckner, Schoenberg, as well as the Strauss family, who composed popular waltzes and polkas in the 19th century. Vienna is also associated with great men of science and medicine, such as Sigmund Freud, Anton Mesmer, and Karl Landsteiner.

Vienna is Austria's economic focal point. Numerous firms producing metal products, precision instruments, and electrical goods are situated in the area.

Vienna is divided into 21 districts, of which the Inner City, surrounded by the Ringstrasse, a broad boulevard (avenue) planted with trees, is the centre. In the Inner City is the cathedral of St. Stephen with its towering spire. Southwest of the cathedral is the Hofburg, until 1918 the palace of the emperors of Austria. It consists of buildings and courtyards, and houses the national library of Austria, which includes many papyri (see PAPYRUS). The treasures of the emperors are kept in a special wing.

Vienna has a famous university, dating from the 14th century, and many fine churches and museums of history and art. The opera house, where some of the world's greatest players and singers can be heard, was built in the 1860s.

In the southern outskirts are the Prater, a wooded park beside the River Danube, and the Wurstelprater, which is the fairground of Vienna. In the western part is Schoenbrunn Castle, once the summer residence of the imperial family. In the surrounding gardens the Empress Maria Theresa built a zoo for her children. This later developed into the Vienna Zoo.

Vienna is an ancient city. The Celts (see CELTS) built a settlement on the site of the present city which the Romans made into a fortress town called Vindobona. The Emperor Marcus Aurelius is supposed to have died there in AD 180. After the fall of the Roman Empire, Vienna was of little importance until the 12th century. It became rich and important when the Habsburg family came to Austria and made Vienna the capital of their growing empire. (See AUSTRIAN EMPIRE.)

ZEFA

The National Theatre (Burgtheater), Vienna, is one of several 19th-century buildings along the Ringstrasse, a wide leafy boulevard round the city centre.

The Turks, who were trying to overrun Europe, besieged Vienna in 1529 and 1683, but were beaten back. After the second siege, lilac, which they brought from the East, was planted in Vienna and later spread to the rest of western Europe. The Turks also brought coffee to Vienna and in the city western Europe's first coffee-shop appeared.

After the first defeat of Napoleon and his banishment to Elba (see NAPOLEON, EMPERORS OF FRANCE), European statesmen met at Vienna to decide on the ownership of certain parts of Europe. This meeting is known as the Congress of Vienna (1814–15). During the 19th century the city, as the capital of the Austro-Hungarian Empire, grew larger and more magnificent. In 1857 the old city walls were pulled down and the Ringstrasse built in its place. Around this were erected a series of splendid buildings: the opera house, the city chambers, and the parliament building, among others. In 1918 after World War I, the empire was split up and Vienna became the capital of a comparatively tiny Austrian state. In 1938 Vienna was occupied by Nazi Germany and did not become fully independent again until 1955 when, 10 years after the end of World War II, the allied powers of Britain, France, the United States, and the USSR ceased their occupation. The city now has the headquarters of several international organizations, among them the International Atomic Energy Agency.

VIETNAM occupies the eastern part of the Indo-Chinese peninsula in Southeast Asia. It is a long narrow land, bordered to the north by China, to the west by Kampuchea and Laos, and to the east and south by the South China Sea. Vietnam was formerly divided into two republics, North Vietnam and South Vietnam, but since 1976 it has been one country again.

Vietnam is a mountainous land. Most of the people live in two lowland deltas, where the land is flat and the soil is rich. In the north the delta at Tonkin is formed by the Red River and its branches the Claire and Black rivers. Situated in the delta are Hanoi, the capital city (see HANOI), and the sea port of Haiphong. The Mekong delta in the south is larger and also densely populated. It contains Ho Chi Minh City, formerly known as Saigon. Vietnam is a warm, monsoon land with high rainfall and thick forest. Severe typhoons occur in late summer and autumn.

FACTS ABOUT VIETNAM

AREA: 331,653 square kilometres (128,052 square miles).
POPULATION: 61,218,000 (1986).
GOVERNMENT: Communist republic.
CAPITAL: Hanoi.
GEOGRAPHICAL FEATURES: Two major deltas, the Red River and the Mekong, are important lowland areas. A coastal plain lies on the east, and a mountainous, forested region covers much of the rest of the land.
CHIEF PRODUCTS: Rice, cassava, sorghum, maize; coffee, tea, rubber; handicrafts.
IMPORTANT TOWNS: Ho Chi Minh City, Hanoi, Haiphong.
EDUCATION: Free and compulsory up to 12 years of age.

Originally, large areas of the land were covered in forest, bamboo, and mangrove vegetation. Much has been destroyed by primitive cultivation methods, and recently by bombing and massive deforestation during the Vietnam War (on which there is a separate article). Grassland and shrubs cover much of the highest land. Wildlife includes elephants, tigers, bears, pythons, and crocodiles.

The Vietnamese people are much like the Chinese in appearance. Their religion is a mixture of Buddhism, Taoism, and Confucianism.

ZEFA

Ho Chi Minh City was the name give to Saigon after the Communist takeover of 1975.

They are mostly village dwellers and three-quarters of the population are farmers. Rice takes up more land area than all other crops put together. Other crops include rubber, maize, sugar, bananas, coconuts, pepper, tea, tobacco, and sweet potatoes. Fishing is also important, and livestock including buffalo and pigs are raised. The south is the richer agricultural area, while the north is more industrialized and has mineral resources which include coal, salt, tin, iron, and zinc.

ZEFA

A typical landscape with terraced fields in the Dalat region. Danhim dam is in the background.

History

The history of Vietnam can be traced to the ancient kingdom of Annam which lay in the north of the country. The Chinese dominated the country until the 9th century AD, when the Annamese established their independence.

French missionaries came to Annam in the 16th century, and in 1802 the French helped the leader of the southern dynasty to become emperor of a united Annam. A French military expedition established the southern province of Cochin China as a French colony in 1867. In the next 40 years, Tonkin, Annam, Cambodia, and Laos were united by France as French Indo-China.

The most tragic years of Vietnam's history came after World War II (1939–45). During the war, the French were driven out and Vietnam was occupied by the Japanese. When the Japanese were defeated in 1945, the country was occupied by the Allies and split at latitude 16°N, with Communist China controlling the north. France resumed power in the south but came into conflict with the Communists and a war began which lasted from 1946 to 1954 when a settlement was reached at Geneva.

In the following years the government in the south attempted to establish its authority by force, but met resistance. This grew during the 1960s into civil war between government forces and Communist sympathizers sponsored by North Vietnam and China. The government received increasing support from the United States as well as other nations. It eventually became clear that this help was not going to bring victory for the south and the United States began to withdraw troops from 1969, until in 1973 a ceasefire was negotiated and the US withdrew all forces. However, the ceasefire did not last and the North eventually proved victorious capturing the southern capital of Saigon in 1975. The article VIETNAM WAR gives a full description of this period of Vietnamese history from 1946 to 1975.

In 1976 North and South Vietnam were reunited to form a single country. Yet unity did not bring peace. In 1979 the Vietnamese attacked Kampuchea and installed a new government there. To "teach Vietnam a lesson", China invaded northern Vietnam and a short war was fought, in which neither side won a clear victory. Tragedy followed. Thousands of people of Chinese origin, living in Vietnam, were forced to leave the country. Many took to the sea in small boats. About 250,000 refugees reached the safety of other countries, including the United States, Canada, Australia, and Britain. But perhaps as many "boat people" drowned. In the 1980s Vietnam's continuing involvement in Kampuchea caused serious quarrels not only with China, but also with non-Communist countries in Southeast Asia.

VIETNAM WAR. The Vietnam War was a military conflict that started in French Indo-China in 1946. At the beginning, the war was a struggle for Vietnamese independence from French rule. Eventually it developed into a conflict of grave international concern in which the United States became a major com-

Camera Press

Many Vietnamese live in small villages and grow rice in flooded fields. The long war caused great suffering.

batant. Australia too sent forces to fight in Vietnam. The war lasted until 1975, when Vietnam was unified under Communist control (see VIETNAM). The war did enormous damage to the countryside and towns of Vietnam, and also affected neighbouring countries such as Laos. The long and costly US involvement in the Vietnam War had a great impact on people in the United States, and continues to influence the attitude of many Americans towards foreign wars.

Origins of the War

Throughout World War II, French Indo-China was occupied by Japan. Until March 1945, the local French administrators, police, and soldiers were permitted to continue in office. Then the Japanese proclaimed Vietnam (the Indo-Chinese provinces of Tonkin, Annam, and Cochin China) an independent state and restored the former emperor, Bao Dai, as its head. When World War II ended in 1945, the Allies occupied Vietnam. The country was divided at the 16th parallel, with China in command of the north and Great Britain of the south. In the south, the British helped the French back to power.

In the north, Vietnamese nationalists led by Ho Chi Minh, founder of the Indo-Chinese Communist Party, joined to form the Vietnam League for Independence, or the Viet Minh. The Viet Minh formed a government with Ho Chi Minh as its head, and proclaimed independence in the name of the Democratic Republic of Vietnam (DRV). The DRV controlled the north at the war's end.

France and the DRV became involved in disputes over the future of Vietnam. Chief among these differences was the dispute over Cochin China, the southernmost province of Indo-China. This dispute led to fighting between French and Viet Minh troops. In November 1946 the French attacked Haiphong. The Viet Minh retaliated by assaulting the French in Hanoi. This opened the Vietnam War.

Defeat of the French

When the fighting began, the French had an apparent military advantage. But the countryside belonged to the Viet Minh guerrillas. The Viet Minh had popular support, while the French did not. In 1949 the French restored Emperor Bao Dai, but kept real power over the government of the country.

The DRV received aid from the new Communist government of China. The United States backed France and the Bao Dai government, paying an increasingly large share of the cost of waging the war. The war went badly for the French, and also spread into neighbouring Laos. Finally, in 1954 the French fortress of Dien Bien Phu fell to the Viet Minh and the conflict shifted to the negotiating table.

A conference at Geneva, Switzerland, negotiated a settlement which divided Vietnam in two. This division was intended to be temporary, until an election was held to decide whether or not the two parts of Vietnam should reunite.

South Vietnam's Fate

In 1955 Ngo Dinh Diem, premier of South Vietnam, replaced Emperor Bao Dai as head of state. The harsh actions of Diem's government

During the 1960s, when fighting ranged throughout South Vietnam, helicopters (right) were a key means of transport for US and South Vietnamese troops. War became a constant feature of life for the inhabitants. Farmers (below) continue work as bombs explode near by. In February 1968, Saigon became a battlefield (below right).

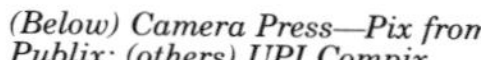

(Below) Camera Press—Pix from Publix; (others) UPI Compix

displeased many Vietnamese. In 1956 the government refused to hold elections to decide on unifying Vietnam as set out in the Geneva settlement. Diem sought to establish his authority by force.

An anti-government guerrilla movement developed which attempted to overthrow Diem, and this struggle grew into civil war. The anti-government group, the National Liberation Front (NLF), included former supporters of the Viet Minh. It sought withdrawal of foreign troops from Vietnam and the unification of north and south. In 1961, Communist North Vietnam began supplying the NLF with training and equipment.

The NLF was referred to by the Saigon government as *Viet Cong*, meaning Vietnamese Communists, although it was not originally a Communist organization. During the early 1960s, much of South Vietnam came under Vietcong control.

Several attempts were made to overthrow the Diem regime. A popular protest headed by Buddhist monks and students led finally to a successful takeover by a military group in 1963. But Diem's military successors were also incapable of ending the civil war.

The United States became deeply involved in South Vietnam. The US supplied military and economic aid, and also sent advisers to help the South Vietnamese forces. On 4 August 1964, two US destroyers were reportedly attacked by North Vietnamese patrol boats in the Gulf of Tonkin. In retaliation, the United States attacked North Vietnamese military installations. This was the first US attack on North Vietnamese territory. By 1965 the US policy had shifted to direct participation in the war.

The US Involvement

In the mid-1960s the Vietnam war evolved into an international conflict. Troops of the South Vietnamese government were assisted by US, Korean, Australian, New Zealand, Thai, and Philippine units. The Vietcong drew support, mainly supplies, from the Soviet Union and China.

Between 1965 and 1967, the United States increased its Vietnam forces to about 500,000. US aircraft bombed North Vietnam targets to prevent troop and supply movement. But in February 1968 the NLF launched a devastating attack on South Vietnam.

In March 1968, US President Lyndon B. Johnson ordered a partial halt in the bombing of North Vietnam in order to start peace talks. On 13 May peace talks began in Paris, France, and in October all the bombing of the North was stopped.

In 1969 the United States, led by newly elected President Richard M. Nixon, began to reduce its troop strength in Vietnam. Nixon's policy of "Vietnamization" consisted of gradual withdrawal of US troops and their replacement by South Vietnamese forces.

The peace talks in Paris, made little or no progress. In April 1972, North Vietnam launched a major invasion of the South. The US retaliated with air raids, and for the first time bombed the northern port of Haiphong. President Nixon ordered a blockade of North Vietnam, which called for harbours to be mined and rail lines to be bombed. The war's heaviest bombing was directed against North Vietnam.

Peace Agreement

In January 1973, a cease-fire agreement was signed by the United States, North and South Vietnam, and the Vietcong. By April all US troops had been withdrawn from South Vietnam.

In the winter of 1975 Communist forces launched a new attack. In a three-week period South Vietnam lost nearly two-thirds of its territory. Several provinces were abandoned without resistance. With Communist troops near the capital, Saigon, President Thieu resigned in an attempt to achieve a negotiated settlement, but the Vietcong pressed on. They captured the city on 30 April 1975. The Saigon government, then under General Duong Van Minh, surrendered, finally ending some 30 years of war. In 1976 South Vietnam was reunited with the North.

VIKINGS. From the 8th to the 11th centuries AD the coasts of Christian Europe were frequently raided by fierce warriors from the Scandinavian countries of Norway, Sweden, and Denmark. At first they came to plunder, but later they conquered land for themselves and settled down as farmers. They were also great traders. In time, therefore, the Viking raids developed into a movement of exploration and conquest. Icelandic Vikings reached America long before Columbus did, although, as they did not settle, their voyages did not become widely known.

The Vikings caused great misery and terror on their raids, for they robbed churches of their treasures, drove away cattle, killed people, and burned their homes. They were unafraid of death, and sometimes in the midst of battle they were overcome by a fighting madness which was known as going *berserk*, a word which is still used. Some idea of the kinds of actions that they admired can be got from reading the legends they told about their heroes and their gods. (See NORSE LEGENDS.)

The British Isles were raided by Norsemen, or Norwegian Vikings, in the 9th century. They settled in the Faeroes (or Faroes) and Shetlands and Orkneys, in Caithness, the

Science Museum, London

A model of a Viking ship of about AD 900. This is a hafskip, or deep-sea vessel, used for long voyages.

Hebrides, and the Isle of Man, in Dublin and southeast Ireland, and in the northwest of England. One Viking, Olaf Tryggvason, after spending the early part of his life in the usual Viking manner of raiding and plundering, came to the Scilly Isles off Cornwall and, according to legend, was converted to Christianity there by a hermit.

The Norsemen also went to Iceland, where their descendants live today, and settled along the southwest of Greenland. The leader of this expedition was Eric the Red. It was these Greenland Vikings, led by Eric's son Leif Eriksson, who reached North America. Leif Eriksson set out from Greenland in about 1002, searching for a land to the west which some sailors had sighted when they were blown off their course to Greenland. He landed on a part of the North American coast where wild grapes grew and the winters were mild, probably between Nova Scotia and Cape Cod. (See also ERIC THE RED; LEIF ERIKSSON.)

The Vikings from Denmark went south and raided the coasts of the continent of Europe. Some ships ventured as far as Spain and Morocco and even Italy.

The Danish Vikings also coveted England, and in 865 the sons of the great leader Ragnar Lodbrok landed in England and occupied East Anglia and Northumbria. This territory, where the Danes settled down to farm, was known as the Danelaw.

Towards the end of the 9th century the Danes began to invade southern England and might have conquered it had it not been for Alfred the Great (see ALFRED THE GREAT). The kings who followed Alfred continued his struggle, and by 954 the last Viking king had been driven out, although many Danes still remained in England. England was not yet free from Viking invasions. Danes, Norwegians, and Swedes laid waste large areas towards the end of the 10th century. The English king Ethelred was too weak to resist them and his country was taken by Sweyn Forkbeard, king of Denmark, in 1013. A year later Sweyn died and his son Canute became king of England, as well as ruler of Denmark and much of Norway (see CANUTE).

In 1066 William I invaded England from the south. In the same year a Norse king, Harold Hardrada, invaded England from the north. He ravaged Yorkshire but was finally defeated by Harold, king of England.

The Swedish Vikings conquered the lands east of the Baltic Sea. They sailed down the River Dnieper to the Black Sea and down the River Volga to the Caspian Sea, trading with the Greeks and Arabs, who called them the "Rus". The Slavonic peoples over whom the Swedish Vikings ruled took the name of Russians from them in the course of time.

VILLA, Pancho (1878–1923), was a powerful military leader of the Mexican Revolution. He was born Doroteo Arango, in San Juan del Rio, Mexico. He changed his name to Francisco Villa, but became known as Pancho.

In 1909 he joined Francisco Madero's revolution against President Porfirio Diaz. While in the service of Madero, Villa was jailed for insubordination by Victoriano Huerta, Madero's chief military leader. Villa escaped and fled to Texas. After the assassination of Madero, and Huerta's establishment of a new tyrannical government, Villa returned and joined forces with the aspiring political leader Venustiano Carranza. Because of his military victories, Villa's importance and power grew.

Culver Pictures Inc.

Pancho Villa was a powerful leader of the Mexican revolution who, with Emiliano Zapata, once controlled most of Mexico.

When the Huerta government fell, he and Carranza began fighting for control. Villa established an alliance with Emiliano Zapata, the powerful Indian leader in southern Mexico. Between them they managed to control most of the country.

Villa was inevitably defeated, however, because of his unwillingness to assume civilian control of the country and his inability to agree to orderly processes. From a crest of complete power in 1915, he was slowly forced into retreat and later into obscurity by the Carranza forces. In desperation he crossed the border to raid Columbus, New Mexico, in 1916, hoping that United States intervention would follow and embarrass the Carranza government. A United States expedition did pursue Villa but without success. Villa was finally induced to retire in 1920, and was assassinated three years later.

See also MEXICO.

VILLAGE. Villages may be described as communities where the people have close contact with the countryside. They are smaller than towns, usually with less than 1,000 people, and are found all over the world.

More than 4,000 years ago in prehistoric times men built villages of houses on upright posts in the lakes of Europe. Other villages built at the same time were on hilltops. Some time later, about 3,500 years ago, a village built entirely of stone was set up in Skara Brae in the Orkney Islands north of Scotland, and this can still be seen.

In a typical British village, houses cluster round a church that may have stood since medieval times. Thatched roofs can still be seen in many of the villages of England. Some houses have whitewashed walls; others have beams of dark timber. In Cornwall, Wales, Scotland, and the north of England the houses are often built of local stone. Perhaps the most

British Tourist Authority

Castle Combe, Wiltshire is thought to be one of the most beautiful villages in England.

lovely villages of England are those of the Cotswolds, built in yellow-grey stone.

In the Middle Ages the population of a typical village in Europe was as low as 50 people. The houses were modest wooden buildings with thatched or turfed roofs. Each house had a small piece of land enclosed by a fence, but this was rarely used as a garden, for few vegetables were then grown. Around the village were ploughed fields, meadows, and woodland. The ploughed fields lay open, instead of being divided up by hedges. Each villager had a certain number of unfenced strips in the ploughed fields and the right to take a certain amount of hay from the meadow, which all the villagers held in common. He also had the right to keep a number of animals in the woodland.

A village organized in this way was known as a manor, and the way in which the people of a manor lived is described in the article MANOR. Over the manor was the lord, who controlled it. The villagers rented their strips from him. Sometimes they worked on the part of the village land called the lord's domain (because he owned it) and their work counted as rent. Sometimes the rent payment was in the form of goods. Later, the rent began to be paid in money.

Towards the end of the Middle Ages some lords and richer villagers started to enclose their own land by hedges. At first it was used for sheep farming and later, in the 18th century, for experiments into methods of increasing the size of crops. Thus the village ceased to be a community working its land and using its woods in common. Many villagers suffered great hardship from the loss of their land during the enclosures, as this movement was called.

Settlers in North America made their first homes in villages on the same pattern as those they had left in Europe.

In the 18th and 19th centuries came the great changes known as the Industrial Revolution (see INDUSTRIAL REVOLUTION), which changed the whole way of village life. The cloth, furniture, and other goods which villagers had made at home, either to sell or for their own use, could now be made cheaply and quickly in factories. Villagers had to go to the fast-growing towns to find work, and this is still happening today in many countries.

ZEFA

A Ghanaian village. As elsewhere in Africa, most villagers are kinsmen, and land is held communally.

Nowadays, even small and remote villages have a good deal in common with cities. People who work in cities have bought homes in villages, travelling to the city to work each day, or living in the city and visiting the village home at weekends. Farming, which used to employ most country people, now needs far fewer workers than in the past and so in devel-

South Royalton, Vermont, USA. In Vermont more than half the people live in villages.

oped countries a village tends to have a mixture of people and occupations. In developing countries, such as parts of Africa, many people still live and work in villages and their main activity is farming.

In North America some of the most beautiful villages are to be found in New England. They have white-framed buildings, a church, town hall, shops, and usually some large homes in spacious grounds owned by the wealthier members of the community. This style was copied in other parts of the United States, particularly in the northern part of the Midwest, where there are attractive villages and small towns.

See also TOWN AND CITY.

VINEGAR. The word vinegar means "sour wine", from the French words *vin* (wine) and *aigre* (sour), for if wine is not properly bottled it turns sour from contact with the air. This sourness is due to acetic acid, caused by a bacterium (a microscopic living thing). The action of yeast on the sugar in the grape juice produces alcohol and carbon dioxide (see FERMENTATION). The bacterium then causes the oxygen in the air to combine with the alcohol and forms acetic acid and water.

Wine is used to make vinegar in countries where wine is made, but in other countries, such as Britain, a brewing of malted barley is used. Vinegar can also be made from apples (cider vinegar), sugar, or rice. It is sometimes flavoured with herbs, such as tarragon. Whatever alcoholic liquid is used is pumped into a vessel which is capable of holding up to 45,000 litres (about 12,000 US gallons), although it is only half filled. In the middle of the vessel is a stage on which layers of birch twigs are placed, and below this air holes are bored in it. The liquid is then pumped over the birch twigs through a sparge, which is just like the sprinkler used for watering gardens. Thus a large amount of liquid is exposed to the air. The process takes about six days, but at the end of them the vinegar is still not fit for use. It has to be kept for some months in large storage vessels for the right flavour to be produced.

In Scotland most of the vinegar used is distilled, a term which is explained in the article DISTILLATION.

Vinegar has many uses. It is used in pickling foods—onions, cucumbers, and herrings, for example. Mixed with olive or other vegetable oil it is added to salads. It is also eaten with greasy foods such as fried fish, and meat becomes tender when it is cooked in vinegar. It can also be used for treating wasp stings.

VIOLA see VIOLIN FAMILY.

VIOLET flowers have five petals, two at the back, one at each side, and one bigger one at the bottom which has a spur (a drawn-out part of the base of the petal). The flowers hang gracefully from the top of slender stalks. Most violet plants are small, 5 to 7 centimetres (2 to 3 inches) high, and their leaves are generally long-stalked. Some plants have roots that creep underground and some have runners that creep above the ground and start new plants. The flowers do not always produce seed when the pollen from one kind is carried to the stigma of another (see POLLINATION), and so the plant also bears flowers that never open. In these flowers self-pollination takes place, which means that the pollen falls on to the stigma inside the closed flower and thus makes certain that seeds are produced. The fruit opens in three sections, each of which contains many seeds. Violets may be annuals or perennials.

Alan Beaumont

Violets are sweet-scented spring flowers that like to grow in shady conditions.

There are about 500 species of violet. Many are found in meadows or damp woods, and they bloom in the spring. North America has a large number of species, including the bird's-foot violet (*Viola pedata*), named from its deeply cleft leaves. Violets have been cultivated for hundreds of years. It is known that the Parma violet (*Viola odorata*), which has large double flowers, has been grown in Turkey, Persia, and Syria since about AD 900 or earlier. Today is it grown in France and Italy to produce oils used in perfume. Violets are also used to make sweet syrups, the flowers are candied, and the leaves are used for salads.

Pansies also belong to the violet family, Violaceae (see also PANSY).

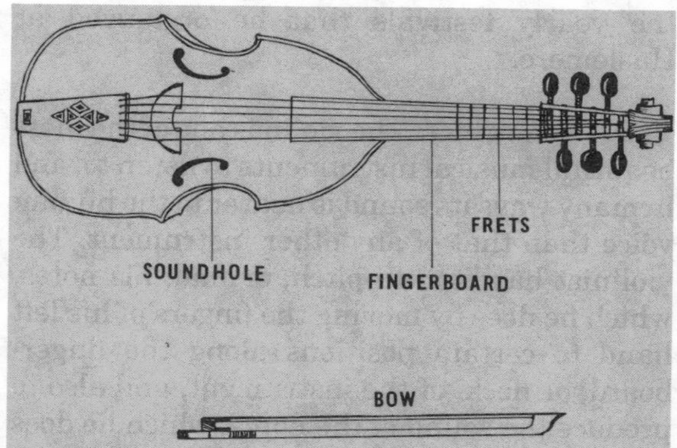

The viol, an old-fashioned musical instrument, has C-shaped soundholes and a fingerboard with frets.

VIOL FAMILY. The viols belong to a family of stringed instruments that is older than the violin family and developed along different lines. Music was already being written for viols in the 15th century and it is known that they existed long before that. Viols had a shape that resembled that of the later violin, except that the back was flat. They were held downwards, resting on the knees instead of under the chin like the violin. The largest were gripped between the legs. The sound-holes in the body of the instrument were roughly in the shape of a *c* (in the violin they are like an *f*). There were usually six strings. The positions on the fingerboard, where the fingers of the left hand held down the strings to form the different notes, were marked by ridges called frets.

The bow had a large outward curve and was held above the hand not below it, as the violin bow is. There were four main kinds of viols, the smaller higher in pitch and the larger lower. They are called the treble, alto, tenor and bass. A wealthy family often had what was called a chest of viols. This was actually a set of six instruments and the term came from the fact that they were kept in a chest specially made to hold them. In the 15th century the set usually consisted of two trebles, two tenors, and two basses, but in the 16th century and later it more often contained two trebles, an alto, a tenor, and two basses.

Because the bass viol was held between the legs it became known by the Italian name viola da gamba (literally "viol of the leg"). The violone was a double bass viol, an octave lower than the viola da gamba. A type of viol that lived on into the 18th century was the viola d'amore. This was a treble viol fitted with "sympathetic" strings that were made to vibrate when the ordinary strings were played. Its tone was very sweet. In the late 18th century Haydn wrote a number of sonatas for a type of bass viol called a baryton. It had "sympathetic" strings, too.

The best viol music was that written in England during the 16th and early 17th centuries. Composers such as John Dowland and Orlando Gibbons wrote lovely pieces for what was called a consort of viols. The music included pieces called fancies and other pieces known as divisions.

In the 18th century the viols went out of fashion, for people preferred music that was written for the louder-toned violin (see VIOLIN FAMILY). However, in the 20th century the thinner tones of the viols have been heard again because interest in old music has revived. This was largely due to the work of Arnold Dolmetsch, a Frenchman who settled in England and started a workshop at Haslemere in Surrey where he made copies of many old instruments, including the viols. He and his family gave concerts of old music at the yearly festivals that he organized at Haslemere.

VIOLIN FAMILY. The violin is one of the most beautiful musical instruments to listen to, and in many ways its sound is nearer to the human voice than that of any other instrument. The violinist has both to pitch, or find, his notes, which he does by moving the fingers of his left hand to certain positions along the fingerboard, or neck, of the instrument, and also to produce the sound of the notes, which he does by drawing his bow across the strings.

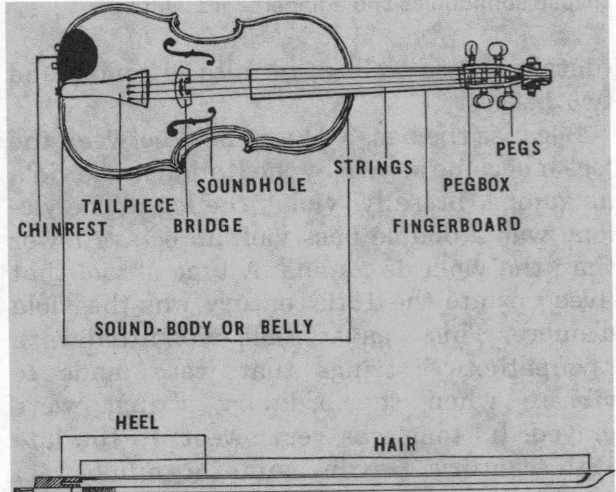

The parts of a violin and its bow. The strings are of finely spun metal or of catgut, which comes from a sheep's intestines. The pegs are used to tighten or slacken the strings during tuning.

The earliest violins date from the 16th century. Nobody knows for certain where they originated, but some people believe they came from Poland. However, we do know that, by the end of the 16th century, the best were being made in Italy, chiefly at Cremona in north Italy.

Though it is a small, lightweight instrument, the violin consists of no fewer than 84 separate pieces. The main parts of a violin are the fingerboard along which the strings are stretched, and the case of wood called the soundbody or belly, which increases the volume of the sound. A bridge made of thin wood carries the strings from the end of the fingerboard to the tail piece, which is fixed to the end of the belly. The strings are made of catgut or finely spun metal. Two soundholes in the shape of an *f* are carved out of the middle of the belly, allowing sound vibrations to escape from the body of the instrument. The violinist holds the instrument firmly under his chin by means of the chin-rest. This is fixed to the left of the tail piece and is slightly raised from the belly. Usually in order to strengthen the grip of his chin and collar-bone on the violin, a violinist places a pad between the back of the violin and his body. With the fingers of his left hand he alters the length of the strings by stopping them (pressing them down) along the fingerboard. With his right hand he draws the bow across the strings in the open section between the end of the fingerboard and the bridge. More than one string may be stopped and played at a time, so that the violinist can produce some chords, as well as single notes.

The greatest Italian makers of violins were Nicolò Amati (1596–1684), Antonio Stradivari (*c.*1644–1737), and Giuseppe Guarneri (1698–1744), who was often called Giuseppe del Gesu. The instruments they made are still the best that have ever been made, although fine violins have also been produced in several other European countries, including England, where the family of Hill has been making musical instruments since the 18th century. The great maker of violin bows was a Frenchman, François Tourte (1747–1835). The shape of the violin has changed only very slightly since the 16th century. In some later violins the bridge is higher so that the bow does not so easily touch the string next to the one being played, and the fingerboard has been lengthened so that higher notes may be reached.

There are four members of the violin family. Apart from the violin itself they are the viola, the cello, and the double bass. The viola is rather larger than the violin and is played in the same way. Its tone is more mellow and less penetrating than the violin's. The cello (short for violoncello) is much bigger and deeper in pitch. The seated player supports the cello between his or her legs, and

ZEFA

A string orchestra consists of first and second violins, violas, cellos, and double basses.

it rests on a metal rod or spike. The double bass, which developed from the violone, is the lowest in pitch in the viol family and is so large that it is played standing up or perched on a high stool. The strings of the violin, viola, and cello are tuned in fifths, that is to say there is an interval of five notes between every two strings (for an explanation of intervals, see HARMONY). The strings of the double bass are tuned in fourths.

The open, or full-length, strings of the violin are G, D, A, and E. The strings of the viola are a fifth below these, that is to say by counting five notes down you arrive at the viola's open, full-length strings which are C, G, D, A. The cello is tuned exactly like the viola except that the strings are an octave lower. The open strings of the double bass are E, A, D, G. Sometimes the double bass has a fifth string tuned to low B or C.

These four instruments of the violin family form two-thirds or three-quarters of the modern symphony orchestra (see ORCHESTRA). In orchestras today there are about 20 first violins, a slightly smaller number of second violins, about 14 violas, 12 cellos, and 8 double basses.

The use of violins in orchestras dates from the time of the great Italian composer Claudio Monteverdi (1567–1643). Violin-playing as we know it today, especially solo violin playing, began with another Italian, Arcangelo Corelli (1653–1713), who was a great composer, player, and teacher of violin music. Following after him other Italians wrote remarkable music for the violin, the most important of them being Antonio Vivaldi and Giuseppe Tartini. Their works are often played today and they no longer seem as difficult as they once did. Landmarks in the repertoire of the solo violin were the so-called partitas of Johann Sebastian Bach, the greatest of the German baroque composers. In the first half of the 19th century the great Italian violinist Niccolo Paganini wrote such difficult music that only he himself was able to play it at the time, although today there are several violinists who play it well. Later in the 19th century new methods and styles of violin playing were created in Paris and Brussels with Martin Marsick, Pablo de Sarasate, and Eugène Ysaÿe. In central and eastern Europe there were still other violinists, among them Joseph Joachim, who were beginning to find new things that the violin could do. Outstanding violin soloists of the 20th century have included the Russian-born American violinist Jascha Heifetz, the American-born Briton Yehudi Menuhin, the Russian father and son David and Igor Oistrakh, the Israeli-born American Itzhak Perlman, the Korean-born woman violinist Kyung Wha Chung, and the Briton Nigel Kennedy.

The tone, or sound-colour, of a violin depends both on the instrument and on the player—on his wrist movements as he presses the bow on the strings, and on his manner of stopping the strings. If he wants a warm tone he allows his fingers to waver on the strings, giving the note a rounder tone quality. This manner of stopping is called *vibrato*. If he wants a loud, harsh tone he plays with the bottom of the bow, called the heel. For special effects he plucks the string with his fingers instead of using the bow. This effect is called *pizzicato*. He may draw the bow very near the bridge for a certain kind of hollow tone. On the bridge he may place a mute (a small piece of wood or metal that lessens the vibrations of the strings) to soften the tone. Or he may stop one of the strings in two places so as to produce a high thin tone. These notes are called harmonics. All these effects make the violin a rich and varied instrument. These same methods also broadly apply to the other instruments of the violin family.

Two British viola players, Lionel Tertis (an Englishman) and William Primrose (a Scotsman), achieved international fame during the 20th century. Many modern composers have now written solo works for the viola, and although it has not quite the same interest for most people as the violin, musicians are beginning to appreciate the rich, full colour of its tone. Outstanding works for the viola have been written by Brahms, Paul Hindemith (himself a good viola-player), and Sir William Walton.

The first musician of modern times to show the beauties of the cello was the Spaniard, Pablo Casals, and he is still looked upon as the "father" of modern cellists. He is remembered for his wonderful performances of the unaccompanied *Suites* for cello by Bach. Outstanding cellists of the later 20th century have included Julian Lloyd Webber and Ralph Kirschbaum.

The double bass is rarely used as a solo instrument. There have, however, been three remarkable double bass players, the Italians Domenico Dragonetti and Giovanni Bottesini in the 19th century, and the 20th-century Russian-born musician Serge Koussevitzky, who was also a great conductor. As well as playing music especially written for the double bass he used to transpose (change) music originally written for the violin so that it became suitable for the deeper notes of the double bass. All these artists exploited the topmost notes of the instrument, which are hard to play because of the finger-stretching involved.

See also CHAMBER MUSIC and VIOL FAMILY.

VIPER. Snakes of the viper family are very dangerous because of their poison. All 200 species have long fangs attached to a small movable bone in the mouth. This bone is hinged, and when not in use the fangs are folded back in the snake's mouth. When it bites and injects poison into the wound the fangs are erected. A viper's poison causes a breakdown of the blood vessels, and extreme swelling around the wound. The bites of some vipers can be fatal.

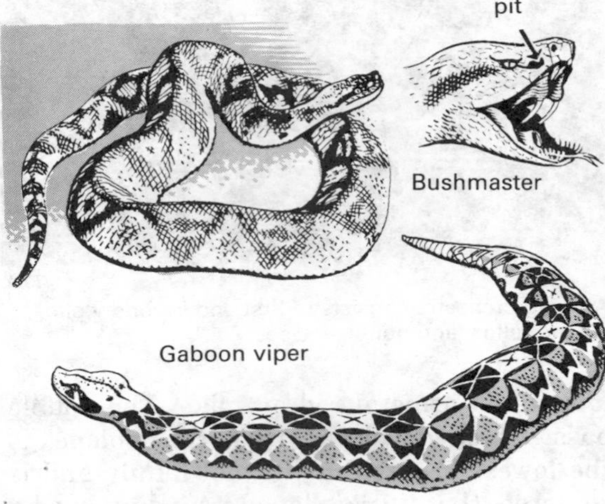

Snakes of the viper family.

The viper family is divided into two groups: true vipers and pit vipers. Pit vipers, which are found only in southern Asia and America, have a deep pit between the eye and the nostril. This is heat-sensitive and alerts the snakes when warm-blooded creatures, on which vipers prey, are near. The rattlesnake, copperhead, moccasin, and bushmaster are all pit vipers. (See RATTLESNAKE).

One of the best-known vipers is the adder (*Vipera berus*) of Europe. It can be recognized at once by the clear zigzag pattern down its back. (See ADDER.) Other true vipers are the saw-scaled viper (*Echis carinatus*) from the deserts of North Africa, the large puff adder (*Bitis arietans*) from dry parts of Africa, the gaboon viper (*Bitis gabonica*) from the African forests, and Russell's viper (*Vipera russelli*) from Asia.

Most vipers are thick snakes with large flat heads, but there are exceptions, such as the small-eyed burrowing vipers, and the slender tree vipers.

Most vipers give birth to live young. The few that lay eggs include the African night adder (*Causus rhombeatus*), and the bushmaster

(*Lachesis muta*) of South America. This is the largest poisonous snake of the New World, with an average length of about 1.8 metres (6 feet).

VIREO is a small insect-eating bird, 10 to 18 centimetres (4 to 7 inches) long. Vireo comes from a Latin word meaning greenish, and these birds are sometimes called greenlets. Their plumage (feathers) is greenish or yellowish olive, olive-brown, or grey on the upper part of the body. The lower part may be white, whitish, yellow, or grey. The cap (head feathers) may be a contrasting colour, sometimes black or reddish brown.

The wings may be long and pointed or short and rounded. The strong bill is slightly hooked. About 42 species are found in South and Central America, north through Canada, and in the West Indies. About 12 species live in the United States.

Vireos live in the forests and forest edges, and in garden trees quite close to houses. They feed mainly on insects and their larvae, which they search for high up in the foliage of trees. They sometimes eat fruit, such as berries. Most vireos are migratory, that is, they winter in the warm south, then return to the north early in the spring. The song of the vireo is cheerful and, in some species, very musical.

The red-eyed vireo (*Vireo olivaceus*) is probably the most common vireo in the United States. Its deep, cup-shaped nest is lined with grasses and often decorated with bark and paper. These small, well-built nests are slung by cobwebs from the small, outer branches of a tree. The vireo lays two to five white, lightly speckled eggs. Both parents help to feed and care for the young birds.

The red-eyed vireo breeds from Canada to Argentina. It has a cheerful song and calls from morning to night.

Other kinds of vireo may build their nests higher or lower in the trees than the red-eyed. The yellow-throated and warbling vireos (*Vireo flavifrons, V.gilvus*) like nesting spots more than 5 metres (16 feet) above the ground.

VIRGIL, or **VERGIL** (70–19 BC). One of the great long epic poems of the world is the *Aeneid* (see AENEID), and its author was the Roman poet Virgil. The poem tells of the adventures of the Trojan hero Aeneas and how he came to Italy and helped to found the future Rome. The poem not only was a heroic tale but also contained the story of Rome throughout the ages, and of the glorious events in its history, culminating in the greatness it achieved under its emperor Augustus. Thus the *Aeneid* served a political purpose, reminding Romans of their ancient pride, and how much they owed to Augustus' good management of the state.

Virgil's full name was Publius Vergilius Maro. He was born on 15 October 70 BC on his father's farm at Andes, not far from the town of Mantua, in northern Italy. He studied at Cremona, Milan, and Rome, and when his education was finished he returned home to live with his family. From 49 to 42 BC, Roman politics went through a violently turbulent period, and after the murder of Julius Caesar in 44 Italy was racked with civil war. In 42 many people's land was confiscated to be given to the victorious soldiers. Virgil's family's farm would have been taken from them, but fortunately Virgil was already becoming known in Rome as a man of letters, and Octavian himself, who later became the Emperor Augustus, commanded that the farm be given back. Virgil showed his gratitude in a book of ten pastoral poems called the *Eclogues*, in which he praised the beauty of the countryside and its

BBC Hulton Picture Library

This bust, said to be of the Roman poet Virgil, is in the Capitoline Museum, Rome.

simple life and predicted peace under the rule of Augustus.

For a time Virgil lived in Rome and there made many friends, among them Augustus' minister, the wealthy Maecenas, who gave great help and encouragement to poets. Another friend, the poet Horace, described how Virgil was loved and admired by everyone who knew him, not only for his work but also because he himself was so good and sincere a man. It was at Maecenas' suggestion that Virgil wrote his poem called the *Georgics*, from the Greek word *Georgos*, which means "farmer". This work, in four books, told of the work of the countryside through the seasons: cultivating the fields, looking after trees, especially the olive-tree and the vine, rearing sheep, cattle, and horses, and keeping bees. The *Georgics* contains many mythological digressions, including the story of Orpheus and Eurydice.

It took Virgil seven years to finish the *Georgics*, but he spent even longer on the *Aeneid*, on which he began work soon afterwards, in the year 30. In fact he had not finished it to his own satisfaction when, arriving back from a short trip to Greece, he died of a sudden illness at Brundisium on 21 September 19 BC. When he realized he was dying Virgil asked his friends to burn the whole poem rather than let it be published without the improvements he wanted to make, but, luckily for readers ever since, his friends disobeyed him.

VIRGINIA is a state on the east coast of the United States. It was, as a colony, the first permanent settlement in British North America. It was the colony in which American nationhood was formed. There in 1669 was founded the House of Burgesses, the first democratically elected legislature in America. The state is sometimes called Old Dominion and the Mother of Presidents, which is no exaggeration. American presidents George Washington, Thomas Jefferson, James Madison, James Monroe, William Henry Harrison, Zachary Taylor, John Tyler, and Woodrow Wilson were all Virginians.

The Land

Virginia is located in the southeastern part of the United States. Along its irregular northern boundary line, it is bordered by Maryland, the District of Columbia, and West Virginia. The northern border would have been more regular had not West Virginia seceded (withdrawn) from the state at the onset of the American Civil War. Kentucky is to the west, while Tennessee and North Carolina are to the south. To the east it faces Chesapeake Bay and the Atlantic Ocean, with a coastline of 180 kilometres (112 miles). The state, at its greatest length (along the southern border) is 708 kilometres (440 miles). The greatest width, north to south, is 315 kilometres (196 miles).

The state is made up of three natural regions: the Coastal Plain, the Piedmont Plateau, and the Appalachian Highland of the west. The Coastal Plain stretches inland for about 160 kilometres (100 miles) at some places. It includes the cities of Newport News, Norfolk, and Richmond (the capital). Along the North Carolina border is the Great Dismal Swamp, a swamp area about 50 kilometres (30 miles) long and one of the more

The State capitol building, Richmond, Virginia, was designed by Thomas Jefferson.

Courtesy, Virginia State Chamber of Commerce

remarkable ecological wonders of North America. The plain is fairly flat, although there are some hills. Across Chesapeake Bay is a disconnected portion of the plain called the Eastern Shore. It is part of the Delmarva Peninsula.

The Piedmont (meaning "foot of the mountains") lies between the Plain and the Blue Ridge Mountains. It ranges in width from 64 to 290 kilometres (40 to 180 miles).

The Appalachian Highland is part of the long mountain chain that crosses eastern North America from north to south (see Appalachian Mountains). The region itself can be divided into three parts. Along the eastern rim are the Blue Ridge Mountains. To the west of this range is the Valley and Ridge region; and in the far southwestern section of the state is a portion of the Appalachian Plateau. The most fertile soil of Virginia is in the Valley and Ridge section, also called the Valley of Virginia.

Virginia has a mild climate, although the western highlands are cool. Summers can be hot in the lower elevations, but winters are cool rather than cold. The growing season ranges from 150 days in the southwest to 240 days along the coast.

The People

The massive growth of the federal government and the expansion of the state's industrial base since World War II (1939–45) have given Virginia a population as diverse as any state. About 80 per cent of the people are white, descendants of European immigrants over a period of more than 350 years. About one-fifth of the population is black. Nearly 70 per cent of the population was urban in 1980. The greatest growth in population has taken place in the urban corridor south of Washington, DC, from Alexandria to Richmond, and south-east to Norfolk.

The Economy

Colonial Virginia developed a plantation economy based on cotton and tobacco. The plantations stretched along the rivers of the Plain and Piedmont making the state a very rural colony, compared to Massachusetts and New York. This economy was destroyed by the American Civil War and never returned. For decades the state struggled to recover from the ravages of the war. Through soundly managed government it survived but did not prosper, until World War II brought new industry, jobs, and expanded military installations. Today the federal government is the state's largest employer. Many government workers live in the state, and many more are connected to military establishments, such as the huge Norfolk Naval Base. The Air Force, the Coast Guard, the Marines, and the National Aeronautics and Space Administration (NASA) also have facilities in the state.

After government employment, manufacturing has the second largest segment of the labour force. The Newport News Shipbuilding and Dry Dock Company is one of the largest firms of its kind in the world. Other industries provide processed food, textiles, clothing, tobacco products, fertilizer, explosives, chemicals, furniture and other wood products, paper, and paper products.

The death of the cotton plantation did not mean the end of agriculture. Farming is more productive and diversified than before the American Civil War. Tobacco, grown in the southern Piedmont, is the main cash crop. Varieties of livestock, including dairy cattle, sheep, pigs, chickens, and turkeys, provide a large proportion of farm income. Peanuts are grown in the southeast. Other crops are apples, cherries, pears, peaches, plums, potatoes, maize, hay, wheat, and green vegetables.

Courtesy, Virginia State Chamber of Commerce

Oyster fishing in Chesapeake Bay, a large inlet on the Atlantic coast of Virginia.

Fishing is a major industry along the Chesapeake Bay coasts. Menhaden, one of the main catches, is used for fertilizer. Other catches are oysters, crabs, mackerel, and sea bass.

Mining thrives throughout much of Virginia. The Piedmont has much granite. Coal mines are located in the southwest. Lead, zinc, manganese, gypsum, and salt are also found there. Limestone, from the Valley of Virginia, is used for fertilizer, soap, glue, glass, paint, cement, soda, and materials for road-surfacing.

Virginia also prospers because of its tourist industry. Historical sites, such as colonial Williamsburg and the battlefields of the American Revolution and the Civil War, are popular. Visitors also go to George Washington's Mount Vernon home, Jefferson's Monticello, and the birthplace of Robert E. Lee. The scenery, too, attracts many people to the shores of Chesapeake Bay or the beautiful mountains.

Education

Virginia's public (state) school system was late in developing. The plantation owners educated their children privately and would not allow schools for blacks. No system of public schools was started until 1846. Adequate funding had to await the post-Civil War era, however. Today all counties and cities have school boards. Attempts were made to prevent school integration during the 1950s and after, but they were over-ruled by the courts.

Higher education has always presented a bright picture. There are several outstanding colleges and universities. Best-known, apart from Jefferson's University of Virginia, is the College of William and Mary. It is located in Williamsburg and was founded in 1693, making it the second oldest college (after Harvard) in the United States.

History

Virginia was named after Elizabeth I, the Virgin Queen. But it was King James I who gave the Virginia Company of London the right to start a colony. About 100 colonists left for America, and Jamestown was founded on 14 May 1607, as the first permanent settlement. Captain John Smith was leader of the colonists, but he was forced to return home after two years. He was succeeded by John Rolfe. In 1612 Rolfe raised a small tobacco crop from seeds that had been brought from the West Indies. Soon, trade in tobacco was the colony's primary means of support.

There were few problems during the first decades, but about 1660 resentment against British rule emerged. In 1676 there was a rebellion led by Nathaniel Bacon against

ZEFA

Replicas of 17th-century English ships re-create a colonial atmosphere, at Jamestown, Virginia.

Governor William Berkeley. It was unsuccessful, but Bacon's Rebellion is noted as the first colonial revolt against England.

Virginia prospered greatly during the 18th century, as plantations spread inland to the Piedmont. Tobacco remained the staple crop, but cotton was grown as well.

FACTS AND FIGURES

AREA: 105,566 square kilometres (40,767 miles).
POPULATION: 5,787,000 (1987).
MOUNTAIN RANGES: Appalachian, including the Blue Ridge, Allegheny, and Shenandoah. Highest peaks: Rogers, 1,743 metres (5,719 feet); White Top, 1,682 metres (5,520 feet); Hawksbill, 1,234 metres (4,049 feet); Elliot Knob, 1,359 metres (4,458 feet).
RIVERS: Potomac, Rappahannock, Tork, James.
CITIES (1985): Virginia Beach, 312,584; Norfolk, 283,219; Richmond, 221,857; Newport News, 156,545; Hampton, 122,617; Chesapeake, 114,486; Portsmouth, 104,577; Alexandria, 108,346; Roanoke, 101,967.

In the years immediately following the French and Indian War (or Seven Years' War), resentment against England began to grow, as Parliament made greater demands on the colonists for financial support. The Stamp Act and other legislation aroused the feelings of the colonists against "taxation without representation".

When the American Revolution came, several Virginians were prominent in the military and political decisions which guided it. A number of battles were fought within the state's boundaries, and the final conflict was at Yorktown in October 1781. (See AMERICAN REVOLUTION.)

From the end of the American Revolution to the Civil War, slavery divided not only the nation, but Virginia as well. There were several attempts to abolish it, but none succeeded. After the notorious Nat Turner Rebellion of 1831 when many white people were murdered, the General Assembly tried once more to get rid of slavery, but no agreement could be reached on how to do it. When the crisis came in 1861, Virginia reluctantly left the Union to join the Confederate States, and Virginian Robert E. Lee became the South's leading general. (See also SLAVERY; CIVIL WAR, AMERICAN; LEE, ROBERT E.) During the war the counties in the west separated to form West Virginia.

After the war Virginia was designated Military District Number One by the federal government. Finally, in 1870, Virginia was readmitted to the Union. After 1877, when the period known as Reconstruction ended throughout the South, the state was left to run its own affairs. By this time the large plantations had been broken up into smaller farms and a greater variety of crops were being grown.

The state's economy remained desperate for some time. Debts and devastation from the war plagued Virginia for decades. The white rural aristocracy, once back in power, proceded to deprive blacks of most civil rights (see CIVIL RIGHTS, UNITED STATES).

Virginia did not really recover from the Civil War until after World War I (1914–18), when Governor Harry F. Bird, straightened out the state's finances and set it on the road to agricultural diversification and industrialization. He, his family, and their associates dominated the state's affairs until the 1970s.

VIRGIN ISLANDS. East of Puerto Rico in the West Indies are the Virgin Islands, which are divided between Great Britain and the United States. The Virgin Islands belong to the Leeward Islands (see LEEWARD ISLANDS) in the

Charlotte Amalie, St. Thomas island, is built on five foothills, and faces a fine landlocked harbour.

ZEFA

Lesser Antilles. The British Virgin Islands are a colony, whereas the Virgin Islands of the United States are an "unincorporated territory", although its people are American citizens.

The Virgin Islands are all small, and although there are about 100 of them they are mostly uninhabited. Sugar, bananas, citrus fruit, and vegetables are grown in the cultivated parts and the islanders keep cattle and other livestock. Tourism is an important industry. There is also some manufacturing industry. The climate is mild and healthy.

There are 36 islands in the British Virgin Islands, of which 11 are inhabited. The chief ones are Tortola, Anegada, Virgin Gorda, Jost van Dyke, Peter Island, Beef Island, and Salt Island. There is a small airport on Beef Island. The capital is Road Town, on Tortola. Around Tortola are scattered a number of the smaller islands, one of which, Norman Island, is said to be the one on which Robert Louis Stevenson based his novel *Treasure Island*. Most of the population is black, descended from African slaves.

The American Virgin Islands, of which there are 53, cover a much larger area. The most important islands are St. Croix, St. Thomas, on which stands Charlotte Amalie, the chief town, and St. John. Most of the people are black or of mixed descent. The islands are administered by a governor, elected every four years. The inhabitants also elect a non-voting representative to the United States Congress.

The Virgin Islands were discovered by Christopher Columbus in 1493 and named after the virgin martyr St. Ursula and her companions. The British took possession of Tortola in 1666, and more settlers came to other islands in 1680. These have remained British ever since.

In the 17th and 18th centuries St. Thomas, St. Croix, and St. John were known as the Danish West Indies, because at that time Denmark was the country which had the most power in the Virgin Islands. However, the islands were captured and used by the British from 1807 to 1815 (during the Napoleonic Wars) and afterwards the Danish power declined. After a good deal of hesitation on both sides, Denmark sold its islands to the United States in 1917.

VIRUS AND VIRUS INFECTION. Viruses are the smallest known living things. If 1 or 2 million viruses were placed side by side, their total length would measure about 1 centimetre (0.4 inch). Viruses are sometimes grouped together with bacteria as germs, or microbes, but in fact they are very different (see GERMS). Viruses have a simple structure and cannot multiply by themselves. In order to reproduce,

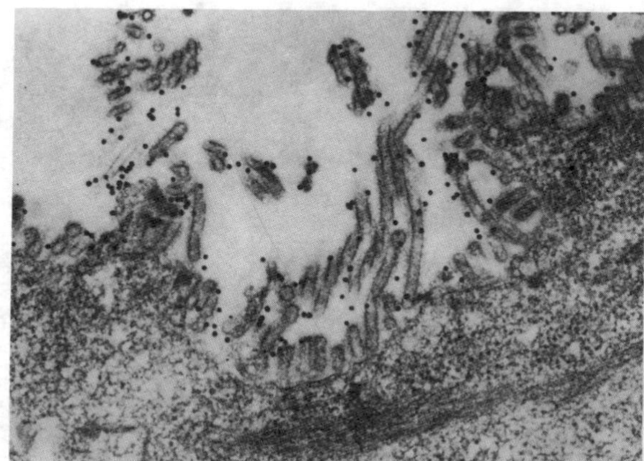

Science Photo Library

Influenza viruses (black dots) infecting cultured cells, magnified 20,000 times.

therefore, they must exist within another living cell and use the host's food and energy. When they do this they damage the host cell and cause disease.

A complete, freely-existing virus particle is called a virion. It has an outer shell, or coat, termed a capsid, made of small molecules of protein fitted together like building bricks. Inside is a molecule of nucleic acid, either DNA or RNA, which is the virus's genetic material, or genes. It is arguable whether a virion is actually a living thing, since it does none of the things we normally associate with life, such as grow, breathe, or move.

When the virus finds a host cell the nucleic acid passes inside and adds itself to the host's genetic material. In the normal workings of the host cell, the genetic material is used as the "blueprint" for building new molecules. In this case what is built are the parts for new virus particles. These either pass through the host's cell wall one by one, or collect until the host cell eventually bursts to release hundreds of new virions.

Science Photo Library

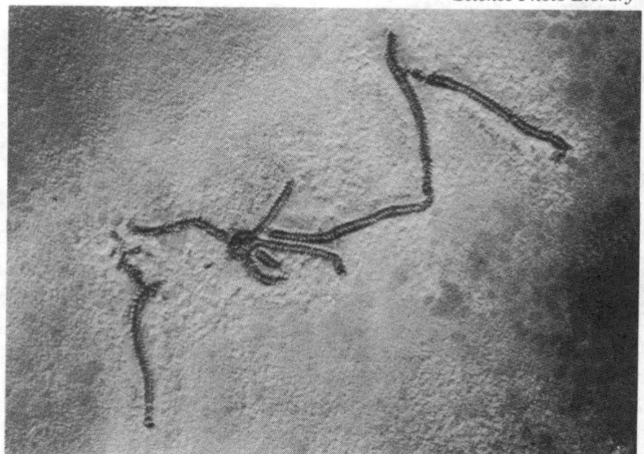

Virions (virus particles) of the measles virus, magnified 50,000 times.

Science Photo Library

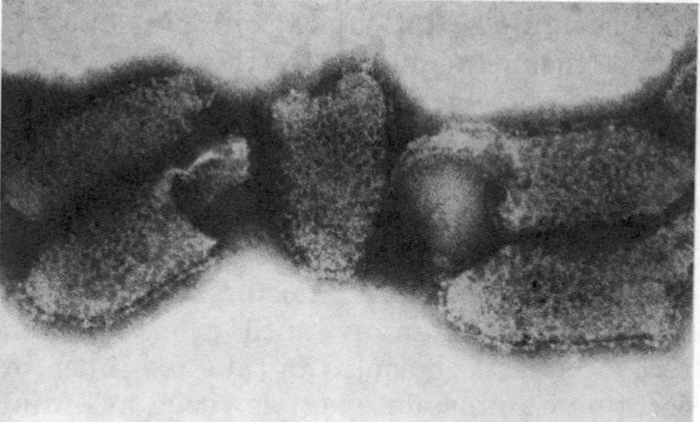

Rabies viruses, transmitted to man by the bite of an infected animal, multiply in the brain's nerve cells. The cells are magnified 140,000 times.

Viruses that infect bacteria are known as bacteriophages, or phages. They are very important to genetic engineers, who use them to transfer genes (the bits of nucleic acid) (see GENETIC ENGINEERING). The phages "stitch" the genes into certain bacteria along with their own nucleic acid, so that the bacteria will produce whatever the genes instruct—a new drug, for example.

Many diseases of human beings, animals, and plants are caused by viruses, including German measles, chickenpox, mumps, rabies, yellow fever, hepatitis, influenza (flu) and the common cold, and AIDS. Cold sores and warts are also due to viruses, and viruses play a role in certain types of cancer. Viruses do not survive well in soil or dust, and so most infectious diseases caused by viruses are spread directly from person to person or animal to animal. Virus diseases are difficult to treat because it is hard to kill the virus without also destroying the host cell. Antibiotic drugs, which are successful against bacteria, affect hardly any viruses. However, some virus diseases, such as polio, smallpox, and measles, can be prevented by vaccination (see VACCINATION AND INOCULATION).

VITAMIN. The word vitamin comes from *vita*, the Latin for "life", for everyone must eat a certain amount of vitamins to keep alive and in good health. Vitamins are tiny chemical compounds found in most foods. Their existence was discovered in 1911 by a Polish scientist, Casimir Funk.

Vitamins are known by letters of the alphabet (vitamins A, B, C, and so on). Tiny quantities of them are enough for the needs of the body, and no one who eats a good quantity of different kinds of food need worry about lack of vitamins. For most people, nothing is gained from taking excessive vitamins as they cannot be stored in the body and so are discharged. For certain diseases, doctors recommend taking extra vitamins until the body has recovered. It is harmful to take too much of certain vitamins, for example vitamins A and D, and a varied diet prevents this. If people live on only one or two kinds of food, they do not get their proper share of vitamins and develop "vitamin deficiency" diseases, such as scurvy and beriberi.

Vitamin A is formed in growing plants, and animals take it into their bodies when they eat the plants. It is always found connected with fat in the animal body. Besides helping to prevent infection, vitamin A is important to the health of skin, teeth, and bones. It also has an important effect on eyesight. People who do not have enough develop night blindness, which means they cannot see in dim light, and if they have still less they may become completely blind. Vitamin A is easy to obtain, as there is a good deal in milk, egg-yolk, liver, and vegetables such as lettuce, carrots, spinach, and turnips. It is lacking in white bread.

Vitamin B is often called the B complex. For many years it was thought to be one vitamin, but it is now known to be at least ten different vitamins. These were called vitamin B_1, vitamin B_2, and so on. However, even apparently single B vitamins are made of more than one substance, so the B vitamins are now referred to by their chemical names.

Vitamin B_1 (thiamine) is necessary for the prevention of some nervous diseases. People who do not take enough of it become nervous and irritable, and certain nerves are inflamed. This may even lead to paralysis of the limbs. Beriberi is a food deficiency disease caused by lack of vitamin B_1, and it affects people in the tropics whose diet includes rice with the husk removed. Their nerves are inflamed and they become paralysed, particularly in the hands and feet.

ZEFA

Vitamins are obtained from many different foods. Among the foods illustrated above, grapes are a source of vitamin A; lemons and green peppers, sources of vitamin C; and eggs provide vitamins A, B, and D.

Besides being found in whole ears of corn and rice, vitamin B_1 is also found in yeast, milk, fresh fruits and vegetables. It does not last long in the body and must be constantly replaced.

Vitamin B_2 (riboflavin) is found in milk, liver, yeast, lean beef, green leafy vegetables, and bananas. Lack of it causes a stunting of growth, loss of weight, and soreness of the eyes, mouth, or nose. Vitamin B_3 (niacin) also called vitamin PP, is found in chicken, turkey, liver, fish, lean meats, and legumes. The disease pellagra, which affects the skin and causes weakness and wasting away, is due to a lack of vitamin B_3 in the diet.

Vitamin C (ascorbic acid) is found in fresh

fruit, particularly citrus fruits such as oranges, and in raw cabbages, turnips, and tomatoes. The body is unable to store vitamin C for any length of time, so it must be replaced continually, as it is a very important vitamin. People who do not get enough vitamin C develop the disease known as scurvy, in which the bones, joints, and gums are affected. Many sailors used to get scurvy because they had no fresh fruits and vegetables on board ship.

Vitamin D is important to babies because it prevents rickets, a disease that causes them to grow up with deformed bones. Adults lacking vitamin D develop a similar disease, osteomalacia. Vitamin D is found in great quantities in cod-liver oil, liver, and egg yolk.

Vitamin E may be necessary for the reproduction of new living things, but the effects of the lack of it in human beings are not clear. It is found in a good many foods and can be stored for a long time in the body.

Vitamin K, which was discovered some time after the others mentioned here, is necessary for the clotting of the blood. It is contained in all green-leaf plants, especially spinach, cabbage, and cauliflower. There is a certain amount in liver, too.

VLADIVOSTOK, which means "Rule of the East", is a port in the extreme southeast of Siberia in the Soviet Union, on the Sea of Japan. It is close to Manchuria (on the west) and North Korea (on the south). Vladivostok is the most important city in Siberia and the terminus of the Trans-Siberian Railway. (See SIBERIA; TRANS-SIBERIAN RAILWAY.)

Vladivostok has a fine harbour, but it freezes during the winter and has to be kept open by ships called icebreakers. The city is the centre of Soviet whaling, crab-catching, and fishing. A variety of industries have grown there including ship and railway repair, instrument and radio manufacture, and food processing. There are also many research and educational establishments, making it the educational centre of the Soviet Far East.

Vladivostok was founded in 1860 as a military base to protect Russia's growing interests in the East. In 1872 Russia's main naval base on the Pacific was transferred there, and it has been the key naval base of the area ever since. In the 1950s it was closed to foreign vessels because of its military importance, and international maritime trade now goes through nearby Nakhodka. The population of Vladivostok is 600,000 (1985).

Novosti

Vladivostok looks on to Golden Horn Bay. It is the largest port on the Soviet Union's Pacific coast.

VOGEL, Sir Julius (1835–99). Julius Vogel was a New Zealand statesman who became his country's prime minister. He urged large-scale public works as a boost to the economy.

Vogel was born in London, England. At the age of 17 he emigrated to Australia to join in the gold rush in Victoria. He quickly established himself in business and later was successful in journalism, although not in politics. A gold rush again proved the attraction when he moved to Otago, New Zealand, in 1861. He founded the *Otago Daily Times*, a newspaper which is still published. He was elected to the New Zealand parliament in 1863 and soon became leader of the opposition. As colonial treasurer from 1869 he wielded more power than anyone else in the country. He successfully proposed that New Zealand should speed its development by building railways, roads, and telegraphs with money borrowed from London.

Vogel was twice prime minister (1873–75 and 1876). He urged Britain to take over Fiji in 1874 (see FIJI). He was largely responsible for the abolition of provincial governments in 1876. He was New Zealand's agent-general in London from 1876 to 1880, but later returned to serve in Sir Robert Stout's government (1884–87). Vogel was made a knight in 1875.

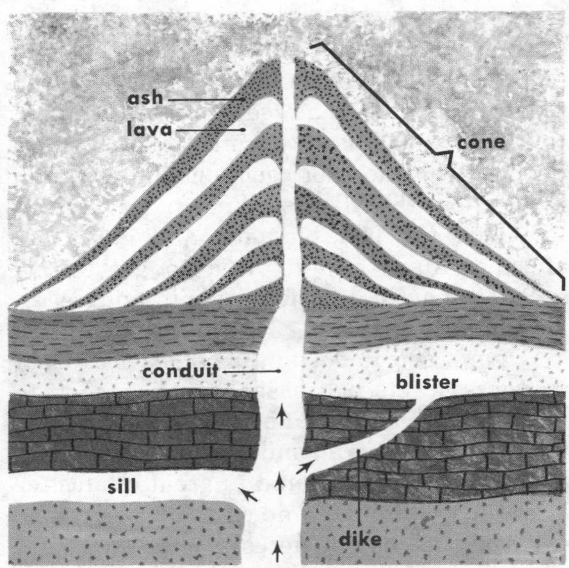

A cross-section through a volcano and the underlying layers of rock.

VOLCANO. A place, usually but not always a mountain, where molten rock from the Earth's interior pours out at the surface is called a volcano. The molten rock—called *magma* before it reaches the surface and *lava* when it can be seen in the open—comes up through a pipe drilled by the magma itself or through a fissure formed where the crust has been pulled apart. The temperature of molten lava is around 1,200°C (2,200°F), that is, between yellow-hot and white-hot. Explosions which blow the lava to fragments are frequent, especially in the early history of a volcano. The fragments can be anything from fine dust or ash to large blocks or "bombs" as they are called. Many explosions are caused by water, either sea-water or well water, coming into contact with the lava before it reaches the surface. Others, and usually the most dangerous, are caused by gas, mainly superheated steam and carbon dioxide, dissolved in the lava itself.

There are many different kinds of lava: some are thin and runny, others are stiff and sticky. By far the commonest of the thin and runny kind is *basalt*, a heavy, black rock when cool and hardened. The commonest of the stiff and sticky kind is *rhyolite*, which is pale biscuit in colour and is really just molten granite. Runny basalt lava erupts in fountains which can reach 600 metres (2,000 feet) in height. It runs downhill in streams, spreading out over large areas. Great thicknesses of basalt, made up of many lava flows piled one on another, can be seen in parts of the northwestern United States and the Deccan plateau of India. A famous exposure occurs in the Giant's Causeway of Northern Ireland.

Eruptions of lava are frequently preceded by explosions which throw out large amounts of ash and cinder. A cone-shaped mountain made up of layers of ash and lava like a layer cake builds up to form a volcano. The lava and ash are poured out from the top of the cone, where there is a hollow crater. When the cone reaches a very large size, lava may erupt from smaller cones on the slopes of the main cone.

Sticky rhyolite lava tends to form not streams but dome-shaped masses in the crater of the volcano. These are very dangerous. From the base of these domes, gassy rhyolite lava, really a compressed froth, explodes out sideways. The result is a nuée ardente (glowing cloud) eruption. The lava, consisting of myriads of red-hot fragments suspended in the air, rushes downhill destroying everything in its path. Great clouds of fine ash are also emitted.

Volcanoes normally erupt for short periods and then remain dormant (quiet) for long periods. During dormant periods, the lava may bubble and boil in a lava lake in the crater, or it may solidify. Solidification can mean the end of volcanic activity for good, that is, the volcano becomes extinct. But more usually it means that the next eruption will be explosive. This is because only a heavy pressure of gas will be sufficient to blow out the plug of solidified lava in the throat of the volcano. Many volcanoes "smoke" between eruptions; the "smoke" is mostly hot steam escaping from the lava below.

As explained in the article EARTH, the Earth has two different kinds of crust, *continental* and *oceanic*, and beneath them both is the mantle. New oceanic crust is constantly formed at the mid-ocean ridges by the squeezing out of molten rock from the mantle. Many volcanoes are situated on the mid-ocean ridges and in the ocean basins. The highest of these oceanic volcanoes sit above the water level as islands, such as the Hawaiian Islands and Iceland. The lava in these oceanic volcanoes is almost entirely basaltic. Around the shores of the Pacific Ocean and in the northeast Indian Ocean, the oceanic crust plunges back into the Earth's interior in deep oceanic trenches. Where this happens, a chain of volcanoes forms above the descending plate of oceanic crust. The chain of volcanoes may form a string of islands, such as the Aleutian Islands in the North Pacific, or it may be situated on a mountain range at the edge of a continent, such as the Andes of South America. The lava from volcanoes formed over sinking oceanic crust, and particularly from volcanoes along the edge of a continent, is likely to be explosive. The dangerous volcanic eruptions of recent times, such as Krakatoa, Katmai, and Mont Pelée were of this type.

Famous Volcanoes and Eruptions

The greatest eruption of the last 100 years was that of Krakatoa, an island in the Sunda Strait between Java and Sumatra in Indonesia. A large volcano in the sea had erupted a long time previously and formed a collection of small islands, one of which was Krakatoa. In August 1883, after earthquakes and a smaller eruption, a series of terrific explosions destroyed most of Krakatoa and part of Rakata, another island. The noise of the explosions was so great that it was heard 5,000 kilometres (3,100 miles) away in the Indian Ocean and in Australia. No other sounds have been known to have reached so far. The sky was darkened 250 kilometres (150 miles) away and dust filled the atmosphere, causing brilliant sunsets and dawns in many parts of the world for months afterwards. The eruption sent enormous waves travelling over the oceans. More than 36,000 people living near the sea on the islands of Java and Sumatra were drowned by these waves.

Mont Pelée on the island of Martinique in the West Indies began erupting violently in May 1902. The force of the explosion, instead of being directed straight up into the air, broke through a gash in the rim of the mountain. It sent a mighty nuée ardente in the form of a cloud of glowing, white-hot gas and dust down the side of the mountain, overwhelming the city of St. Pierre which lay in its path and killing about 30,000 people. The only person in the city who survived was a black man, Joseph Surtout, convicted of murder and kept locked deep underground in the city jail. He remained there for four days without food or water before being rescued. Many of the ships in the harbour were burnt by the fiery dust or overwhelmed by the huge waves stirred up by the boiling sea.

An eruption brought the Valley of Ten

Thousand Smokes in Alaska into existence in 1912. On 5 June of that year a new eruption in the valley sent out a stream of glowing lava particles which swallowed up everything in their path until they reached the end of the valley, where the trees were turned to charcoal. The next day, Mount Katmai, at the head of the valley, exploded, its three-peaked, snow-covered crown being blown apart, leaving a crater 4 kilometres (2.5 miles) wide. The eruption covered Kodiak Island, 160 kilometres (100 miles) away, with ash 30 centimetres (12 inches) deep. Strange to say, no one was killed in this great eruption.

The valley was not discovered until three years later, when not ten thousand but millions of jets of steam were to be seen spurting through its floor. Today many jets can still be seen in the valley. They are of course steam, not smoke.

The eruption that took place in 1980 at Mount St. Helens in the Cascade Range, southwest Washington State, was one of the greatest ever recorded in North America. An earthquake preceded the eruption, opening a crack on the volcano's north side. This side then bulged out and fell away in an avalanche. An explosion followed carrying debris out to a distance of 20 kilometres (12 miles), and destroying 260 square kilometres (100 square miles) of forest. The eruption left 66 people either dead or missing.

Vesuvius, in the Bay of Naples in Italy, is a perfect example of the explosive kind of volcano, and is the only active one on the mainland of Europe. There is nearly always some activity going on inside the crater and usually some smoke drifting from it. Its eruptions are of the same type as those of Mount St. Helens.

Now and then Vesuvius erupts violently. This happened in AD 79 after many centuries of quiet. Without warning the top of the volcano blew off and great quantities of ash descended on the surrounding plains. Pompeii was buried by this ash and Herculaneum by mud after intense thunderstorms had turned the ash to mud so that it flowed like lava. Many people were killed. The shapes of their bodies were preserved in the ash at Pompeii. This has now been cleared so that visitors can walk the streets and see the city more or less as it was in AD 79. There were only occasional outbursts until 1631. (See POMPEII.)

Since then the volcano has remained active, with more violent eruptions at intervals, the last of which happened in 1944.

On the island of Sicily in the Mediterranean is Mount Etna, the largest volcano in Europe and second only to Vesuvius in fame. Like Vesuvius, it is usually crowned with smoke. North of Sicily are the Lipari Islands which include Stromboli, another active volcano. Its fires can always be seen at night, so it is known as the "lighthouse of the Mediterranean". These islands also include Vulcano, where there was an eruption in 1888.

Iceland is an island of volcanoes, the best known being Hekla and the volcanic island of Surtsey off the coast. None of these, however, is active all the time, and many remain quiet for so long that they become covered with ice and snow. As a result, if there is an eruption, the snow and ice are melted by the heat and sweep down in floods.

The North Island of New Zealand contains many volcanoes, extinct, dormant, and active. In 1886 Mount Tarawera was split into two parts when a 12 kilometre-long (7.5 mile-long) fissure (crack) formed and ash covered an area of about 10,000 square kilometres (4,000 square miles). As in Iceland, there are many hot springs and geysers in this region. (See GEYSER.)

Hawaii has two active volcanoes, Mauna Loa and Kilauea. Mauna Loa, which does not erupt violently, produces more lava than any other volcano and in 1950 it produced the biggest flow ever recorded. In 1935 the city of Hilo was threatened by a lava flow from Mauna Loa, which advanced at the rate of 2 kilometres (1.25 miles) a day. The United States Navy Air Force dropped bombs on the lava and so opened new channels down which it flowed away from Hilo.

Kilauea generally pours out its lava quietly, but in 1924 it exploded violently. Its crater is 10.7 square kilometres (4 square miles) in area and has a floor of cooled and solid lava.

Courtesy, Gernsheim Collection, The University of Texas At Austin (centre); Ewing Galloway (top and bottom)

Some volcanoes erupt much more explosively than others, depending on the composition of their lavas. The volcanoes Botak, Bromo, and Semeru, in Java (top) are examples of the most explosive type. Mount Vesuvius (centre) in the Bay of Naples, in Italy, is of the intermediate kind and not so explosive. The volcanoes of Hawaii, in the Pacific, are among the least explosive. Mount Kilauea is shown here (bottom). Note that the most explosive volcanoes have the cones with the steepest sides.

There are, however, lakes and fountains of liquid lava that at intervals of years rise and break through the mountainside to flow in red-hot streams towards the sea.

FAMOUS VOLCANOES

NAME	REGION
Africa	
Nyamlagira	Zaire
Ngorongoro	Tanzania
America	
Chimborazo	Ecuador
Cotopaxi	Ecuador
Katmai	California, USA
Lassen	California, USA
Mont Pelée	Martinique
Mount St. Helens	Washington, USA
Okmok	Aleutian Islands, USA
San Miguel	El Salvador
Soufriere	St. Vincent, West Indies
Antarctica	
Erebus	Ross Island
Asia	
Fujiyama	Japan
Krakatoa	Indonesia
Mayon	Luzon, Philippines
Merapi	Java, Indonesia
Mihara	Japan
Oceania	
Bagana	Solomon Islands
Kilauea	Hawaii
Mauna Loa	Hawaii
Ngauruhoe	New Zealand
Ruapehu	New Zealand
Tarawera	New Zealand
Tongariro	New Zealand
Europe	
Askja	Iceland
Etna	Sicily, Italy
Hekla	Iceland
Santorin	Greece
Stromboli	Italy
Surtsey	Iceland
Vesuvius	Italy

VOLE is the name of a small rodent related to rats and mice. The easiest way of distinguishing voles is by their noses, which are very blunt and rounded. Voles are northern animals, living in North America, Europe, and northern Asia. In North America they are often called meadow mice.

There are about 45 species of vole that live in a wide variety of habitats from swamps and meadows to woodlands and deserts. They often make runways under low vegetation and dig short burrows. They eat nearly their own weight of plant material each day in seeds, roots, and leaves. Their voice is a high-pitched

The bank vole is reddish brown with a white chest. It lives along the base of thickets and hedgerows.

squeak. As they are fond of grass roots and shoots, some voles do a good deal of damage to farmers' crops. Sometimes they are found in such large numbers that they become a plague.

Water voles (*Arvicola*) are found only in Europe and Asia, and are often wrongly called water rats. The body is between 15 and 23 centimetres (6 to 9 inches) long, with a tail about two-thirds that length, and its coat is very dark brown. Water voles are often heard diving with a loud plop into the water of rivers, canals, and ponds.

See also RODENT.

VOLGA RIVER. By far the longest European river is the Volga, which flows 3,690 kilometres (2,293 miles) through the Soviet Union from its source in the Valdai Hills to the Caspian Sea. Astrakhan, Volgograd, Kuybyshev, Kazan, and Gorky are five great towns on the Volga's banks.

The Volga drains the water from an area of more than 1 million square kilometres (386,100 square miles). It has the largest series of barrages and reservoirs in the world. A series of giant dams have created huge artificial lakes, so that the Volga has almost ceased to be a river in the normal sense. Hydroelectric power stations have been built and the water flow is controlled so that navigation is easier, and the river is no longer blocked by ice jams in spring.

The river is the chief waterway of the Soviet Union and of great economic importance to the country. The fisheries of the Volga are important particularly for sturgeon, the fish from which caviar comes. Oil from the Caspian oilfields and wheat from the steppes are taken up the Volga to the northern industrial towns. Timber, grain, and machinery are brought down it.

The Volga is linked by canals to other rivers, including several draining into the Black Sea and to the Baltic and the White seas. The Moscow canal built in 1932–37 gave access to Moscow for large craft. The Volga-Don canal, completed in 1952, opened the whole system to seagoing ships and formed a direct link between the Volga and the Donets Basin industrial area. The Volga-Baltic waterway, reconstructed in the 1960s, completed the connection between the Volga and the seas surrounding European Russia. Regular passenger services ply along the Volga, making increasing use of fast hydrofoils.

VOLGOGRAD in the southwest of the Soviet Union stretches some 65 kilometres (40 miles) along the high west bank of the Volga River, about 560 kilometres (350 miles) from the Caspian Sea.

Although a market centre for agricultural produce, the city is in an area where the rainfall is insufficient for plentiful crops and it is important chiefly for its industries. Raw materials for these are carried on the Volga and also on the Don River, which is connected to the Volga by a canal. The city has important iron and steel works and manufactures farm tractors, machinery, ships, railway equipment, and motor vehicles. Natural gas and by-products from the oil refinery serve as the basis of a growing chemical industry. About 15 kilometres (10 miles) upstream of the city a huge dam across the Volga provides electricity and also collects water for irrigation (see also VOLGA RIVER).

The city was formerly Tsaritsyn, a fortified town on the river, and a trading centre for many years. In the period shortly after the

ZEFA

Volgograd, on the River Volga, was rebuilt after destruction in World War II.

Russian Revolution of 1917 the town was held by the Soviet leader Joseph Stalin against the anti-revolutionary troops. In 1925 it was renamed Stalingrad in his honour.

Stalingrad was the scene of a decisive land battle of World War II. In August 1942, the Germans, trying to cross the Volga, attacked the city fiercely but were finally encircled and forced to surrender. Much of Stalingrad was destroyed in the fighting and after the war the city was rebuilt and repopulated. It grew in importance with the opening of the Volga-Don canal and the completion of the barrage and hydroelectric power station.

Following Russia's re-evaluation and criticism of Stalin's rule, the city was renamed Volgograd in 1961. There are many technical institutes and a university. The population is 974,000 (1985).

VOLLEYBALL is a popular team game in more than 100 countries. It was invented in 1895 by William G. Morgan, physical director of the Young Men's Christian Association in Holyoke, Massachusetts. He wanted a game for businessmen which was less strenuous than basketball. Modern volleyball is played by two teams of six, with up to six substitutes allowed.

The ball is the same size as a soccer ball, but slightly lighter. The game is played on a court, rectangular in shape and measuring 18 metres (60 feet) by 9 metres (30 feet). Across the court is a net 2.43 metres (8 feet) high for men, 2.21 metres (7.25 feet) high for women. Two attack lines are marked 3 metres (10 feet) from the net on either side.

Play begins with a service. Standing in the service area behind the base line, the server hits the ball with his hand or arm over the net. Once it has crossed the net, the other team may touch the ball up to three times before returning it. But no player may touch the ball twice in succession. The object is to hit the ball over the net in such a way that it bounces on the floor or cannot be returned by the other team. If the ball goes out of play, the receiving team wins the rally.

If the serving team wins the rally, they score a point. If the receiving team wins, they take over service. The first team to reach 15 points by a margin of two points wins the set. A game consists of the best of three or five sets.

The art of good volleyball is team play: passing the ball up close to the net (first

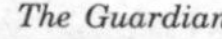

The Guardian

Volleyball players at the net.

touch), and setting up a high ball (second touch) so that an incoming player can spike (smash) it down over the net (third touch). Two or three opposing players may jump together to try to block the spike. If they fail, the rest of the team try to control the ball before it bounces and then start their own attack.

The International Volleyball Federation was set up in 1937. World championships were first held in 1949 (for men only) and in 1952 for men and women. Volleyball has been an Olympic sport since 1964.

VOLTAIRE is the pen name of François Marie Arouet (1694–1778), the greatest of the writers and thinkers who lived in France in the 18th century, during the years leading up to the French Revolution (1789–99). He lived a long life and he never stopped writing about the right of a person to be free and to think for himself. He attacked the government for oppressing people's lives. He also attacked the Church which, he felt, did not allow freedom of faith. He pointed out all the weaknesses of the society in which he lived and helped to prepare the way for the upheaval of the French Revolution (see FRENCH REVOLUTION).

François Marie Arouet was born in Paris. He attended the Jesuit college of Louis-le-Grand in Paris, and there learned to love literature and the theatre. He became the wit of Parisian society, but was always in trouble with the powerful people whom he mocked and wrote about. Before he was 24 he had been exiled from Paris and then imprisoned in the Bastille. Following the success of the first of his plays, *Oedipe*, in 1718, he took the name Voltaire.

From 1726 to 1729 he lived as an exile in England. He saw a society where there was far more freedom than he had known in France and far greater tolerance for the opinions and beliefs of others.

Back in France, Voltaire turned his interest to history and philosophy, and in 1734 published *Lettres philosophiques* (Philosophical Letters), a landmark in the history of thought. This outspoken work caused such a stir that he was again in trouble with the political and religious authorities, and he fled to the château of a friend at Cirey in the Champagne region. Here he lived with Mme du Châtelet for 15 years, studying, writing, and from time to time travelling in Europe.

For some years King Frederick II (the Great) of Prussia had been inviting Voltaire to visit his court. In 1750, after the death of Mme du Châtelet and the poor reception given to some of his plays in the 1740s, he accepted the invitation and spent the next three years in Berlin. He often quarrelled with the king, however, and finally left for Geneva.

In 1758 Voltaire wrote what became his most famous work, the short novel *Candide*. It tells of the adventures of the young man Candide and his companion Dr Pangloss. They see and suffer such great misfortunes that Candide cannot believe, as did the philosopher Leibnitz, that the world he lives in is "the best of all possible worlds". He ceases to travel and finally discovers that the secret of happiness is "to cultivate one's garden".

Early in 1778, at the age of 83, Voltaire returned to Paris for the rehearsals of his play *Irène*. He received a tumultuous welcome. The excitement was too much for him and he was taken ill and died on 30 May.

Only a few of his many works are still read, but Voltaire has remained through his total work and life an outstanding figure in French literature.

VULTURE. When an animal of the warm countries of Africa, Asia, or southern Europe dies in the open, large numbers of vultures quickly descend from the sky and soon pick its bones clean. Although their feeding habits seem unpleasant, these birds are really very useful, as the dead bodies of animals (called carrion) would rot and attract flies if they were left untouched.

There are many kinds of vulture and they are mostly large birds, often about 1 metre (3 feet) in length, with no feathers on their heads or necks. This feature allows them to thrust their head deep into a dead animal's body easily and without fouling any feathers. In many, this bare skin is coloured. The beak is strong and hooked and the feet are large and clumsy. Generally vultures walk along the ground with slow and solemn movements, but occasionally they run, flapping their large wings as they do so.

Vultures are keen-sighted and strong-winged. They soar high above the ground and watch for their food. When one bird spots a dead animal, it swoops down and other vultures, seeing it descend, follow it and join in the feast. Sometimes vultures eat so much that they are unable to fly away afterwards.

Old World Vultures

The bearded vulture (*Gypaetus barbatus*) is a bird of the mountains, and it is common in the Himalayas of Asia. It has stiff black bristles over the nostrils and a beard of bristles under the chin, from which it gets its name. It is also called the lammergeyer or lamb eagle, and the bone-breaker. This last name comes from its habit of carrying bones to a great height and then dropping them to get at the marrow inside. The bearded vulture builds a great nest of sticks in places that human beings cannot reach. Once it nested in the Swiss and Austrian Alps, but it was exterminated (killed off) there about 1884. It has a wingspan of nearly 3 metres (10 feet).

The black vulture (*Coragyps atratus*) is one of the biggest and heaviest of flying birds, weighing 12.5 kilograms (27.5 pounds), and has a wingspan of 2.7 metres (9 feet). It ranges through southern Europe, the central steppes, and the highest mountains in Asia, nesting in tall trees.

New World vultures include the king vulture of the tropics (top left), the long-winged, long-legged turkey vulture (top right), and the Andean condor (bottom), one of the largest flying birds, with a wingspan of over 3 metres (10 feet).

The Egyptian vulture (*Neophron percnopterus*) is small and almost pure white. It is one of the few animals to use a tool, in this case a rock, with which it breaks open the tough shells of other birds' eggs.

The palm-nut vulture (*Gyphohierax angolensis*) of western and central Africa has a bare orange face and a yellow beak. It is unusual in that it eats mainly plants, although it sometimes feeds on dead fish.

New World Vultures

There are also American birds of a different family which are known as turkey vultures. They are found from Canada to Cape Horn. Their habits are similar to those of true vultures, but they also catch their prey alive.

The mighty condor (*Vultur gryphus*), which lives in the Andes Mountains of South America sometimes measures more than 3 metres (10 feet) from wing tip to wing tip and is the largest flying bird. It rises high into the air and hovers on spread wings, supported by thermal air currents.

The Californian condor (*Gymnogyps californianus*) is one of the world's rarest birds. About 40 remain in the San Rafael Mountains near Santa Barbara in southern California. Their feeding grounds are open land near the coast where they take mainly fresh carrion. They lay a single egg every other year. The nesting area is now protected by law.

The king vulture (*Sarcoramphus papa*) is the most colourful of all vultures: the head, and neck are red, yellow, and bluish. This bird ranges from southern Mexico to Argentina, where it soars in flocks over the rain-forests.

WADING BIRDS (or shorebirds) include 200 species of bird related to gulls, skuas, and auks. They get their name from feeding in or around water. Most waders have a brown,

NHPA/L. Campbell

Small wading birds—dunlin and turnstone—feed on small marine animals exposed by the receding tide.

black, or white plumage that camouflages them on their nest, which is usually on the ground in open country.

Waders are rather small birds, the largest being the curlews, up to 60 centimetres (2 feet) long. Stilts have unusually long legs on which they wade in the water of muddy shallows.

Different Bills

Curlews have a long downwardly curved beak, with which they probe mud for worms and small crabs. Most waders have similar long and slender bills to pick up small invertebrate animals. The avocet has an upturned bill which it sweeps sideways through the water. Sandpipers and snipe have a sensitive movable tip at the end of the upper bill with which they find food. Oystercatchers have a strong bill, flattened at the end to form a wedge used to prise open shellfish such as mussels. Turnstones have a short, flattened bill that is slightly upturned at the end. They use it to overturn pebbles and shells in search of food. Seed snipe are unusual among waders since they have a short, cone-like bill to pick up seed.

Migration

Waders are strong fliers, and after the breeding season they come together in flocks to feed, especially along estuaries and coasts. Many waders, such as the greenshank, nest in the far north and at the end of the summer they migrate many thousands of miles into the southern hemisphere. Waders are fast fliers; a ruddy turnstone was found to have covered over 3,200 kilometres (2,000 miles) after just four days.

Waders are popular with birdwatchers because of their graceful form and whirring flight. In the northern hemisphere one can see many different wading birds during autumn and winter feeding on coastal mud flats. (See OYSTERCATCHER; PHALAROPE; PLOVER; RUFF; SNIPE; TURNSTONE.)

WAGNER, Richard (1813–83). William Richard Wagner was a German composer whose revolutionary theories had a tremendous effect on the development of opera. He was born in Leipzig, now in East Germany, on 22 May 1813. As a boy, he was lazy at school, but developed an interest in music and poetry. After briefly attending Leipzig University, he travelled from town to town serving as music director for several small opera companies. He longed to go to France, where operas were very popular, but could not leave Germany because of debt. In 1839 he and his actress wife finally managed to dodge their creditors and escape to Paris. During three years in Paris, Wagner made few friends among his fellow musicians and had to borrow money continually. He was forced to spend hours on routine work for a music publisher, while his mind was bursting with musical ideas.

In 1842 he returned to Germany to produce his opera *Rienzi*. The performance was a success, and Wagner immediately became famous. *Rienzi* was based on Italian history, but all Wagner's other operas took their plots from legend. In the following years three more of his operas, *The Flying Dutchman* (*Der Fliegende Holländer*), *Tannhäuser*, and *Lohengrin*, were presented, the last at Weimar by Franz Liszt, who became his champion and whose daughter Cosima he later married. (See LISZT, FRANZ.) Because of Wagner's new ideas in operatic composition, these works were not appreciated.

During the 1840s, Wagner became increasingly involved in revolutionary activities in Germany. Forced to leave the country in 1849, he took refuge in Zurich, Switzerland. There he spent ten years struggling with poverty and illness. Despite the unfavourable conditions, these years were among the most productive of his whole life. After studying the ancient sagas of the "Nibelundgenlied" and the old Icelandic *Eddas* (see SAGA), Wagner began a series of four pieces called music dramas based on its legends. This cycle of operas, called *The Ring of the Nibelungs* (*Der Ring des Nibelungen*) (1854–74), included *The Rhinegold* (*Das Rheingold*), *The Valkyrie* (*Die Walküre*), *Siegfried*, and *The Twilight of the Gods* (*Die Goetterdämmerung*). He stopped work on *The Ring* to write two other operas, *Tristan and Isolde* (1857–59), a tragedy based on a Breton tale set in Cornwall, England, and *The Mastersingers of Nuremberg* (1862), a comedy set in 15th-century Germany.

BBC Hulton Picture Library

The German composer Richard Wagner invented a new kind of opera called music drama.

After Zurich, Wagner lived in Venice, Lucerne, Paris, and Vienna. In Vienna he again fell into financial difficulty and had to leave to avoid imprisonment for debt. Fortunately, however, in 1864 King Ludwig of Bavaria became interested in his works. Under the king's patronage, several of Wagner's operas were performed in Munich, including the two just mentioned. The composer was given a home in Bayreuth, now in East Germany. There he finally finished *The Ring* and saw its first complete performance in 1876 in a theatre built especially for his works. Wagner spent the rest of his life in Bayreuth, but died while visiting Venice, on 13 February 1883. A yearly festival honouring him is still held in the theatre at Bayreuth.

Wagner's operas are among the most powerful and emotional ever written. Wagner had some unique ideas about the opera as a form of art. He believed that the music and the drama should be fused together into a single spectacle. This blending of orchestra, voices, scenery, and story was later called "music drama". Wagner was one of the few operatic composers who wrote not only the music but also the libretto (the words of the opera). While he stressed the importance of drama, he also increased the size of the orchestra and made it a more important element in the opera. Until his time, operas had been divided into songs, called arias, and either musical dialogue, called recitative, or straight spoken dialogue. Wagner, however, felt that music should flow continuously throughout the opera and did away with the old tradition. Another characteristic of his music was the use of the *leitmotif*, or "leading theme", a short musical phrase used to identify a specific character, mood, or setting. The leitmotif added greatly to the expression of emotion and helped to unify the story and the music.

Wagner's ideas of music drama are most fully worked out in *The Ring*. With these ideas he also coupled a new approach to harmony largely influenced by Liszt. His revolutionary method of writing opened the way that eventually led to Schoenberg's invention of atonal music. This music is described in the article SCHOENBERG, ARNOLD.

See also MUSIC; OPERA.

WAGTAIL. The group of birds known as wagtails can at once be recognized by the way they run along the ground, their heads nodding and their long tails moving rapidly up and down. They are about the size of a sparrow but have longer legs and are more slender and dainty. When they take wing they rise and dip in long curves as they move through the air. Their nests are made of plant materials and lined with hair and feathers. They feed mainly on insects which they will snap up in mid-air.

Wagtails are so named because they flick their long tails up and down.

Wagtails are birds of the Old World, and only the yellow wagtail (*Motacilla flava*) breeds regularly in North America, in Alaska. One of the commonest of the European species is the pied wagtail (*Motacilla alba*), which, as its name shows, is a black and white bird. In winter both male and female have a crescent-shaped black patch on the breast, black on the top of the head, a white throat, and a grey back. In summer, however, the back and throat of the male become black. Its wings are black with a double white bar, those of the female being greyer.

Pied wagtails utter a sharp sound like "tsch-izzik" and also a twittering song. Except in the breeding season these birds will roost together in large numbers, sometimes in reed beds or on the roofs of buildings. They have been known to spend the night on a tree in the centre of a large town, but they prefer open country. They nest in a hole in a wall, tree, or bank.

The grey wagtail (*Motacilla cinerea*) has grey upper parts, yellow under parts, and a longer tail than the other species. Grey wagtails are usually found near water and are particularly fond of swift-flowing streams.

The yellow wagtail also has yellow under parts, but its upper parts are greenish and it has a shorter tail. It is mostly found in marshy meadows and cultivated fields. It builds its nest on the ground, among plants in fields, or in a bank or wall.

The willie wagtail (*Rhipidura leucophrys*) of Australia is one of the fantails, which also has the habit of wagging its tail.

WAKEFIELD, Edward Gibbon (1796–1862). Some of the early British colonies in New Zealand and South Australia were founded according to a plan suggested by E. G. Wakefield. He was born in London of a well-known Quaker family (see FRIENDS, SOCIETY OF). He began a diplomatic career but in 1826 disgraced himself by eloping with a schoolgirl heiress. He was sent to Newgate prison for three years, and there wrote his *Letter from Sydney*, pretending it was written by a settler in Australia. Most people believed his claim and the book was widely read.

The book explained that colonists were being granted huge stretches of land but could find no one to help them clear and cultivate their land. Wakefield urged that the plots should be much smaller, and that they should be sold at prices that would allow a settler to buy his plot from his earnings over about four years. Part of the money the settler paid for his plot should be used to bring out more settlers and part should be spent on building churches and schools.

Wakefield's ideas were tried out in South Australia in 1836 and in the following year the New Zealand Association was formed in order to colonize New Zealand on the Wakefield plan. The first settlers under the plan landed at Port Nicholson (Wellington harbour) in 1840. Later Wakefield helped to found other colonies in New Zealand, especially the important Church of England settlement at Canterbury, South Island, in 1850. In 1853 Wakefield arrived in New Zealand himself. His health failed and he died at Wellington in 1862.

Although his ideas were not accepted in every detail, Wakefield's work was valuable. He showed that colonies must be properly planned and developed if they are to be granted self-government.

WALES is part of the United Kingdom of Great Britain and Northern Ireland. It is surrounded on three sides by the sea, the Irish Sea being on the north and northwest, St. George's Channel on the southwest, and the Bristol Channel on the south. On the east is England. It covers an area of 20,768 square kilometres (8,019 square miles), and its population is 2,811,800 (1985).

Celtic Picture Agency

Conway, North Wales, is a tourist centre and one of Europe's finest medieval walled boroughs.

There are eight Welsh counties. They are Clwyd, Dyfed, Gwent, Gwynedd, Mid Glamorgan, Powys, South Glamorgan, and West Glamorgan.

Like the rest of the United Kingdom, Wales is governed by parliament at Westminster. It also has its own capital, Cardiff, and its own language. The Welsh name for the country is *Cymru*.

Llynnau Mymbyr (Mymbyr Lakes), Snowdonia, North Wales, with the peaks of the Snowdon Horseshoe in the background.

Celtic Picture Agency

Land and Climate

The west coast of Wales is at once noticeable for its two great bays: Caernarfon Bay in the north, bounded by the island of Anglesey and the county of Gwynedd, and Cardigan Bay, which is even larger. South of Cardigan Bay the county of Dyfed extends out to the sea. This is the most westerly county of Wales and the nearest to Ireland, although it does not extend as far west as Cornwall in England.

Wales is a country of hills and mountains. In the northwest there are mountains more than 600 metres (2,000 feet) high, with some peaks more than 900 metres (3,000 feet) high. Snowdon at 1,085 metres (3,560 feet) is the highest point.

Around the upland regions of Wales is a coastal fringe of lowland which is very narrow at some points along the north and west coast. Lowland areas include the Vale of Glamorgan in the south, and Anglesey. The central uplands are broken by rivers flowing in all directions through deep valleys. As Wales is a small country, the rivers that do not extend beyond its boundaries are rather short. They include the Clwyd, Conway, Mawddach, Dyfi (or Dovey), Ystwyth, Teifi, and Taff.

In the northwest the River Dee flows through Cheshire to the sea, and its broad mouth divides part of Clwyd from England. The mouth of the River Severn cuts off Gwent and South Glamorgan from the English counties of Gloucestershire, Avon, and Somerset. The Wye flows through England for part of its course, while the Usk reaches the sea in Gwent.

Like the rest of the western British Isles, Wales has a mild, damp climate. The high regions are slightly cooler than the lowlands and have a heavy rainfall, particularly in the mountains. This rainfall is, however, very useful, not only to Wales but to England as well. Large cities such as Liverpool and Birmingham, which need a great deal of water for their huge populations, get most of it from reservoirs at Vrynwy and the Elan Valley. There are large hydroelectric power stations in north and west Wales and nuclear power stations in Gwynedd. In south Wales there is an important coalfield.

In early times much of Wales was wooded, but the great forests have been cleared away. However, much of the upland area, where farming is difficult, and has been replanted with trees.

Atlantic seals breed on Ramsey Island off Dyfed and on small islands off the coast of Gwynedd. On Grassholm Island, not far away, is a great colony of gannets. Rare species including the chough, kite, polecat, and pine marten are also found. Rare alpine plants grow in Snowdonia.

People and Culture

The Welsh are a Celtic people, which means that they are descendants of the ancient inhabitants of Britain. (See CELTS.)

Welsh, the native language of Wales, closely resembles Breton, another Celtic language spoken in Brittany in France, and Cornish, which died out as a regular spoken language in Cornwall in the 18th Century. Welsh was spoken by nearly all the inhabitants of Wales until late in the 18th century, and it remained the language of the ordinary people for about another 100 years. As industry spread in Wales, mainly from the east, many English, Scots, and Irish workers moved in, and as a result Welsh gave way to English in many industrial areas. The coming of radio, films, and television all helped to increase the amount of English spoken in Wales.

About a quarter of the population of Wales is able to speak Welsh. One per cent of the population speak Welsh only. Most of the Welsh-speaking people live in the north and southwest. Today, much effort is given to preserving Welsh language and culture. There are Welsh language programmes on radio and television.

Literature in Welsh dates from the 6th century. The earliest literature was written in verse, by a number of poets, chief of whom were Aneirin and Taliesin. Their poetry captures the heroism of the Welsh chieftains. This tradition of epic poems, as well as prose, continued with the famous collection of epic tales, the *Mabinogion*, in the late 11th century.

Welsh was saved from possible extinction as a language by the translation of the Bible in 1588 by Bishop William Morgan. After this many Welsh writers echoed the majestic prose of the Welsh Bible. This was particularly so during the Methodist revival in the 18th century when the Methodist Church become established in Wales. The hymns of William Williams (1731–91) are the finest examples of this revival.

Literature by Welsh writers, but written in English, is known as "Anglo-Welsh". The finest writer in this tradition is the poet Dylan Thomas (on whom there is a separate article).

The traditional culture of Wales is a spoken one in which poetry, prose, and singing play a great part. The Welsh tradition of choral singing is world famous. The special festivals of Wales, known as eisteddfodau (pronounced "eye-steth-VOD-eye"), encourage the Welsh music and literature. The greatest of these is the Royal National Eisteddfod of Wales, which is entirely in Welsh. (See EISTEDDFOD.)

Most schools in Wales teach Welsh as a subject and many use the language for other teaching too. Certain colleges train teachers in Welsh. The University of Wales has colleges at Aberystwyth, Cardiff, Bangor, Swansea, and at Lampeter.

The British government has a Secretary of State for Wales with special responsibility for Welsh affairs but many Welsh people wish to regard Wales as a separate country, rather than as a part of England.

British Tourist Authority

The Rhondda Valley is a mining area in the county of Mid Glamorgan, South Wales.

Towns and Occupations

Nearly two-thirds of the population live in the south, working in industries based on the south Wales coalfield. The population is much more scattered in the hills and valleys of the north.

Celtic Picture Agency

The Norman castle in Cardiff's city centre was built by Robert FitzHamon on the site of a Roman fort.

The largest cities of Wales are Cardiff (South Glamorgan), Swansea (West Glamorgan), and Newport (Gwent). The Rhondda Valley (Mid Glamorgan) is traditionally a coal-mining area. Swansea is a seaport on the Bristol Channel and an industrial centre. Cardiff, the capital of Wales, has a separate article.

Farming and forestry are the most important occupations in the rural areas of Wales. The farms on the upland regions are small and their owners keep cattle and sheep.

Celtic Picture Agency

A sheep "mart" in Aberystwyth, West Wales. Sheep are the main source of income for Welsh hill farmers.

The slate industry of north Wales employed thousands of men in the 19th century, in some of the largest slate quarries in the world. The industry began to decline in the early 20th century but is returning to prominence both as a commercial operation and as a tourist attraction.

The south Wales coalfield was first developed in the 19th century, and until World War I it was one of the main coal-producing areas in the world. After World War I there was less demand for Welsh coal, one reason being the increased use by other countries of their own coal. During the 1930s there was widespread unemployment and much misery in south Wales.

Today the main Welsh contributions to Britain are steel, tinplate, and coal (particularly anthracite coal). Steel and tinplate are produced in the south Wales coalfield area, and other industries have been introduced. These have included a range of occupations from motor-vehicle production to electronics. Further west the fine natural harbour of Milford Haven in Dyfed has one of the major oil refineries and tanker anchorages in western Europe. The opening of the Severn Bridge linking southeast Wales with the Bristol area has lead to greater economic activity in the region.

In the northeast of Wales is the coalfield of Clwyd. This, although much smaller than that of south Wales, contains many industries besides coal-mining. These include steel, bricks, chemicals, paper, and textiles.

The tourist industry in Wales is one of the most economically significant activities in the United Kingdom. Round the coasts are many flourishing resorts. Snowdonia is popular for camping, walking, and climbing holidays. Pony-trekking is popular in mid-Wales. International and club Rugby matches attract many people during the winter months.

History

When the Romans came to Britain in the 1st century AD the people of what is now England and Wales were Brythonic Celts, and the

Brythonic version of the Celtic language later became Welsh. The Brythons were by no means confined to England and Wales; from an early date a Brythonic tribe called the Votadini held territory in Strathclyde, southwestern Scotland. In spite of much resistance from the Britons of Wales, the Romans occupied the country before the end of the 1st century, building fortresses at Chester and Caerleon in Gwent, and Caernarfon in the northwest, and Carmarthen in the southwest.

Even before the Romans left Britain, Goidelic Celts from Ireland had begun to attack the shores of Wales and to settle there. Legend says that a prince called Cunedda went to Wales from Scotland and drove the Irish from North Wales. This area was later called Gwynedd in his honour. The Anglo-Saxons attacked Wales at the end of the 5th century. In face of this new enemy, the Brythons and Goidels joined together under the name *Cymry*. It was the Saxons who called them Welsh, which means "foreigners".

During the 6th century a number of monks, whom the Welsh called saints, set up their cells (homes) and churches in Wales, some of which became monasteries of the Celtic Church. The Welsh had by now been converted to Christianity, partly as a result of Roman influence and partly because of Wales's links with the Celts of Gaul (France) who were Christian.

Wales became divided into several kingdoms, the main ones being Gwynedd (north Wales), Powys (mid-Wales), Dyfed (southwest Wales), and Morgannwg and Gwent (southeast Wales). Although these kingdoms had some strong rulers, the good effects of their reigns did not last because when they died their lands had to be shared among all their sons, and it was impossible to build up a strong and lasting kingdom to oppose invaders. Under Offa, King of Mercia (757–96), the Saxons were able to fix a boundary between England and Wales and to build a great embankment along it called Offa's Dyke. Parts of this remain today.

Over the next three centuries, Wales was united by such figures as Rhodri Mawr and Hywell Dda, but the unity was only temporary. The threat of the Saxons was always the unifying factor.

After the Normans had conquered England in 1066, they attacked Wales and took some of the best lands, building castles to hold down their conquests. The Welsh princes, however, put up a stout resistance against the invaders. Under Llywelyn ap Iorwerth, sometimes called Llywelyn the Great, Gwynedd became the most powerful principality in Wales and Llywelyn ap Gruffudd, his grandson, was recognized by King Henry III of England as Prince of Wales. It was this Llywelyn who led the Welsh in their last struggles against the English king Edward I. In 1277, Llywelyn was defeated, but five years later he rebelled again and was killed in a skirmish near Builth.

The conquering Edward took Llywelyn's lands and made them into the shires (counties) of Anglesey, Caernarfon, and Merioneth (now Gwynedd), while other lands which Edward held in Wales became Flintshire, Cardiganshire, and Carmarthenshire, all of which were then ruled by the king's officials. Edward ended the line of Welsh princes by beheading Llywelyn's brother Dafydd, and built castles and towns in Wales. These, which include Caernarfon and Harlech, can still be seen today.

At Caernarfon Castle in 1284 Edward's son, who later became Edward II, was born. In 1301 he was made the first English Prince of Wales (see also WALES, PRINCE OF). The rest of Wales was held for the king by various powerful barons who were known as Marcher lords, and were descended from the early Norman castle builders who had set up lordships in the Marches (borderlands) and extended them into Wales. After Edward I's conquest, the Marcher lords shared the administration of Wales with leading Welshmen who had links with the earlier Welsh princes. Occasional quarrels arose between them and in 1400 one of these developed into a full national rising under Owain Glyn Dwr, generally called in English Owen Glendower. Until 1405 it looked as though Glendower's rising might succeed, but the English managed to put it down. (See GLENDOWER, OWEN.)

In order to try to prevent another rising from breaking out, the English parliament passed a number of laws which forbade, among other things, any Welshman to carry arms or to own land in England or in the English towns in Wales. Under King Henry VIII, this situation was reversed, and Welsh people were put on the same footing as the English by the Acts of Union of England and Wales, passed in 1536 and 1542. Through this legislation, Wales became "part of England" and the Marcher Lordships were formed into the seven new shires of Denbigh, Montgomery, Radnor, Brecon, Glamorgan, Pembroke, and Monmouth. There were Welsh members of parliament and the laws of England were applied to Wales. English became the official language of Wales.

WALES, PRINCE OF. The title "Prince of Wales" can be given only to the eldest son of a British sovereign. He is the heir apparent, that is, the person who will succeed to the throne. Prince Charles received the title in 1958, when he was nearly ten. He was the 21st prince of Wales since Edward I gave the title to his own son.

Edward did this because in 1282 he finally conquered Llywelyn, prince of Wales, and took his lands. In order to please the Welsh and also to have an English ruler over the conquered lands, he made his son Edward prince of Wales in 1301. Edward had been born at Caernarfon Castle in Wales in 1284, so the story is not true that Edward presented his son to the Welsh as a baby, telling them that they now had a prince who could speak no English.

Popperfoto

The Prince and Princess of Wales visiting the Brixton Enterprise Centre, London.

Most, although not all, of the eldest sons of British sovereigns have been given the title of prince of Wales since Edward I's day. When a sovereign reigns for a long time, the same person may hold the title for many years. Both George IV (the son of George III) and Edward VII (the son of Queen Victoria) were prince of Wales for nearly 60 years. When, however, the sovereign has no son, there is no prince of Wales at all. There was not one between 1509 and 1610, nor between 1936 and 1958.

The title of prince of Wales is given by the sovereign. The prince is invested with it at a special ceremony at Caernarfon Castle. The investiture of Prince Charles in 1969 was the first since 1911. When he becomes king the title ceases to exist until he proclaims his own eldest son prince of Wales. But the heir apparent immediately receives the title of earl of Chester. There are several other titles which the eldest son of the sovereign inherits straight away, as soon as he becomes heir apparent. These are duke of Cornwall, duke of Rothesay, earl of Carrick, baron of Renfrew, Lord of the Isles, and prince and great steward of Scotland.

The heir-apparent, whether or not he is made prince of Wales, has a special badge consisting of a crown of fleur-de-lys and crosses encircling three ostrich plumes. Below are the German words *Ich dien*—"I serve". Edward, the Black Prince, was given this name because he sometimes wore the three ostrich feathers on a black surcoat (see HERALDRY). There is no truth in the story that he took them from the blind king of Bohemia who was killed at the Battle of Crécy, since the badge had already been used for some years by the English kings.

The prince of Wales's coronet is similar in design to the royal crown but has only one arch.

WALLABY. Many small members of the kangaroo family of marsupials, or pouched animals, are known as wallabies. The name comes from a word in the language of the Australian aboriginals. Wallabies live on the mainland of Australia, in Tasmania, and in the island of New Guinea and other neighbouring islands.

It is rather difficult to say just where the kangaroos end and the wallabies begin. They belong to one big group and are sometimes divided into kangaroos, large wallabies, and small wallabies. They have strong back legs, much smaller front legs, and move along by jumping. The largest wallabies are about 90 centimetres (35 inches) long from the nose to the base of the tail, and their tails are about 60 centimetres (24 inches) long. The smallest wallabies are less than 60 centimetres (2 feet) tall.

Barnaby's Picture Library

Bennett's wallaby lives in Tasmania. Wallabies enjoy eating the bark of trees.

Wallabies are mostly found in scrub country, where they can find shelter from their enemies among the low bushes. These enemies include the dingo (the Australian wild dog) and the enormous wedge-tailed eagle. All wallabies live only on plant food, such as grass, leaves, fruits, and the bark of trees.

Many wallabies have been killed for their fur, particularly the black or swamp wallaby (*Wallabia bicolor*). One that used to be more common than it is now is the red-necked wallaby (*Macropus rufogriseus*) of the dry forest country of eastern Australia.

A rather distinct group of wallabies, known as the rock wallabies, is found only in Australia itself. These animals have attractively coloured fur, and a tail that is thin at its base. Rock wallabies thump their feet on the ground when they are alarmed. They live in very rocky country and make remarkably nimble leaps over this rough ground. Another group is the hare wallabies, so named from their speed and habit of dodging when chased, and also for their long ears and thin legs. There are also three species of pademelons, small, stocky wallabies with short hind limbs and pointed noses. A similar-looking animal is the short-tailed scrub wallaby or quokka (*Setonix brachyurus*) that lives only on two offshore islands of Western Australia.

WALLACE, Alfred Russel (1823–1913). This English naturalist developed a theory of evolution independently of Charles Darwin (see EVOLUTION; DARWIN, CHARLES).

Wallace developed his interest in natural history as a boy, while catching lampreys (eel-like fish) on the banks of the River Usk in Wales. At the age of 25 he became a professional naturalist, travelling the world to observe nature and collect specimens for museums.

Wallace had become friendly with another famous naturalist, Henry Walter Bates. In 1848 they set off together on a journey to

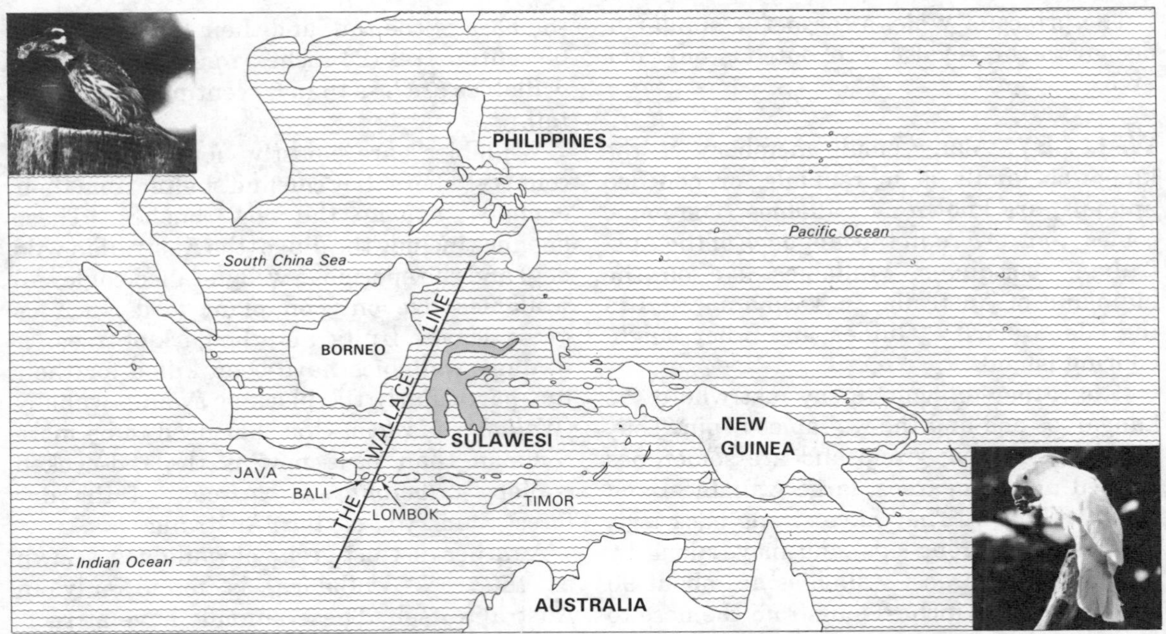

NHPA/E. Hanumantha Rao (top left); NHPA/ANT (bottom right)

Alfred Russel Wallace found a striking contrast between the animal life of the island of Bali and that of neighbouring Lombok. The strait between the islands and the line continuing northwards, known as Wallace's Line, separates Oriental animals such as the barbet (top left) from Australian animals such as the cockatoo (bottom right).

South America and travelled 1,600 kilometres (1,000 miles) up the Amazon River. Wallace was overwhelmed by the beauty and variety of nature in the tropics. After four years he left Bates and travelled home, unfortunately losing most of his specimens when his ship caught fire. Undaunted, he set off again in 1854 on an eight-year trip to Southeast Asia.

Wallace suffered bouts of fever as he worked in the tropical forests. During one of these in Ternate, Indonesia, as he tossed and turned, the idea of natural selection suddenly came into his mind. "Then at once I saw, that the ever present variability of all living things would furnish the material from which, by the mere weeding out of those less adapted to the actual conditions, the fittest alone would continue the race . . . There suddenly flashed upon me the idea of the survival of the fittest."

Wallace knew that Darwin, back in England, was working on a similar idea, so he hurriedly wrote him a letter. Darwin was astonished, when the letter arrived, to see that Wallace had almost exactly the same ideas as himself. The two wrote a scientific paper together, and presented it to the Linnean Society in England in 1858. Darwin went on to write his world-shattering *On the Origin of Species*, and Wallace was content to let him take the limelight.

Wallace also wrote books on the distribution of animal species (zoogeography). He noticed the sudden change in animal species when travelling west to east through the islands of Malaysia and Indonesia. In zoogeography today this distinction is known as Wallace's Line.

WALLACE, Sir William (*c*.1270–1305), is Scotland's national hero, for it was he who began his country's long struggle for independence from England. There are so many legends about him that it is difficult to separate what actually happened from what was made up later by poets and story-tellers.

Wallace was a knight's son and was probably born in Renfrewshire, where his father had an estate. However, the date of his birth is not known, nor is anything known about his life as a young man. He first appears in history early in 1297, a few months after Edward I had deposed the king of Scots, John Balliol, and stationed English soldiers in Scotland. With a few supporters Wallace attacked Lanark and killed the English sheriff there. He then gathered more men and marched to Scone in Perthshire.

Other risings broke out in different parts of Scotland, and King Edward sent the earl of Surrey with an army to put them down. Surrey overtook a Scottish army at Irvine in Ayrshire and forced it to surrender. Wallace and his men did not yield, however, and laid siege to the castle of Dundee. When Surrey marched north to Stirling, Wallace and another young general, Andrew de Moray, met him with their combined forces. On 11 September 1297, having waited until half the English army had crossed a narrow bridge over the River Forth, the Scots attacked and destroyed it. Surrey and the rest fled, but Andrew de Moray was wounded and died soon afterwards.

This, the Battle of Stirling Bridge, led to the recovery of Scotland for a short time. The English garrisons were driven out and Wallace with his army crossed the border, besieged Carlisle, and laid waste the country as far as Newcastle. After returning to Scotland, Wallace was knighted and became known as Guardian of the Kingdom.

In the summer of 1298, King Edward marched north with a large army to reconquer Scotland. Wallace retreated slowly past Edinburgh and Linlithgow, laying waste the country as he went, so that the English were half-starved when at last he turned to fight them on 22 July. But King Edward had archers, and the English longbow, then a new weapon in war, broke the ranks of Wallace's spearmen. The Scots were completely defeated with great slaughter.

Wallace escaped but he no longer had the same influence in Scotland, although the resistance he had begun continued. On 5 August 1305 he was captured near Glasgow and taken to London, where he was condemned to death in Westminster Hall without trial and was executed on 23 August.

The memory of Wallace's deeds became an inspiration to the Scots. Even Robert Bruce, who was crowned king seven months after Wallace's death, was not considered a greater hero (see BRUCE, ROBERT).

WALLFLOWER. There are several species of wallflower, sweet-smelling plants of the mustard family. The cultivated wallflower is the European plant (*Cheiranthus cheiri*) that blooms in May, earlier than most garden flowers. The plants are about 30 centimetres (12 inches) high and the stems bear many flowers, each of which has its own little stalk. Wallflowers have richly scented blossoms of bronze, purplish, red or golden yellow, and the

ARDEA

The European wallflower grows wild on cliffs. Seeds from cultivated plants often sprout from garden walls.

leaves are long, strap-shaped and rather tough. The stems are often woody and generally have several branches.

Wallflowers are usually grown as biennials, which means that they bloom in their second year. They prefer a cool climate and they grow easily on any well-drained soil.

The western wallflower (*Erysimum asperum*) is a perennial plant of western North America. It grows to 90 centimetres (3 feet) high, with fragrant yellow flowers. It is found in a range of poor-soil habitats, from sand dune and prairie to open ponderosa parkland in the Rocky Mountains.

WALLPAPER. At various times in history the walls of houses have been decorated with paintings, plaster-work, wood panelling, tapestry hangings, and also paper. In England the oldest wallpaper known was discovered on a ceiling in Christ's College, Cambridge, and it had been made in the early part of the 16th century. In those days paper was very precious, and so the maker of this wallpaper, who was a printer, did not use new paper. Instead he decorated the back of a printed proclamation issued by King Henry VIII. He printed the design in the same kind of black ink as he used for his other jobs, because making wallpaper was then a side-line of the printers' trade. The pattern was a copy of the kind of pattern used on the lengths of velvet which were hung on the walls of rich people's houses. In fact, wallpaper was at first just a cheaper substitute for hangings made of fabric, sometimes it was actually called "paper tapestry".

Since those days, however, there have been many changes in the way wallpaper is made and designed, and now it is one of the most popular ways of decorating the walls of rooms. One change has been in the making of paper itself. (See PAPER AND PAPER MAKING.) When paper was made by hand it could only be produced in fairly small sheets which were then pasted together to form "pieces" or rolls of wallpaper. At the beginning of the 19th century, however, a machine was invented to produce paper in long continuous sheets, and

Above left: Hand-painted Chinese wallpaper depicting beautiful Oriental landscapes. **Above right**: The use of flocked paper dates from the early 18th century.

Above: The use of wallpaper spread from England to America. In the early 20th century, paper friezes became popular. **Right**: Figured paper used in a colonial tavern. **Below**: A chrysanthemum wallpaper pattern designed by 19th-century English artist William Morris.

Temple Newsom House, Leeds/The Wallpaper Manufacturers Ltd. (top left and right); Lexington Historical Society, Inc. Lexington, Mass./The Wallpaper Manufacturers Ltd. (above and right); Courtesy, Arthur Sanderson and Sons Ltd. (below).

since then wallpaper has been made in continuous sheets too.

Patterns and designs have also altered. When wallpaper was still a new idea, the patterns continued to be made in imitation of the patterns on fabrics, such as damask or embroidery. Later, people could buy paper that looked like wood panelling or marble. Towards the end of the 17th century, wallpapers were brought to Europe from China, and the designs on them were hand-painted and different on each piece. People who had a room decorated with a Chinese paper at that time never had exactly the same pattern all round the room, whereas nowadays patterns are "repeated" at regular distances on nearly all wallpapers.

In the 18th century, new designs became fashionable, including flower patterns and stripes, papers that looked like satin or velvet, and others with the design embossed on them, that is, raised up on the surface of the paper so that you can feel it if you run your finger over it. In France there were papers decorated with beautifully drawn countryside scenes. Today there are all these kinds of designs and many more, made in a great variety of colours on easily-hung papers and vinyl materials. There are designs specially suitable for kitchens and bathrooms on paper coated so that it is washable and cannot be spoilt by steam.

Wallpaper-Printing

As wallpaper became popular, it began to be made by craftsmen who specialized in wallpaper and not simply by ordinary printers. At first the printing was done by hand, but from the 18th century onwards machines were invented which could print much more quickly. Hand-printing is still used today for the more expensive wallpapers, even though most are made by machine.

One way of printing by hand is called *block printing*, in which the design is cut on a block which is then wetted with colour and pressed on to the paper. The method of making the velvety-looking papers is called *flocking*. The pattern is printed on in gum instead of paint, and then shavings of wool are sprayed on so that they stick to the gum. Patterns on borders are sometimes made by the method called stencilling, and for larger patterns a special kind of stencilling called *screen printing* is used.

The most usual methods of machine printing are *roller printing* and *embossing*. For roller printing the paper passes under rollers with paint on them, and the colours are transferred to the paper as it runs through. Rollers are also used for embossing. The paper passes between two rollers, one with the pattern rolled on it, the other with the pattern in hollows; as the two rollers press the paper between them they stamp the pattern into it.

Another machine you would see in a wallpaper factory is the one for *grounding*. All wallpaper is given a first coat or ground of paint to prevent it becoming yellow as it gets older. The paper is drawn along under a set of moving brushes that put on the paint and smooth it out.

WALNUT.

There are about 20 species of walnut. The one that is most often grown commercially for its nuts is the English walnut (*Juglans regia*), native to western Asia. It is said that it was brought to Britain by the Romans, who called it the nut of Jupiter, the chief of their gods. It was not cultivated much until the 16th and 17th centuries.

Walnut trees do best in a fairly warm climate and a deep, dry soil. Often they grow 30 metres (100 feet) tall. The bark is thick, grey, and deeply furrowed; the buds black and covered with short, fine hair; and the leaves are made up of oval leaflets. The male flowers

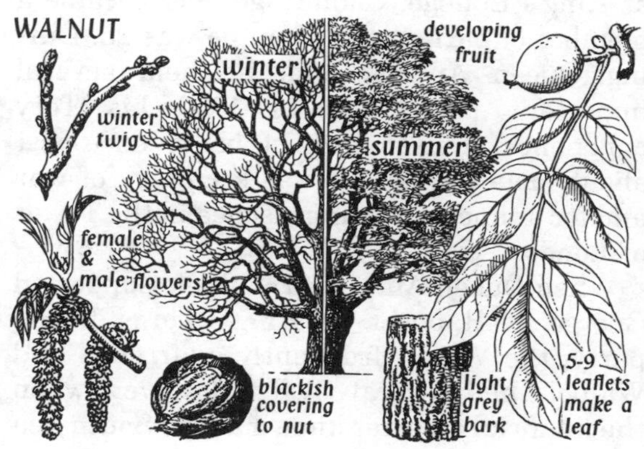

are thick green catkins and the female flowers are small and rounded. They develop at the end of the shoots. The nuts are not true nuts but what botanists call drupes. A skin covers the oval, brittle shell, inside which is the white nut, covered with a papery brown skin. Walnuts are picked green for pickling. Walnut oil, especially popular in France, is used as a salad dressing, and for cooking.

Walnuts are grown on a large scale in California, France, Italy, China, and Turkey.

Two North American species, the black walnut (*Juglans nigra*) and the butternut (*Juglans cinerea*), have edible nuts. The black walnut is also grown for its valuable timber, as an ornamental tree, and for a dye found in the fruit husks.

The wood of walnut trees is finely grained and polishes well. It does not warp (shrink or swell) when made into furniture and it resists insects, although beetles and larvae (grubs) may attack a growing tree.

In country regions of Italy the walnut is known as the witches' tree under which nobody should sleep. The Greeks dedicated the tree to Artemis, goddess of the moon, and the Romans to Jupiter. King Solomon is said to have grown walnut trees.

The hickory and pecan are American trees related to the walnut that also produce edible nuts (see HICKORY; PECAN).

WALPOLE, Robert (1676–1745). Sir Robert Walpole, who is generally regarded as Britain's first prime minister, was the son of a Norfolk squire. He was educated at Eton and at King's College, Cambridge, and became a member of parliament when he was 25. During Queen Anne's reign he held several important posts, but in 1712 his Tory opponents accused him of being dishonest about money when he was secretary of war and for a time he was imprisoned in the Tower of London.

When Queen Anne died Walpole supported George of Hanover as King George I. His party, the Whigs, frequently quarrelled and Walpole had several rivals. However, when the financial disaster known as the South Sea Bubble occurred, it was Walpole who was called on to settle the disturbance. He became chancellor of the Exchequer and first lord of the Treasury in 1721.

BBC Hulton Picture Library

Sir Robert Walpole maintained his position of leadership in England for 21 years, from 1721–42.

George II succeeded his father in 1727 and Walpole at first remained powerful. He was an extremely skilful politician, the first to realize that the British government must work by means of the House of Commons. Various troubles, however, made him less popular, and in 1737 Queen Caroline, George's wife and Walpole's friend and ally, died.

Frederick, prince of Wales, was Walpole's enemy and the Tories were angry with Walpole because of his attempts to keep the peace. To quieten them, in 1739 he declared war against Spain, which was quarrelling with England over America, but his popularity continued to decline and in 1742, two days after he had been made earl of Orford, he was finally defeated. He retired to Houghton Hall in Norfolk. He died in London in 1745 and was buried at Houghton.

WALRUS. Seals, sea-lions, and walruses are sea-living mammals closely related to each other. While seals and sea-lions are easily confused, the walrus can easily be distinguished, for it is the only member of the group with

Above: A thick fringe of sensory bristles helps a walrus to locate its shellfish food. **Right**: Walruses are sociable animals and live in large herds.

Russ Kinne/Photo Researchers Inc./Karl W. Kenyon/National Audubon Society

tusks. These, which may be as much as 60 centimetres (24 inches) long, are the upper canine teeth which grow down below a mass of bristly whiskers resembling a heavy moustache.

Walruses live only in the Arctic, being found in herds of varying size, usually close inshore or on ice floes. They are heavily built animals, weighing up to 1,300 kilograms (2,860 pounds) and measuring more than 3 metres (almost 10 feet) in length. The head of a walrus is rounded, without visible ears, and seems too small for the great thick neck and huge wrinkled body which becomes almost hairless in old age. The hind flippers are separated and on land the walrus can therefore waddle about awkwardly. In water, however, the great beast moves gracefully and swiftly.

The walrus feeds mostly on molluscs (shellfish) and crustaceans which are dug or scraped from the muddy sea bottom with its tusks. Walruses breed between April and June and during the fortnight or so that they are ashore they neither eat nor drink. Only one baby is born at a time and the mother looks after it by herself, perhaps for up to two years.

Eskimos hunt walruses for their meat and thick layer of fat, or blubber, that provides both food and fuel. The bones and skin are also used, and the ivory from the tusks is especially valued.

See also SEAL.

WALTON, Izaak (1593–1683), was an English writer noted as the author of *Lives*, a collection of biographies, and the *Compleat Angler* (1653), a book on fishing.

Walton was born at Stafford, the son of an alehouse keeper. As a young man he moved to London and became an ironmonger. His first wife died in 1640 after bearing seven children, all of whom died young. He married again and had two children, who survived.

Throughout his life Walton had many friends who were writers and men of learning. One was the poet John Donne, then the vicar of a local church, with whom he often went fishing. His first *Life* was of Donne (see DONNE, JOHN). Others were written on Sir Henry Wotton, George Herbert, Richard Hooker, and Dr Robert Sanderson.

The *Compleat Angler* was so popular during Walton's lifetime that five editions of it were published. Not only does it describe the art of angling, but it also gives a picture of the peace and simple pleasures of country life. When it first appeared Walton did not claim authorship and in recent times a similar book was discovered called *The Arte of Angling*, written in 1577, on which Walton's book is thought to have been based.

WALTON, Sir William (1902–83). The English composer Sir William Turner Walton was born in Oldham, Lancashire. Both his parents were professionally involved with singing, his father being a choirmaster and voice teacher and his mother being a vocalist. Walton sang in his father's choir as a boy, learned the piano and violin, and taught himself to compose. He studied at Oxford but failed to get a degree.

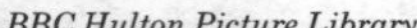

BBC Hulton Picture Library

The composer Sir William Walton, photographed in 1971, is best known for his orchestral music.

During the 1920s Walton spent most of his time in the company of the Sitwell family, whom he had got to know at Oxford. He made his reputation as a composer with such works as *Façade* (1923), a light piece for chamber ensemble written to accompany a poetry reading by Edith Sitwell; the *Sinfonia Concertante* for piano and orchestra (1928); and the overture *Portsmouth Point* (1926). These works were brash, jazz-influenced pieces of little emotional substance. His beautiful viola concerto of 1929, however, marked a deeper level of musical composition and the beginning of his maturity. During the 1930s and 1940s Walton composed several film scores, notably for the Shakespeare films of Laurence Olivier, *Henry V* and *Richard III*. After World War II he went to live on the island of Ischia, in the Bay of Naples, Italy, where he died after a long fight against lung cancer.

Walton's finest works include the oratorio *Belshazzar's Feast* (1931); the operas *Troilus and Cressida* (1954), and *The Bear* (1967); a beautiful violin concerto; and two symphonies.

WAR AND WARFARE. Warfare has changed over the centuries as weapons have become more devastating. The battles fought in ancient times were as different from present-day warfare as the spear is different from a modern guided missile.

The most important landmark in the history of warfare is the introduction of gunpowder and firearms in the 14th century. They revolutionized the conduct of battles, which were thereafter often fought at long range. Previously, armies had to get close to each other, within bowshot range. Most wars have been won by the nations with the most highly developed weapons. The Germans might have won World War II if they had developed their rocket weapons earlier. Japan was compelled to make a quick surrender when the United States was the first to develop an atomic bomb.

Types of Weapon

There are three main types of weapon. The first, and earliest, are those used by hand for stabbing, clubbing, cutting, or thrusting. Examples of such weapons are the spear, the lance, and the sword. Next there are shooting weapons, which fling some object designed to cause damage at the end of its flight. The object itself is called a missile. The bow and arrow and the catapult are early examples of shooting weapons. Thousands more were developed after the introduction of gunpowder. All guns, from the musket and cannon through the rifle and machine-gun, as well as modern bombs, torpedoes, and guided missiles, are examples of shooting weapons. Lastly there are the weapons of the booby-trap type which are designed to be set off by an enemy. An ancient weapon of this type was the pit with sharpened stakes driven into its floor and concealed by a flimsy roof spread with soil. A typical modern weapon of the trap kind is the mine.

There are articles on the main weapons, including BOMB; BOW AND ARROW; CATAPULT; GUIDED WEAPONS; GUN; MINE; SWORD; TORPEDO. Developments in warfare at sea are described in NAVAL BATTLES.

Michael Holford

The Assyrians developed the use of cavalry. Here King Ashurbanipal goes into battle in the 7th century BC.

Warfare in the Ancient World

The first historical accounts of organized warfare come from Egypt. In ancient Egypt soldiers belonged to a special caste, or social group. At first the Egyptians fought only on foot. Their weapons included a rather ineffective infantry bronze sword, a bronze-tipped spear, and a wooden shield large enough to protect the whole body. Later the shield was covered with metal. The light infantry (slingers and archers) had no shields and no armour.

Against the early Egyptians the Assyrians pitted heavy infantry and cavalry. The Assyrians used two types of chariot: a light chariot for two horses and two men, and a heavy chariot for three horses and up to four men. They also introduced the idea of archers riding

Michael Holford

A wall carving from the tomb of Queen Hatshepsut in Thebes depicts soldiers carrying spears and shields.

on horseback and the extensive use of body armour. Assyrian infantrymen carried a short spear and a round shield, but no sword. They wore a bronze helmet. Assyrian archers were equipped with helmet, body armour, and a long wicker shield.

Later, the Egyptians too made extensive use of chariots. They learned this method of fighting from the Hyksos, a people who dominated Egypt from about 1700 BC.

In these very early times battles were rather haphazard affairs. When an army was ready to fight it drew up on a broad front on some flat, open plain. If the enemy desired battle it drew up also. Otherwise it stayed away. No effort was made by either side to choose a favourable position or to force a fight on an unwilling opponent. No reserve troops stood by.

The Warriors of Greece

During the Golden Age of Greece (500–300 BC) practically all able-bodied men were warriors at some time or another because the Greek city-states continually warred with each other. The fiercest war was the Peloponnesian War (see PELOPONNESIAN WAR) which broke the power of Athens. Of all the city states Sparta put the most emphasis on military preparedness. Every boy was trained for fighting from the age of seven. At 20 he became a fully fledged soldier, remaining in active service until he was no longer physically fit. Slaves called helots did all the ordinary labour.

In Athens all able-bodied men between the ages of 16 and 60 were liable for military service. Other Greek cities had similar laws.

Until the 5th century BC the horse was rarely seen in Greek armies. Then cavalry was introduced and became widely used. But saddles and stirrups had not been invented. Greek foot soldiers were of two classes, the *hoplites*, or heavy infantry, and the *psiloi*, or light infantry. The hoplites, drawn from the upper classes, wore body armour (helmets, breastplates, and greaves or leg armour) and carried shields. The psiloi had no body armour and carried bows or slings. Greek tactics varied, but in general the hoplites massed for battle in a formation which was called a *phalanx*, with the psiloi on their front and flanks. During the 4th century BC the phalanx reached its greatest perfection under King Philip II of Macedonia and his son Alexander the Great. Its smallest unit consisted of 16 hoplites. Sixteen such units in a solid square of 256 men made a *syntagma*, four syntagmas a *chiliarchia*, and four chiliarchias a phalanx of 4,096 officers and men. This total was increased by a certain number of attached troops: cavalry and light infantry. Alexander made great use of cavalry, especially on the wings of his forces.

The hoplite's principal weapon was a spear, the *sarissa*, 5 metres (17 feet) long. The first five ranks of the massed infantry levelled these in front of them, so that an enemy faced a wall of overlapping spear points. Rear ranks held their spears upright or resting on the shoulders of those in front.

The Roman Legions

The Romans developed an organization resembling the phalanx which they called a *legion*. In 197 BC they defeated the Macedonian phalanxes at the Battle of Cynoscephalae. This battle marked the end of the phalanx.

The Roman army under the Republic was made up of citizen-soldiers. Service in the army was considered a high honour and for the citizen to be deprived of it was a mark of shame. The infantry included five classes

Michael Holford

Citizen-soldiers of the Roman Republic, about 100 BC. The Roman army was first and foremost an infantry army, although it did use cavalry. The soldier's shield gave protection against swords, spears, and arrows.

ranged according to wealth. The cavalry and the highest class of the infantry were drawn from the richest citizens. Boys were called to service from the age of 17 upward, passing into the reserves at 47. During the wars with Carthage in the 3rd century BC heavy infantry of the legion consisted of three types: the *hastati* (first line), aged 25 to 30, the *principes* (second line), 30 to 40, and the *triarii* (third line), 40 to 50. Young men of 17 to 25 formed the light infantry (*velites*). The three lines of heavy infantry were subdivided for drill purposes into *maniples*, which consisted, in the first two lines, of 120 men, in the third, of 60.

The Roman legion drew up for battle in a much more flexible formation than the phalanx, relying for success on its swords and lances rather than on a mass of spear points. Its greater mobility finally overcame the phalanx. Roman cavalry was formed into *alae*, or wings, of 900 horsemen composed of ten *turmae* of 90 each, drawn up in three ranks. One maniple of each of the three lines of infantry, plus 120 velites and a turma of cavalry made a *cohort*, with a minimum of 450 men. Ten cohorts made a legion.

The chief Roman weapon was a sword, the *gladius*—straight, double-edged, and 50 centimetres (20 inches) long. Soldiers in the first two lines bore in addition a *pilum*, a short, heavy lance, and a *hasta*, or light lance. The third line carried, instead of the pilum, a spear 3 to 4.5 metres (10 to 15 feet) long and several darts. The arms of the velites included a javelin and seven darts. For armour, hastati and principes wore leather helmets reinforced with iron, leather and metal breastplates, and iron greaves on the legs. They carried large, curved, rectangular wooden shields, covered with leather and reinforced with iron.

The Middle Ages

The Roman empire collapsed under attacks from barbarian invaders. From the 7th century AD until near the end of the 13th century there existed throughout Europe what has become known as the feudal system (see FEUDALISM). Small groups of invading barbarians, strongly armed and equipped, estab-

Mansell Collection

At the battle of Agincourt in 1415 the use of the long bow gave the English the advantage.

lished themselves at strategic points, built powerful castles, and levied tribute from all the inhabitants in the area. The ordinary people were held in subjection as serfs. They were virtually slaves, subject to military service under their lord for 40 days each year. The knights, of high birth, served first as pages to the local lord from the age of seven and became squires at 14. They learned to use arms, becoming knights at about 21.

During the Middle Ages chain mail and, somewhat later, plate mail made up the armour worn by knights (see ARMOUR). Soldiers of lesser rank sometimes wore padded leather coats, but the serfs were unprotected and never mounted. The ordinary foot-soldier was no match for a mounted knight unless armed with a longbow. An arrow 1 metre (1 yard) long shot from such a bow would pierce most armour. As well as strength and skill, the archer needed courage to stand his ground until the charging horsemen were within easy range. Sometimes archers were placed behind rows of sharpened stakes to protect them.

The longbow helped the English to defeat the French at Crécy and Agincourt. This

King Gustavus Adolphus of Sweden attacked and took Frankfurt during the Thirty Years War.

Mary Evans Picture Library

development of an efficient missile weapon was of great significance. When men fight hand to hand with swords or spears the numbers actually using their weapons at any moment are likely to be roughly equal on both sides. If one side has more men than the other, it is difficult to use the extra men effectively. If, however, the fighters are armed with missile weapons, there is really no limit to the number of such weapons that can be aimed at the enemy. In such a case the side with more men has a probably overwhelming superiority in fighting strength.

The Introduction of Gunpowder and Firearms

Early in the 14th century the introduction of gunpowder quickly resulted in the development of much more deadly missile weapons. The principle of the firearm is the same as that of the blowpipe. A missile is blown out of a tube. The exploding gunpowder shot out the missile with enough force to pierce armour, and knock down stone walls. However, there were many difficulties to overcome before guns became really efficient.

One of the first problems was how to set light to the gunpowder while at the same time taking aim. Many devices were tried, the most common being the slow-burning match and the fuse. In both, a spark of flame travelled slowly along a length of material. The interval of several seconds from the time of lighting until the flame reached and exploded the gunpowder was used by the gunner to steady his weapon and take aim. Guns based on this principle were called matchlocks. The arquebus was a matchlock and was the first effective gun to be used as a hand gun, a personal weapon.

The trouble with these early guns was that the firer took so long to reload that he had to be protected while doing so. Therefore each infantry unit came to be composed of musketeers and pikemen (pikes are long spears). Nevertheless the introduction of gunpowder soon brought a new era of warfare. Castles were unable to withstand artillery bombardment, while the lead musket ball easily pierced the armour of the knights.

The new era in warfare may be said to date from the time of Gustavus Adolphus of Sweden (1594–1632). He understood and used the shock value of a cavalry charge. He also drew up his infantry in two lines with a third in reserve, and he established real field artillery. His infantry lines in battle formation were six ranks deep but opened out to form three only. The front line kneeled so that the rear two could fire over it.

Towards the end of the 17th century the matchlock began to be replaced by the faster-firing flintlock. The musketeer took aim and then pressed a trigger, which caused a spark from a flint to explode the gunpowder immediately. As the time taken to reload decreased, the musketeers' guard of pikemen became unnecessary. For protection at close quarters the musketeers were given short swords or daggers to fix to the end of their firearms. Thus developed the bayonet, which is now the only survivor of the thrusting spear.

Cavalry were at first armed with both swords and pistols, but this proved unsatisfactory because in order to aim their pistols they had to halt. They thus wasted all the dash and speed of their charge. In the English Civil War (1642–51) both sides taught their cavalry to charge with the sword alone. By the time of Frederick the Great of Prussia, who was crowned in 1740, the pike had been wholly replaced by the musket. He too forbade his cavalry to fire while mounted, and instructed mounted troops to use only swords. He increased the proportion of cavalry in his forces. At first he neglected artillery but later used it to crush the Austrians at Leuthen.

The 19th Century

The next military commander to make his mark in the history of warfare was Napoleon Bonaparte, who kept Europe in a turmoil from 1795 to 1815 (see NAPOLEONIC WARS). Napoleon's infantry adopted a new open order of fighting. It was based on lessons learned in the wars in America. There both the Indians and the white woodsmen fought from carefully chosen cover, slaughtering European troops

Mary Evans Picture Library

Napoleon Bonaparte developed fighting methods based on surprise and rapid manoeuvre.

Mary Evans Picture Library

Improved, faster weapons, such as breech-loading rifles, were first widely used in the American Civil War.

who attacked in mass formation and could see nothing at which to fire. Napoleon's infantry formed up in three ranks and his cavalry in two. He made extensive use of small columns in surprise manoeuvres and in assaults. These tactics proved effective against an enemy who was not experienced in them. The trouble was that Napoleon's tactics required well-trained, seasoned soldiers. Eventually he used up his reserves and had to use raw recruits in the old-fashioned mass formation and to increase considerably the proportion of artillery.

Many of the early difficulties with firearms were the result of ignorance about metals and unreliable methods of manufacture. The early artillery guns were particularly inefficient. Although they made a lot of noise they were very inaccurate, had a short range, and were liable to burst, doing more damage to the gunners than to the enemy.

With the development of steel and the use of machine tools it became possible to make strong and accurate firearms which could be depended on to give the same result each time they were used. Quick reloading was achieved by using a breech which opened and closed like a door at the rear of the gun instead of loading from the muzzle, or front end. Instead of firing solid iron cannon balls, guns fired hollow, pointed, cylinder-shaped shells, filled with explosive and containing a fuse. The fuse was designed to burst the shell when it hit the ground or target. To make the shell travel in a straight line the inside of the gun was shaped with twisted grooves called rifling. The rifling caused the shell to spin and thus to keep a steady flight. Rifling was also introduced into muskets and this caused them to be known as rifles.

Most of these improvements came in the second half of the 19th century. They increased the certainty of infantry fire and had a tremendous effect on war tactics. Opposing forces in battle could now be separated by long distances. An individual soldier with a rifled musket could hit targets several hundred metres distant. For the same reason artillery, formerly in the forefront of the battle lines, was now withdrawn to the rear.

During the American Civil War (1861–65) the metallic cartridge and the breech-loading rifle first saw wide military use. Guns capable of rapid fire caused far more destruction and casualties than ever before. Rifles that could be quickly reloaded were known as "magazine rifles". They were soon followed by revolvers, automatic pistols, and machine-guns, all of which reloaded themselves automatically after firing a shot. About 1884 Hiram Maxim invented the first successful entirely automatic machine-gun. Earlier partly mechanical machine-guns were used in the American Civil War and the Franco-Prussian War (1870–71).

During the second half of the 19th century gunpowder began to be replaced by more reliable and powerful explosives, such as ballistite and cordite for shooting the shells out of guns, and by much more damaging explosives for bursting the shells. It became possible to hurl projectiles to distances formerly undreamed of. An example is the 120-kilometre (75-mile) range of the "Paris Gun" used by the Germans in World War I. Rifles and machine-guns became effective over distances of 3,200 metres (3,500 yards) and more.

World War I

The results of the technical advances of the late 19th century began to appear in World War I (1914–18). Machine-guns, simplified and greatly improved, assumed a new and vital importance. Whichever side possessed them in greater numbers was usually victorious. At first neither side could make much impression on the other in open warfare. After some weeks a new type of fighting known as trench warfare developed. Opposing armies dug trenches along a front hundreds of kilometres in length. Massed artillery bombardment was followed by violent infantry attacks, most of them inconclusive and all resulting in appalling loss of life. Meanwhile new means of destruction were constantly appearing.

Aircraft began to play an important part for the first time in warfare. The earliest missiles dropped from aircraft were spikes and darts. It quickly became clear that far more damage could be done by dropping bombs filled with high explosive. These burst when they hit the

Acme

Left: A typical scene in Toul, France, during World War I as the US artillery rolled on its way to the front. **Right**: An Allied soldier stands guard in a long slit trench on the Somme River, France, a World War I battleground.

Imperial War Museum

World War I brought into use new weapons, explosives, and combat techniques developed in the late 19th and early 20th centuries.

ground and their flying fragments killed anyone near by. At first bombs were dropped only on military targets such as trenches, camps, gun positions, ammunition dumps, and railways. Later, civilian targets were also attacked. As aircraft became larger and more powerful they were able to carry heavier bombs. By the end of World War I, squadrons of bombers were able to cause considerable damage and kill many people in a single raid on a city. Aircraft were also valuable for carrying out reconnaissance missions such as scouting over enemy lines.

A new and particularly horrifying weapon was used by the Germans. Poisonous gases were released from rows of huge cylinders, to be carried by favourable winds into enemy trenches, or were fired in explosive shells. To protect soldiers against the effects, gas masks were hurriedly designed, manufactured, and rushed to the front. (See CHEMICAL WARFARE.)

A clumsy mechanical monster called the tank appeared. It was heavily armoured, moved on caterpillar tracks, and housed a crew which operated its armament of light cannon and machine-guns (see TANK). Soon a special type of small cannon, the anti-tank gun, was developed to combat it. Flame throwers, squirting burning oil through long tubes, were also introduced. (See WORLD WAR I.)

When the war ended in 1918, most nations reduced their armies and navies. But Germany went to work to invent and perfect new weapons for use in a war to come. Bigger and better tanks, weighing up to 70 tonnes (77 US tons) and armoured to withstand the shellfire of most guns, appeared. Aircraft were designed with speeds above 650 kilometres (400 miles) an hour. Whereas in the past aircraft had carried a single machine-gun, they now mounted six or eight and sometimes one or more small cannon in addition.

Self-sealing fuel tanks were installed in air-

The military techniques of World War II brought greater suffering to civilians than in previous wars. Here Russian women follow the battle trail of the German invasion, hoping to find their dead.

Dmitri Baltermanz, from the "Twelve Photographers" Exhibition including the Huntingdon Hartford Collection

craft, plugging holes automatically when hit by machine-gun bullets. Armour was added to protect pilot and crew. Bombsights were improved to a point where an aircraft could hit a target from a height of 6,000 metres (20,000 feet). Soldiers were equipped with parachutes and trained to jump in full equipment from aircraft in flight. They learned how to land behind enemy lines and carry out surprise attacks.

Large bodies of troops were moved from place to place and landed quickly in transport planes. When World War II broke out all these developments were ready to be exploited. Aircraft were destroyed from the air before they could get off the ground. Troop movements by railway were made impossible by the bombing of important rail centres.

An old rule of warfare forbade a deep penetration through hostile lines on a narrow front for fear the enemy might close the gap behind and bottle up the penetrating force. This rule was successfully broken by fast-moving columns of tanks, motorized artillery,

Paramount/UPI—Compix

Left: Hitler's invasion of Poland in 1939 introduced the blitzkrieg (lightning war)—a single, massive surprise attack. **Above**: A German infantry man, carrying a grenade, signals his comrades to advance.

and motor-drawn infantry. The machine rather than the man now seemed to rule the battlefield.

World War II Tactics

In World War II (1939–45) there was a complete revolution in battle tactics. The trench warfare characteristic of World War I practically disappeared in the face of modern developments. On the other hand, old-fashioned siege tactics were at times necessary, particularly in the German attack on Stalingrad (now Volgograd) in the Soviet Union. The battles of World War II demanded of the generals extreme flexibility and instant comprehension of what tactics would best suit the immediate need. Combined task forces moulded air, sea, and land forces into the mightiest military forces ever known.

Destruction by air came from aircraft such

Brown Brothers

The bombs developed by both sides in World War II were enormous. One could destroy a large building.

Courtesy, US Army AAF Photo

World War II paratroopers learned to jump in full equipment, ready for action the moment they landed.

as the US B-29, dropping incendiary (fire) and explosive bombs. V-2 rockets and V-1 flying bombs, launched by the Germans, caused damage and terror. Huge bombs were developed, whose blast alone was enough to cause the collapse of buildings. In heavy bombing raids on cities, any pretence that these weapons were aimed solely at the enemy armed forces was given up. It was hoped to destroy enemy factories making war material. But if those were missed, the bombs would probably destroy the homes of the factory workers. This policy, which was called strategic bombing, was followed by both sides.

Infantry, in new, highly mobile tactical formations, followed the spearhead attacks of tanks and armoured weapons to consolidate ground wrested from the enemy. Whole infantry divisions, with their full complement of arms and equipment, dropped from the skies by parachute to cut enemy supply lines in rear areas. On foot, the infantryman with his new semi-automatic rifle, his improved machine-guns, and his flame throwers was formidable.

His support came from field artillery with armament ranging from the highly mobile Bofors to the deadly "Long Tom" field pieces, mortars, and howitzers.

At sea there were equally important developments, particularly in the use of submarines and aircraft carriers. (See NAVY; SUBMARINE.) Sea power was used to support land attacks, as in the D-Day landings by Allied armies in France in June 1944. As ships' guns blasted enemy positions, landing vessels opened to disgorge men, tanks, and artillery on to the shore.

Courtesy, Signal Corps Photo

In World War II sea power was used to support land assaults. Here American troops attack the Philippines.

After the surrender of Germany, the United States launched the greatest destructive force yet known, the atom bomb, against Japan. The attacks on Hiroshima, destroyed by a single atom bomb on 6 August 1945, and Nagasaki, wrecked by another three days later, forced Japan's immediate surrender. (See WORLD WAR II.)

War in the Atomic Age

A far-reaching development of missile weapons had been achieved by the Germans during World War II. Their V-2 rocket was able to carry about 1 tonne (1 US ton) of high explosive over a distance of about 320 kilometres (200 miles). Although not very accurate, the V-2 rockets had more than twice the range of any gun. After the end of World War II all the leading countries hastened research to develop guided missiles which were driven by rockets or ram-jets and could be steered towards the target by radio. (See GUIDED WEAPONS; JET PROPULSION; ROCKET.)

The larger guided missiles, such as the ICBMs (inter-continental ballistic missiles), were designed to have a range of about 8,000 kilometres (5,000 miles) and to carry nuclear warheads. The development of these immensely powerful weapons tended towards the reduction of conventional armies, navies, and air forces and their associated weapons. For one thing, countries simply could not afford large armed forces as well as these very expensive guided weapons. In the second place, an attack with long-range nuclear guided weapons would, it was thought, be so overwhelming and quick that conventional armed forces would be unable to stop it or to have any effect at all.

On 25 June 1950 the armies of North Korea crossed the 38th parallel of latitude and invaded South Korea. Bloody fighting followed in Korea as the opposing forces surged back and forth across the frontier. The weapons of the conflict were similar to those used in World War II except that they had been improved. They included jet aircraft, giant Pershing tanks, powerful bazookas, 75-millimetre recoilless rifles, heavy mobile artillery guns and howitzers, high-fragmentation grenades, automatic rifles, and machine-guns. The war lasted until July 1953. (See KOREA, SOUTH).

The Vietnam War began in 1946 as a conflict between France and its Vietnamese colony. Eventually it became a war between South Vietnam, supported by the United States, and North Vietnam, supported by the Soviet Union and China. As in Korea, tanks, air power, and large land armies played key roles. But guerrilla attacks, dense jungle, and advanced weaponry introduced new factors. To combat guerrillas, United States bombers dropped bombs and chemicals in an attempt to destroy the foliage hiding the guerrillas. Helicopters played an important part because of the rugged terrain (see HELICOPTER). Guided missiles and electronic equipment became vital weapons. (See VIETNAM WAR.)

Later conflicts have included a long struggle between Iran and Iraq, in which once again chemical weapons were used, and the continuing fighting between Arabs and Israelis, which has affected Middle East affairs for many years.

The threat of war with nuclear weapons is ever-present as long as such weapons exist in the hands of the world's super-powers.

WARBLER is the name of four different groups of bird that get their name for their warbling song, or because they resemble birds with such a song.

There are about 300 species of Old World warbler, mainly drab, brownish birds with sweet melodious calls. They feed chiefly on insects and spiders, actively searching the vegetation for food. In the autumn they migrate south to Africa and southern Asia.

In Europe, among the first of the commoner warblers to arrive in spring are the chiffchaff (*Phylloscopus collybitus*) and willow warbler (*Phylloscopus trochilus*). Both these birds are slender and dainty with greenish-yellow plumage. It is not easy to tell them apart until they start singing. The chiffchaff repeats, over and over again, the sounds that have given it its name, while the willow warbler has a plaintive little song ending on two descending notes. Both birds live in woodland and copses (small groups of trees) but the willow warbler is also found in places where there are bushes but no trees. The nests of both birds have domed roofs and are lined with feathers.

The wood warbler (*Phylloscopus sibilatrix*), which has greenish-yellow upper parts and a yellow throat, is found in woodland. It has a loud trilling song which continues unbroken for a time and is rather like the sound of a coin spinning on a marble table. The blackcap (*Sylvia atricapilla*), which also arrives in early spring, has one of the sweetest songs. Only the cock has a "cap" of glossy black feathers, the hen's cap being rust-coloured.

The New World warblers or wood warblers are also small, active, insect-eating birds but their calls are not so sweet, and they are more brightly coloured. For example, the male Blackburnian warbler (*Dendroica fusca*) has a bold-patterned black and orange plumage. This warbler sings from treetops and builds its nest at the end of the branch of a pine or spruce tree. It lives deep in the forests of eastern

Alvin E. Staffan from National Audubon Society (left); Allan D. Cruickshank from National Audubon Society (above).

Two North American warblers. The yellow warbler (left) builds its deep cup-shaped nest in the upright fork of a tree or shrub. The magnolia warbler (above) prefers to build its shallow nest in small conifers and to line it with tiny rootlets.

Canada and the northeastern United States. The Parula warbler (*Parula americana*) of eastern North America is another distinctive bird, with blue upper parts and a chestnut breast-band. Its song is a rapid trill-buzz sound and its nest, gourd-shaped, is made mainly of lichens.

Although several species of warbler may feed and breed in one area, they do not compete with each other for food or space because they have different habits. Some may feed in the tree canopy and nest near the ground, while others may both feed and nest in shrubbery. Most New World warblers go south during the winter.

In Australia the name warbler is given to little fan-tailed, brown, green, and yellow birds, that include the white-throated warbler (*Gerygone cantator*) which can be found nesting in gardens in the suburbs of Brisbane and Sydney.

Among the old world chat-thrushes, there are three species of morning warbler that get their name because they sing sweetly at dawn.

WAR OF 1812 was fought between the United States and Britain. In some ways it was a strange war. The United States declared war on Britain to protect its sailors and shipping. Yet in the United States the West, which had neither sailors nor shipping, was for the war, while New England, which had both, was against it. Even more strange was the fact that the greatest victory of the United States took place after the war had officially ended.

Origins of the War

From 1800 to 1815 the Napoleonic Wars were fought between France and most of the other European nations. In 1803, after a short truce, Britain and France continued their war. The United States found it was becoming harder to stay neutral. Each of the warring nations tried to blockade the other. To do this, both sides were seizing ships of the United States, the largest neutral commercial nation. In 1806 and 1807 France said it had the right to capture any ships trading with Britain or carrying British goods. The British answered with similar orders against trade with France or its allies. Because Napoleon Bonaparte's armies controlled most of Europe, this greatly hurt United States trade.

Britain made things more difficult by her practice of stopping United States ships to search them for British subjects. If British sailors were found they were impressed, or forced to serve on British ships. Often United States sailors were taken by mistake. This angered many people in the United States.

War almost started in June 1807. The British warship *Leopard* had ordered the *Chesapeake*, a United States frigate, to stop and be searched for deserters. When the *Chesapeake's* captain refused, the *Leopard* fired on the *Chesapeake*, killing and wounding a number of men. After taking off four deserters, the British allowed the *Chesapeake* to return to port.

Had President Thomas Jefferson asked for a declaration of war, the country would probably have been more united than it was to be five years later. But Jefferson wanted peace. Instead of asking for war, he asked Congress to pass an Embargo Act. This act provided that no ship with cargo could leave a United States port for a foreign country. The embargo did not work. It was difficult to enforce, and the merchants wanted to trade, even if it meant trouble with the British and French. For this reason the embargo was repealed in 1809. Under James Madison, who became president that year, similar efforts were made to stop British and French attacks on United States shipping. (See JEFFERSON, THOMAS; MADISON, JAMES.)

Events in the West increased the demand for war. As people moved westward, difficulties grew between the whites and the Indians. Under the leadership of Tecumseh, the Indians began to unite. They hoped to keep the white settlers from taking more of their lands.

In November 1811 the governor of Indiana Territory, William Henry Harrison, invaded Tecumseh's lands. The Indians attacked his men but were driven off in the Battle of Tippecanoe. This led to more Indian attacks on the northwestern frontier. In the southwest, also, the Indians were becoming more restless. (See TECUMSEH.)

Westerners believed that the British were behind Tecumseh's plan and that they had given the Indians guns and gunpowder. For these reasons the West wanted war with Britain. Westerners claimed that such a war would also make it easy to capture Canada, and, if Spain should fight as an ally of Britain, it might even be possible to take Florida.

In the elections of 1811 and 1812 many new representatives were elected to the United States Congress. A group from the South and the West led by Henry Clay and John Calhoun shouted for war. John Randolph of Virginia called them "War Hawks". Their shouts were successful and on 18 June 1812, Congress declared war. Meanwhile, no one in the United States knew that on 16 June the British, fearing war, had ordered an end to attacks on United States shipping.

Madison's war message said that the war was to defend sailors and ships of the United States. Yet New England shipowners preferred the possible losses of neutrality to the certain losses of warfare. Both the South and the West, however, wanted the war.

The War Begins

The main plan of the United States was to conquer Canada. (See CANADIAN HISTORY, section on The Beginning of British Canada.) The population of the United States outnumbered that of Canada by about 15 times. Yet the result was a series of defeats. The first defeat took place when William Hull, governor of Michigan Territory, was told to invade Canada. Instead, in August 1812 he was forced to surrender Detroit to the British. Earlier, the garrison at Michilimackinac surrendered to the British, and the garrison at Fort Dearborn (the future Chicago, Illinois) was massacred by the Indians.

A few months later United States troops invaded Canada across the Niagara River. Under Captain John E. Wool the United States troops took a strong position on Queenston Heights. In the fighting the British commander, General Isaac Brock, was killed. As fighting continued, Wool needed more soldiers, but the New York militia refused to cross the river into Canada to help. Instead, they watched the British drive the United States soldiers back to the river where they were forced to surrender.

The United States record in sea fighting was far better. The navy had about 16 warships and other smaller ships. This was few when compared with the 100 or more ships that England sent to fight. But the United States ships were well designed, well built, and well manned.

In 1812 there were a series of United States naval victories. The *Essex* captured the

Courtesy, New Haven Colony Historical Society

Although the United States land forces suffered a series of defeats during the early stages of the War of 1812, the Navy was largely victorious at sea. A contemporary engraving by Michele Carne illustrates the battle and victory of the American ship *Constitution*, commanded by Captain Isaac Hull, over the British ship *Guerriere*.

Minerva and, shortly afterwards, the *Alert*. The *Constitution*, commanded by Captain Isaac Hull, won a brilliant victory over the British *Guerrière*. The *United States*, under Captain Stephen Decatur, defeated and captured the British frigate *Macedonian*. The United States sloop *Wasp* took the British *Frolic*. The *Constitution*, now commanded by William Bainbridge, destroyed the British frigate *Java*.

Such victories surprised the British and pleased the people of the United States. But the British had a great many ships. From 1813 most of the United States warships were blockaded in ports or captured by British squadrons.

In 1813 the United States again planned to invade Canada. First, however, it was necessary to control the Great Lakes. During the winter of 1812–13 a small fleet of warships was built on Lake Erie. Captain Oliver Hazard Perry was placed in charge. On 10 September 1813 Perry won a victory over the British squadron at Put-in-Bay. The way was now open for the invasion.

This time the troops were led by William Henry Harrison, the hero of Tippecanoe. Because of Perry's victory, the British burned Detroit and tried to withdraw. Harrison caught up with them and on 5 October 1813 won an important victory at the Battle of the Thames. Tecumseh, who had fought with the British, was killed during the battle. Another invasion of Canada, under General Henry Dearborn, resulted in the capture of the city of York in what is now Ontario.

By 1814 Napoleon had been defeated in Europe. The British were able to give much more attention to the war with the United States. But now they faced a better United States army. Old and incompetent military commanders had been removed and, instead of state militia, more of the regular army troops were being used.

In July 1814 United States troops under General Jacob Brown crossed the Niagara River and took Fort Erie. The Battle of Lundy's Lane, near Niagara Falls, was fought three weeks later. After fierce fighting the British received reinforcements and the United States troops withdrew.

The greatest blow to United States pride occurred in August 1814. Some 4,000 British soldiers under General Robert Ross were landed by naval ships near Washington, DC. They easily captured the city and burned the

Library of Congress, Washington, DC

American forces suffered a demoralising defeat in 1814 when a British force under the command of General Robert Ross captured the city of Washington, DC. The Capitol, the president's house, and other government buildings were burned. President Madison barely escaped capture by the enemy.

Capitol, the president's house, and other public buildings. The defeat was unexpected. In fact, President Madison and others had gone to watch the British being turned back. Madison barely escaped capture, and a meal prepared for him in the president's house was eaten by British officers. The British then tried to capture Baltimore, Maryland, but failed. It was during the British naval bombardment of that city that "The Star-Spangled Banner" was written. (See BALTIMORE.)

The next month the British tried an invasion of the United States by way of Lake Champlain. They had to give up their plan when a United States naval squadron defeated a British fleet off Plattsburg Bay on Lake Champlain. Captain Thomas Macdonough won this battle for the United States. His victory prevented the invasion of New York by 11,000 British troops.

Early in December 1814 the British forces set out to capture New Orleans, Louisiana. The Tennessee Indian fighter, Andrew Jackson, was in charge of the city's defence. The British commander Sir Edward Pakenham despised the United States militia and marched his men in close formation toward the United States positions. On 8 January 1815 a terrible battle was fought during which Pakenham and more than 2,000 British soldiers were killed. United States losses were 8 killed and 13 wounded. The soldiers under Jackson fought from behind banks of earth while the British troops marched towards them in the open. The unprotected British were no match for the sharpshooting frontiersmen.

Results of the War

The Battle of New Orleans had no military value, for the Treaty of Ghent, signed on 24 December 1814, had made peace between Britain and the United States. The news had not yet reached the United States. But the Battle of New Orleans was notable for two reasons. It made Jackson a national hero, and it gave people in the United States the mistaken idea that the War of 1812 was a United States victory. (See JACKSON, ANDREW.) The peace treaty did not show any such victory. Boundaries were to be as before the war. Other problems were to be discussed by future commissions.

One result of the war was that it brought two military men, Jackson and Harrison, closer to the presidency. Another result was the growth of manufacturing in New England because the war cut off imports from Britain. The war also increased patriotism in the United States: the national anthem was written and the flag became more important as a symbol.

It was an unhappy and perhaps needless war. But soon afterwards friendly relations began between the United States and Canada. The Rush-Bagot agreement of 1817 stated that no large warships were to be kept on the Great Lakes. The boundary line west of the Great Lakes was extended along the 49th parallel to the Rockies. The war also helped to unite the scattered Canadian communities.

WARSAW (Warszawa in Polish) is in the centre of Poland and is the capital of the country. It stands on the west bank of the River Vistula, which here flows through a sandy plain. The earlier capitals of Poland were Gniezno in the 10th century and Cracow from the 11th to the end of the 16th century. Warsaw probably grew around a fort built in the 12th century, when the youngest son of King Boleslaw III set up his rule in the surrounding region of Mazovia. Later, Mazovia became part of the Polish kingdom, and because of its central position, Warsaw was made capital during the reign of King Sigismund III Vasa (1587–1632).

Warsaw soon entered a stormy period of history. In 1655 and 1656 and again in 1702 it was captured by the Swedes. In 1794 it was stormed by the Russians and in the following year became a frontier town of Prussia. In 1806 it was occupied by the French and in 1807 was made capital of the Duchy of Warsaw which, after Napoleon's defeat, was given to Russia by the Congress of Vienna (1815). The Duchy then became a kingdom with the Tsar (emperor) of Russia as King of Poland.

In 1830 the Poles rebelled against the Russians, but a year later Warsaw was retaken by

Andrzej Zborski

People enjoying the music of Frederic Chopin by his monument in Lazienki Park, Warsaw.

the Russians after great bloodshed. Another rising in 1863 also failed. This time the Russians tried to blot out even the name of Poland, and so they called it "Vistula Land" with Warsaw as its ruling city (see POLAND). In World War I, Warsaw was occupied by the Germans in 1915, and recovered its position as capital of the restored state of Poland in 1918. In 1920 the Russian army was defeated by the Poles a few kilometres east of the city. In World War II most of Warsaw was destroyed, first when besieged by the Germans in 1939 and five years later when the Poles rose against the Germans. On the second occasion Soviet troops took Praga, which is an industrial suburb across the river from Warsaw, and stopped there while the capital was destroyed. They drove the Germans from the ruins in January 1945.

Warsaw had many magnificent buildings, including a magnificent royal palace, many palaces built by the Polish noblemen, and churches. The beauty of Warsaw's buildings was recorded by the famous architectural painter Canaletto (1697–1768), and so accurate were his paintings that the Poles used them to guide the rebuilding of the old city, which had to be begun from the foundations after World War II. The largest building in Warsaw is the Palace of Science and Culture, which was completed by the USSR as a gift to Poland in 1955.

Development since World War II has changed Warsaw into one of Poland's most important industrial centres, with steelworks, factories making motor vehicles and tractors, electrical, chemical, and printing works, and many others. In the old days, Warsaw was famous for its thousands of small shops selling hand-made goods, and its tailors and shoemakers have regained their importance.

Warsaw is the centre of Poland's road and rail systems. It has a great river port at Zeran and the international airport of Okecie is a few kilometres from the city centre.

The population of Warsaw is 1,659,400 (1986).

WART. Most people have had warts at some time or other, usually on their hands. This kind of wart is a bundle of fibres covered with an overgrowth of skin. It is caused by a virus growing in the skin (see VIRUS). Warts appear to spread to some extent from person to person, and so they are common among children and young people, but they may come on at any age. Sometimes old people have warts on the face or neck. A whole crop of warts may appear suddenly and then disappear weeks or months later.

If a person wishes, a wart can be removed by a doctor, who will burn it away with acid or kill it by freezing. If it is only partially removed, the place will bleed a good deal and a new wart may grow there.

In adults rather different wart-like growths are often due to repeated slight irritation or infection of the skin. These are not true warts. They are more difficult to remove permanently than the other kind. In older people, especially chimney-sweeps and people who work with coal-tar, the single raised wart may last for years and slowly become a kind of cancer of the skin.

The Latin word for a wart is *verruca* and this

is the name often used for the painful warts that may occur on the soles of the feet.

WARTHOG. This member of the pig family lives in open and partly forested areas of Africa. It was given its name because it has growths like large warts on each side of its enormous head. The warthog has two pairs of tusks, both of which curve upward. Those on the upper jaw, which are always larger than those on the lower one, sometimes stick out well over 30 centimetres (12 inches).

New York Zoological Society

Both male and female warthogs have two pairs of tusks; those of the lower jaw form sharp weapons.

The wart hog measures up to 75 centimetres (30 inches) high at the shoulder and may weigh about 100 kilograms (220 pounds). It has a greyish-brown skin which is nearly hairless, except for some long bristles which form a mane on its neck and back. It feeds mostly on roots, berries, and other vegetable matter. The animal lives in burrows in open woodland areas and two or three females with their young will often band together. When it goes to its burrow, a warthog will turn round and go in backwards, so that its head is left sticking out and its tusks can attack any enemy.

WARWICKSHIRE is a county in the midlands of England; in fact, because of its central position, it is sometimes called the heart of England. It is bordered to the east by Leicestershire and Northamptonshire, to the south by Gloucestershire and Oxfordshire, and to the west by Hereford and Worcester. To the north are the great industrial cities of Birmingham and Coventry, which are at the centre of the West Midlands region (see WEST MIDLANDS). Warwickshire has an area of 1,981 square kilometres (765 square miles) and a population of 479,700 (1985).

In the east, the River Avon enters Warwickshire from Northamptonshire and winds across it in a southerly direction through a broad, flat valley. This is rich farm country. Past Stratford-upon-Avon, where William Shakespeare was born, the river flows through many orchards until it crosses into Hereford and Worcester.

The Avon valley once divided Warwickshire into the woodland of the northwest and the feldon, or field country, of the southeast. The woodland was the great Forest of Arden, which extended unbroken to where Birmingham stands today. The forest has now gone, but many farms and small hamlets of black-and-white half-timbered houses remain where they were first built in clearings of the forest. The names of Hampton in Arden and Henley in Arden are a reminder of this woodland.

The feldon country was always more open, and the first settlers built villages from which they went out to work in the surrounding fields. Kineton is a large village of this kind and Southam is a small market town.

Further south, the land rises suddenly to Edgehill and the Cotswold Hills. Here, and in the limestone ridge which ends with Meon Hill, south of Stratford, is the highest ground in the county. Beeches grow on the slopes of the hills and the fields are enclosed by stone walls. Many houses here are built of deep yellow stone from quarries in Oxfordshire.

Towns and Industries

The most important activity in the county is farming, both arable and dairy. The main crop grown is wheat. Fruit and vegetable growing is also important, particularly in the valley of the lower Avon, where there are orchards of fruit trees.

Warwick, the county town, is on the Avon northeast of Stratford. The river flows past a mighty towered castle on a rock. Much of it dates from the 14th and 15th centuries, but it was much rebuilt later, and is now open to the public. Although a great fire broke out in Warwick in 1694, many old buildings can still be seen there. It also has some light industry.

Nuneaton, close to the Leicestershire border, is a small industrial town which grew up on the Warwickshire coalfield. It has brickmaking works, engineering and textile industries, and stone quarries.

Cephas Picture Library/Mick Rock

The half-timbered Lord Leycester Hospital (1415) in Warwick, a town with many fine old buildings.

Rugby, in the east, was little more than a village until the 19th century. It became a railway junction and manufacturing town, and remains famous for the public, (fee-paying) school, which was reformed by Dr Thomas Arnold in the 19th century to become the model for public schools in Britain. At this school the game now called rugby football began in 1823 (see RUGBY FOOTBALL).

Leamington Spa, east of Warwick, gained its name from the mineral waters there. (A spa is a town where people go to bathe in or drink mineral waters for their health.)

History

The Forest of Arden proved a barrier to settlement in Warwickshire for many centuries. Prehistoric people seem to have settled only on the gravelly region called Dunsmore Heath around Rugby. The Romans made roads: Watling Street along the boundary of Warwickshire and Staffordshire, and the Fosse Way across the southeast. Alcester, a small town near the border with Hereford and Worcester, dates from Roman times, and many Roman coins have been found there.

The first Anglo-Saxon settlers came into Warwickshire along the Avon valley, probably from Northamptonshire. Their burial places have been found at Stratford and at Bidford-on-Avon, to the west. This land became part of the Saxon kingdom of Mercia in the 7th century. Ethelfleda, who was the daughter of Alfred the Great and Queen of Mercia, built a fortress against the invading Danes at Warwick in 914.

The earls of Warwick were among the most powerful men in England during the Middle Ages. Richard Neville, Earl of Warwick, played such a part in the Wars of the Roses, supporting first one then another claimant to the throne, that after his death he became known as "Warwick the Kingmaker". (See ROSES, WARS OF THE.) The earls of Warwick of the Beauchamp family lie under magnificent tombs in the Beauchamp Chapel, which is part of St. Mary's Church in Warwick.

In the reign of Elizabeth I occurred the birth of Warwickshire's most famous son, William Shakespeare, at Stratford in 1564. Because of this, Stratford is now not only a market town but a tourist centre visited by people from all over the world. (See SHAKESPEARE, WILLIAM; STRATFORD-UPON-AVON.)

At Kenilworth, just north of Warwick, is a great ruined castle where Queen Elizabeth I was entertained by her favourite, Robert Dudley, Earl of Leicester. He held magnificent pageants to entertain the queen, both in the castle grounds and on the lake which then lay below the walls.

The first great battle of the English Civil War was fought in 1642 at Edgehill. The armies of Oliver Cromwell and Charles I met on level ground below the hill, but neither side won a decisive victory.

Mary Ann Evans, whose pen name was George Eliot, was born at Arbury Farm, Chilvers Coton (near Nuneaton) in 1819. She wrote about Warwickshire in several of her novels, including *Adam Bede*. (See ELIOT, GEORGE.)

WASHINGTON. Man-made boundaries sometimes fail to match natural ones and those of Washington State, situated in the far northwest corner of the continental United States, are good examples.

The high mountains of the Cascade Range cut through the state from north to south, creating what ought to be two states from the point of view of climate, society, and economics. Eastern Washington makes up two-thirds of the state. It is an agricultural region with a continental climate, not very different from states of the upper Midwest. Its trade is linked eastward, towards Idaho, Montana, and other landlocked states.

Western Washington, on the other side of the Cascades, has more in common with the coastal areas of Oregon and California. The climate is completely different, wet and mild compared to the much drier east. Its trade also faces west, towards Alaska and the nations of the Pacific Rim. It is in the western region that three-quarters of the state's population lives, in cities stretching south from Bellingham near the Canadian border through Everett, Seattle, Tacoma, down to the capital at Olympia. There is more industry here than agriculture.

Washington is the only state named after a president. It is also the smallest state in the Far West in area. In population, however, it is second only to California in the region. Along with Oregon and California, Washington is rich in natural resources, both in minerals and vast forests.

The Land

Washington is bordered on the north by the Canadian province of British Columbia, on the east by Idaho, on the south by Oregon, and on the west by the Pacific Ocean. The mighty Columbia River cuts through the state from the north and runs along most of the Oregon border. At its greatest length, Washington is 570 kilometres (354 miles) from east to west. The greatest width is 381 kilometres (237 miles).

Although smaller in area than the other western states, Washington has more diversity of terrain than most. There are seven natural regions: the Olympic Peninsula, the Willapa Hills, the Puget Sound Lowland, the Cascade Mountains, the Columbia Basin, the Okanogan Highlands, and the Blue Mountains.

The Olympic Peninsula is in the far northwest, directly south of Canada's Victoria Island. The term "peninsula" seems somewhat misleading when looking at a map, but the area is surrounded by water on three sides. The dominant feature of the peninsula is the Olympic Mountain Range, reaching nearly 2,440 metres (8,000 feet). Precipitation can be as much as 3,550 millimetres (140 inches) annually in the rain-forests of the peninsula.

Immediately to the south of the Olympic Mountains are the Willapa Hills. These are low-lying tree-covered hills not more than 915 metres (3,000 feet) above sea-level. Here, too, annual rainfall can be heavy, up to 1,900 millimetres (75 inches).

The coastal Olympic Peninsula and the Willapa Hills are separated from the Cascade Range by the Puget Sound Lowland, which runs south from the Canadian border to Oregon. It has a mild climate and relatively flat terrain. Most of the state's population lives within this region, and the state's best harbours are there, along with most of the industries.

The massive Cascade Range borders the Lowland in the east for its entire length. It has peaks ranging from 1,220 metres (4,000 feet) in the south to more than 2,440 metres (8,000 feet) in the north. The most spectacular of its peaks is Mount Rainier, the fifth highest mountain in the adjoining 48 states, at 4,392 metres (14,410 feet). Another peak in the range, Mount St. Helens, gained instant worldwide fame on 18 May 1980, when it erupted with the force of a large atomic bomb. It was the first volcanic eruption in the continental United States since 1917 and far more violent than earlier ones. (See also CASCADE MOUNTAINS.)

In the northeast corner of Washington are the Okanogan Highlands, a southern extension of the Canadian Rockies. Here the peaks are lower and less rugged than in the Cascades, reaching heights of from 1,220 metres (4,000 feet) to 2,440 metres (8,000 feet). The Highlands are the richest source of minerals in the state.

To the south of the Highlands and covering most of eastern Washington is the Columbia Basin. It is a dry, desert-like plateau with an elevation of from 305 to 760 metres (1,000 to 2,500 feet). Much of the plateau is irrigated for farming by water from the Columbia River and its tributaries.

Bob & Ira Spring

Riders stop for a rest, and to admire the view in Mount Rainier National Park, Washington.

The Columbia River is one of the great rivers of North America. In volume it carries more water than any river system except the Missouri-Mississippi combination. Its course flows about 1,942 kilometres (1,207 miles) from Canada through western Washington to the Oregon border, then on to the Pacific. The river's water power produces one-third of the hydroelectric power generated in the United States. The Grand Coulee, completed in 1942, is the largest of the Columbia's dams to harness water for irrigation and electric power. (See COLUMBIA RIVER.)

In the southeastern corner of Washington are the Blue Mountains, the smallest of the state's regions. The region consists of plateau and small mountains, which rise to heights of from 610 to 1,220 metres (2,000 to 4,000 feet). The area is thinly settled, but there is some agriculture and livestock grazing. The Snake River flows north along the eastern edge of the Blue Mountains, then changes direction to go west and merge with the Columbia.

The People

Washington was originally part of the Oregon Country to which pioneers came over the long Oregon Trail during the second half of the 19th century. Most of the early arrivals were from the East and the Midwest and most of them were Protestants. Washington is probably the most Protestant state in the Union. Immigrants from Norway, Sweden, and other European countries soon added to the original settlers. Coal miners from England, Wales, Finland, and Poland came around 1900. Germans farmed the uplands in the eastern part of the state, while Chinese arrived to help build the transcontinental railways. Japanese moved into the Puget Sound Lowland to farm, and after World War II Filipinos joined them.

The state's population is nearly three-quarters urban and centred in the major cities of the west, which although they are some distance from the sea are not landlocked. The most heavily built-up area is around Puget Sound, where Seattle is the largest city (see SEATTLE). The second largest city is Spokane, in the eastern part of Washington. It is a trading and railway centre for the Columbia Basin.

The Economy

Aircraft and timber are the two leading industries. The Boeing Corporation, a maker of aircraft and aircraft parts, was in the post-World War II period the largest employer in Washington. Its fortunes rose or fell, depending on the needs of the United States Defense Department and the whims of airlines. Massive lay-offs in this single industry harmed all of western Washington.

The state's huge timber industry has been subject to similar ups and downs. The state's forests contain about four per cent of the nation's commercial forest area. As home construction and other timber-using business declined, Washington's income fell and unemployment rose.

Dozens of products are made from trees, including pulp, plywood, paper, cardboard, containers, and furniture. There are shipyards in some of the cities on Puget Sound, and there is an enormous volume of trade, both export and import, conducted through Seattle and other ports. Other industries include food processing, aluminium refining, petroleum refining, chemical production, steel manufacture, and mining.

FACTS AND FIGURES

AREA: 105,566 square kilometres (40,767 square miles).
POPULATION: 4,463,000 (1986).
MOUNTAIN RANGES: Olympic, Cascade, Blue, Kettle River. Highest peaks: Rainier, 4,392 metres (14,410 feet); Adams, 3,751 metres (12,307 feet); Baker, 3,285 metres (10,778 feet); Glacier Peak, 3,213 metres (10,541 feet).
RIVERS: Columbia, Snake, Skagit, Chehalis, Skykomish, Spokane, Yakima, and Okanogan.
CITIES (1985): Seattle, 495,190; Spokane, 175,732; Tacoma, 161,625 (1980); Bellevue, 73,903; Everett, 54,413; Yakima, 49,826; Bellingham, 45,794.

Coal mining, once prosperous, has fallen on hard times because of petroleum use. The chief minerals now are sand, gravel, cement, stone, zinc, and uranium ore. There is some gold produced in the northern Cascade Range and in the Okanogan Highlands.

Agriculture flourishes on one-third of the state's land. The best-known crop is probably the Washington Delicious apple. Other activities include dairy farming, poultry raising, bulb growing, and vegetable and berry growing. Hay, hops, alfalfa seed, cranberries, filberts (hazelnuts), barley, sugar beets, potatoes, beans, peas, maize, pears, and peaches are grown in eastern Washington. Melons, plums, and grapes are grown in the Yakima Valley.

Commercial fishing, mainly on boats out of Puget Sound, brings in salmon, halibut, flounder, perch, tuna, oysters, cod, and crabs. Much of the fish, as well as other food products, are processed within the state.

Education

In 1854 the first territorial legislature passed a public (state) school law. Today the State Board of Education sets requirements which must be met by the state's 300 school districts. All children must attend school from the ages of 8 to 15. Most higher education in Washington is gained through state-supported schools. The oldest and largest is the University of Washington, at Seattle, founded in 1861. Washington State University, at Pullman, was established in 1890.

History

English exploration of Washington began in 1778 with a voyage by Captain James Cook, discoverer of the Hawaiian Islands. George Vancouver sailed into Puget Sound in 1792 and named many of the inlets, islands, and mountains. Meriwether Lewis and William Clark reached the area from the East in 1805 on their long overland exploration of the Northwest (see LEWIS AND CLARK EXPEDITION). The Columbia River was discovered and named in 1805 by Robert Gray, a trader from Boston.

These explorations aroused the interest of fur companies. John Jacob Astor's Pacific Fur Company built Astoria on the Oregon side of the Columbia River in 1810 (see also ASTOR FAMILY). Missionaries to the Indians followed the fur traders, but there was no significant settlement in the territory until after Marcus Whitman opened a mission near Walla Walla in 1836. He returned east to encourage settlers to come to the Oregon Country, as it was then called. The first arrivals, in the early 1840s, went to the Willamette Valley of Oregon. It was not until 1844 that settlers first decided to go north of the Columbia River.

In 1846 Great Britain and the United States signed a treaty dividing the Oregon Country from Canada along the present border. Within a few years settlements sprang up at many places on Puget Sound. The Oregon Territory was organized in 1848. In 1853 Congress divided the area and established the Washington Territory north of the Columbia. The territory grew quite slowly at first and was not admitted to the Union until November 1889.

During the next decade there were gold strikes in the Yukon and Klondike territories of Canada and Alaska. The gold rush helped populate the Puget Sound cities, as they became shipping ports for goods to the miners and recipients of gold and other commodities from the north. The state's major undertaking early in the 20th century was harnessing the Columbia River for irrigation, navigation, and electric power.

WASHINGTON, Booker T. (1856–1915).

Booker T. Washington was an American educator who became a leader of black Americans in the difficult days soon after the slaves in the southern parts of the United States received their freedom.

He was born a slave on a plantation in Virginia in a one-room cabin with an earthen floor and no windows. All black slaves were freed when, in 1864, the American Civil War ended with a victory for the Northern states (see CIVIL WAR, AMERICAN). However, Washington and his family were desperately poor and he worked in the coal and salt mines of West Virginia from the age of nine. From his small wages he saved enough money to pay his fees at a night school, and learnt to read and write at a time when few black children could do so. He grew up determined that others too should have the benefits of education.

BBC Hulton Picture Library

Born a slave before the American Civil War, Booker T. Washington worked all his life for the education of blacks in America.

At the age of 17 he went to a school at Hampton, in Virginia, where he learnt the trade of a bricklayer. But he was soon working as a schoolmaster. In 1881 when a college to train black teachers was opened at Tuskegee, in Alabama, Washington became its first principal. The college was short of money and many of the students had received only a poor school education, but Washington achieved remarkable results. He believed that blacks and whites could and should live together in friendship, and he thought that when the blacks had been better educated there would be a better understanding between the two races. He became the recognized leader of black Americans and won high regard from white and black alike. Washington wrote the story of his life in a book called *Up From Slavery*.

Meanwhile the college at Tuskegee prospered and by the time Washington died it had more than 1,500 students and nearly 200 teachers. It led the way in improving the lot of black people and helped them towards taking their rightful place as respected citizens of the United States.

WASHINGTON, George (1732–99).

George Washington, the first president of the United States of America, was born near Fredericksburg, Virginia, on 22 February 1732.

Early Life

His father Augustine Washington owned extensive estates, but as he died when George was only 11, and there were nine other children, George's education was both scrappy and short. However, by the time he was 14 he had learnt something about surveying (see SURVEYING) and made beautiful maps. He earned his first money when at 16 he joined an expedition that went to survey the unknown country along and beyond the Shenandoah River in western Virginia. On his return he

Courtesy, Metropolitan Museum of Art

George Washington, US President, 1789–97.

was made public surveyor for Fairfax county in Virginia and once more went into the wild interior. The year 1752 brought him land of his own, for his half-brother Lawrence died and Washington inherited the estate of Mount Vernon on the banks of the Potomac River. In the same year he was given the rank of major and was made adjutant of one of the four districts into which Virginia was divided for military purposes.

Army Career

The French, who were then growing powerful on the Ohio River, started to order British settlers to leave areas that had been claimed for Britain. In 1753 the governor of Virginia sent young Major Washington with a message to the French commander that he was to withdraw. To deliver this message Washington had to travel over 800 kilometres (500 miles), nearly to Lake Erie, by boat, on foot, and on horseback. His account of this journey was one of the first reliable descriptions of life in the regions across the Allegheny Mountains.

The French did not withdraw and Washington, now a lieutenant-colonel, was sent with several hundred men to enforce British claims to the Ohio River lands. In May 1754 he captured a French party and killed their leader. However, the French counter-attacked and Washington surrendered, but he and his men were allowed to return to Virginia. In 1755 he was in battle against the French once more, this time so ill with fever that he rode on a pillow instead of a saddle. He showed great bravery and when General Edward Braddock was killed he helped to bring the defeated army safely out. Virginia made him a colonel and commander of its troops. He had to protect a thinly settled frontier nearly 650 kilometres (400 miles) long with only about 700 rather poor troops. He became ill again but recovered in time to take part in the capture of Fort Duquesne, which was where the city of Pittsburgh now stands. Washington then left the army, and early in 1759 he married and settled down to the life of a landowner and tobacco-planter.

Commander-in-Chief

The most famous part of Washington's career was yet to come. As a member of the House of Burgesses (parliament) of Virginia, he was

Culver Pictures Inc.

George Washington with Martha Custis, a wealthy widow whom he married on 6 January 1759, and her two children.

drawn into the disputes which, in 1775, led to war between Britain and its American colonies. (See AMERICAN REVOLUTION.) When the people of Massachusetts revolted against Britain and asked the other colonies to help them, the Second Continental Congress appointed Washington commander-in-chief of the revolutionary armies. His job was not an easy one, for the 13 colonies were jealous of one another. Although they had set up the Congress, it was not strong enough to make the leaders of all the states carry out its orders. The soldiers under Washington's command were volunteers and they went home when they felt like it. Washington reached Boston, however, bluffed the British, and made them sail away with their fleet.

After this he went to defend New York, which the British were attacking. Heavily outnumbered, he was defeated and made his famous retreat across the state of New Jersey. Most of his army deserted and the remainder was in rags. However, at Christmas 1776 Washington captured a British outpost and turned his country's despair into confidence. After this he both suffered defeats and won victories, often turning defeats into victories. He and his starving, almost naked army spent the winter of 1777–78 in camp at Valley Forge, Pennsylvania. Then the spring brought help to the Americans, for France joined them against Britain. In 1781 at Yorktown in Virginia the British were defeated. Two years later the peace treaty was signed and Washington went back to Mount Vernon. But he soon returned to public life. The colonies, now free from British rule, joined to form the United States of America and in 1789 Washington was chosen as the first president of the new country.

United States President

George Washington was inaugurated on 30 April 1789, with John Adams as vice-president. The new government was only a skeleton. The Constitution, for example, provided for federal courts, but none had been set up. Legislation by Congress was needed to get the system of courts into operation. The Constitution said that the government could collect taxes and set up a currency system, but this would take time.

Washington was a good administrator. He created what is now called the president's cabinet. He invited Thomas Jefferson, the Virginian who had drafted the Declaration of Independence, to be his secretary of state. To handle the difficult financial problems he invited Alexander Hamilton to be secretary of the treasury. Henry Knox, commander of his artillery during the Revolutionary War, was Washington's choice for secretary of war. Edmund Randolph, a brilliant lawyer from Virginia, was the attorney general. These four men formed the first cabinet. (See HAMILTON, ALEXANDER; JEFFERSON, THOMAS.)

The new administration faced three major tasks. First in importance was the problem of amending the Constitution. In several states, friends of the proposed government had promised that if the Constitution were adopted, amendments would guarantee civil rights. By 1791 acceptance of the first ten amendments, now known as the Bill of Rights, had been ratified (confirmed).

A second major task was setting up the machinery for operating the government. Before this could be done a great many laws had to be passed. The newly created departments (treasury, war, and state) had to be legally established, and laws providing for their operation had to be passed. Much of Washington's effort during the next few years was devoted to such elementary but necessary work.

Finally the new government had to find ways to pay its expenses. Taxes had to be raised and debts paid off. The Tariff Act of 1789 brought in much needed revenue from duties on goods brought into the country. Excise taxes were introduced. Farmers in Pennsylvania rebelled against duties on whisky in 1794. Washington sent in the militia of four states and compelled their submission.

Strong disagreements developed within the cabinet. Jefferson defended the powers of the states while Hamilton felt the central government needed more and more power. When

Courtesy, Virginia Conservation Commission

Mount Vernon, George Washington's home in Virginia, looks just as it did when he and his family lived there.

Washington encouraged Hamilton to set up a federal bank, Jefferson withdrew from the cabinet.

During these early years the new national government had troubles with Europe. Several months after Washington became president, the French Revolution began. When this revolution involved France in war with other European countries the French government appealed to the United States for help. However, Washington insisted on the United States preserving its neutrality.

Relations with Britain were very strained as Britain continued to interfere with United States trade. The Jay Treaty of 1794 postponed war for a few years, giving the United States a much needed breathing space. Trouble with Spain was also postponed by the Pinckney Treaty of 1795, setting the Florida and Louisiana boundaries.

Washington was unanimously re-elected for a second term in 1792 but he refused to consider a third term. In 1797 he retired from public life and was at last free to enjoy Mount Vernon. However, he died two-and-a-half years later on 14 December 1799, and was honoured by all Americans as the "father of his country" and the founder of the United States. He was buried at Mount Vernon which he loved so well.

WASHINGTON, DC. Washington, District of Columbia is the capital and 16th largest city of the United States. It is one of the few cities of the world founded especially as a national capital, and as the capital, Washington is among the most important cities in the United States. It is the seat of national government where elected leaders and representatives from throughout the United States gather to serve the nation. It is the city where laws and policies that govern the land are enacted. Its streets are often jammed: with civil servants, with tourists visiting the many historic sites and national monuments, with shoppers, with flag-waving political party supporters, or beribboned diplomats crowding a presidential inauguration.

Washington and the District of Columbia are the same place. The city occupies an area along the Potomac River between the northern part of Virginia and the southern part of Maryland. Much of Washington is wedged between the Potomac and Anacostia rivers. Algonkian-speaking Indians called the longer of the two rivers the *potomack*, or "trading place".

The location of the city, once a trackless marsh and meadow, was chosen because it was close to both the geographical and population centres of the original 13 states that stretched from New Hampshire to Georgia. Also, it could be reached upriver by boat on the Potomac River. Much of the land on which the city was built is low and sandy.

Following the American Revolution the newly formed United States needed a capital city. Various sites, including Philadelphia, were proposed. However, Congress passed a bill in 1790 giving permission for a site to be chosen somewhere near the Potomac River. This section of land was to be called the District of Columbia after Christopher Columbus; the city to be built on it was to be named Washington in honour of the first president.

In 1791 President George Washington chose the site where the city now stands, and selected Pierre Charles L'Enfant, a young Frenchman who had fought in the American Revolution, to design the city. L'Enfant planned the city with broad avenues lined with trees, majestic buildings, and monuments.

Washington is divided into Northwest, Northeast, Southeast, and Southwest sections. The Capitol stands at the point where these sections meet. Streets that run north and south from the Capitol are numbered. Streets that run east and west are lettered. Diagonal streets are named after states. From the Capitol and the White House, avenues extend out like spokes of giant wheels. Pennsylvania Avenue is the widest street in the city. Every four years, presidential inaugural parades proceed down Pennsylvania Avenue between the Capitol and the White House.

Washington, DC, is the headquarters of all branches of government. The President of the United States lives in the White House (*left*). The Capitol (*below left*) houses the Senate and the House of Representatives. The Supreme Court building (*below right*) houses the nation's highest court of law.

White House Photo (left); courtesy, Washington Area Convention and Visitors Bureau (below left); Cary Wolinsky/Stock, Boston (below right).

David W. Corson/A. Devaney, NY

The Jefferson Memorial, one of the splendid statues and memorials that grace Washington's open spaces, was dedicated on the 200th anniversary of his birth.

Buildings and Monuments

Washington, DC, has become a city of famous buildings and monuments. These include the following:

Capitol Building. Construction of the Capitol building was begun in 1793 when President Washington laid the cornerstone for the building. Made in three sections, the north (Senate) wing was completed in 1800; the south (House of Representatives) wing in 1807; and the huge middle section, or Rotunda, in 1827. The dome was not completed until the American Civil War (1861–65).

Historical paintings and statues of famous Americans are housed in the Rotunda and Statuary Hall. The Rotunda is occasionally used for the lying in state of great American citizens, when members of the public can pay respects at the coffin before burial. The huge bronze *Statue of Freedom*, weighing nearly 6,800 kilograms (15,000 pounds), stands on top of the Capitol Dome.

The Congress, offices of the congressmen, and both the Supreme Court and the Library of Congress were once all together in the Capitol. Today congressmen have their offices across the plaza from each wing of the Capitol; the Supreme Court and Library of Congress are in separate buildings. (See also CONGRESS OF THE UNITED STATES.)

Jefferson Memorial. Erected in the beautiful setting of the Tidal Basin, the Jefferson Memorial was begun in 1938 and dedicated in 1943 as a memorial to the third president. It is a round, domed building encircled by 66 marble columns. A statue of Jefferson stands inside.

Library of Congress. Founded in 1800 for the use of the members of Congress, the library was destroyed by British troops during the War of 1812. Later, in 1897, it was relocated in a new building across from the Capitol. Rapid growth of the collections required an annex, and a white marble addition was completed in 1939. The third building was opened in 1981. Today, the library is one of the largest and best equipped in the world. Its large rare book collection includes a copy of the Gutenberg Bible, printed about 1456. (See LIBRARY.)

Lincoln Memorial. Dedicated to the 16th president, this white marble memorial building is noted for its statue of President Abraham Lincoln. Construction of the building was begun in 1915 on the anniversary of Lincoln's birth and it was dedicated on Memorial Day in 1922. Lincoln's famous Gettysburg Address and Second Inaugural Address are engraved on bronze plaques inside the building.

National Archives Building. Some of the most valuable documents of United States history are housed in this building. The Declaration of Independence, the Constitution of the United States, and the Bill of Rights, collectively referred to as the "Charters of Freedom", are preserved there. The Archives also include other famous documents such as the Emancipation Proclamation and one of the copies of the Louisiana Purchase Treaty. The National Archives were created by a Congressional act in 1934. (See also BILL OF RIGHTS; CONSTITUTION OF THE UNITED STATES; DECLARATION OF INDEPENDENCE.)

Smithsonian Institution. The Smithsonian Institution was founded in 1846. It was built with money provided by an English scientist named James Smithson, to be used for the increase and spread of knowledge.

The Institution includes some of the city's

ZEFA

The Lincoln Memorial was designed by Henry Bacon on a plan similar to that of the Parthenon in Athens. It houses a colossal seated statue of President Lincoln.

best-known landmarks. Some of these are the Museum of Natural History, the Freer Gallery of Art, and the National Gallery of Art. One of the Institution's most popular attractions is the National Air and Space Museum, which houses the Wright brothers' aircraft; Lindbergh's *Spirit of Saint Louis*, the first single-seater plane flown across the Atlantic; and several of NASA's space-flight capsules and satellites.

Supreme Court Building. Located east of the Capitol, the Supreme Court building is an impressive white marble structure where nine justices make up the highest court in the United States. The building was completed in 1935. At the entrance two rows of large marble columns support a *pediment*, or triangular roof, with nine sculptured figures. In the centre is the *Goddess of Liberty* with the scales of justice in her lap. Each year the court hears more than 4,000 cases.

Washington Monument. Completed in 1884, the Washington Monument was built as a memorial to the first president. Construction began in 1848 but was interrupted in the 1850s because of lack of money. The point at which work resumed can be seen as a colour change today. A hollow obelisk (a four-sided shaft with a pyramid top) standing some 169 metres (555 feet) high, it can be ascended by visitors either by a lift or by walking up 898 steps.

ZEFA

The Washington Monument (1885) is a memorial to George Washington, first US President.

White House. This is the home and office of the president of the United States. It is described in the article WHITE HOUSE.

Pentagon and Arlington National Cemetery. Located across the Potomac River in Arlington County, Virginia, is the Pentagon. This huge Department of Defense building employs about 22,000 persons. More than half of these are civilians. It is the headquarters for the Joint Chiefs of Staff, the top military officials of the US Army, Navy, and Air Force.

(Left) Paul S. Conklin; (below) Harold M. Lambert Studios—Frederic Lewis

Some of the soldiers who gave their lives in the wars fought by the United States are buried at Arlington Cemetery (left). The Pentagon (above) is the headquarters of the Department of Defense.

The Pentagon, so called because it is five-sided, was built in only 16 months during World War II. It actually consists of five pentagon-shaped buildings nested within each other and connected by corridors. Covering just under 14 hectares (34 acres), the building is often called a "city in itself". Its 28 kilometres (17.5 miles) of corridors offer exhibits, shopping, and dining facilities.

Arlington National Cemetery, located northwest of the Pentagon, is situated on the former estate of Robert E. Lee, the Confederate general in the Civil War. It was seized by the Union as a prize of war. The cemetery is the burial ground of well-known military and government officials. Some soldiers from every war in which the United States has been involved, including the American Revolution and Civil War, are buried there. The Tomb of the Unknowns, a memorial to all American war dead, is there. President John F. Kennedy and Robert F. Kennedy are also buried there.

People and Employment

Since its beginning Washington has been a city whose major business has been the governing of the United States. It never developed as a port or industrial city. It is also an important centre of tourism.

The growth of government in and around the city has attracted people from all parts of the United States. Two-thirds of those who work in Washington live outside the District of Columbia. Of the people who live in the city less than half were born there. The population is often called *transient*, meaning many people reside only temporarily within the city.

A large number of workers is needed to run the numerous federal government agencies. While some are elected or appointed to government positions, many are hired through the Civil Service Commission. Jobs range from clerical tasks to the complex duties of those who form policies and direct agencies.

Large organizations, such as the American National Red Cross, the Daughters of the American Revolution, the US Chamber of Commerce, and the various labour unions, have national headquarters in the city. Among international organizations represented in Washington are the World Bank, the Inter-

Courtesy, Washington Area Convention and Visitors Bureau (left); Paul S. Conklin (right)

The first Smithsonian Institution building (above left) was built in 1846 and designed by James Renwick. Other branches of the Smithsonian include the famous Museum of Natural History (above right).

national Monetary Fund, and the Organization of American States.

Representatives of foreign nations, such as ambassadors, envoys, members of the diplomatic service, and foreign correspondents, also work in Washington. These people give the city a distinctly international flavour. About 125 foreign embassies are located in Washington.

Washington, DC, is a major centre of culture as well as a centre of government. The city has musical, theatrical, and sporting events throughout the year. The mild climate, averaging 24°C (75°F) in summer, presents ample opportunity for outdoor activities.

Transport

The opening of the Metro rapid transport system in 1976 greatly helped to improve public transport in the city. A vital link between city and suburbs, the Metro's eventual 161-kilometre (100-mile) system will provide improved commuter service for the capital region. The Metro includes both rail and bus transport. About 50 subway and 37 surface stations provide access to the Metro.

Washington also has regular bus services and freeways that lead around and into the city. Several bridges provide access to the city across the Potomac and Anacostia rivers. There are several airports serving Washington including Dulles International Airport.

The population is 626,000 (1986).

WASP. The yellow and black wasps (*Vespa* or *Vespula*) that enter buildings in the early autumn or make themselves a nuisance at a picnic, come from nests where they live with many hundreds or even thousands of sister-wasps and their mother, the queen. Each nest is started by the queen wasp. She comes out of her winter sleep in the spring and chooses a place in which to set up home, in the ground or perhaps in a hollow tree, according to the kind of wasp she is. The nest she makes is usually grey and hangs down from the roof of the nesting place, attached by a little stalk. It is the size of a golf ball and feels like paper.

Social wasps, as wasps that live in colonies are called, build their nests out of paper made from wood pulp which they obtain by scraping wood fragments from posts or dead trees and chewing them with saliva into a paste. The queen does this as skilfully as her daughters, the workers. Her nest is a small comb of cells which contain at the same time eggs, grubs, and pupae. The comb is protected by layers of paper called envelopes.

The nest begins to grow rapidly as soon as the queen's first brood of workers come out of their cocoons. By the end of the summer there may be as many as eight combs in a big nest, lying one above the other and separated by short pillars of wood pulp so that the wasps can move freely.

In the autumn hundreds of young queens and males fly from the nest and mate, the

NHPA/Stephen Dalton

The ruby-tailed wasp is a parasitic insect that lays its eggs in the nests of other wasps and bees.

queens afterwards finding a sheltered place in which to pass the winter, while the males die with the coming of cold weather. The old queen and the workers also die and the empty nest, if in the ground, soon falls to pieces.

Other social wasps include the paper wasps (*Polistes*) that build a single circular tier of cells attached by a narrow stalk to the underside of a ceiling or similar structure.

The hornet, or giant hornet (*Vespa crabro*) as it is known in North America, is a large, formidable insect 3 centimetres (over 1 inch) long. It defends its nest against intruders, but otherwise does not readily attack.

Wasps are useful insects, as they catch and kill great numbers of flies and caterpillars, using them as food for the grubs in the nest. They are also very fond of sweet things such as ripe fruit.

Solitary Wasps

Not all wasps live together in colonies. There are also solitary wasps; each female makes her nest and provides food for her young without help. There are no worker wasps. Solitary wasps do not kill the insects they capture straight away. Instead they paralyse them with their sting and lay their eggs on them, so that they remain fresh for the hungry grubs that hatch from the eggs. Each kind of solitary wasp preys on one particular kind of insect. The habits of these wasps are very varied and they have many different ways of making their nests. For example, even among a single genus, one may paralyse small weevils, while another may catch only small bees as food for its young.

Thread-waisted wasps (*Ammophila*), are mainly black and red and have a long thin body. The female catches a single large caterpillar for each of her young and drags it to her burrow, perhaps as much as 45 metres (150 feet) and often over very rough ground. She pulls the caterpillar into her burrow by backing in herself. As soon as she has laid her egg, she fills up the burrow by scraping in sand with her front pair of legs. What is particularly interesting about *Ammophila* is that the female then picks up a tiny pebble with her jaws and uses it to make the spot that marks her nest firm and smooth.

All these are digger wasps, making burrows in the ground. Others make tunnels in rotten wood. Among these are the many different kinds of *Crabro*, nearly all of which store their nests with two-winged flies. There are many kinds of solitary wasp in the warmer parts of the world. A European example is *Eumenes*. Its mud-pot nest is about the size of a large

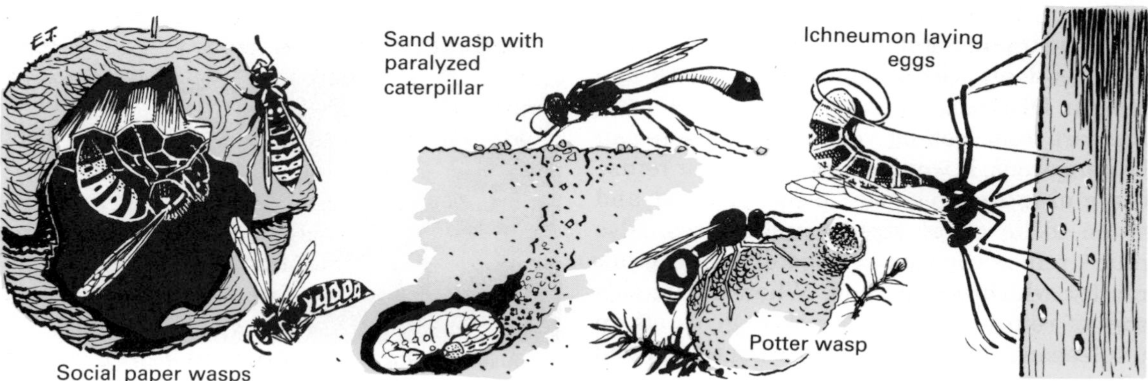

pea, built on to a twig of heather. The pot is stocked with small caterpillars before the female lays a single egg in it. The following summer the young wasp bites its way out and flies away.

There are also spider-wasps, or pompilids. They do not fly much but run rapidly over the ground in search of their prey. Their movements are extremely nimble but curiously jerky. Having stung a spider, the wasp seizes it by a leg and drags it to her burrow. Some pompilids found in the tropics, especially in South America, are among the largest known wasps. Their sting is said to be very painful and they attack and paralyse some of the largest spiders known.

The insect known as ichneumon fly is actually a close relative of the wasp. They are very numerous and live mainly on other insects (see ICHNEUMON FLY).

WASTE DISPOSAL. What happens to the rubbish produced daily in every household? Centuries ago some of it would have been left lying on the floors of people's houses and some would have been thrown into the streets. Since then there has been a huge increase in population, and a greater crowding together of people into large towns and, more important still, a general desire to improve living conditions. Therefore more attention has been paid to the proper disposal of waste matter. The problem is complicated by the fact that modern waste is no longer primarily natural waste. It contains metal, glass, and plastics which can remain in the environment for years without decomposing.

Liquid waste is known as sewage and its disposal is dealt with in the article SEWER AND SEWAGE DISPOSAL.

Apart from looking very untidy, waste can be dangerous. It would be dangerous for refuse containing broken bottles, pieces of metal, and so on to lie about streets and houses. Also much refuse consists of vegetable and other matter which will go bad. When damp, this sort of refuse rots very quickly, gives off an unpleasant smell, and encourages the spread of rats and disease-carrying flies. In order to safeguard health and to keep streets and the surroundings of houses tidy, there must be an organized system of refuse storage and disposal.

For this three things are necessary. The first is that all refuse shall be properly stored, the second is that the refuse shall be collected as frequently as possible in order to remove it before it rots, and the third is that the refuse shall be disposed of in a sanitary manner.

It is necessary to store refuse in such a way that flies and other pests cannot get at it. The most suitable container is a metal or plastic bin, which can be cleaned, or a non-returnable paper or plastic sack. Collections are usually undertaken by public utilities, private companies, or local authorities on a regular schedule. The frequency depends, among other things, on the financial resources available to employ staff and provide machinery, and on the local climate. Rubbish rots more quickly in warm weather and so in hot countries collections are usually made more than once a week. This may also happen in city centres where there are a large number of food stores and restaurants. Not everywhere is rubbish collected from private houses. In rural France, for instance, people have to put their rubbish in large communal bins placed in the streets.

Modern collection vehicles usually have a "compaction plate" which breaks up the rubbish and squashes it together to increase the load it can carry.

J. R. Karrach

A refuse collector in Amsterdam. The refuse is immediately emptied into a crusher to reduce its bulk.

Another way to dispose of household rubbish is by putting it through a grinder into the sewage system. The rubbish is put down the kitchen sink accompanied by water and is ground up by an electric motor into small particles. Not all rubbish can be treated in this way: metal and plastic cannot be ground up and large bones also provide a problem. In some places where many grinders have been installed, sewage treatment plants have had to put in extra machinery to deal with the increase in sewage. The system has been most successfully used in hospitals and large industrial plants.

Destroying and Saving Refuse

The methods of disposal most generally used are controlled tipping and incineration (burning). Controlled tipping is the tipping of refuse into disused gravel pits, quarries, and other holes in the ground. It is sometimes called "sanitary landfill" to distinguish it from simple dumping. In the past there were public dumps outside many towns where people would take their rubbish and these became breeding grounds for flies, rats, and other pests. Controlled tipping is done by putting the refuse down in layers and covering each layer with soil; by preventing papers or other debris from being blown away; and by seeing that no refuse is left uncovered. Many authorities have used this method to fill in unsightly pits and have afterwards levelled the site, planted trees, sown grass seed and so transformed useless and ugly areas into parks and open spaces for recreation.

Until recently, much rubbish was tipped into the sea instead of dumping it on land. It is now accepted that this causes pollution and it has been largely banned (see POLLUTION).

An alternative to burying is burning, or incineration. By incineration most of the combustible (burnable) material found in the refuse is burned in a specially designed furnace or incinerator. One very important advantage of this method is that all offensive matter is made harmless, and substances that might breed flies and disease-carrying organisms are destroyed. The heat produced by incineration is often used to drive machinery and to provide hot water. The Turkish baths of Cairo (Egypt) were heated for many centuries by the heat produced by burning the city's refuse. Refuse can be burned in special power stations to provide energy. The refuse is passed over a magnetic separator to remove tins and pieces of iron, and then burned to provide the heat needed to drive turbines and generate electric power. The problem with incineration is that it can cause air pollution and many old incinerators are now disused for this reason. However, modern incinerators have been designed to process certain waste before incineration and so prevent pollution.

With all methods of refuse disposal, some form of salvage, or saving of usable materials, should be undertaken. Many waste disposal schemes include plants to recover from refuse such materials as metals, glass bottles and jars, paper, and cardboard which can be recycled, or reused (see RECYCLING).

Street Cleaning

Even if there is an efficient method of collecting rubbish from homes, shops, restaurants, and places of employment, waste may still be disposed of in the streets. In most cities there are penalties for dropping litter and allowing pets to foul the footpaths, but in many places they are not rigidly enforced. Even where people obey the rules, the streets still need to be cleared of fallen leaves, dust, and dirt. Waste disposal authorities are usually responsible for providing street cleaning in cities. Vacuum machines similar to household vacuum cleaners may be used to suck up fallen leaves. In winter, the streets must be kept clear of snow and ice.

Hazardous Waste

Radioactive waste and toxic (poisonous) chemicals pose special problems in waste disposal. They must be disposed of so as not to cause danger to anyone coming into contact with them. (The disposal of nuclear waste is explained in the article NUCLEAR ENERGY.)

WATER is one of the commonest of all substances, and without it life would be impossible. The seas and oceans cover about seven-tenths of the Earth's surface, but water is also contained in the soil, in the atmosphere, and in all living things. About two thirds of the human body consists of water, and water also forms a large part of the food we eat, especially vegetables and fruit.

Water was believed to be an element, or distinct single substance, until 1781. Then the English chemist Henry Cavendish (1731–1810) proved that water was really a compound of two elements: hydrogen and oxygen. He did this by showing that when hydrogen was burned in oxygen, water was formed. In 1806, Sir Humphry Davy confirmed this by electrolysis, that is, he passed an electric current through water and obtained the two gases hydrogen and oxygen. (See DAVY, SIR HUMPHRY; ELECTROLYSIS.) Water is so unlike the elements composing it that Cavendish's discovery was one of the most startling in the history of chemistry.

Water exists as a substance in three states: ice, which melts at 0°C (32°F); liquid water; and steam, which is formed when water boils at 100°C (212°F). Water expands (swells) on freezing by about 10 per cent. At 4°C (39.2°F) it is at its densest, or occupies the least volume (space); thus it is unlike most liquids, which have their maximum density at their melting point. Pure water at 4°C (39.2°F) is often used as a reference substance for scientific measurements. For example, 1 cubic centimetre of pure water at this temperature weighs exactly 1 gram; in other words it has a density of 1 g/cm^3 and provides the standard for measuring the relative densities (specific gravities) of solids and liquids (see DENSITY). The original definition of the metric unit of volume, the litre, was the volume of 1 kilogram of pure water at 4°C (39.2°) and at standard atmospheric pressure. (See MEASUREMENT; WEIGHTS AND MEASURES.)

Pure water is rarely found in nature. This is because water is able to dissolve so many substances from the air, the soil, and the rocks. The saltiness of sea-water is caused by the mineral substances which are dissolved from the Earth's surface by rivers and carried down to the sea. (See OCEAN AND OCEANOGRAPHY.) The Sun's heat causes the surface sea-water to evaporate, or change into vapour, leaving behind the salts and other minerals (see EVAPORATION). This explains why the seas are so much more salty than the rivers flowing into them.

Falling raindrops dissolve the gases in the air to some extent. These gases are chiefly nitrogen and oxygen, with some carbon dioxide. Lightning flashes change some of the

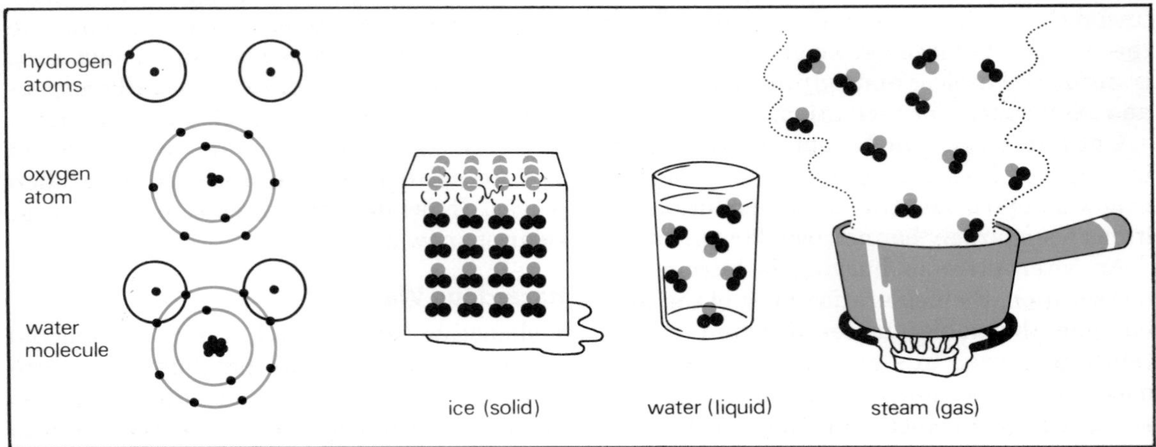

A water molecule consists of two atoms of hydrogen linked with one of oxygen. In ice the molecules are held close together and can only vibrate back and forth. Heat melts ice to form liquid water, in which molecules move about more freely. Further heat turns water to steam, in which molecules are free to move anywhere.

nitrogen into oxides of nitrogen that react with rainwater to form nitrous or nitric acids. These acids are washed down into the soil and help to fertilize it (see NITROGEN).

The kind and amount of solid substances dissolved by rainwater in any particular district depend chiefly on the type of rock present and on the dissolved gases in the water. Chalk and limestone combine with water containing carbon dioxide to form calcium bicarbonate, (calcium hydrogencarbonate) which dissolves in the water. Substances in the soil such as gypsum (calcium sulphate) are also dissolved by water. These dissolved substances, chiefly salts of calcium and magnesium, are the main cause of "hard" water, in which soap lathers poorly and leaves a thick scum.

Spas are places where people go to "take the waters". The waters in question usually rise from deep springs. They are often hot and contain dissolved salts such as sulphides which have medicinal value.

NASA/Science Photo Library

Water dominates the planet Earth. Oceans of salt water cover about 70 per cent of the surface. Water evaporating from seas and rivers forms clouds. It returns to the surface in the form of rain.

Pure water can be obtained from water containing salts by the method known as distillation. The process of distillation is occasionally used to supply the crews of ships at sea with fresh water (see DISTILLATION).

To be pleasant to drink, water must contain small quantities of dissolved gases and mineral substances. Chemically pure water (distilled water) is flat and tasteless. Water used for drinking must, however, be free from the bacteria that cause such diseases as typhoid fever and dysentery. (See BACTERIA.) These bacteria may be contained in water that has passed through soil containing dead animal or vegetable matter. Polluted (foul) water of this kind is more likely to come from shallow wells or streams fed by surface drainage than from deep wells. The safety of public water supplies is ensured by treating the water with chlorine gas, which destroys the bacteria.

Dissolved oxygen in water enables animals and plants to live in it. Fish, and such animals as water snails, oysters, and crayfish, absorb oxygen from water as it passes over their gills. Water plants absorb oxygen through cells on their surface. Oxygen in water also helps to keep it clean by assisting the decay of waste matter and dead things.

Rainwater containing carbon dioxide is a weak acid capable of dissolving limestone. This results in the formation of caves, gorges, potholes, and underground rivers in limestone districts. When water containing dissolved limestone evaporates, the limestone is deposited, sometimes in the form of crystals and coloured by iron or other impurities. The stalactites and stalagmites in some limestone caves, formed from dripping water during many centuries, are an impressive sight. (See STALACTITE AND STALAGMITE.) When water is boiled the same chemical process occurs, only much more rapidly. The calcium carbonate is then deposited in the form of "fur". In kettles this is a nuisance, while in large boilers or central heating pipe systems it not only causes a waste of fuel but also can block pipes. Therefore various chemical methods have been developed to remove the calcium carbonate from the water before it is used. This is called softening the water.

Life on the Earth is kept going by a continual process of water distribution. The oceans provide the great reservoir for the world's supply, and the Sun provides the energy for distributing water from this reservoir over the Earth's surface. The Sun's heat evaporates the water, which is gathered into clouds which can be thought of as masses of "water dust". When these particles of "dust" are big enough they fall as rain, hail, or snow to sustain plant and animal life. This is called *precipitation* and is the process by which water gets into the soil. Plants absorb water from the soil and return a lot of it to the air by a process called transpiration. Evaporation, precipitation, and transpiration make up the "water cycle". (See RAIN.)

Falling rain and flowing streams gradually change the face of the Earth. By means of huge dams, some of the water can be stored before it can reach the sea again. Water from these artificial reservoirs drives turbines for producing electricity, or flows through pipes to the taps in faraway towns and cities. (See DAM; TURBINE; WATER POWER; WATER SUPPLY.)

A chemical reaction in which water is added to another substance is called a hydration reaction. There is a separate article on DEHYDRATION which is the term for the removal of water from a substance.

WATER BUG. An interesting example of the way in which insects become fitted to live in a strange, new environment is shown by the water bugs. Most insects live on land and fly through the air. When they take to the water, they have to solve the problem of breathing, for insects are air-breathers. They also must solve the problem of moving, for most insects have slender legs unsuited to swimming.

Gerald Cubitt/Bruce Coleman

A waterboatman stationed on the water undersurface. It breathes from an envelope of air stored round its body and under its wings.

Pond, or water, skaters have bodies covered with soft, silvery down, which folds about them a covering layer of air. Their legs are long and hairy, and they can move rapidly over the surface of the water. The brown water scorpion (*Ranatra*) has near its tail a breathing tube which it projects above the surface of the water like a periscope. Its long, slender body makes it look like a floating twig. The familiar grey-and-black water boatman (*Corixa*) uses one pair of legs for oars. This pair is hairy and longer than the others. It always takes a supply of air beneath its wings when it goes under the surface. Some of the larger species of water boatman (*Notonecta*) are also called backswimmers.

Water bugs are cousins to scale insects and lice. Like them, they have mouths made for piercing and sucking. They generally live on the body juices of other insects, but they sometimes attack worms. The giant water bug, or electric light bug (*Lethocerus americanus*) of North America, which flies from pond to pond at night, preys upon small fish and tadpoles. Its oval body is brown and it has a very long beak. It grows up to 10 centimetres (4 inches).

See also FRESHWATER LIFE.

WATERCRESS, which is at its best in late autumn and early spring, is very useful for salads at a time when there is little fresh greenstuff available. It is rich in vitamin C and has a pleasant, hot flavour.

The scientific name of watercress is *Nasturtium officinale* and it is a member of the cabbage family, Cruciferae. It is quite a common plant in clear streams and ditches. During early summer, heads of small white flowers appear. The fruits are long and narrow and scatter their seeds in late summer. Watercress is found wild in Europe and Asia and has been introduced into North America and New Zealand.

Small quantities of watercress are cultivated in shallow pools known as watercress beds. These are made near a clear stream,

A–Z Collection

Watercress is grown on a commercial scale in beds, such as this one in Hampshire, southern England.

preferably coming from chalky soils. The stream is dammed up so that a steady stream of water flows over the ponds to a depth of about 15 centimetres (6 inches). Cuttings of watercress are planted in the ponds, and after only a few months the shoots are ready to gather.

Watercress can, however, be grown in any damp place, even in ordinary soil, where it sends out creeping branches which root along their length. Cuttings taken from a bunch bought in a shop are easy to grow provided that they are kept continually damp.

WATERFALL. Wherever a river or stream plunges down a steep slope, a waterfall or cataract is liable to form after some time. Any hard band of rock will resist the downward erosion of the river so that the edge of the band eventually becomes a ledge over which the water falls, cutting away more swiftly the softer rocks immediately downstream until a waterfall results.

The layers of soft rock beneath the cap rock may continue to be worn away, thus undercutting the cap rock, the edge of which finally breaks off. In this way the whole waterfall may slowly but steadily move upstream. The great Niagara Falls, on the Niagara River between Canada and the United States, have moved upstream in this manner a distance of about 11 kilometres (7 miles) since they were first formed some 30,000 years ago.

Although often beautiful and majestic, waterfalls prevent a river from being used by ships and boats. Canals are built to bypass such obstacles. To allow ships to pass between Lake Ontario and Lake Erie without using the Niagara River, the Welland Canal, which was first opened in 1829, was built along a line about 19 kilometres (12 miles) west of the river.

If the water can be led through pipes instead of being allowed to plunge over a waterfall, it can be taken to a power station at the foot of

Picturepoint

Pistyll Rhaeadr waterfall, in Clwyd, Wales. The water, which drops 73m (240ft), has worn away the rock and created a natural bridge, near the foot.

the falls and used to drive turbines for producing electricity. (See TURBINE; WATER POWER.) If all the stream is sidetracked in this manner the waterfall is reduced to a mere trickle or ceases. This is what has happened to the Reichenbach Falls in Switzerland.

Many of the world's spectacular waterfalls are in remote regions which are difficult to reach, although Niagara Falls and the Victoria Falls in Zimbabwe are exceptions. The effect produced on the eye by a waterfall depends more on its height and width and on the surrounding scenery than on the volume of water flowing. The Guaira Falls on the Parana River between Brazil and Paraguay, and the Khone Falls on the Mekong River in Laos, have probably a larger flow than any others. The height of the tallest waterfall, which pours down the sheer wall of Auyan Tepui in southeast Venezuela, known as Angel Fall, is not accurately known because approach to it is very difficult except by air and the top is usually hidden in the clouds. Its height is usually given as 807 metres (2,650 feet).

Here is a list of some of the most famous waterfalls (there are separate articles IGUASSU FALLS; NIAGARA FALLS; SUTHERLAND FALLS; VICTORIA FALLS).

WATER LILY. As their name suggests, water lilies grow in water. In more northern parts they are among the loveliest of wild flowers when in the summer their large white or yellow flowers open among their big round leaves on a pond or lake. Water lilies have special arrangements for growing in still water. Their roots are very long and can creep in the mud at the bottom of the pond and their leaves, which may be 25 centimetres (10 inches) across, have long stalks and float on the water. The yellow water lily has other leaves as well that are completely covered by the water. The flowers may either float or rise just above the surface of the water. The fruit is shaped like nuts or berries. Some of the fruit grows under water, so that when it ripens the seeds float away.

Water lilies belong to a family called Nymphaeaceae and they grow in temperate and tropical parts of the world. Many of the tropical ones are brightly coloured—blue, purple,

GREAT WATERFALLS OF THE WORLD

NAME	PLACE	HEIGHT metres	feet
Africa			
Victoria	Zimbabwe–Zambia	108	354
Tugela	South Africa	948	3,110 (in three plunges)
Kalambo	Zambia–Tanzania	215	705
Asia			
Gersoppa (Jog)	India	253	830
Khone	Laos	70	230
Australasia			
Sutherland	New Zealand	580	1,903 (in three plunges)
Wollomombi	New South Wales	482	1,581
Europe			
Mardalsfoss	Norway	517	1,696
Gavarnie	Pyrenees, France	427	1,401
North America			
Niagara	Canada–USA	48 and 51	157 and 167
Yosemite	California, USA	739	2,425 (in three plunges)
Takkakaw	British Columbia, Canada	503	1,650 (in three plunges)
South America			
Angel	Venezuela	807	2,648
Iguassu	Argentina-Brazil-Paraguay	82	269
Kaieteur	Guyana	226	741
Guaira	Brazil–Paraguay	114	374

red or yellow—and they are often sweet smelling. The lovely lotus flowers, which include the sacred lotus (*Nelumbo nucifera*) of India and the Egyptian lotus (*Nymphaea lotus*), are kinds of water lily. The sacred lotus of India probably used to grow in the River Nile in Egypt, but it is not found in that river any more. (See LOTUS.)

The biggest of all water lilies is the Amazon or royal water lily (*Victoria amazonica*), which has leaves about 2 metres (6.5 feet) across, like huge green plates with turned-up edges. The flowers are about 30 centimetres (12 inches) across and have deep rose-purple centres

A–Z Collection

Water lilies have showy flowers, with petals arranged in a spiral. Some only open in the morning or evening.

fading to white on the outside. This lily grows in the Amazon River in South America, where in some places the water is completely hidden for long stretches by its vast leaves.

Water lilies are often planted in lakes and ponds, to add to the beauty of gardens and parks.

WATERLOO, BATTLE OF. Today people still say "he has met his Waterloo" when someone who has been successful for a time is at last defeated. Waterloo was the final defeat of the French emperor Napoleon I, who had returned from his exile on the island of Elba and marched with an army across France, determined once again to make himself the master of Europe. The battle that prevented him from accomplishing this was fought on 18 June 1815, and was centred on the village of Mont St. Jean in Belgium. Waterloo was another village to the north of the battlefield.

Napoleon's opponents were the British and the Prussians (Germans). Soldiers of other nationalities, particularly Dutch, also fought with the British. The leader of the British forces was the Duke of Wellington, and the Prussians were under Field Marshal Gebhard von Blücher. (See WELLINGTON, DUKE OF.)

The Russians and Austrians were also in alliance with the British and the Prussians, who in June 1815 were waiting for them to join them. On 16 June, however, the French attacked the Prussians at Ligny, south of Mont St. Jean, and defeated them. Wellington, after holding a French attack under Marshal Ney at Quatre Bras to the west of Ligny, came to their aid. But at the end of the day he was in an awkward position and likely to be defeated.

The next day, 17 June, the Prussians retreated and Wellington decided to go to Mont St. Jean and prepare to give battle there, provided he could be sure that Blücher would support him. He sent a message to Blücher, telling him of this decision, but it was some time before he received an answer. The French under Napoleon did not give chase until the

BBC Hulton Picture Library

The Duke of Wellington at the battle of Waterloo.

afternoon, and Wellington succeeded in reaching Mont St. Jean before night. At two o'clock the next morning he received an answer from Blücher, saying that he would be able to come to his support, and Wellington decided to stand and fight.

Rain had fallen on the afternoon of 17 June and during the night, and the fields were sodden. Napoleon waited for the ground to dry before lining up his men and guns opposite Wellington's forces. The British had meanwhile taken up a position behind a low ridge which sheltered them from much of the enemy's gunfire. In front of the ridge were two farms, Hougoumont and La Haye Sainte, and the British occupied both these.

Ney was sent against Wellington's men, while Marshal Grouchy attacked the Prussians. After heavy fighting, Ney unsuccessfully attacked La Haye Sainte and then led his cavalry (horsemen) against Wellington's foot soldiers. Again and again the French cavalry attacked, but the foot soldiers stood firm and the remains of the force were driven back down the ridge. Then at about half past four in the afternoon Prussian troops arrived.

La Haye Sainte was finally captured about an hour and a half later, but the Prussians were firing on the road where the French retreated. Napoleon then decided to use his older and more experienced troops, known as the Old Guard, which until then he had held back. The Old Guard drove back the Prussians and for a time the fortunes of the French improved. The British, however, succeeded in overpowering them, and at eight o'clock in the evening the Old Guard gave way and British, Dutch, and Prussians swept down on them. Two battalions of the Old Guard covered the line of retreat and marched away in order, although pursued by the Prussians.

Napoleon himself rode away from the field of battle towards Paris. The disaster of Waterloo was so great that it was plain he could do nothing but abdicate as emperor. He made an attempt to escape to America, but finding that this was impossible he surrendered to the British, whom he described as "the most powerful, the most determined, and the most generous of my enemies". The British exiled him to the island of St. Helena, and there he died. (See NAPOLEON (EMPERORS OF FRANCE).)

On the battlefield of Waterloo about 45,000 men were left dead and wounded. Of these, about 15,000 were British and Dutch and about 8,000 were Prussian.

WATERMARK is a design put into paper during manufacture which can be seen when the paper is held up to the light. It is often used on banknotes to prevent counterfeiting (faking).

The use of watermarks dates from the second half of the 13th century, when they were used in Italy. The first watermarks consisted of designs such as crosses, circles, and triangles which could be formed by twisting wire. The wire was then sewn on to the mould on which the paper was formed and an impression was left on the paper. This method is still used in the manufacture of hand-made paper, such as that from which banknotes are made.

About the middle of the 19th century it became possible to make watermarks of more detailed designs, such as portraits. The design is first modelled in a sheet of wax and then imprinted by an electrical process on metal stamps known as dies. One of these dies is an *intaglio* (with lines carved into the metal) and one is a *cameo* (with the design cut in relief, so that it stands out from the background). Closely woven brass wire gauze is then put between the two dies under great pressure until the same impression as the original wax design appears on it. In making sheets of paper by hand, water drains away through this wire and the pulp from which the paper is made is left in the same thickness as the wax sheet and with the watermark in it.

This kind of watermark, too, is used only for hand-made paper and is very clear. When (as is usually the case) paper is manufactured on machines and watermarks are put on it, a wire mesh roll known as a dandy roll is used (see PAPER AND PAPER MAKING). The design of the watermark is made in relief on the surface of this and it is rolled over the paper *after* it has been made, not while it is actually in process of being made. As a result, the watermarks of machine-made paper are much less clear.

WATER POLO was first played in Britain in the 1870s and was called "football in the water". The game is played by swimmers, and has something in common with both soccer and basketball, the object being to throw the ball into the opponent's goal. The first rules were prepared by the Amateur Swimming Association in 1888, and in 1908 the International Water Polo Board was formed in London.

Features of water polo are team play and passing the ball from one player to another. The players control the ball, pass, and move into the open spaces while the defenders "mark" their opponents and try to catch their passes. Each team has seven players: a goalkeeper, two backs, a half-back, and three forwards, together with four substitutes.

ZEFA

The defending goalkeeper, in the red hat, uses both hands to save a shot from an opponent in black.

The game is played in a stretch of water which must not be more than 30 metres (32 yards long) and 20 metres (21 yards) broad. The goals are 3 metres (10 feet) wide, and the crossbar is placed 2.4 metres (8 feet) from the bottom of the pool. The water must be at least 1 metre (3 feet) deep.

The ball used for water polo is like a soccer ball. When playing it, the players, except for the goalkeeper, are allowed to use one hand only. To pick it up, they press the ball gently down on the water and then flick the wrist over. The ball then comes up into the palm of the hand. In order to throw the ball forward with any force, a player raises his shoulders clear of the water.

The game lasts for 20 minutes of actual play (four periods of five minutes each). A time-keeper subtracts the periods of stoppages such as corners and the scoring of a goal.

Water polo may be played by women, using a slightly smaller ball and field of play, but it is mainly a men's game. Until about 1920, British teams always won in international matches, but since then the leading countries at water polo have been Hungary, Italy, the Netherlands, the USSR, and Yugoslavia.

WATER POWER. Water flowing down rivers or falling from heights has great energy. For many centuries such running water has been used to turn water-wheels to drive machinery and mills. That use of water power has generally given place to what is called hydroelectric power. ("Hydro" is a word which comes from Greek and means "having to do with water".) In a hydroelectric power scheme the water drives machines called turbines. The shaft of each turbine is connected to the shaft of another machine called a dynamo, or electric generator, which produces electric current as long as the water continues to drive the turbine. The current is led through cables (wires) to wherever it is required. (There are separate articles DYNAMO; ELECTRICITY; ELECTRIC POWER; TURBINE.)

Water Wheels and Water Mills

Until steam engines were introduced in the 18th century, all machines in industry that were too big to be worked by hand or by animals were driven either by wind (see WIND POWER) or by flowing water.

In a water wheel the energy of the flowing or falling water turns the wheel attached to a shaft that drives machinery, for example, a mill. One of the commonest kinds of water mill in the past was the flour mill, whose heavy stones were turned by the wheel in order to grind wheat into flour.

To stop a water wheel, the flow of water to it must be cut off. This made it usual to place the wheel in a side channel instead of in the main stream. This channel, the mill stream, has fitted at the upstream end a *sluice gate* which is adjusted to control the amount of water flowing or to shut it off completely. The entering stream is called the leat, or head race, and the leaving stream is called the tail race.

The commonest type of water wheel found in Europe from the 13th century onwards was the *overshot wheel*. In this type, water is led to the top of the wheel, which is about 60 centimetres (2 feet) below the head race. Around the rim of the wheel are fixed curved blades forming buckets into which the water flows. The difference in weight between the full buckets on one side of the wheel and the empty buckets on the other side forces the wheel to turn. As each bucket nears the bottom it spills out water into the tail race. The diameter (height) of the overshot wheel is slightly less than the difference in level between the head and tail races. Wheels of 6 to 7.5 metres (20 to 25 feet) in diameter were common and some were more than 21 metres (70 feet).

Barnaby's

A 300-year-old water mill near Wrexham, in Wales. Water is one of the oldest sources of power.

Overshot wheels are quite efficient and waste only about one-quarter of the energy of the falling water. However, they turn rather slowly and so are generally fitted with gearing to increase the speed of the machinery driven from the shaft. (See GEAR.)

The *undershot wheel* makes use of the speed

of the water flowing beneath it. The water strikes the lower blades and forces the wheel to turn. These wheels are much less efficient than those of the overshot type, and when flat blades are used about three-quarters of the energy of the water is wasted. By fitting curved blades the efficiency is doubled. Undershot wheels have long been used in Europe, especially along the River Rhine.

The breast wheel owes its name to the breast or casing built close to the wheel rim between the head race and tail race. In this type, water enters the wheel at about the level of the axle where it exerts the greatest useful force on the buckets, and the breast prevents it from spilling out of the buckets until they are almost level with the tail race. The breast wheel combines the principles of the overshot and undershot wheels.

A more modern form of water wheel is called the Pelton wheel, which is a type specially designed to turn at high speeds under the influence of powerful jets of water which has fallen from a great height. Pelton wheels and water turbines are explained in the article TURBINE.

Estimating the Power

The amount of energy in falling water depends on its *head*, that is, the distance through which it falls under the action of gravity. During its descent it increases in velocity, as do all falling bodies. For example, water falling from a head of 150 metres (492 feet) enters the turbine at a speed of 195 kilometres (121 miles) an hour. Falling from a head of 1,650 metres (5,413 feet) its speed would be 640 kilometres (398 miles) an hour. The type of turbine chosen for a hydroelectric power station is decided primarily by these water conditions.

The power obtainable from the generator (its generating capacity) is expressed as kilowatts (kW) or as megawatts (MW). One megawatt is 1,000 kilowatts or 1 million watts. In theory 1 litre of water weighing 1 kilogram falling through a distance of 102 metres (or conversely 102 litres of water falling through 1 metre) in 1 second should produce 1 kilowatt of electrical power. (In Imperial units, 1 gallon of water weighing 10 pounds should produce 1 kilowatt of power in falling 74 feet in 1 second.) In practice it is less than this because some of the energy is used to overcome friction in the pipelines and in the machine. See POWER.

In large installations the water flow is measured in cubic metres a second (cubic yards a second).

Power Resources

Countries such as Switzerland, Italy, Sweden, and Norway with little coal or oil to burn in steam power stations, have developed their resources of water power. In countries where water, coal, oil, and gas are available there is a choice of electricity obtained from water power, diesel engines, gas turbines, and steam power stations. For steam power stations, in turn, there is a choice between burning coal or oil as fuel and using nuclear reactors (see NUCLEAR ENERGY). The final decision, therefore, is often a difficult one which depends on complicated circumstances.

Supplies of water power exist only in certain areas, usually in mountainous regions. A hydroelectric power station costs at least three times as much to build as a coal-burning one of the same power and one-and-a-half times as much as a nuclear power station. However, the *running* costs of the hydroelectric power station are very much less because it does not have to buy fuel and fewer staff are needed.

Hydroelectric Power Stations

A hydroelectric power station can be built either in a hilly or mountainous district where plenty of rain falls or in a river valley. In the first case, a storage space is made at a high place into which water drains from the largest possible area of the surrounding slopes. This area, called the *catchment area*, is often occupied by a lake. The outlet from the catchment area is blocked by building a dam across it. Usually this greatly increases the size of any existing lake.

Water from the base of the dam is led through tunnels or pipes to the power station, which contains the turbines and electrical generators. The pipes through which the

(1, 2, 3, 5) Courtesy, North of Scotland Hydro-Electric Board. (4) Keystone

1 Strong steel pipes lead water from a reservoir down to the power station. **2** The water turbines in the power station drive dynamos. **3** Below the power station the water carries on into the river. **4** The water flowing through some types of turbine forces round huge, bladed propellers. **5** Loch Lednock, an artificial lake formed by the dam, supplies a power station at Dalchonzie, Scotland.

water flows down to the turbines are called *penstocks* and are usually made of steel, as they have to be very strong. The pressure caused by the head of water tending to burst them may be enormous. With a head of 1,650 metres (5,413 feet), which is the highest yet used, the pressure at the bottom of the penstock is more than 1.5 kilograms on each square millimetre (2,135 pounds per square inch) of pipe surface. Often tunnels have to be driven through the hills and mountains; the tunnels are lined with concrete or steel to strengthen them.

To prevent sudden pressure surges that might burst the penstock when the turbine to which it is connected is shut off, *surge shafts* may be fitted. These are open-topped pipes with their upper ends at a higher level than that of the water behind the dam. They are usually connected to the top of the penstocks.

The *power house* is usually built at the lowest convenient level near a watercourse or lake into which the water can flow after it has been through the turbines. The channel leading the water from the turbines is called the *tail race*.

If electricity is supplied to a generator, it turns as an electric motor and can then drive a turbine which acts like a pump. In pumped storage schemes generator motors are driven by electricity during off-peak hours, when demand for electricity is low, to pump water from a lower reservoir to one at a higher level. The stored water can then be released from the higher reservoir to drive the water turbine-generators again and supply power to the grid at peak periods.

River Power Schemes

For a hydroelectric power station built on a river, the general plan is to build a dam across the river. This raises the level upstream of the dam, producing a head of water depending on the height of the dam. The water collects on the upstream side of the dam, often forming a large lake, which ensures a steady flow even when the river shrinks during the dry season. Dams of this kind may also be used to control flooding.

Courtesy, Washington Power Company

The rush of water from a dam is turned into electricity at the Long Lake power plant, Washington.

The power house may be built on the dam or inside it, or just downstream of it. The water flows through the turbines and into the river below the dam. Not all the water of the river flows through the turbines. The rest passes downstream by *spillways*, which are usually arranged just below the top of a dam, rather like the overflow of a bath.

On any particular stretch of river having a fairly steady slope, it is often possible to build a whole series of dams, one downstream of the other. An example of this is the Tennessee River in the United States, which has its main stream dammed in nine places, as well as 13 other large dams across its tributaries (see TENNESSEE VALLEY AUTHORITY). The dams on the River Tennessee vary in length from about 800 metres to 2.3 kilometres (0.5 to 1.4 miles). The level of the river is altered by as much as 50 metres (164 feet) at one dam and by as little as 21 metres (69 feet) at another. This series of dams makes it possible to obtain huge quantities of power from the Tennessee and its tributaries. Other examples are the Waikato River in New Zealand and the Snowy Mountains Scheme in Australia (see SNOWY MOUNTAINS SCHEME).

A river water-power scheme of a somewhat different kind is that supplied by the Hoover Dam between Nevada and Arizona, United States. Here the deep Black Canyon had made it possible to build a dam 223 metres (732 feet) high. Upstream of the dam has formed Lake Mead, which is 185 kilometres (115 miles) in length. Lake Nasser, formed by the Aswan High Dam over the River Nile in Egypt, is four times the size of Lake Mead. The world's largest man-made lake covers 5,000 square kilometres (1,930 square miles) and is part of the Kariba Dam scheme over the Zambezi River between Zambia and Zimbabwe in southern Africa. Some of the largest water-power schemes are in the USSR. That at Krasnoyarsk on the Yenisei River has a capacity of 6,000 megawatts.

Tidal and Wave Power

The rise and fall of the tides (see TIDES) can be used to produce power. Modern designs for tidal power stations depend on building a dam across the mouth of a river or sea inlet in a place with a large tidal range. If tunnels are made through the dam, water will enter through them while the tide rises and flow out of them as the tide falls. Turbine-generators mounted in the tunnels are turned by the flow.

The difference in level between high and low tide can seldom be more than 10 metres (33 feet), compared with 160 metres (525 feet) or more for ordinary hydroelectric power stations. With a small head, a great volume of water is needed to do a useful amount of work. Thus a tidal power station requires the trapping of a lot of water above the dam.

The first big tidal power station was built in France in 1966. It is at the mouth of the Rance River near St. Malo in Brittany. The dam is about 800 metres (0.5 mile) across and has 24 tunnels through it. Mounted in each tunnel is a 10-megawatt turbine-generator. The turbines have reversible blades so that they drive the dynamos for a period during each flood and each ebb.

Tidal power stations have been proposed for Passamaquoddy Bay, an inlet of the Bay of Fundy between Canada and the United States, and also for the Severn Estuary in Britain.

Wave power depends on the energy of sea waves. In mid-Atlantic, for example, this averages about 90 kilowatts for every 1-metre (3.3-foot) length of wave. In storm conditions this may increase to as much as 5 megawatts per metre. One device for harnessing this power consists of a long flexible bag, partly filled with water; as the waves reach it, the bag is compressed and the water inside is forced through turbines. No full-scale wave-power generator is yet in operation, but research is being carried out, especially in Norway and Japan.

Despite the great developments that have taken place in harnessing water power, mainly in the United States, Canada, Australia, New Zealand, and Europe, the world's oceans and rivers remain a vast and still largely untapped source of energy.

WATER SKIING as a sport began in France in the 1920s. Skiing on snow was already a popular winter-sports pastime, and the French had the idea of taking to the water on skis. The water skier may use one or two skis, which are wider than skis used on snow. Most water skis also have a stabilizing fin beneath (like the keel of a yacht), although the special skis used for tricks are flat underneath. (This enables the skier to make a complete 360° turn.)

The skier stands upright on the skis, holding on to a wooden handle at the end of a towline 23 metres (75 feet) long. The towline is

ZEFA

A slalom skier pulls the towrope taut and leans inwards, gathering speed to cross the boat's wake.

fastened to the stern of a motorboat; as the boat speeds along at up to 55 kilometres (35 miles) per hour, the skier is towed behind.

Slalom water skiing involves winding in and out of a course marked by buoys in the water, often crossing the wake of the motorboat. Another water ski event is jumping. Here the skier is pulled up a waxed ramp, aiming to hit the bottom of the ramp at the highest possible speed by cutting sharply across the boat's wake. The expert ski-jumper can leap about 50 metres (160 feet). Other forms of water skiing are racing, kite flying, and barefoot skiing.

A pioneer of water skiing in the 1920s was an American named Ralph W. Sammuelson. There are now clubs all over the world, and international championships. Water skiing may be enjoyed on a lake or at sea, although calm water is really essential. In cold climates, the skiers wear rubber wet-suits, which provide insulation against the cold. Being buoyant, the suit also helps the skier to float while he or she is putting on the skis in the water.

Even if you are a good swimmer, you should always wear a life jacket when water skiing. The life jacket not only provides buoyancy, but also helps to cushion the body against falls.

WATERSPOUT. A waterspout appears as a dark funnel-shaped cloud tapering downwards, and is an eddy of whirling and rising air which carries up water from an ocean or from a lake. There are two types of waterspout. Some begin over the land as tornadoes (see TORNADO), and others form over the sea as whirlwinds which are caused by the uneven heating of the surface.

The tornado-type waterspout may be a terrifying thing causing severe damage and loss of life. It is caused by the meeting of warm and cold air masses in the atmosphere. In the south and east of the United States, hot and moist tropical air travelling northwards from the Gulf of Mexico may meet cold and dry air coming from the north. If these air masses pass over the sea, their different directions and speeds cause a rising spiral movement which sucks up water to form a waterspout.

The whirlwind type of waterspout seldom causes damage because it usually moves slowly, occurs in fair weather, and can be avoided by vessels which have engines. It is believed to be caused by a mass of air near the surface becoming warmer than the surrounding air, and thus rising. If this rising air is directly below a rain-producing cloud of the kind called cumulo-nimbus, a waterspout may be formed. The base of the cloud forms a conical pointed shape whose long tip spreads downwards towards the sea. Beneath it the sea is whipped up and a cloud of spray forms. The point of the descending cloud dips into this cloud of spray and at the same time the waterspout appears as a column of water. Most of these waterspouts are about 5 to 10 metres (15 to 30 feet) thick and may be 60 to 120 metres (200 to 400 feet) high, although much thicker and taller ones have been seen.

Courtesy, US Weather Bureau

A waterspout over Lake Huron, in North America.

WATER SUPPLY. Although we can live for quite a long time without food, we must drink water (in one form or another) regularly and frequently to stay alive and healthy. As well as using water for drinking, we use it in many other ways at home and in industry. But because it costs very little, we tend to take it for granted.

Water comes from clouds and rainfall, rivers, boreholes, and reservoirs. In developed countries public authorities are usually responsible for managing the whole "water cycle". (See RAIN.) In addition to supplying tap water and keeping an adequate supply for fire-fighting, they take it and treat it after use, drain the land, prevent floods, control pollution, and look after amenities such as fishing, swimming, and boating.

The total amount of water on Earth is fixed, and is estimated to be about 1,360 million cubic kilometres (326 million cubic miles). Of this, about 97 per cent is sea-water, covering nearly three-quarters of the Earth's surface, and is undrinkable unless the salt is removed. A supply of fresh water has always been one of man's necessities, and from the earliest times villages and settlements were built near streams and rivers. Originally these same streams were used as drains and sewers until people discovered that polluting their water supply in this way caused disease. (Polluted water is water which has been made foul or dirty).

Today, most water is supplied from reservoirs (see RESERVOIR) taking their supply from nearby rivers, or from boreholes drilled into the "aquifer" layer in the ground that naturally stores water that has seeped down through porous (spongy) layers of rock and sand. In soaking through these layers, the water is filtered to some extent, and as long as nothing but rainwater sinks through the soil, then this well (or borehole) water is safe for drinking after removal of sand, and chlorination (described later). (See also ARTESIAN WELL.)

In parts of the world where there is low rainfall, water may be taken from the sea, and used for drinking after removal of the salt (desalination). This may be achieved by *distillation* using heat, sometimes the Sun's, to evaporate the water from the salt and then condensing or cooling the water vapour to form pure water. (See DISTILLATION; EVAPORATION.) An example of a sea-water desalination plant is at Rosarito Beach, Mexico; it has a capacity of 34 million litres (9 million US gallons) per day. Consideration has also been given to the possibility of towing icebergs (which contain little salt) to dry countries.

Reservoirs ensure that when water is plentiful it is conserved as a reserve in case of drought. They are also an important preliminary stage in the natural purification of water on its way to the tap. The comparative stillness of the water allows the bigger solid impurities to settle, and the large surface area allows the oxygen in the air to get to work on the other impurities. From the storage reservoirs the water is taken for treatment. Methods vary, but the effect is the same. Water treatment is merely the intensification of natural processes.

First comes primary filtration, one method of which uses rapid filter beds. For this method to be effective, fine particles in the water are first made to stick together or *coagulate*, and this is done by adding a chemical, aluminium sulphate. The water then sinks through a layer of coarse sand at the rate of 6 metres (20 feet) an hour, leaving behind the larger suspended matter. It passes finally through a layer of shingle into perforated pipes, which carry it away. Every day the filter beds are drained down; and then compressed air is forced out through the perforated pipes to loosen the dirt, which is washed away by a reverse, upward flow of clean water. This simple cleansing operation takes only half an hour or so. The filter bed is then refilled with unfiltered water from the storage reservoir and the process begins again.

After this comes secondary filtration. The principle is the same as in primary filtration, but in these beds the sand is finer. Minute natural organisms in the sand feed on bacteria in the water and help purify it further. At intervals the top 25 millimetres (1 inch) or so of dirty sand is removed by skimming, and after being washed it can then be re-used. Meanwhile the water is being taken to the final stage of treatment.

Water flows from the river and the reservoir into filter beds. From there it is piped into individual homes.

The final process of water treatment is chlorination. The water passes through a covered tank where chlorine is used to combine with the hydrogen in the water to release oxygen, which destroys any remaining bacteria by a process similar to burning. (See COMBUSTION.) Chemical methods can also be used for softening the water, that is, removing calcium carbonate and magnesium hydroxide which the water may dissolve from rocks and which cause "scale" to be desposited in plumbing systems and kettles when the water is heated. It is then clear, safe to drink, and ready for pumping into the mains.

In some parts of the United States and Britain fluoride is added to the water to help strengthen children's teeth and reduce tooth decay (see FLUORINE AND FLUORIDE).

Trunk mains carry the water underground or overground, and whatever is not used by consumers goes into water towers or service reservoirs. From the service reservoirs, a network of large pipes runs beneath the streets, and from these mains, a service pipe, usually about 13 millimetres (0.5 inch) in diameter, brings water direct to the water tank of each house (see PLUMBING). To enable the water to reach the water tank of, for example, a four-storey building, it must be at a pressure of 2.9 to 3.6 kilograms per square centimetre (40 to 50 pounds per square inch).

Every day, water samples are tested to ensure safety. Samples come from all stages of water treatment. Water Authorities have special responsibilities for keeping a constant check on pollution throughout the whole system. (See also DRAINAGE; SEWER AND SEWAGE DISPOSAL.)

History of Water Supply

Although modern technology is very different, the principle of water supply is an ancient one. Ancient Rome, and many other cities, had piped supplies, public baths, and fountains. In some places the Romans built huge underground cisterns (tanks) of stone in which water was collected during the rainy periods as a reserve to be used in dry periods. In this way garrisons could be kept where otherwise they would soon have died of thirst.

As more and more people began settling in towns, the difficulties of obtaining water supplies increased. Wells and rivers were the usual sources for a town's water and river water was easily polluted. Dirt and rubbish from the streets, refuse and sewage from houses on the riverside and from places further upstream, cattle wallowing in the river outside the town—all these helped to pollute the water. Where the stream flowed fairly rapidly much of the dirt was washed away, but it is not surprising that there were quite frequent outbreaks of dysentery, typhoid fever, and cholera.

The Romans overcame the dangers of pollution by collecting the water in places well away from their cities and leading it along channels called aqueducts. Water from the Apennine Mountains reached Rome by an aqueduct as early as 313 BC. Later, tunnels were driven through mountains and great arches carried aqueducts across valleys. Some of these magnificent Roman aqueducts still exist, for example near Nîmes in France, and at Segovia and Tarragona in Spain, where they are still used. (See AQUEDUCT.)

Wells are less likely to become polluted than are streams but they are more difficult to cleanse once this has occurred. A well sunk on a farm, for example, must be properly sealed on its sides, or drainage from the farmyard will seep into it through its walls. Thus, where wells are used, great care must be taken to protect them from pollution by local surface drainage (see WELL).

Small artificial lakes made by building a dam across the lower end of a valley are often used as reservoirs. From the reservoir the water is led through tunnels, covered channels, or large pipes to the pumping station outside the town. If the main reservoir is at a much higher level than the town, one or more auxiliary reservoirs are built between the two so as to reduce the pressure of water. The auxiliary reservoir is kept filled from the main source and supplies the next "pressure break" or the pumping station. If there were no pressure breaks and the water were led direct to people's houses, the pressure might easily burst the pipes and taps there. (The pressure caused by a "head", or height of water, of 30 metres (100 feet) is 3 kilograms per square centimetre (42 pounds per square inch).)

As countries have become more and more industrialized, the amount of water used has increased considerably. Many factories use great quantities of water, much of which must be fresh. (Examples of this are the plastics, paper, and metal-plating industries.) The amount used daily in people's homes has also greatly increased, partly due to higher standards of cleanliness, and to the use of domestic appliances such as washing machines. In areas where people still have to fetch and carry their water from wells or pumps, the average daily consumption is seldom more than 18 litres (4.7 US gallons) per person. But, when there is a piped supply, with lavatories, washbasins, and baths and showers, people may use more than 225 litres (59 US gallons) a day each. The Thames Water Authority in southern England, one of the largest in the world, is responsible for an area of 12,900 square kilometres (5,000 square miles), and supplies on average 3,820 million litres (1,009 million US gallons) of water *each day*.

Courtesy, Thames Water

The draw-off tower of a reservoir where the water begins its journey through the filtration system.

In the United States and many other countries water usage is measured by a meter, and the customer is billed according to the amount used. In a few countries, including Great Britain, water is paid for by the collection of a tax, or water rate, charged according to the size of the house.

WATSON AND CRICK. The American biologist James Dewey Watson (born 1928) and the English biochemist Sir Francis Harry Compton Crick (born 1916) are most famous for their discovery of the structure of DNA, the "molecule of life".

When animals and plants breed they pass their genes to their offspring. Genes are contained in chromosomes, microscopic thread-like objects found inside every cell. The genes are the 'instructions' for how to build and run new cells, anything from a bacterium to the cells in the body of a blue whale. They control many aspects of life: how the body develops, its size, shape and colour, as well as the chemical reactions that go on inside it (see HEREDITY AND GENETICS).

For many years scientists puzzled over how such complicated instructions could be packed into a space as small as the inside of a cell, and how the instructions were copied so accurately that a creature's offspring looked very much like its parents.

Biochemists such as Maurice Wilson and Rosaline Franklin found that the instructions seem to be in the form of large molecules called DNA (deoxyribonucleic acid). From 1950 to 1953 they collected and purified DNA and photographed it by a special method called X-ray diffraction, which gave an intricate pattern of lines and dots on a screen.

Watson and Crick, who were working at Cambridge University, England, studied the photographs and much other information. Finally, in 1953 they worked out the structure of DNA. Each DNA molecule was made of thousands of chemical subunits, strung in a line like beads on a necklace. The "necklace" was coiled like a long spring shaped like a helix. In each chromosome there were two DNA molecules, intertwined. In terms of its chemical subunits, one molecule was the "mirror image" of the other.

Camera Press

Watson and Crick photographed with their model of DNA in the Cavendish Laboratory, Cambridge, 1953.

This structure answered the two questions. Firstly, the instructions were shown to be held as a chemical code, based on the order of the subunits on the string. There were just four different subunits, which behaved like a four-letter "chemical alphabet". By arranging the subunits in different orders, thousands of different chemical "words" could be made. This is called the genetic code.

Secondly, the copying process was found to be controlled by the DNA molecule itself. The two coils of DNA separated, then each made a "mirror image" of itself. It then intertwined with the copy. The result was two pairs of DNA molecules, each the same.

In 1962 Watson, Crick, and Wilson were awarded a Nobel Prize for their discovery. Each has gone on to help unravel how the genetic code operates and how the genetic instructions are used by the cell. Their work has had an enormous effect on biology and biochemistry. Much of our understanding of heredity and inherited diseases, and such techniques as genetic engineering, would not exist without it.

WATT, James (1736–1819). It is sometimes said that the great Scottish engineer James Watt was led to invent the steam engine when, as a boy, he watched the lifting lid of a boiling kettle. That story is untrue, but, on the other hand, we *do* know that he was interested in seeing the steam condense into beads of water on a metal spoon. Although Watt did not *invent* the steam engine, he improved it so much that it played a leading part in the Industrial Revolution during the 19th century.

James Watt was born at Greenock on the River Clyde where his father was a builder and shipwright. He attended the Greenock grammar school and helped in his father's workshop, where he showed great skill in making models. At 17 he went to London to learn instrument making, but ill health forced him to return after less than a year. He then became instrument maker to Glasgow University.

In 1764 a model of Thomas Newcomen's "atmospheric" steam engine was brought to Watt to repair. Actually it was not broken or damaged; what was wrong with it was that its boiler was too small to produce enough steam to keep it working. Watt examined it carefully and went on to study the reasons why an engine of the Newcomen type should use so much steam. He studied the pressure, density, and condensation of steam in order to find out exactly what happened. (See CONDENSATION; DENSITY.)

Mary Evans Picture Library

James Watt in his workshop experimenting with ways to improve the Newcomen steam engine.

The Newcomen engine depended on the use of atmospheric pressure to push the piston down after the steam inside the cylinder had been condensed by a spray of cold water. Watt noticed that this spray cooled the cylinder itself, and that before the piston could be lifted again the entering steam had to reheat the cylinder. This waste of heat caused a waste of fuel.

Watt's first improvement was the invention in 1765 of the separate condenser. This was an empty vessel connected to the cylinder by a pipe. The steam was condensed in this vessel, leaving the cylinder hot. He also surrounded the cylinder with a metal case into which steam was admitted, this "steam jacket" helping further to keep the cylinder hot. These improvements led to a great saving of fuel.

Watt's improved engine was first made at the Soho works near Birmingham, in partnership with the English manufacturer Matthew Boulton (1728–1809). They set up in business together in 1775. It was a valuable partnership, as Boulton had a large modern factory and looked after the business side while Watt made inventions and developed them. In 1782 Watt invented the double-acting steam engine. He realized that if the ends were closed, steam could be admitted first to one end of the cylinder and then to the other, making the engine independent of atmospheric pressure. Other improvements were a valve gear to shut off the steam after the piston had travelled for part of its stroke, allowing the expansion (swelling) of the steam to push the piston through the rest of its stroke, and several methods of changing the push-and-pull action of the piston into the turning movement needed for most machinery. You can read more about Watt's development of the steam engine in the article STEAM ENGINE.

Watt also invented the pressure indicator which is used for measuring the power of reciprocating engines. The electrical unit of power, the "watt", is named after him. (See POWER.)

Watt's interests went beyond steam engines. He discovered independently that water is a combination of the gases hydrogen and oxygen. In later life he lived at Heathfield Hall, near Birmingham, where among other inventions he invented a machine for copying sculpture and also a letter-copying press.

WATTEAU, Antoine (1684–1721). Watteau was the greatest painter and draftsman in early 18th-century France.He became famous for the paintings called *fêtes galantes* in which there are beautifully dressed, elegant lords and ladies picnicking in lovely parks, or declaring their love in dainty summer-houses while a guitar plays a serenade. Everything happens in a golden land of make-believe.

Watteau's *Commedia dell'Arte* (1730), one of many paintings he made of a troupe of Italian players who had taken Paris by storm. Pierrot stands in the centre.

National Gallery of Art, Washington

Watteau drew wonderfully well, and used to produce his pictures by making separate drawings first.

His own life was very different from the life of the happy and carefree people in his pictures. He was a workman's son, born in Valenciennes in northern France. When he was 18 he went to Paris hoping to become a painter. For a time he worked in a picture factory making copies of old masters for very low wages. Soon he discovered the delights of the theatre, and in particular the *commedia dell'arte*, a group of Italian actors whose plays included music and dancing, jesters, and pantomime characters such as Pierrot, Harlequin, and Pantaloon. The lighting, costumes, and scenery of their productions influenced Watteau's technique, and he painted many performances.

In 1708 he joined with an artist named Claude Audran who was in charge of the collection of pictures at the Luxembourg Palace. There Watteau was inspired by the work of great painters.

From 1712 he painted on his own, and wealthy patrons began to buy his pictures. He himself was never wealthy, and was often ill. He died of tuberculosis when he was aged only 37.

Among his best-known works are *Mezzetin* (*c.*1718) in the Metropolitan Museum, New York; *The Pilgrimage to the Island of Cythera* (1717) and *Gilles* (1720–21), both in the Louvre, Paris.

WAT TYLER'S REBELLION. Wat Tyler was the leader of the rebellion known as the Peasants' Revolt which took place in England in 1381. At that time the peasants, or agricultural labourers, were the serfs of the lord of the manor, who owned the land on which they worked (see FEUDALISM).

After the Black Death had swept through Europe, killing a third of the population, there was a shortage of people to work in the fields. (See BLACK DEATH.) So the remaining peasants wanted to ask for higher wages. To stop this Parliament passed a law to keep wages low, which caused great discontent.

Then, in 1381, Parliament introduced a poll tax (a tax per head of population) to raise money for a war against the French. Everyone over 15 had to pay a shilling. A shilling was a silver coin worth five pence or about 8 cents, which was quite a large sum of money in those days. There was, therefore, a great deal of resentment at this tax.

In May 1381 riots broke out in Essex and a month later an army of peasants seized Rochester Castle in Kent. Their leader was Wat Tyler, whose work was roofing houses with tiles. From Rochester the rebels moved on to Canterbury, where they released the prisoners from the archbishop's prison. The Archbishop of Canterbury, Simon Sudbury, and John of Gaunt, Duke of Lancaster, were the advisers of the king, Richard II, who was only 14. The peasants blamed them instead of the king for their grievances.

The peasants' army then set off for London. Once inside the city they burnt the palace of John of Gaunt and the prisons of Newgate and the Fleet.

To prevent further trouble it was arranged that Richard should meet Wat Tyler in person, and on 14 June he talked with him at Mile End, just outside London. Tyler demanded measures that would improve the conditions of the peasants. The king promised the rebels that he would abolish serfdom and allow the peasants to buy cheap land, but even while Tyler was talking to the king some other rebels marched on the Tower of London and murdered the Archbishop of Canterbury, who was sheltering there.

The next day Richard rode to meet the rebels at Smithfield with his attendants, including Sir William Walworth, the lord mayor of London. Tyler put forward more demands, showing little respect for the king. Walworth drew his sword and badly wounded Tyler. His followers took him to St. Bartholomew's Hospital but he was later beheaded on Walworth's orders.

Tyler's peasant army was assembled in Smithfield and things would probably have gone badly with the king and his followers if Richard had not bravely taken affairs into his own hands by riding over to the peasants and calling on them to take him as their chief, promising to meet their demands. The peasants, bewildered by what had happened

Mary Evans Picture Library

King Richard, accompanied by the unpopular Archbishop of Canterbury and other advisers, sets off in a barge to parley with the rebellious peasants.

to their leader, followed the king into the open fields round about, where they peacefully dispersed.

This was the end of the disturbances in London, although rebellions in other parts of the country still had to be dealt with. Although the poll tax was lifted, the rising had little effect. Richard was too young to have any real power, and parliament broke all his promises of help for the peasants. Changes for the better only came about slowly for them.

WAVE. Regular disturbances on the surface of water are called waves. Waves also occur in the air, and the expression *wave motion* is used for the vibrations by which sound, light, and radio travel from one place to another. The main difference between water waves and other waves (such as light and radio waves) is that water waves travel at a speed which depends on their wavelength, whereas light and radio waves travel at a constant speed, regardless of wavelength. Sound waves also travel at a fixed speed, faster than water waves but much more slowly than light. The general rules of wave motion apply to waves of all kinds, but the present article is chiefly about sea and water waves. Other forms of wave motion are described in the articles LIGHT; RADIATION; RADIO; SOUND.

In water waves, the disturbance of the water causes a motion that forms the surface into a series of ridges and troughs, or hollows. Each ridge, followed by a trough, moves along the surface. However, the water itself does not advance to any great extent, as was pointed out by the great Italian genius Leonardo da Vinci (1452–1519). He compared water waves with ripples moving across a wheat field, in which the wheat itself remains rooted. When fishing you can see that the float bobs up and down with the waves but does not travel along with their crests, unless it happens to be blown along by a wind.

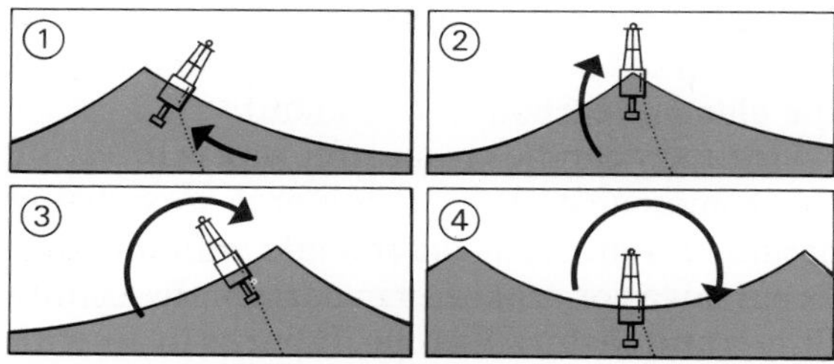

As the wave (travelling right to left) passes, the buoy moves in a circular path from crest to trough.

Each particle of water moves mainly like a cork floating on the surface, moving forwards when the water is above its average level and backwards when it is below it. There is a small overall forward movement, especially in high waves. Viewed from some fixed object like a rock, the particle moves very nearly in a circle. The diameter (breadth) of this circle is the same as the height of the wave, from trough to crest. In shallow water the circle becomes oval in shape.

Most waves are caused by wind. Even a gust of wind blowing over a calm surface raises a ripple, or wavelet, and each ripple takes more energy from the wind. In this way the waves grow in size. The distance between one crest and the next is called the *wavelength*. The *period* is the time between one crest and the next passing a fixed point.

Three things determine the height of waves. They are the *fetch*, or length of the stretch of surface over which the wind blows; the average speed of the wind over the fetch; and the duration of time for which the wind blows. To produce waves 20 metres (65 feet) high, a wind of 30 metres a second (60 miles per hour) would have to blow for about 24 hours over a fetch of 1,000 kilometres (625 miles). Waves 20 metres (65 feet) high are exceptional. Waves higher than this, such as the 24-metre (80-foot) one reported in the North Atlantic by the liner *Majestic* in 1922, and the 34-metre (110-foot) wave reported by the United States ship *Ramapo* in the North Pacific in 1933 are generally freaks caused by the coming together of the crests of two sets of waves travelling in different directions. The highest wave ever recorded on instruments was 26 metres (85 feet) from crest to trough, and was measured by the British weather ship *Weather Reporter* in the North Atlantic in 1972. Winds of hurricane force (35 metres a second or 68 miles per hour) do not necessarily produce mountainous seas because they change direction too rapidly for regular waves to develop. Storm waves in deep water travel at speeds of up to about 100 kilometres (63 miles) an hour.

As waves grow, both their wavelength and their height increase. The wavelength of storm waves is generally about 13 times the height, but steep waves in a shallow sea can grow so rapidly that their height may reach one-seventh of their wavelength. A wave breaks when the water at the crest begins to move faster than the wave itself, and topples forward to form white caps, sometimes described as "white horses". In the smallest waves this happens at a wind speed of 4–5 metres a second (7–10 miles per hour), which sailors call a gentle breeze. (See WIND.)

The surf on a beach is caused by the energy built up by the wind in blowing for many hours over long fetches. When a wave runs into shallow water it grows higher than it was in deep water. This is because the shallow water slows it down, and since it must carry as much

As waves move towards the shore, the water becomes shallower preventing the waves from completing their circular path and causing them to break with the formation of much froth and foam.

ZEFA

energy as before, its height increases until it breaks, releasing the energy. A wave generally breaks when its height from trough to crest is about four-fifths of the depth of the water.

The waves caused by wind are generally mixtures of short and long waves, but when the wind dies away, or when the waves move beyond the area in which the wind is blowing, the shorter waves are left behind and the longer waves take a smooth rounded shape and travel very regularly. Such waves are called *swell*.

When water is sloshed to and fro in a bath, the rise and fall of the levels at the ends continue regularly for some seconds, only gradually dying away. This kind of oscillation occurs on large lakes and inland seas. It was first studied on the Lake of Geneva, between Switzerland and France, and is called a *seiche*.

Earthquakes on the ocean floor produce waves called *tsunamis* which are sometimes called tidal waves, although they have nothing to do with the tides. They travel long distances, at speeds of 600–800 kilometres (375–500 miles) an hour. In the open sea these waves may be only about 1 metre (3 feet) high, but as they slow down in shallower water they rise to many times that height. They cause immense damage by flooding and may even pick up ships and carry them inland.

WAX.

WAX. There are many different kinds of wax. Some are made by animals, some by plants, and others come from minerals. No true waxes are manufactured by people. All can be easily moulded into different shapes and melted, all will keep out water, and all are compounds of the element carbon (see CARBON).

Ordinary candle or paraffin wax is probably the commonest. It is a mineral wax, being obtained from crude oil or shale, and it occurs as earthwax or ozokerite in parts of the United States and eastern Europe. It burns in air with a yellow flame and melts at about 50°C (122°F). When liquid it can be poured into moulds to make waxwork figures. Paper is sometimes surfaced with it to make airtight bags for food which must be kept crisp. All matchsticks are soaked with paraffin wax, and most ordinary polishing waxes are of this type.

The commonest animal wax is beeswax, made by bees in the form of six-sided cells in combs to contain the honey. When full, each cell is sealed with a wax cap. This cap is used by woodworkers to get a fine polish on new wood.

Vegetable wax is found on the bark of some South American trees. One kind, known as carnauba wax, comes from a Brazilian palm. Carnauba wax is used for polishing leather to make it waterproof.

Wax Modelling

Thousands of years ago people realized that wax was very good for making models. The ancient Egyptians for instance, made models of fruit and flowers, and they also used to put wax figures of their gods and goddesses in the graves when people were buried. Children in ancient Greece played with dolls made of coloured wax.

In Roman times modelling in wax became an important activity, because it was a custom for the rich noblemen of Rome to have wax portraits made of themselves. These figures, called images, were greatly treasured and kept in the family, and a family that possessed many was proud of its great and ancient ancestry. The images were carried in the funeral procession when a member of the family died, and they were also brought out and displayed at solemn festivals during the year. One Roman festival was the *Saturnalia*, which was a whole week of holidays, and on the last days people used to give each other presents of wax fruit and flowers.

Later, during the Middle Ages, waxworks were made for Christian churches in Europe. Usually they were images of the saints, which pious worshippers had presented to the church. In England and France, wax figures of kings, queens, and other important people were carried in their funeral processions. These life-sized figures, or effigies, lay on top of the coffins as they were borne to the grave, and sometimes they were left there as monuments until more permanent ones (of stone or brass, for instance) were made.

Usually the effigies were dressed in clothes which belonged to the dead person, and the heads were often modelled from a "death mask". A death mask is a copy in wax made from the actual face of a dead person. First the face is covered with a fine paste-like plaster, which sets hard. It is carefully removed and the inside is then used as a mould, exactly in the shape of the face. Melted wax is poured in and allowed to set. When it is taken out of the mould, it is in the form of a mask, which can be treated and coloured to look very realistic.

A sinister use of wax in the Middle Ages was to make little figures of people who were hated. Long pins were then stuck into the wax in the hope that some deadly injury would happen to the person! Later, wax models were used in medical studies. In the 17th century a Sicilian named Gaetano Giulio Zumbo made wax models to show the effects that the plague had on the human body. In the next century, Giovanni Manzolini and his wife Anna, at Bologna in Italy, made an accurate set of models of various parts and organs of the body and since then wax models have often been used as a clear and useful way of teaching anatomy, that is, the way the body is constructed. Philippe Curtius, a French doctor, became skilled as a maker of these sorts of models, and later he founded a waxworks exhibition in Paris. His niece was Marie Tussaud, founder of the famous waxwork exhibition in London (see TUSSAUD, MARIE).

Wax has also been very valuable to sculptors. It was formerly used in the process of

Madame Tussaud

The pop star Michael Jackson and his lifelike wax effigy in Madame Tussaud's, London.

making statues in bronze (the article MODELLING AND CASTING tells you about this). Sculptors often make wax models of their works before they start to carve them in stone or some other material, in the same way as an artist might make a rough sketch in pencil before he begins on his painting.

Medallion portraits were another form of art executed in wax. They were popular in 16th-century Europe. One of the best wax artists was Antonio Abondio who worked in Vienna and Prague. The craft was revived in the 18th century and Josiah Wedgwood, the English pottery manufacturer, sometimes copied wax portraits in pottery.

During the 19th century wax fruit or flowers were extremely popular. A lady named Mrs. Peachey was appointed Artiste in Wax Flowers to Her Majesty, Queen Victoria. For the Great Exhibition held in London in 1851 Mrs. Peachey made an enormous bouquet of wax flowers which contained almost every variety that was then known. It was displayed hung over a pool containing water plants, and the whole exhibit was enclosed in a glass case 2 metres (6 feet) high.

WAXWING. The waxwings are striking-looking crested birds which get their name from the wax-like patches of scarlet on their wings.

The general colour of the plumage of the common, or Bohemian, waxwing (*Bombycilla garrulus*), including the crest, is brown, but the throat is black, the rump grey, the tip of the tail yellow, and there is yellow and white on the wings. This waxwing is a little smaller than a starling, about 20 centimetres (8 inches) long. Waxwings have a shrill, high call-note and are usually seen in small flocks or parties. They breed mainly in coniferous forest throughout the northern hemisphere. Every few years large numbers of these birds travel south in winter in search of food, generally berries of all kinds. When this happens they often attract people's attention as they are such unusual-looking birds.

The cedar waxwing (*Bombycilla cedorum*) is a smaller, more reddish bird. It is found only in North America, where it is quite common, and it lives further south than the Bohemian waxwing. It is especially fond of cedar berries and will also snatch at insects in mid-air.

The favourite food of waxwings is fruit and berries.

The third species, the Japanese waxwing (*Bombycilla japonicum*) lives in the forests of the Far East. It has no waxy patches on the wing, but has a red tip to its tail.

WAYFARING TREE see VIBURNUM.